BABYLOST

Racism, Survival, and the Quiet Politics of Infant Mortality, from A to Z

MONICA J. CASPER

RUTGERS UNIVERSITY PRESS

NEW BRUNSWICK, CAMDEN, AND NEWARK,

NEW JERSEY, AND LONDON

Library of Congress Cataloging-in-Publication Data

Names: Casper, Monica J., 1966– author.
Title: Babylost: racism, survival, and the quiet politics of infant mortality, from A to Z / Monica J. Casper.
Description: New Brunswick: Rutgers University Press, [2022] | Includes bibliographical references and index.
Identifiers: LCCN 2021023672 | ISBN 9781978825949 (paperback; alk. paper) | ISBN 9781978825956 (hardback; alk. paper) | ISBN 9781978825963 (epub) | ISBN 9781978825970 (mobi) | ISBN 9781978825987 (pdf)
Subjects: LCSH: Infants—Mortality—United States. | African American infants—Health and hygiene. | Indian infants—Health and hygiene—United States. | Maternal health services—United States. | Discrimination in medical care—United States. | Racism—Health aspects—United States. | Maternal and infant welfare—United States.
Classification: LCC HB1323.I42 U6336 2022 | DDC 304.6/4083—dc23
LC record available at https://lccn.loc.gov/2021023672

A British Cataloging-in-Publication record for this book is available from the British Library.

References to internet websites (URLs) were accurate at the time of writing. Neither the author nor Rutgers University Press is responsible for URLs that may have expired or changed since the manuscript was prepared.

♾ The paper used in this publication meets the requirements of the American National Standard for Information Sciences—Permanence of Paper for Printed Library Materials, ANSI Z39.48–1992.

www.rutgersuniversitypress.org

Manufactured in the United States of America

For all the babies, and those who mourn them.

When I get to the Capitol after much difficulty and begin to state the case for the Children's Bureau, I discover a serious handicap. Those men in Congress are really just as fond of children as I am. They are fond of their own children and their friends' children, but they are usually not familiar with what is happening to many American children, and they usually lack the imagination to translate the facts and figures which are presented to them in terms of actual children.

—Grace Abbott, 1931

I thought stillbirth was a thing of history, and then it happened to me, and yet now when I hear of a baby dying I'm just as incredulous. You mean they *still* haven't figured this out? *I want to hear about every dead baby, everywhere in the world. I want to know their names, Christopher, Strick, Jonathan. I want their mothers to know about Pudding.*

—Elizabeth McCracken, 2008

My daughter. Say it—hold it in your mouth, look at the words: born dead. *To be told there is no pulse at the precise threshold of birth—water breaking. To be told to deliver anyway. Death.*

—Lidia Yuknavitch, 2015

I had never seen a dead body before. My baby was my first.

—Kate Inglis, 2018

In many ways, for the mothers and families who lost these babies, the inability and lack of public space to talk about them are a second death. The silence makes us feel as if there is something fundamentally wrong with wanting *and* needing *to remember our children no matter how short their lives may have been.*

—Shannon Gibney and Kao Kalia Yang, 2019

I cannot express how little I care that you hate the photos. How little I care that it's something you wouldn't have done. I lived it, I chose to do it, and more than anything, those photos aren't for anyone but the people who have lived this or are curious enough to wonder what something like this is like. These photos are only for the people who need them. The thoughts of others do not matter to me.

—Chrissy Teigen, 2020

CONTENTS

BABYLOST

INTRODUCTION

Babies matter. And they matter to most, if not all, people on our planet, though in many different ways.

When I was a child, I gradually understood that my grandmother and aunt each had lost a baby. I did not know precise details but recall my mom mentioning it more than once. This knowledge made me sad. I understood that my cousin, Walker Aaron, who died at birth after being strangled on his way through the birth canal, would have been one month older than me. Instead, I was a year older than my next closest cousin, Tim, born fourteen months after his brother's death. Later, tragically and unexpectedly, my aunt lost another child, Chad, at age five. We never met him as they did not live near us then. It was many years before we were able to visit the family gravesite to offer our respects. But we talked to my aunt on the telephone just after her second son died, and I remember—like it was yesterday—the fatigue and sorrow in her usually cheerful voice.

As I grew older, I learned of other lost babies and children. A friend of my sister, married to her high school sweetheart, suffered a stillbirth. Another friend gave birth to a beautiful little girl who died a few days later from a rare illness. Another lost first one twin in utero and then the other a few days later, a ghastly roller coaster of despair, hope, and more despair. Friends and colleagues suffered miscarriages—too many to count. A friend of a friend experienced a late-term miscarriage and had to deliver her stillborn baby. And these were just people I knew personally. I also had read about infant deaths in novels such as Betty Smith's *A Tree Grows in Brooklyn*, Toni Morrison's *Beloved*, and Bobbie Ann Mason's *Feather Crowns*.

Babies everywhere, it seemed, were dying, though few were speaking of these losses publicly.

I have long been fascinated with babies, specifically the practices and politics of imagining, preventing, carrying, delivering, nurturing, fixing, and grieving them. I knew as early as college that I would focus my professional attention on reproduction—my senior thesis was on midwifery—and I also hoped that I would have my own babies someday. And yet, because reproductive loss was a branch of my family tree, I knew that reproduction was fraught. Indeed, in the United States, few issues are as weighted with social and cultural expectations or as heavily politicized. But I was already too invested to be scared away, in large part because reproduction—which is both embodied and deeply consequential for our species—is where politics come out to play, often in deadly ways, especially for women and their babies.

Nearly thirty years ago, while in graduate school, I began a project on fetal surgery, a relatively new boutique procedure for operating on the so-called unborn patient. In addition to interviewing surgeons, nurses, social workers, and others, I observed fetal surgical operations, which prepared me for eventually watching my own (second) cesarean section. That research became my dissertation, then later my first book, *The Making of the Unborn Patient: A Social Anatomy of Fetal Surgery.* In it, I offered an innovative sociological analysis of fetal interventions, drawing attention to significant ethical issues such as the clinical erasure of pregnant women alongside the emergence of fetal personhood. I also situated fetal surgery in historical and contemporary contexts, including vociferous and sometimes violent abortion politics in the United States and elsewhere.

What I did not discuss in the book, but which was very much on my mind, was the high infant mortality rate in African American communities in Oakland, just across the bay from where I had researched fetal surgery at "Capital Hospital." I was struck by the juxtaposition between an expensive, high tech, experimental intervention on a handful of singular, mostly white fetuses, while nearby, Black babies were dying at *two to three times* the rate of white babies, decimating families and communities. This disparity was made more poignant by the abundance of media coverage fawning over every successful fetal surgery ("Look what we did!"), in contrast with the stark absence of stories about reproductive loss. I was witnessing firsthand what anthropologist Shellee Colen called "stratified reproduction."

Though the current project was germinated years ago, while I was immersed in fetal surgery research, I did not launch it in earnest until I was living in Nashville, Tennessee, teaching at Vanderbilt University. There, two related events caused me to dive more fully into studying infant mortality. First, in 2006, I attended a conference on infant death called "Why Our Babies Die," organized by Vanderbilt and Meharry Medical College, one of the nation's oldest historically Black educational institutions. And second, I stumbled across data on high infant mortality rates in nearby Memphis, Tennessee, representative of dire health outcomes across the U.S. South. Together, these suggested there could—*and should*—be sociological investigations into infant death and racism. The data made it obvious that Black communities were especially negatively impacted. But outside of demography and epidemiology, few scholars were paying attention to infant death. I wanted to pick up where sociologist David Armstrong left off in his radical 1986 study of "the invention of infant mortality."

When I began to excavate the practices and politics of infant death, the most pressing and useful question I found myself asking was *Who cares?* That is, in a pragmatist sociological sense, who cares about and is willing to act on commitments to reduce infant mortality rates? This broad question led to other, more pointed questions: Who cares about babies, dead or alive? Who invests in infant survival in the United States, including research to explain and ameliorate health disparities? Who cares about pregnant people, and which pregnant people? Who cares about women's health, and which women? Who cares about mothers, especially those with few resources and little power? Who cares about persistent racial inequalities in the United States that continue to result year after year in premature, preventable death? Who cares about fetuses, abortion, prenatal interventions, and perinatal death, and what do these concerns have to do with the politics of infant and maternal survival? Equally significantly, who cares little or not at all about infant mortality—where are the gaps, elisions, and spaces of disregard? And finally, how do we talk about infant loss—in which registers, in whose voices, and with what consequences for human flourishing?

I started with the basics—framing infant mortality as *a social problem*, just as physician George Newman did more than a century ago.

Every day, small persons die in their first year of life, often quietly and invisibly. They perish from a variety of causes: low birth weight, birth anomalies, genetic diseases, "failure to thrive," inadequate nutrition, violence, stillbirth, poverty, prematurity, and lack of access to care. They die at different ages, some without taking a first breath, others at day 1 or 2 or 6 or 137, and some just shy of their first birthday. These deaths are routine, often preventable tragedies, tiny fissures in the fabric of human evolution. Each death, singly, is an acute loss—a local, specific occasion for grief and commemoration. Infant deaths—like miscarriages, perinatal losses, and stillbirths—are publicly unremarked and largely unrecognized by others beyond grieving parents and perhaps other family members and close friends gathered in private spaces.

Yet taken together, these local misfortunes—Walker, Amelia, Parker, Tyan, Kiara, Malik, Elena, Sophie—are transformed into something greater. One solitary baby's premature death is combined with another and then another and so on, until these excess deaths become a social phenomenon, a collective pattern, a vital statistic. We describe infant loss in the aggregate as *infant mortality*, an arithmetical measure referencing the death of a baby in the first year of life. (The World Health Organization defines *child mortality* as death under age five.) Through population-level quantification, we seek to know how and why babies die. And we seek to understand what these premature deaths mean for families and also for cities, states, and nations tasked with the governance of life and death. Consider, for example, the nature of headlines such as "U.S. Reports New Low in Infant Mortality" and "[Millennium Development Goals] Target on Infant Mortality Not Met."

Infant mortality is political in the fullest sense of the term, connected historically both to *quantities* of death and their measurements and also to *qualities* of life. Yet in relying on "infant mortality" as a conceptual and practical framework for understanding infant death, we move away from grief and loss to a different, more technical register. One that attends not to the emptiness inside a pregnant person's body, the hollow around which they achingly wrap their arms, but rather to numbers, databases, archives, and registries. We move from profound losses experienced affectively to presumably objective statistical rates and from cherished unique babies with gravestones to considering the aggregate, the group, the population, the state. We leave the realm of "my baby died, and it hurts"—expressed privately and intimately—to "infant mortality as a public health problem," firmly transplanting us from hearts, homes, and cemeteries to larger biopolitical worlds of risk, prevention, intervention, governance, and the health status of nations.

Numeric language is preferred, indeed *required*, by clinicians, governments, the World Health Organization, the World Bank, public health experts, nongovernmental organizations (NGOs), and mass media. Infant mortality tells us not about the texture and circumstances of each baby's brief life and death but about frequencies, geographic concentrations, and correlations. Death clusters, and quantitative methodologies help us recognize and chart these. The *infant mortality rate* (IMR) offers a standardized language that enables communication in and across recognizable categories: race, ethnicity, socioeconomic status (SES), gender, city, county, state, nation, globe. Thus rates ultimately help providers, organizations, and states—but not necessarily grieving parents and their families—to communicate and work to assess the situation and formulate possible solutions.

Patterns and aggregates can helpfully allow us to see social phenomena. And *if* we pay attention, we can notice that poor babies and nonwhite babies die more frequently in the United States and globally. We can notice that the United States has more first-day newborn deaths than all other industrial nations *combined*. We can notice that African American and Native American babies die at more than twice the rate of white babies and that some powerful groups in the United States worry less about *this* tragedy and more about declining birth rates among white people. We can notice that babies in some communities, cities, and regions die so often that infant mortality is an established fact of life there, like racial profiling. And we can notice that in other communities, cities, and regions—those that are whiter and those with more economic privilege—the death of an infant is so very rare that it is unexpected and thus especially shocking. Perinatal and infant death, tragically routine in some contexts, in others interrupts the privilege of believing all is right in the world.

My initial aim for this project was to produce a book about the politics of quantification, focusing on how numeric framings of infant death—infant mortality rates—distract us from loss itself. Counting deaths, it seemed to me, minimized lived experiences of grief and loss. Following economist Marilyn Waring, I wanted to know: *Where are the women?* Both dead babies and the people who birthed them—primarily women, but also trans men and genderqueer people—were (and still are) invisible in most discussions of infant mortality. What *was* highly visible were rates, useful for clinical, governmental, and policy purposes. Yet as visible as the shifting rates have been across time, they have not translated into interventions lessening racial disparities in infant mortality. Nor have they inspired many public conversations about the persistent problem of infant death. The numbers, I have found, drain the emotion from loss and fail to inspire care and concern.

As I was working on an earlier version of the book, my beloved stepfather died, quite unexpectedly. After a routine knee replacement, he developed an infection and was dead two weeks later, at age sixty-seven. This was both devastating and life-changing, as my mother suddenly became a widow, and my siblings and I had to figure out how to navigate a world without our dad in it. Grieving, I did not touch the infant mortality project for two years; I could not look at loss and death without weeping. It didn't help that my other projects were also focused on trauma and death, including the harms of gender-based violence. Though it was quite different, I imagined, to lose a beloved parent than a cherished newborn, my dad's death underscored all the ways *death is never merely a statistic*. It is always relational, affective, grief-inducing, and dreadfully permanent.

I understood that it was an immense privilege to be able to step away from infant loss in ways that babylost parents—those who have lost babies through miscarriage, stillbirth, or infant death—could never do. I eventually returned to my infant mortality research but now with a very different project in mind, one that would not unnecessarily create abstractions from lived experiences. This is the book you now hold in your hands (or are viewing on-screen). It is clearly not the standard academic book I originally intended to write, nor does it follow conventional representations of data. Borrowing from the genre of creative nonfiction, I have aimed for accessibility and impact. This book is primarily for babylost parents and those who care for and about them, but also for most anyone interested in babies and their survival and well-being.

Over the past fifteen years, extensive research for this project has included interviews with a wide range of people working on and around infant mortality; participation in workshops and conferences; analysis of clinical, public health, and scientific literature; analysis of memoirs, films, novels, and other cultural depictions of infant loss; conversations with women who have lost babies and the people who have cared for these women; analysis of websites, especially those devoted to baby-loss; media analysis, specifically of news coverage of infant mortality; and analysis of government documents both historical and present-day. When a project takes as long as this one has, it is difficult to ignore new material, whether in the form of epidemiological studies, which are frequent, or memoirs, of which there are too few. What I have learned, sadly, is that there will always be new material until we fix the enduring problem of infant mortality.

To write for a popular audience, I explored a number of forms. I felt an alphabet book could be the right vehicle. For one, alphabet books are a tender reminder of what babylost parents do not get to share with their deceased children. I read many alphabet books to my own girls, and they were critical parts of their early childhood development. To be denied a baby is, ultimately, to be denied the chance to read to and play with that child, to parent that child. I also chose the alphabet book format because it allowed me to usefully organize themes that had emerged from my years of research. Each of the book's fifty-eight entries can be read as a keyword that makes sense of some aspect of infant mortality, primarily in the United States. Ranging from "Absence" to "Zip Code," the entries offer a picture—inevitably incomplete, as not every aspect can be included in one volume—of how infant death moves through and is shaped by various social and cultural factors.

Analytically, I selected entries that in my view most "trouble" our preconceived ideas about infant mortality. What haven't we thought about, talked about, or written about? What aspects of infant death and babyloss have not appeared publicly or been taken up by policymakers? What hidden crevices of infant loss are in dire need of sunlight? What populations have been overlooked? Whose stories are never told or are told only in ways that advantage those in power? Where do pregnant people and parents enter into accounts of infant loss, as those most impacted? How does this book interrupt the formal, numeric register of infant mortality rates to make new spaces for affective considerations of grief and loss? For feelings rather than statistical responses to infant death?

You may ask, How will I read this book?

My answer is, Any way you choose.

Some readers will move through the entries sequentially, as one might when reading to a child or oneself. Others will start with entries that most interest them; the table of contents will be helpful in this regard. *Babylost* may also function as a kind of (partial) encyclopedia or archive, a reference text for activists, caregivers, scholars, and others interested in a specific topic or concern. People who have lost babies may read some entries and skip over others, finding them too close to the bone. And still others may mine this book for ideas about future projects related to infant mortality. I hope this is the case. I would be honored if this book inspired a few dissertations or other studies of the *many woefully understudied aspects of infant loss*, from the relationship between capitalism and infant mortality, to transgender pregnancy and birth outcomes, to infant mortality and pandemics, and well beyond.

The book's underlying argument is this: *infant mortality has been, for far too long, ignored*. Those who study rates and measures, seeking causes in everything from race to socioeconomic status to a father's educational level, will likely disagree with me. But what I mean is this: we have ignored those facets of infant death that might deepen our collective understanding and promote different and better interventions. Because it is not enough to simply *measure* death; we must also be willing to shift practices and structures that will foster deeper understanding and survival. To do so, we must make visible the babies who die and the babylost families who grieve them. If we cannot *see* infant mortality as a *human* problem, a matter of *trauma and loss*, and not simply as a statistical conundrum, then we cannot address it at the roots. We must allow ourselves to be haunted by all the lost babies rather than comforted by or preoccupied with abstractions.

There is another assertion, too, at once poignant and political. It has been the book's pulse, urging me forward even when my own heart was too undone to continue. It is this:

That babies die is a sad fact of life.

That babies die prematurely, from preventable causes, is shameful.

We can and must do more, especially for the most marginalized among us.

Babylost is my modest offering.

A

ABSENCE

In historian Elizabeth Heineman's memoir of babyloss, *Ghostbelly*, she writes, "This is what I want to do. . . . To take that moment, in which Thor will not grow six hours older, and inhabit it fully. . . . And because this is so important, other things can wait. Like crying. Like thinking about Thor's absence. . . . [It] will not last just a moment, not even a stretched-out moment. It will occupy time. First he will be dead a day, then a week, then a month, then a year. I will have the rest of my life to explore it, and its exploration will require the rest of my life."

This passage deftly and painfully captures the ways in which babyloss shapes and is sculpted by time and space. The desolation of absence is strangely flush with the remembrance of presence. For pregnant people, a baby is a solid being inside the womb: moving, kicking, rolling, and otherwise making her presence known. The "thingness" of babies and the corporeal reality of pregnancy—nausea, aches and pains, elasticized joints, weight gain, swollen breasts, penguin-like ungainliness—situate babies as recognizable beings in pregnant bodies and in communal life. A baby felt—*quickened* to use the old-fashioned term—is an anticipated member of the human community.

Babies of a certain gestational age, usually after the first trimester, have heft, names, legacies, and futures. They become tender repositories for the hopes and fears of expectant parents and their families and communities. During pregnancy, women may cradle their bellies with their arms, rest their hands or perhaps a teacup on them as if on a curved shelf, or gaze in wonder (or sometimes dismay) at their silhouettes revealed in full-length mirrors, evidence of fertility in their plump stomachs.

I did all these things, and more.

When my own daughters were born, I immediately desired to touch them. Instinctual or learned behavior: Who knew? It *felt* primal, and I wanted nothing more than to hold their tiny bodies close to my skin, to lick their downy heads. I was fortunate. Despite a terrifying emergency cesarean delivery of my first daughter, more than two weeks past her due date, and a cesarean delivery of my second

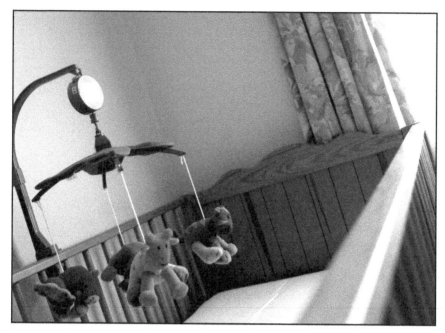

Empty crib. Photo credit: Gary Roebuck / Alamy Stock Photo.

child after thirty-six hours of labor in an attempted vaginal delivery, I held and nursed my babies soon after their births. Their warm, supple matter was breathtakingly familiar and intoxicating.

Some people are not so lucky.

Stillbirth is an especially cruel fate, one that affects 1 in 160 pregnancies in the United States each year. Here, laboring women deliver not-living babies, often unexpectedly—there may be no warning, even with prenatal monitoring. These babies become present in the world as flesh and soft bone; they can be held and caressed, even photographed, by those expecting them. They have names and birth stories, no matter how abbreviated their lives. And yet, these tiny humans are absent consciousness, personhood, and futurity; they are dead on arrival.

Kelly Kittel, author of the memoir *Breathe*, writes, "There is nothing sadder in this world than a dead baby. There is nothing more heartbreaking for a mother than to deliver a baby into this world knowing he is no longer of this world, knowing that it is only a token gesture, like closing the cage door after the dove has flown away."

In her 2008 memoir, *An Exact Replica of a Figment of My Imagination*, novelist Elizabeth McCracken writes, "The first thing we did back at Savary was dismantle the future. That is, Edward broke down the portable crib that had been waiting for a few weeks on my side of the bed. I threw out all my maternity clothes, just threw them away, along with the single package of diapers I'd obediently bought. . . . We tossed out the stuffed hippopotamus from Edward's sister and any other toylike object."

After death, hope seeps away along with the toys and diapers, and absence settles in to supplant physical presence. "Since he died," McCracken laments, "I've never had a dream of him alive."

In "Nadia's Story," Ana Todorović writes wrenchingly of her daughter's still-birth, including the agonizing decision to let Nadia die in utero rather than to "'put her to sleep' with a needle to the heart, after which her birth would be induced and it would be all over." Todorović, a neuroscientist and experimental psychologist, reflects, "My mind will try to build some meaning around her because my feelings take me in that direction, but the idea of a child that *almost was* is something too elusive to be carefully taken apart and then mentally rebuilt. It's just a gaping hole, a hollow, aching absence. One I'm told will grow more comfortable over time."

In stillbirth, a lost baby is barely known to those who mourn him, more a fig-ment of the imagination, to echo McCracken's wistful phrasing. A baby who is born alive but dies within the first year of her life is a different species of being, one who accumulates personality, gestures, familiarity, and prospects as time passes. Babies born alive can be, already are, somebody. Into the abandoned space after such a loss creep specific memories of a life lived, however briefly. Grieving parents may recount weight and matter, the curl of a baby in their arms, but also a particular facial expression, a first giggle, the silkiness of growing curls, gurgles and coos, a milky scent. Or they may feel nothing at all, numb and confused.

A baby who dies during her first year may live for days, weeks, or even months, and the ripple effects of loss—moments lived and shared, history laid down like small footprints—magnify the eventual permanent absence. An abandoned crib, discarded toys, an empty high chair at the kitchen table, a drawer full of carefully folded onesies, a binky still in its package, silence.

To be clear: *there is no better or worse way to lose a baby*, no optimal time or age or circumstance. There are no Olympic games to measure or reward the grief and suffering of moms and dads and other family members. Each loss is achingly unique, and there is ample mourning to be distributed and shared. And yet, while parents are enmeshed in an intricate choreography of presence and absence in the wake of babyloss, infant death *as loss* is still largely absent from public conversation. There is increasing discussion of adult death in hospitals, in hospices, at home, by choice. But infant death is still met with silence.

Instead, a focus on numbers—the infant mortality rate—invites and makes possible abstraction and standardization. Vital statistics are useful, to be sure. But clinical and bureaucratic detachment obscure lived experiences, the messiness of stories. Numbers, rates, charts, and tables hide the fleshiness of loss, the steady pulse of grief, the tears of all the babylost parents and those who love them.

Dead babies are doubly absent, then: they no longer inhabit pregnant bodies and daily lives, nor are they much present in public discourse. They are missing bodies, figments of the imagination, tiny occasions for monumental grief. And their ghostly disappearance is registered in empty cribs and broken hearts.

ABUSE

Sometimes babies die because people hurt them, malevolently or accidentally but nonetheless fatally.

In the United States each year, approximately seven hundred thousand children are abused. Seven percent of infant deaths are caused by injuries and violence, including abuse and neglect. Murder is the cause of one in five injury-related deaths in infants under one year of age.

More often than not—78 percent of the time—the abuser is a parent.

In their first week of life, infants are statistically at greater risk from their mothers; after this period, they are more at risk from male family members, usually a father or stepfather. Homicide risk is highest during a child's first month of life—more than at any other time before age eighteen.

Parents who have abused their infants often report "frustration" stemming from the baby's inconsolable crying. Shaken baby syndrome, which can cause severe brain damage and death, is one—albeit horrific and inappropriate—response to a child in distress.

Parenting, especially mothering, is taxing. An anthropologist friend once shared with me her surprise that exhausted, confused, undervalued, and unsupported mothers do not kill their infants more often.

But sometimes, parents who harm are not frustrated and overtired; they are simply cruel.

Infant abuse may be unfathomable to parents who have lost desperately wanted babies, whom they had hoped to nurture and protect for the entirety of their lives, from cradle to adulthood.

They, and we, might ask: Why would anyone deliberately harm their defenseless baby, especially a tiny, fragile newborn entirely dependent on others for its survival?

Though we can sociologically identify reasons for infant harm, the "why" is sadly rhetorical; it allows us to pose a question about an unspeakable act for which there is no reasonable answer, especially for babylost parents.

ANGEL BABIES

This sweet term of remembrance and endearment designates some babies who have died at birth or during their first year of life. Influenced by religious iconography, angel babies are believed to inhabit both heaven and earth. Their "presence" brings peace and comfort to the people left behind to mourn them, especially parents.

Many babylost parents, particularly mothers, report that when asked how many children they have, they list their living children and angel babies. Some bereaved women share stories of communicating with their angel babies through dreams and conversations.

Support websites (such as stillstandingmag.com), as well as personal stories shared on these sites, make frequent reference to angel babies, "angel moms" (mothers of angel babies), and less often, "angel dads" (fathers of angel babies).

This abundance of angels suggests a fervent longing to believe that lost babies live on, albeit in a different form.

Angel babies, because they are often so small especially if prematurely born, need unique, right-sized clothing for memorials, burial, and cremation. Angel gowns, typically white, are donated or purchased for such purposes. These small, exquisite garments, often created from recycled wedding dresses and other culturally meaningful items, convey a sense of the beatific, evoking tender loss and misfortune. Angel babies are framed through these discourses and practices as wholly innocent and pure, as perhaps they should be.

Of course, the significance of white to denote purity and the proliferation of white angels in Christianity, especially in the United States where evangelicalism has spread widely, invoke racial dynamics of infant death. A white scholar writing about slain teenager Michael Brown once asked, "Why are all the angels white?" And a Black journalist on the other side of the Atlantic Ocean wondered, "Why can't an angel be black?"

We might pose a set of related questions given that death rates for Black and Native American infants in the United States are so much higher than for white infants: Who is deemed worthy of angel baby status, of innocence, in American hierarchies of life, loss, and remembrance? Which angel babies matter, and to whom? Is the grief of "angel moms" and "angel dads" the only legitimate mourning? What about other mothers and fathers, those for whom the angel does not represent their lost child?

AWARENESS

The term *awareness* generally means having knowledge of something or being well informed. In psychology, it can signify consciousness and self-awareness and is at the heart of conversations about sentience and pain. Are animals aware of their own bodies and existence? Are babies, and if so, at what age? And what of grieving mothers and fathers?

In my field—sociology—"awareness" implies that people are social beings: that we have a sense of our communities and the world around us and that we may act on this awareness. For example, on the heels of the Black Lives Matter movement, being "woke" is akin to being aware of racial injustice and prepared to do something about it.

Alas, the opposite of awareness is *ignorance*, or to be lacking in crucial knowledge about social life and people, including babies. Depending on the phenomenon, there may be wide gaps between self-awareness—that which affects us personally—and public awareness. Such gaps in awareness inform what we know and our collective capacity or willingness to act on this knowledge.

I began studying infant mortality because much of the public seemed unaware that babies in the United States, especially babies of color, die at very high, even alarming rates. When I learned many years ago that the African American infant mortality rate was more than twice that of whites and the Native American infant mortality rate nearly as high, I was astonished that we were not discussing this publicly with any sense of urgency or outrage. Was it the case, I wondered, that we just did not care about dying babies, especially Black and Indigenous babies? Why was infant death *not* considered a public health emergency?

The more I learned, the more I came to understand that local awareness of babyloss has *not* generated greater social awareness, and increased awareness has *not* always led to action. Babies die, parents and families grieve, and communities suffer—but this tragedy does not necessarily translate into effective public policy. The missing piece seemed to be *care*. That is, a collective engagement with and willingness to act on knowledge about babyloss, especially as it affects communities of color, does not happen.

More than three decades ago, President Ronald Reagan designated October as Pregnancy and Infant Loss Awareness Month. Proclamation 5890, issued October 25, 1988, recognized "the great tragedy involved in the deaths of unborn and newborn babies." National observance of such losses, according to Reagan, "enables us to consider how, as individuals and communities, we can meet the needs of bereaved parents and family members and work to prevent causes of these problems."

In 2005, the U.S. House of Representatives passed a concurrent resolution "supporting the goals and ideals of National Pregnancy and Infant Loss Remembrance Day." The resolution specifically recognized October 15 as a day of remembrance: "Even the shortest lives are still valuable, and the grief of those who mourn the loss of these lives should not be trivialized."

The nonprofit organization "October 15th"—founded by Robyn Bear, who was influential in the passage of the congressional resolution—was created to increase broader awareness of infant loss: "Too many families grieve in silence, sometimes never coming to terms with their loss. . . . Our goal is to help others relate to our loss."

In the United States, there are more than 200 official recognitions of health awareness, with 145 of these introduced in Congress just since 2005. There are likely many more unofficial observances. One important question is, Do they work? That is, does increasing awareness generate social action, such as policy changes and clinical interventions? Or are awareness days merely to pacify those who care about *x*, *y*, or *z*?

Two public health scholars dug into the literature on awareness events. They found that, without efforts to create healthier social contexts, awareness efforts "might do little more than reinforce ideologies of individual responsibility" and deepen the belief that "adverse [bad] health outcomes are simply the product of misinformed [bad] behaviors." For example, on the October 15th Facebook page, a quote suggested it is women's responsibility to keep their children safe. Katie, a babylost mom, responded, "[Saying] a mother's job is to keep her child safe hurts me as an angel mother. It makes me feel [even more] like the failure I already think I am."

How might greater awareness of infant death lead to actions that reduce death rates *without* making parents, especially mothers, who have lost babies feel like failures? One approach might be for awareness groups to move beyond grief and coping issues to address root causes. That is, many such groups perform awareness by offering empathy, resources, and help just after infant death. These are important. But very few organizations investigate or reference *the causes of preventable infant death*. Alongside a litany of sad remembrances on websites and Facebook pages, there is little to no mention of racism, poverty, environmental injustice, lack of access to health care, violence, or any of the structural factors that can lead to higher infant death rates.

Reading through people's diverse yet strikingly similar stories on site after site, one might be forgiven for believing that all infant deaths are simply individual misfortunes and not part of a larger pattern.

There is little doubt that awareness sites and groups help babylost parents and their families; indeed, many posts convey gratitude for the warm, sympathetic community they find in these spaces. It is vital that people who lose babies are seen, heard, understood, and comforted.

But if awareness of loss could also be translated into action beyond caregiving, including concrete measures that reduce or eliminate infant death, wouldn't this be immensely preferable to the lifelong, often solitary work of simply surviving grief?

B

BABYLAND

Humans have not always buried our dead, nor do all cultures bury human remains. In the United States, cemeteries date only from around the mid-nineteenth century. Prior to that time, many dead were buried in parks, church grounds, and other common spaces. Scholar Keith Eggener understands cemeteries as "liminal" places where the living and dead interact but also as sites of containment. That is, they are places for remembering and also for physically separating the dead from the living.

Some cemeteries in the United States are akin to beautiful parks, lush and verdant landscapes of contemplation and alabaster memorialization. Other cemeteries are unkempt and uncared for, dusty and weed-choked, the last places on earth anyone would seek refuge or consolation. How and where we bury our dead can tell us a great deal about how much their lives mattered, and to whom.

Cemeteries across the United States include unmarked graves alongside those with epitaphs. Such unmarked graves also dot the American landscape outside the bounded spaces of formal burial grounds, for example in backyards and adjacent to churches. And inside many cemeteries, plots for dead babies, which are frequently unmarked, are grouped together in zones of desolation and anonymity often called Babyland.

Though "Babyland" sounds like a mid-twentieth-century theme park, these plots are anything but fun and amusing. They are repositories of grief and loss, and their existence—often in shadowy far corners and dark, distant edges of cemeteries—speaks volumes about how little we acknowledge the deaths of some infants, especially babies from poor families.

Consider Evergreen Cemetery's Babyland in Gainesville, Florida, where more than two hundred babies are buried in mostly unmarked, evenly spaced graves dating from 1939. As one news story noted, "Few of the children lived more than a day, so their markers only bare [*sic*] one date. Even fewer were named." While infants whose families could afford the family plots were likely buried in them, Babyland was for those who did not have financial resources. The babies were mostly interred alone.

Mount Olivet Cemetery, Hugo, Okla. Photo credit: Joseph Novak / Flickr.

The Babyland Renewal Initiative, spearheaded by the Evergreen Cemetery director and community supporters, draws on genealogical research to provide names and birth and death dates for the unidentified graves. "To just have a concrete cylinder for these graves was a little demeaning," one supporter noted, especially given the history of the cemetery, whose first burial was founder James T. Thomas's ten-day-old daughter.

In addition to replacing unmarked graves with named markers, the Evergreen Babyland plot is now watched over by an angel statue engraved with the words, "For all the babies who were never rocked in the arms of their parents, or whose time of rocking was far too brief, may they be rocked forever in the arms of the angels."

There is also a Babyland in Memphis, Tennessee, a city with one of the highest rates of infant mortality in the country. Some seventeen thousand babies are buried there. This "potter's field" in Shelby County gave its name to a 2008 documentary, *Babyland*, focused on the broader structural context of infant loss, including poverty, racism, and government neglect. A promotional site for the film asserts, "The dying babies are a warning of the danger that comes from ignoring the underclass." Asked in the film if the issue is ignored because it is primarily Black babies dying, a social worker responds, "Yes, period."

In 2008, Birthing Project USA (BPUSA)—"the underground railroad for new life"—held a national conference in Memphis to kick off its 2009 "Little Miracles" campaign. According to organizers, "The highlight of the event which brought together community leaders and health care specialists from 20 cities was a historic pilgrimage to BabyLand to commemorate the lives of the babies who have died and to beautify their little burial sites, which are identified by a little silver disc with a number and no name."

BPUSA's mission is to improve birth outcomes for women of color. Public health professional Kathryn Hall-Trujillo founded the organization after holding a dead infant in her arms and realizing at that moment that she had internalized the term *infant mortality* as "counting dead babies." She wanted a different approach, one that would both involve the community *and* recognize that structural factors like racism lead to poor outcomes. The Ashoka website (Hall-Trujillo has been a fellow since 2007) notes that "support and hope may be hard to measure, but Kathryn's results are not."

In contrast to the largely forgotten Babylands of Florida, Tennessee, and other states, in some cemeteries, especially in more affluent communities across the United States, children are remembered with lavish headstones, adornments, and personalized epitaphs. They are named, their birth and death dates acknowledged, and their precious links to other family members noted.

For example, at the Babyland of Forest Lawn Memorial Park in California, where many celebrities including Walt Disney eternally rest, a bronze statue of a baby greets visitors to plots arranged in the form of a heart. This is remembrance sculpted in white marble: "Across the way, a miniature version of Sleeping Beauty's castle at Disneyland marks the entrance to Lullabyland. On the outskirts of the heart, you'll find the graves of mothers who wished to be buried in close proximity to their children."

A photographer, referencing Disneyland's famous tagline, described Forest Lawn's Lullabyland as "one of the Saddest Places on Earth."

A folklorist writes, "The loss of a child is enormous in its levels of grief and sorrow. . . . Because of the strong belief in the innocence and purity of the child, we have a more difficult time coming to terms with the death. It is through the gravemarker and its employing iconography that the memory of the child is immortalized far better than that of the adult. The innocence guarantees a select seat in the afterlife."

But if we accept this interpretation—and some may not—what does it mean for those babies lying in unmarked, solitary graves in forgotten boneyards across the United States, most of them poor, many of them babies of color? Are these babies any less "innocent," any less deserving of recognition and remembrance, any less worthy of being gently entombed and adorned with teddy bears, flowers, and angels?

The way we bury these small dead would seem to suggest they are.

Babyland is, quite literally, taking inequality to the grave.

BLACK INFANT MORTALITY

Everyone dies, eventually. But some people die much too soon.

In the United States, premature death disproportionately plagues Black people, whether they are being shot in the streets by overzealous police, experiencing

·what feminist scholar Lauren Berlant calls "slow death" in jails and prisons, or dying early from preventable causes during and after birth. Black women and babies bear the brunt of "stratified reproduction" in the United States, and their lives and deaths often pass unheeded by those positioned to foster better survival odds.

The Black infant mortality rate is more than twice that of the white infant mortality rate—a disparity that has remained largely unchanged for more than a century. Consider these recent headlines: "Black Babies Face Double the Risk of Dying before Their First Birthday"; "Infant Mortality Rates Are Twice as High for Black Babies, and That Is a Big F*cking Deal"; "Death Rate for Black Infants More Than Double Rate for White Infants"; "Racial Disparity in Infant Mortality Remains Huge Concern in US"; and "Why the Black-White Infant Mortality Gap Exists and How to Eradicate It."

All name a persistent problem: inequality.

Political scientist Annie Menzel has excavated the political life of Black infant mortality across more than a century. She shows how Black infants were left out of popular and medical conceptions of childhood, with white infancy elevated to the level of mattering, or "true babyhood." Efforts to decrease rates of infant death have long relied on racist paradigms that locate pathology inside Black bodies, understood biologically and politically as due to "race traits." Political and public health interventions, Menzel argues, have been willfully decontextualized, targeting individual Black mothers and babies but not the systems that produce debility and death. She denotes "a striking continuity in the devaluation of African American life."

Menzel shows how infant death is made visible and comes to matter politically—*but only for some babies*. White infant death is grievable, with angels; Black infant death is not. Infant mortality is a made-up category, as sociologist David Armstrong argued, with a history in vital statistics, governmental and health interventions, and popular culture. Inside this category are assumptions about whose deaths matter, whose are worth recording and mourning, and whose lives should be prioritized. What Menzel helps us understand is that not only do Black babies die at disproportionately higher rates than white babies; their deaths are accelerated, interpreted, and responded to through racist frameworks that hide the very conditions that overproduce Black death.

In many ways, then, the problem of infant mortality in the United States *is* the problem of Black infant mortality. Our appalling rate globally hinges, in large part, on local racial disparities. With an abundance of research highlighting conditions that speed infant death, including systemic racism, it is clear that infant death in African American communities could be mitigated. As could premature Black death more broadly. There is nothing "natural" about the numbers of Black men, women, and children who die every day from violence, heart disease, pregnancy complications, low birth weight, and other preventable causes.

Eliminating racism would go a long way toward promoting Black survival.

Yet the problem of Black infant mortality is not only about epidemiological cause and effect. It is also about caring, in the pragmatist sense of devoting attention to a matter. That is, infant mortality has not ascended to the status of a social and political emergency *precisely because it is a problem of racism.* Black babies are dying, and yet Black infant mortality does not seem to register as a problem in predominantly white institutional and cultural spaces. But one could argue that if the statistics were reversed—if white babies were dying at two to three times the rate of Black babies—we might well witness a different scenario. One that would involve ample funding, public health initiatives, community interventions, legislation, and other urgent efforts to save lives.

To be clear, in drawing attention to the problem of Black infant mortality, I am not suggesting that babyloss in other communities matters any less. Infant death is grievable, full stop. Babies die, women mourn and suffer, and families and communities are upended across *all* racial groups in the United States. Indigenous women and babies are also particularly at risk for high morbidity and mortality rates. Yet I do want to suggest that the singular experience of loss and mourning, in which babyloss is seen as private, collides with the structural problem of Black infant mortality to shroud infant death. Race and gender intersect to keep infant mortality hidden from the public agenda.

And yet . . .

Black parents and babies matter.

The Black Lives Matter hashtag and movement is a rallying cry to identify and challenge premature Black death and state violence. Predictably there has been backlash, with the hashtag #AllLivesMatter proliferating across social media. The underlying fear, it seems, is that if Black lives are prioritized—seen as grievable—white lives will cease to matter. This is profoundly misguided, and also racist.

Thwarting premature death among African Americans is an ethical and political imperative. It is not, in fact, a distraction from addressing supposedly more important (white) deaths. Indeed, attention to the needs of the most vulnerable— Black babies, Indigenous babies, immigrant babies—can help improve the survival of *all* babies. But efforts to save tender lives cannot advance through racist frameworks that deny structural causes of infant death.

In 1990, the *Black Scholar* published an article that described infant mortality as "an American tragedy." The language of tragedy may be useful in generating concern about infant death, but unmoored from structure and framed as catastrophe—like a hurricane, for example—it may imply an event without attribution of cause. And causes matter. In 2003, pediatrician and public health scholar Paul Wise wrote, "The death of any infant is always a tragedy. But the death of an infant from preventable causes is always unjust."

Black infant mortality is both tragic *and* unjust—and also a political object that shapes how we respond to the ongoing, preventable deaths of Black babies. If infant mortality is an indicator of national health and well-being, then the United States is not well.

Racism is killing too many of us.

Blame

Imagine losing a baby.

Now imagine that you are blamed for this loss.

This happens to far too many women, who are seen as ill-behaved culprits by partners, family members, doctors, the criminal justice system, and even women's health advocates.

Consider this harrowing tale from the *New York Times*: "After Harmony's death, Landrum's life grew more chaotic. Her boyfriend blamed her for what had happened to their baby and grew more abusive. Around Christmas 2016, in a rage, he attacked her, choking her so hard that she urinated on herself."

Blamed to the point of physical abuse in an already volatile, dangerous, life-threatening relationship, while also grieving the loss of her baby. In one study, 16 percent of men blamed their partners for stillbirth. One woman remarked, "He was angry with me for having a stillbirth. I could see it in his behavior."

The word *blame* is rooted in Latin, deriving from the word *blasphemare*, and in Old French from the word *blasmer*, meaning to rebuke, reprimand, condemn, or criticize. Blame denotes culpability, and it is invariably negative. We do not blame people when they do something right; we praise or commend them. We only blame them when they do something wrong.

To be blamed is to be judged, sometimes by the legal system—especially for women of color. For example, an Indiana woman of South Asian descent was arrested and charged with feticide and involuntary manslaughter after her baby was stillborn at home and she sought medical help. Charges were based on her alleged drug use, according to the National Advocates for Pregnant Women, and she spent several months in jail. Blame is intimately woven into the fabric of racism, whether in the criminal justice system or health care.

In 2017, renowned midwife Ina May Gaskin, who is white, suggested that the high infant mortality rate among African Americans was due to Black women's "lifestyle" choices, including illegal drugs and unhealthy eating. She recommended "praying and growing food to reverse mortality rates." Black women's health advocates were quick to respond, including circulating a petition and boycotting events featuring Gaskin. "Unfortunately," wrote Black doula Samantha Griffin, "Gaskin didn't think about the implications of prescribing agricultural work to those descended from slaves." She bitingly noted that midwifery and homebirth "are rich in Black America and pre-date Gaskin."

Blame is also woven into the fabric of gender, such that women are conditioned to accept blame, even when adverse outcomes are not their fault. Kelly Kittel writes, "Somehow, sometime, somewhere, a taciturn movement toward blaming the victim had begun. I was the bad mother, the one who failed to watch Noah, who left him 'alone.'" Another babylost woman in the study mentioned earlier reported, "I still sometimes blame myself for her death, even though I got the autopsy results back."

Such feelings cannot be separated from the widespread cultural phenomenon of "mother blame"—itself anchored in the gendered history of psychology as well as the responsibility of women to reproduce for crown and country. If everybody else is blaming mothers, then why shouldn't mothers blame *themselves* when they lose babies?

Blame has numerous functions, including holding people and institutions morally and legally responsible. It is thus, in a larger sense, about the maintenance of social order. Blame allows us to locate responsibility and agency when things go wrong; it provides meaning and facilitates action. But blaming parents for infant death is fraught. Especially when there is *no* liability, which is the case the vast majority of the time.

Lodging blame with mothers is a misogynistic sleight of hand that draws the eye away from structural causes of infant mortality, such as poverty and racism. Because if women are to blame, then we need not worry about unequal access to health care, violence, environmental toxins, food deserts, or the many other factors that contribute to high rates of infant—and maternal—death.

We *could* work to address structural causes of infant mortality—and many reproductive justice advocates are doing precisely this. It is just so much *easier* to blame women and to target, as Ina May Gaskin did, the "bad" behavior and lifestyle choices of (some) women. Women are potentially malleable; social structures, much less so.

Collectively, we would have to care a great deal more about babies, especially babies of color, than we currently do in the United States. The nation's conservative "pro-life" rhetoric extends rarely to infant health and well-being and almost never to babies and children of color.

In the meantime, when all else fails, let us continue to blame mothers for infant mortality.

After all, they already blame themselves.

BREASTFEEDING

Like some women, I experienced difficult pregnancies and births. With my firstborn, I endured a sudden, frightening, panic-inducing cesarean section. And though I tried to deliver my second daughter vaginally, I surrendered to a C-section after thirty-six hours of painful labor.

I am grateful every day that my children lived. Their survival, and my own, are reflections of my many privileges, including access to quality obstetric care.

After such challenging deliveries, to my surprise, one aspect of motherhood worked beautifully: breastfeeding. My firstborn would not take a bottle, and so during her first six months of life, I was solely responsible for sustaining her. She nursed like a champion, and I loved the closeness of feeding her. She would have kept nursing, too, if I had not become pregnant with her sister. Explaining to my precocious toddler that my body would now need to make special milk for the new baby, as it did for her, I weaned her at nineteen months.

My birthing and nursing experiences were both incredibly meaningful to me and were also not especially unique. Lots of women breastfeed and have done so for millennia, as babies usually thrive on mother's milk, and nursing can bring profoundly satisfying physical and emotional connections.

Yet the biological act of nursing babies—the word *mammal* comes from the word for breast, *mamma*—is not precisely the same thing as the social (or political) act. Some aspects of breastfeeding ignite confusion and even outrage about women's breasts, gender roles, motherhood, and the care and feeding of infants. Still today, it is deemed scandalous in many parts of the country to nurse a baby in public. And shamefully, many babies dine on their mothers' bodies hidden in unclean public restrooms or closets. While it may be natural for mammals, including humans, to nurse their young, breastfeeding is heavily policed and managed.

Breastfeeding figures prominently in "official" versions of motherhood and infant survival. Medical and public health experts have weighed in as strong advocates of breastfeeding, if not always of pregnant and laboring women. The American Academy of Pediatrics recommends exclusive breastfeeding for six months and continued breastfeeding for a year while other foods are introduced. Similarly, the World Health Organization recommends exclusive breastfeeding for six months, with continuation to two years *or beyond*: "Virtually all mothers can breastfeed, provided they have accurate information, and the support of their family, the health care system and society at large. Colostrum, the yellow sticky breast milk produced at the end of pregnancy, is recommended by WHO as the perfect food for the newborn, and [breast] feeding should be initiated within the first hour after birth."

Despite these uniform *recommendations*, breastfeeding is not universal, nor can all parents nurse their babies. And some may not want to, for a variety of quite legitimate reasons. In the United States, according to the CDC, most babies (more than 80 percent) start out nursing, but fewer than half of infants are exclusively breastfed for three months, and only about a quarter are exclusively breastfed for six months. Around 17 percent of infants are given formula within the first two days of life. The CDC suggests these rates show that "mothers may not be getting the support they need from health care providers, family members, and employers to meet their breastfeeding goals." The Healthy People 2020 initiative sought to improve breastfeeding rates, including workplace lactation support.

Some scholars, such as political scientist Joan Wolf, contest the recommendations noted above. In her acclaimed book *Is Breast Best?*, Wolf asserts that an overemphasis on breastfeeding is based on cultural expectations of "total motherhood" and efforts to eliminate all risk from children's lives. She challenges the evidence that breastfeeding is optimal, noting that "despite numerous theories, scientists have been largely unable to demonstrate *how* breast milk works in a baby's body to protect or promote health. . . . When studies find an association between breastfeeding and reduced risks . . . it is not at all clear that one causes the other, and the conclusion that breastfeeding confers health benefits is far less certain than its proponents contend."

While Wolf agrees that "on average breastfed babies are healthier," she takes issue with the idea that breastfeeding *causes* better health, arguing that "women who breastfeed are [also] more likely to do other things that make their babies healthier."

Predictably, many breastfeeding advocates have not appreciated Wolf's scholarly intervention. She admits, "I've been placed in the same camp as Holocaust deniers and advocates of cold fusion. I've been accused of hating mothers and children. I've also been called a lesbian (gasp) and a feminist (double gasp). One person called me a gender-confused cow." (Wolf is herself a mother and unambiguously human.)

Calling forth some of the same data Wolf rejects, breastfeeding is also linked directly to infant mortality as an important preventive strategy. Authors of a 2012 study assert, "It is well-known that breastfeeding saves and improves the quality of lives even in relatively clean, industrialized contexts. In an analysis of data from the 2005 National Immunization Survey, researchers calculated that if 90% of infants were exclusively breastfed for 6 months, 911 deaths would be prevented. . . . The association between breastfeeding behaviors and infant health outcomes are the subject of a large literature that, despite limitations, establishes breastfeeding as the 'gold standard' against which alternative feeds should be evaluated." These authors also delve into *how* breastfeeding confers benefits, contra Wolf, including a deep dive into antibodies, gut bacteria, and hormones.

Focused on Indiana, which like other states faces high Black infant mortality rates, a 2017 article declared, "Breastfeeding is a key piece of the infant mortality puzzle." The author was Jerome Adams, former Indiana State Health Commissioner and former U.S. Surgeon General. He wrote, "Infant mortality is one of Indiana's most persistent health concerns. Our state has lost 3,000 infants before the age of one in the last 5 years. In 2015 alone, 613 children died before their first birthdays. Our journey to find answers to this problem has spurred efforts to build a comprehensive and evidence-based plan to increase breastfeeding rates, a goal that will impact the health of all Hoosiers for generations to come."

As part of its efforts, the state created a new position—breastfeeding coordinator in the Office of Women's Health—implemented a state breastfeeding plan, and established the Maternal Child Health (MOMS) helpline. Though opting for a "holistic view," enhanced breastfeeding is the cornerstone of the plan.

International research supports the U.S. data on breastfeeding and infant mortality. An oft-cited 2006 study focused on Ghana determined that "promotion of early initiation of breastfeeding has the potential to make a major contribution to the achievement of the child survival millennial development goal; 16% of neonatal deaths could be saved if all infants were breastfed from day 1 and 22% if breastfeeding started in the first hour." Similarly, a 2015 longitudinal study in Ethiopia found that "infant mortality in the northwest part of the country is still very high. Exclusive breast feeding is the strongest predictor of infant survival in this predominantly rural setting where hygienic standards are poor." And in 2018, Kenya's Ministry of Health and the nongovernmental organization PATH announced that human breast milk would be freely available by donation for babies who cannot be breastfed. Elizabeth Kimani-Murage, head of maternal and child well-being at the African Population and Health Research Center, remarked, "Despite improvements in infant mortality, neonatal mortality is reducing at a very slow rate, so those are the children we want to target."

The World Economic Forum has taken a position as well, citing maternal vaccination and breastfeeding as "the two best ways to reduce infant mortality." Taking up the United Nations Sustainable Development Goals (SDGs), including the commitment to end preventable newborn and child deaths, the forum describes breastmilk as a "readily available" resource. Noting that breastfeeding has a more significant positive impact than maternal vaccinations, the report states, "Breast milk is the perfect nutrition for a baby. . . . Best of all, mothers create new antibodies in real time, which help strengthen young immune systems." However, the report's author laments, "rates of breastfeeding and breast-milk consumption are well below desired levels. Only 40% of infants worldwide are breastfed exclusively until they are at least six months old."

The connection between breastfeeding and infant mortality has been picked up by the media; it is too compelling not to be. For example, a 2018 magazine article reports, "Research has shown that in countries with poor water quality, early breastfeeding leads to lower infant mortality rates. But in 2017 alone, about 78 million babies were not breastfed within the first hour of life, most of them born in low- and middle-income countries." The article also discusses increased rates of cesarean section, which can lead to delayed breastfeeding, and also women's socioeconomic status, topics often left out of media coverage touting breastfeeding's benefits. As the author notes, "Mothers cannot be expected to do it alone."

As important as breastfeeding is deemed to be for infant survival, it is rather astonishing how relatively few supportive resources are available, especially for poor women, women of color, and transgender people. Many parents, in fact, do attempt to go it alone. These include single moms and women with partners who may not understand how to help; those in hostile workplaces, at risk of public censure or hypersexualization; and those with little guidance or support from health care professionals. The situation is changing in the United States with the advent of doulas (trained professionals who provide support and comfort to mothers before, during, and after birth), childbirth educators, in-hospital breastfeeding support, and other resources. Yet too many women are unable or unwilling to continue trying to nurse, especially when they return to work. Also, pumping milk is difficult for many (as it was for me), and breast pumps are prohibitively expensive and not uniformly covered by health insurance.

Additionally, educational campaigns about the importance of breastfeeding are not equivalent to providing resources and assisting workplaces and public spaces to be more welcoming to nursing mothers. Claiming breastfeeding is the key to infant health without offering material resources and tangible support may do more to make women feel guilty for not breastfeeding than actually encourage them to nurse their babies. Advocating breastfeeding while simultaneously cutting reproductive access and services is especially duplicitous and harmful to women and babies.

The political gap between knowledge and practice can be striking. In 2018, the U.S. State Department undermined a World Health Assembly resolution from Ecuador promoting breastfeeding—and did so in the interests of formula makers. The *New York Times* reported, "The intensity of the administration's opposition to the breast-feeding resolution stunned public health officials and foreign diplomats. . . . During the deliberations, some American delegates even suggested the United States might cut its contribution to the W.H.O." A British breastfeeding advocate commented, "What happened was tantamount to blackmail, with the U.S. holding the world hostage and trying to overturn nearly 40 years of consensus on the best way to protect infant and young child health."

Beyond government officials playing politics with women's health on a global stage, breastfeeding is also politicized in ways that create barriers and lead to stark disparities. This is especially the case for African American women who suffer from the highest rates of maternal and infant death from preventable causes. Regina Smith James of the National Institute on Minority Health and Health Disparities writes, "Despite the many benefits of breastfeeding, African American mothers have the lowest rate of breastfeeding initiation and duration. . . . *The Surgeon General's Call to Action to Support Breastfeeding* noted that even while researchers control for family's income or educational level, breastfeeding rates for African American infants are lower than for White infants at birth, 6 months, and 12 months."

James identifies several reasons for these disparities, including new mothers returning to work earlier, giving birth in settings that provide formula rather than support breastfeeding, lacking knowledge on the subject, perceiving it as an inconvenience, and feeling embarrassed about breastfeeding, among others.

Lactation counselor Kelly Glass deepens this understanding, situating Black women's breastfeeding in a historical and political context. She suggests that bigotry and racism play a pivotal role, along with lack of access to quality health care. She also acknowledges the disparity "may have to do with the legacy of slavery: Some Black women have been reluctant to breastfeed . . . because slaves were often forced to nurse their slaver masters' children." She further notes that infant formula was "aggressively marketed to Black communities." In short, Glass believes "the health-care system has turned its back on women of color. Put simply, Black mothers often lack the community resources they need to successfully learn about and initiate breastfeeding."

Journalist and maternal-infant health advocate Kimberly Seals Allers posits an even stronger message: the discourse of choice in breastfeeding contributes to Black infant deaths. She writes, "Stereotypes about who breastfeeds and who doesn't, supported by media images, suggest breastfeeding is for white women of privilege; black women, on the other hand, have been stereotyped as good caretakers for other people's children but distrusted as capable parents of their own."

Allers found Black women's breastfeeding repeatedly unsupported by health care professionals who offered them formula more often, thus further limiting any choice they might make about breastfeeding. She avows, "We must end the dangerous conversation of breastfeeding as a 'choice' without a deeper discussion as to how black women's choices are shaped by their circumstances. . . . We must put black mothers and infants at the forefront of the breastfeeding conversation."

Taking a more institutional approach, health psychologist and lactation consultant Kathleen Kendall-Tackett advocates for enhanced diversity among International Board Certified Lactation Consultants (IBCLCs), noting that most doulas and IBCLCs are white, middle-class women like herself. She writes, "The low pay, or lack of job opportunities for IBCLCs who are not also nurses, means that there are limited opportunities for women without other sources of income to be in this profession. . . . We need to recognize the structural barriers that make it difficult for young women of color to enter our field."

Clearly, breastfeeding has been firmly incorporated into the fight against infant mortality—in spite of its limitations, including barriers, disparities, and harmful cultural stereotypes. But what does it mean to lodge responsibility for saving babies solely with lactating women? New mothers are already primarily responsible for nurturing their babies, whether they breastfeed or not. Emphasizing breastfeeding as "the" solution, as many commentators do, places the burden of preventing infant death on mothers rather than distributing it more widely among other family members, communities, and society writ large. Breastfeeding as a panacea for infant death—especially for Black infant death—provokes precisely the question of who is responsible for saving babies' lives.

When I nursed my own daughters, I felt a powerful sense of pride that I was single-handedly (or, rather, double-breastedly) sustaining them. Nobody else could do it; just me. I was woman and animal; hear me roar.

Yet that enormous burden—keeping my babies alive—meant also that I was exhausted, drained (in all senses of the term), and hypervigilant. I barely slept, no matter how tired I was. It is no wonder I experienced the "baby blues" with my firstborn. Though the sense of duty and care to keep my children alive and safe has never left me, it has been shared across time and space with other family members, friends, caregivers, and institutions, such as schools, and also, as they grew older, with my daughters.

I worry that telling women their babies will die if they do not breastfeed and enshrining this message in public health campaigns adds yet more pressure to mothering, as if it isn't already enough of a struggle to bring a new life into the world and care for it. Moreover, if women are solely responsible for keeping their babies alive with precious breastmilk, what happens when babies die anyway, as too many do and all too often? Will women be punished if they haven't breastfed? Or just blamed and shamed? And what of mothers who transmit the "wrong" substances into their babies after being encouraged to breastfeed? Will they be charged with criminal homicide when their infants die from ingesting drugs, as a Pennsylvania woman was in 2018?

Here is what I know for sure: breastfeeding can be both joyful and very, very challenging. Many, perhaps most, women do it because it is perceived as "natural" and expected. It is also low-cost, financially speaking—certainly cheaper than formula. But many other women do not breastfeed because they are not supported to do so, or for other valid reasons.

I also know this, and it pierces my heart:

There is a cruel irony in making breastfeeding a linchpin of infant survival when babylost women cannot nurse their young at all. Dead babies cannot suckle. There are few more devastating experiences in the world than attempting to express breastmilk for an infant who is no longer alive to need it.

C

Children's Rights

Children matter.

Or, rather, they *should* matter in a just world.

Sometimes, too often, they do not.

The United Nations Convention on the Rights of the Child recognizes that "children need special consideration" and "should be brought up in the spirit of the ideals proclaimed in the Charter of the United Nations." Governments should act in "the best interests of the child," including ensuring "to the maximum extent possible the survival and development of the child." Nation-states have an obligation "to diminish infant and child mortality" and "to ensure appropriate pre-natal and post-natal care for mothers."

The convention was "the most widely and rapidly ratified human rights treaty in history," and yet the United States is the *only* U.N. member state *not* a party to it. Though it was signed in 1995, "no US President then or since has sent it to the Senate for ratification." Somalia and South Sudan were also longtime holdouts, but those countries eventually ratified it in 2015. "So now we're completely on our own," according to a human rights researcher with the ACLU.

One of the aims of the convention—and of various U.N. initiatives that followed, including the Millennium Development Goals (MDGs) and the Sustainable Development Goals (SDGs)—is to improve infant and child mortality. There is still much work to be done. UNICEF reports that, annually, "one million children die the day they are born," 80 percent from premature birth, infection, and complications from birth. Another 2.5 million perish within the first month of life.

Such a staggering number of deaths: 3.5 *million* babies every year, gone.

UNICEF executive director Henrietta Fore laments, "Given that the majority of these deaths are preventable, we are failing the world's poorest babies."

Indeed, we are.

Closer to home, there is broad consensus that the U.S. infant mortality rate is "a national embarrassment," a term that appears frequently in media coverage. In

2017, fifty-four countries had better infant mortality rates than the United States, well below other developed nations.

The lowest infant mortality rate in 2017 belonged to tiny, wealthy, relatively homogenous Monaco, where one in fifty-six people is worth at least thirty million dollars and the literacy rate is nearly 100 percent. Afghanistan, one of the poorest countries in the world and frayed by a long history of armed conflict—in which the United States is heavily implicated—had the highest rate, with more than 110 babies per 1,000 dying before their first birthdays. In both cases, infrastructure as much as policy contributes to the survival odds. (By 2020, Monaco had slipped to the number two spot, displaced by Slovenia, but Afghanistan was still the worst.)

While it is easy to single out our own shameful vital statistics in the United States, it is important to note that 169 countries had *higher* infant death rates in 2017. Of course, none of these 169 countries boasts of having the greatest health care system in the world, despite overwhelming evidence to the contrary. Out of eleven industrialized countries in a 2017 study, the United States ranked dead last on health care outcomes, access, and equity.

Ironically, also tragically, we have the most expensive health care system in the world. Here, health care is not considered a human right. Rather, it is a privilege and a commodity; our health care system is "for profit." Those with money and insurance are generally able to secure better care. Those without, do without. Consequently, many become ill and die. We do as poorly on most other measures of morbidity and mortality as we do with regard to infant death.

The United States is, in a word, sick.

And despite a robust "pro-life" rhetoric from conservatives that centers on the unborn and their right to life, in practice, there is no *actual* right to life, or to living. Not only are we not a party to the U.N. Convention on the Rights of the Child, thereby actually foreclosing core rights that children in many other nations hold. But also, our institutions are set up in such a way that babies and children—and their parents—are profoundly disadvantaged, especially if they are poor, nonwhite, disabled, undocumented, and/or lack access to quality health care.

If we truly cared about life, babies would not die immediately after birth or in their first year from overwhelmingly preventable causes. If we truly cared about the unborn, we would care about the bodies that produce them and remake our institutions to foster life and thriving rather than vulnerability, illness, and death, for parents and their offspring.

We would recognize preventable infant death as a violation of human rights.

And we would ratify the U.N. Convention on the Rights of the Child.

Because children matter—and not just to our future as a species.

CIA's WORLD FACTBOOK

The loss of an infant is a profoundly personal experience, one rarely discussed publicly. And yet, infant death is also a grave matter of national security, of keen interest to the U.S. Central Intelligence Agency.

The CIA grew out of the Japanese "sneak" attack on Pearl Harbor in 1941. It was formally created in 1947 through the National Security Act. Harry S. Truman, who assumed office after President Roosevelt's death in 1945, wanted a global information network that could prevent surprises like Pearl Harbor. "When I took over," he wrote, "the President had no means of coordinating the intelligence from around the world."

An almanac filled with information about hundreds of countries, the CIA's *World Factbook* is based on the kind of intelligence gathering Truman imagined. It was first published as a classified document in 1962 and then in unclassified form in 1971. The *Factbook* went "online" in 1997, making it more widely accessible.

Categories of the CIA's *World Factbook* include "land, water, people, government, economy, communications, and defense forces." Infant mortality data are included alongside other demographic data, and the infant mortality rate is seen as a key indicator of a nation's health. Tracking rising infant mortality rates is one means for knowing which countries are in danger of collapsing or failing, with high or climbing rates signposting trouble. Knowing which states might collapse is useful for U.S. government officials reliant on global intelligence gathering. The *Factbook* is also used widely by NGOs, scholars, and others as it is considered a definitive and up-to-date resource.

The most recent *World Factbook* (2021) reports the U.S. infant mortality rate at 5.22 deaths per 1,000 births, slightly better than the United Arab Emirates at 5.25. Astonishingly, *fifty-one countries have better infant mortality rates than the United States, including Latvia, Slovakia, and Cuba.* However, we are far from the worst nation, Afghanistan, with a continued staggering rate of 106.75 deaths per 1,000 births, worsened by decades of military intervention there.

Given that infant mortality rates of some cities and communities in the United States *exceed* the rates of many developing nations, perhaps we should consider the United States itself a collapsing or failed state? By the CIA's *World Factbook* logic and metrics, we threaten our own national security with our persistent inability to keep (some) babies alive.

CONGRESSIONAL BLACK CAUCUS

"Silence. The beeps are no longer heard, the monitors are no longer on, and the peaks and valleys that represent life now display a flat line. The smallest medical equipment is removed, the lamps turned off, and a mother and father attempt to absorb the unthinkable. Into the world early and gone far too soon, a void has been created that cannot be filled. Today, the village lost a child."

Surprisingly, this poignant passage about infant death appeared not on an online forum curated for babylost parents but rather on the website of the Congressional Black Caucus Foundation (CBCF), the nonprofit, nonpartisan offshoot of the Congressional Black Caucus (CBC). Founded in 1976, the CBCF's mission is "to advance the global black community by developing leaders, informing policy, and educating the public," including on matters of health.

Established in 1971 on the heels of the civil rights movement by thirteen founding members, including Shirley Chisholm (the only woman and an expert on child welfare), the CBC has long been considered by many to be "the conscience of Congress." The CBC has taken up issues important to African Americans that many white policymakers have not, including very early attention to apartheid in South Africa. In its formative years, members aimed "to present a unified voice for black America"—a goal that became increasingly difficult as more members joined. Some have questioned whether the CBC has ever, or can ever, truly represent a diverse Black citizenry.

Black infant mortality has been a "going concern" of the CBC and the foundation for decades. Given that Washington, D.C. has long had one of the highest Black infant mortality rates in the nation, it would have been impossible for Black legislators to ignore the issue of infant death in their own backyard, especially when prominent Black activists nationally and locally were calling attention to disparities. Yet beyond support for Medicaid, the Women, Infants, and Children (WIC) program, and various efforts to combat poverty, there has been little *direct* federal action on infant mortality since the early twentieth century.

For example, the short-lived National Commission to Prevent Infant Mortality, established in 1985 during the Reagan administration, did not single out race and was not a program of the CBC; rather, it was spearheaded by Florida senator Lawton Chiles, who was white. That may be, in part, why the effort was not sustained; it did not address the needs of the most vulnerable, and it was tied to elected office.

This has changed only recently.

Years of tireless activism and reporting on Black maternal and infant mortality seem, finally, to have spurred action. Representative Robin Kelly (D-Illinois), chairwoman of the CBC's Health Braintrust and cochair of the Congressional Caucus on Black Women and Girls, introduced the Mothers and Offspring Mortality and Morbidity Awareness (MOMMA's) Act in May 2018. The bill would have supported the Alliance for Innovation on Maternal Health, extended federal aid to providers and advocates, provided technical assistance to programs working on evidence-based care, and improved vital statistics collection at the national and state levels. Unfortunately, it died in committee.

Representative Lauren Underwood (D-Illinois), Senator (and, as of 2020, Vice President elect) Kamala Harris, and other members of the Black Maternal Health Caucus introduced the Black Maternal Health Omnibus Act of 2020. An umbrella for nine individual bills aimed at addressing high maternal mortality rates among Black women, the act would "fill gaps in existing legislation to comprehensively address every dimension of the Black maternal health crisis in America." Writing in the *Hill*, March for Moms executive director Katie Shea Barrett stated, "The U.S. has the highest maternal mortality rates in the developed world. . . . Congress must take action and pass the Momnibus and the MOMMAs Acts so that families have what they need to grow with dignity."

This legislation was the first in decades that took seriously the preventable tragedy of maternal mortality and morbidity, especially for Black women. The Momnibus and MOMMA's Acts were, in a word, groundbreaking. They were especially significant in their explicit recognition of racism: "A growing body of evidence-based research has shown the correlation between the stress associated with one's race—the stress of racism—and one's birthing outcomes. . . . African-American women remain the most at risk for pregnancy-associated or pregnancy-related causes of death. . . . African-American women are three to four times more likely to die from pregnancy or maternal-related distress than are White women, yielding one of the greatest and most disconcerting racial disparities in public health."

Though the focus of the legislation was primarily on maternal mortality, inclusion of the word *offspring* concretized the relationship between maternal and infant health and survival. As women's health activists have long asserted, if pregnant and birthing people are healthy, then there is a much greater likelihood their babies will be healthy too. Investing in women's health matters for maternal *and* infant survival—and, of course, for women themselves.

It is indeed worth celebrating legislation that centers Black women and aims to save lives. But let us pause a moment to reflect:

In 1899, W. E. B. Du Bois published *The Philadelphia Negro*, demonstrating a link between racism and persistent health disparities, including infant mortality. His ideas challenged notions that were often used to legitimate inequality at that time, such as innate Black inferiority, demonstrating instead structural aspects of Black "afflictions," including poverty. The issue of infant death was deeply personal to Du Bois, whose firstborn son, Burghardt, had perished from diphtheria before the age of two, a devastating tragedy the sociologist lamented at length in *The Souls of Black Folk*.

Well more than a century passed between Du Bois's astute accounting of Black survival and the maternal health legislation described above—a century that included the Sheppard-Towner Act, the Great Society, civil rights activism, the women's movement, Black Lives Matter, and epidemiological and demographic research on all manner of causes of maternal and infant mortality. If celebration of long-awaited achievements has a reverse image, perhaps it is shame. The shame of knowing for so many years *how* to keep Black mothers and babies alive and nevertheless failing to do so.

CUBA

There is a Cuban saying: "We live like rich people, and we die like poor people."

The Republic of Cuba—or Cuba—lies in the Caribbean Sea where that body of water meets the Gulf of Mexico, south of the United States and east of Mexico's Yucatán Peninsula. The archipelago's island neighbors include Haiti and the Dominican Republic, Jamaica, the Cayman Islands, and the Bahamas. Originally inhabited by the Indigenous Ciboney and Taíno people, the islands were colonized

Circulo Infantil/"Kindergarten." Photo credit: Wladislaw Peljuchno / Unsplash, published August 9, 2018.

by the Spanish in the fifteenth century. Conquest, wars, slavery, and occupation mark Cuba's history, culminating in revolution and communism under Fidel Castro beginning in 1959.

The relationship between the United States and Cuba, since well before the tense, thirteen-day Cuban Missile Crisis of 1962, has been vexed, shaping, among other things, the migration of Cubans to the United States and their political allegiances. Following Castro's revolution, the population of Cubans in the United States grew from 79,000 in 1960 to 439,000 in 1970. The Mariel boatlift in 1980 brought 124,800 more refugees to Florida, and subsequent migrations by sea "prompted the two governments to renegotiate new migration terms."

The collapse of the Soviet Union in 1991 ushered in a fresh era of connections with the United States, including a rapprochement in 2014, with President Obama and Cuba's President Raúl Castro (brother of Fidel) normalizing diplomatic and economic relations.

In 2016, there were 1.3 million Cuban immigrants in the United States, enriching our diverse nation with their culture, history, language, and delicious food. There is a reason Cuba holds a special place in the American imagination. That same year, Cuba received nearly four million visitors, a 13 percent increase over the previous year, with the greatest increase in visitors traveling from the United States. The era of "economic reform" and cultural exchange, it seems, was upon us; something frankly unimaginable in the middle of the last century.

A remarkable fact about Cuba is that it has an excellent health care system, which has consistently had much better outcomes than our own more expensive system. Fidel Castro aspired for Cuba to be a "world medical power" and "the bulwark of Third World medicine." There, unlike in the United States, health care is enshrined in the constitution as a human right. This means the government must find efficient and effective ways to ensure better health and survival for its people.

Cuba operates its health care system at roughly 10 percent the cost of ours but spends more of its total GDP on health care than many other poorer nations, investing in primary, preventive, and community health: "Family doctors work in clinics and care for everyone in the surrounding neighborhood. At least once a year, the doctor knocks on your front door (or elsewhere, if you prefer) for a check-up." In Cuba, primary care and prevention are mandatory: "If the system is going to take care of people in dire situations, people must also let the system take care of them before those dire situations occur."

Cuba's infant mortality rate is especially enviable.

Prior to the Castro revolution, the rate was extraordinarily high. In 1970, for example, there were 9,173 child deaths, with an infant mortality rate of 38.7. Comparatively, Cuba ended 2018 with its lowest infant mortality rate in history, just four deaths per thousand births—4.0. This places it below the U.S. rate as a whole and much lower than the rate for African Americans in the United States. The rate is comparable to that of Cuban Americans.

Factors linked to Cuba's low infant mortality rate include universal health care, a government-run centralized system, mandatory vaccinations, investment in medical education, and scientific innovation: "By taking measures to prevent diseases and postpartum complications, physicians are able to avoid birth obstacles that would not only increase infant mortality rates but also mother postpartum deaths."

A public health scholar who traveled to Cuba wanted to know how the country has maintained far better survival rates than the United States. She wrote, "Cuba has healthy infants because the health system and those working in it actually care about them. Despite a range of serious political and economic problems that Cuba still faces, its attention to the basic needs of the population was reflected in much of what we saw, even as casual observers, in our short time in the country. . . . At the national level, Cuba has the political will to assure that pregnant women and their offspring thrive. Can we learn anything from Cuba? What prevents the United States from demonstrating this same concern?"

One answer to this question might be *communism*. Or, rather, the fear of socialized medicine and national health care—of "socialism"—that has long plagued the United States. In recent years, several politicians, including Senators Tom Harkin and Bernie Sanders, created firestorms when they publicly praised Cuba's health care system. Conservative media are rife with criticism of Castro's Cuba, and responses to praise of its successes invoke laden terms like *propaganda*, *repression*, and *manipulation*.

Yet as one physician, commenting on Cuba's health care system, noted, "Now that Fidel Castro has passed on, history will long debate his complex legacy. From a healthcare standpoint, however, Cuba has demonstrated that a poor country can dramatically improve the health of its population through long-term, consistent investments in primary care and public health. Even if those investments depended on the authoritarian rule of a long-reigning communist dictator who made many other errors, Cuba's example shows what very basic health care services can accomplish when the political will to apply them exists."

While politicians and pundits engage in ideological skirmishes, babies in the United States continue to die at much higher rates than those in Cuba. And the people who care about pregnant women and babies continue to try to find ways to keep them alive.

For example, on Chicago's South Side, in the Englewood neighborhood, as in so many African American neighborhoods in the United States, infant death is worrisome. Losses have generated concern and efforts to reduce "alarmingly" high death rates. Because resources are limited, "[doctors] are thinking creatively, which has led them to look at an unlikely role model: Cuba. . . . In an effort to tackle the high rate, medical professionals in Chicago are now working with their counterparts in Cuba to learn about new approaches, including seeking out women of childbearing age in the Englewood neighborhood to ask them about everything. Really, everything."

This effort—rooted in proven community-based health care learned from a resource-poor nation—is funded by the W. K. Kellogg Foundation, "which has also paid for some American health care workers to visit Cuba." During home visits, health care professionals ask women about topics ranging from mold and rodent infestations in the home to cavities and dental care. Based on women's answers, they are then placed into different risk groups for follow-up, a direct method borrowed from the Cuban model. Higher-risk women receive additional home visits and care.

The basic idea is familiar to advocates for health prevention: identify problems, intervene early, and hopefully avoid disasters—here, infant and maternal injury and death. An epidemiologist connected to the project states, "What we are hoping to discover is issues in Englewood that truly impact health, that are not being collected, that the doctors cannot see when they come and see [a] woman, and prescribe her one pill."

Study participants are excited and would like to "scale up" this model to see if it might work for other health problems in underserved parts of the city. Experts believe it is worth exploring, but caution that in Cuba, when problems are identified, they are addressed quickly: "although Cuba is not as wealthy as the U.S., it makes more resources available to at-risk women." In the United States, it is not merely a question of resources but rather the *allocation* of resources. Poor African American women in Chicago simply do not have the same access to resources as white women in more affluent neighborhoods, from primary health care, to high-risk intervention, to abundant and healthy food options.

As with so many issues, we come back to political will and thorny questions of ideology. Are lessons imported from a small communist archipelago, a nation anathema to so many U.S. politicians including many Cuban American

Republicans, worth translating to the U.S. context? What barriers must be breached to make possible universal health care, or at least better primary care in poor neighborhoods, where Black mothers and babies die at much higher rates?

It would be easy to say, "Yeah, we could do it, if we were willing to expend those resources," but I doubt we will. Cuba—as politically complicated as it is—has demonstrated that nations can do more with less, for many more people.

D

Mothers grieve the loss of their infants. It is expected of them. A mother who does not grieve her dead child must be an unnatural woman, a monster.

But fathers also become babylost, with splintered hearts, partners to comfort, and limited spaces in which to navigate and disclose their own sorrow. Too often, they must be stoic and strong, with cultural expectations of proper masculinity in full bloom: "Minimize. Suck it up. Keep it to yourself." In other words, act like a man!

Steven, whose daughter, Avery, was stillborn, posted on his partner's blog: "It's well known that dads can often be forgotten, not intentionally, but with everything our partners have been through it's hard to focus on yourself or for other people to focus on us."

"Men Lose Babies, Too" is the title of an article originally published in *Psychology Today* that suggests "it is a mistake to paint the masculine experience of loss with one broad stroke. This costs more than we know."

As Steven noted, "Everyone grieves differently, there is definitely no right or wrong way but if there was anything I could share with you guys from a male perspective, it is to just be there for each other as a couple, remember that you guys are in this together."

The online magazine *Reconceiving Loss* offers a rare space where men can share experiences and also find community and support. The site includes stories, poems, songs, artworks, videos, and podcasts—a spectrum of creative outlets for grief of infinite magnitude. Contributions from men highlight that their experiences, while diverse, can be radically different from women's.

Michael, whose son was stillborn, writes, "Rarely does one hear fatherhood spoken of as a longing. Pregnancy is supposed to be the exclusive province of women; they grow the baby within their body; nothing a man can feel or imagine can come close to that. And the pain of feeling that life snuffed out—of nurturing something with your bodily essences—and feeling it die inside you—how can a man's experience compare to that?"

Terry, whose wife suffered a miscarriage, recalled, "I felt my role was to be practical; to deal with the doctors and nurses and be the person who would sort everything out so that she at least didn't have to think beyond her own personal suffering. But in fact what she really needed was to also see that I was grieving, too. I just didn't know how to let all that out. . . . Everyone was asking after Caroline. But only one person asked how I was coping with it all—and that happened to be a fellow man who had been through miscarriage himself."

Supermodel Chrissy Teigen documented on Instagram the stillbirth of her son, Jack, at twenty weeks. Husband John Legend, award-winning musician, was by her side, his grief fully on display in Teigen's posts and subsequent media coverage. With more than thirty-three million Instagram followers, Teigen made public the couple's anguish in ways we seldom see.

She wrote, "I had asked my mom and John to take pictures, no matter how uncomfortable it was. I explained to a very hesitant John that I needed them, and that I did NOT want to have to ever ask. That he just had to do it. He hated it. I could tell. It didn't make sense to him at the time." Legend, no stranger to publicity, later remarked, "I didn't know that we could experience this grief and also share it, but when we did, it really meant so much to so many people. And it was such a powerful experience for me to learn that. I'm just grateful that my wife was courageous enough to do it."

Efforts are underway across the nation to bring more men into conversations about infant mortality—though not quite in the ways one might expect.

One clue can be found in a 1999 study, which found that the absence of a father's name on birth certificates in Georgia was a risk factor for premature infant death. A more recent study in 2010, also investigating birth certificates, found that "absent fathers" contributed to lower birth weights; "the neonatal death rate of father-absent infants was nearly four times that of their counterparts with involved fathers."

Of course, a name on a birth certificate does not mean paternal involvement.

The 2010 study also found that "the risk of poor birth outcomes was highest for infants born to black women whose babies' fathers were absent during their pregnancies. Even after adjusting for socioeconomic differences, these babies were *seven times more likely* to die in infancy than babies born to Hispanic and white women in the same situation" (emphasis in original).

"For many dads, [preventing infant death] is about taking responsibility," says the coordinator of a program in Racine, Wisconsin, to include fathers in efforts to reduce infant mortality. "After they get through blaming the mom for everything, they get it and tend to take responsibility."

Filmmaker Spike Lee—whose wife, Tonya Lewis Lee, produced a superb documentary about Black infant mortality, *Crisis in the Crib*—also encourages fathers to be more involved to ensure their babies make it to age one and also "grow up to become productive members of society."

The Fatherhood Empty Shoes Memorial project in northeast Florida is designed to draw fathers more fully into community efforts. The Jacksonville metropolitan area has one of the highest infant mortality rates in the country. The empty shoes, small and haunting, are displayed in barbershops, the traditional domain of men.

Barber Lamont Foy Sr. commented, "In the barbershop, we typically talk about sports, social and political issues." He was "shocked" when he learned about the high infant mortality rates: "It's terrifying and sad. I wish we didn't have to have this discussion."

In Milwaukee, another city with very high infant mortality rates among African Americans, several programs target fathers. An official with the United Way of Greater Milwaukee commented, "Until now, we've been sadly and inappropriately dismissive of the role of the father in birth outcomes. . . . We cannot continue to focus only on the health care of the expectant mother."

On the one hand, given the high rates of preventable infant death in Black communities, it makes good sense to focus on Black men and their role in healthy pregnancy outcomes. Black men care and grieve too—as Chrissy Teigen's images of John Legend poignantly reveal. At the same time, it feels suspect that so many community programs, especially those serving men of color, target "absent" fathers.

One is uncomfortably reminded of the 1965 Moynihan Report, shaped by the white sociologist/politician's obsession with "the Negro family," including Black women having "too many children too early" and chronically unemployed or missing Black fathers.

There is a very fine line in the United States between race and racism. Following W. E. B. Du Bois, we might even call it "the color line."

Surely, we can include *all* men in efforts to improve infant mortality without assuming or pathologizing the categorical absence of only some men. Many fathers, regardless of race or ethnicity, go missing routinely and in doing so, make women's lives that much harder.

Indeed, it is masculinity itself—the imperative to "suck it up"—that gets in the way of grief and its expression for so many men. And grief withheld can be volcanic, paralyzing, even lethal, for those who grieve. A 2017 survey of 303 men revealed that 21 percent of dads self-harmed and 80 percent reported a decline in their mental health after the loss of a baby.

Writer Daniel Raeburn, whose daughter, Irene, was stillborn, notes that "society tends to assume that the man has no emotions about this kind of loss. This is, in part, the fault of men. We don't talk. . . . My memories of that time are of being absolutely alone." He goes on to recommend grief groups: "Men tend to clam up around women more than they do around other men. I have had great conversations with other dads about loss when their wives and partners weren't around."

There is yet another way in which fathers matter in relation to infant mortality: as gestational parents. Transgender and nonbinary people with uteruses can and do give birth, and while they may assume a variety of parental identities, "dad" is a common one. This is especially (but not only) the case for transgender men who become pregnant and give birth.

Trystan Reese of the Family Equality Council, who gave birth to a son in 2017, told NBC News, "You can be a man and have a baby . . . and [trans men and nonbinary people] are starting to see that it is possible and that hasn't always been the case."

The Trans Pregnancy Project at the University of Leeds seeks "to provide an in-depth understanding of the feelings, experiences and health care needs of trans people (including trans men, transmasculine people and non-binary individuals) who wish to, or become, pregnant." Though there are no statistics on how many trans people globally become pregnant or give birth, the Trans Project's research suggests that "a growing number of trans people are choosing to start their own families in this way."

Transgender people have unique health care needs and experiences. A Rutgers University study found that up to 30 percent of transgender men have unplanned pregnancies. Health care for transgender parents ranges from limited to hostile to dangerous, especially when pregnant: "The whole process is difficult—it really is tailored for women, essentially, in the language and everything about it." A 2016 study found that 30.8 percent of transgender people delayed or did not seek treatment, which has significant implications for health, including pregnancy outcomes.

And though there is scant research on transgender birth and infant death, a study in the *New England Journal of Medicine* reported on the tragic case of Sam, a thirty-two-year-old transgender man whose baby was stillborn after he was misdiagnosed in the emergency room. The authors of the study note, "After discharge from the hospital, Sam reestablished care. . . . Though he had not planned or expected the pregnancy, he was heartbroken at the loss of his baby and had a major depressive episode."

Babylost dads, in all their variety in twenty-first-century America and beyond, live somewhere between presence and absence, hope and grief, prevention and recovery, connection and isolation. Their places remain to be seen, and their stories should be more widely known.

DEPRIVATION

To be deprived of something is to lack basic necessities; deprivation is a social ill, and it may be profoundly damaging to lives and livelihoods. Sociologist Peter Townsend defined deprivation as "a state of observable and demonstrable disadvantage, relative to the local community or the wider society or nation to which an individual, family or group belongs."

Babylost women are deprived of their infants and their dreams of motherhood, compared to women for whom these dreams are realized. The loss is shattering, but so too is the deprivation; loss and deprivation are not, in fact, the same experiences.

Synonyms for *deprivation* are stark in their meanings and social implications: poverty, impoverishment, privation, need, hardship, want, distress, dispossession, withdrawal, removal, divestment, forfeiture, loss, absence, unavailability, dearth, ruin.

As embodied beings, we require oxygen, food, and water to live. Shelter and safety also foster survival; lack of these speed death. Beyond the necessities, we need

Rhesus monkey. Photo credit: Science History Images / Alamy Stock Photo.
An infant rhesus monkey (Macaca mulatta) with its cloth surrogate mother during an animal experiment. Maternal deprivation experiments performed by Harry Harlow of the University of Wisconsin in the 1950s involved separating infant monkeys from their mothers and rearing them with surrogate mothers made of wire or cloth. The monkeys were kept in partial or total isolation, in wire cages or in "pits" or "wells of despair." These experiments found that comfort, security, and affection are necessary for a monkey's healthy psychosocial development.

creative activity, interaction, movement, love, pleasure, and the means to provide for ourselves and our families.

Humans, like our nonhuman primate kin and other species such as elephants, are deeply social creatures. Interaction and love are, especially for young children, as essential as food and water. These are not fluffy, optional add-ons to the basics; they are fundamental to development. To be deprived of love can be as deadly as gasping futilely for oxygen.

Most parents live in fear of losing their children; we watch our newborns like mama bears, ever vigilant they are still breathing in the night. As our children age and become increasingly mobile, we strive to ensure they do not wander off at the supermarket, tumble down a staircase, toddle in front of a car, or worse.

Given the fear that surrounds parental loss of children and children's own fear of *being lost*, it is astonishing and disturbing that psychological experiments in the mid-twentieth century deliberately separated and isolated babies from their mothers (or leveraged forced institutional separations, such as in hospitals) and profited intellectually from doing so.

The work of British psychologist John Bowlby, whose research was funded by the World Health Organization, illustrated the negative effects of what he called "maternal deprivation." In 1952, Bowlby wrote, "When deprived of maternal care, the child's development is almost always retarded—physically, intellectually, and socially—and . . . symptoms of physical and mental illness may appear. Such evidence is disquieting."

René Spitz, an Austrian American psychoanalyst, had earlier coined the term *hospitalism* to describe such separation effects, conducting his research on children in a foundling home. Short-term deprivation could be overcome, but longer-term emotional deprivation led to negative health consequences, and even death. Spitz's work inspired Bowlby's research agenda and later studies, leading ultimately to theories of attachment and separation that fostered changes in childcare, including recommendations that parents spend more time with their children.

Given the context and historical period in which Spitz and Bowlby were working, the onus of care was placed firmly on mothers, in what one critic described as "an awe-inspiring responsibility." The very name of the theory—"maternal deprivation"—centers on mothers, though later interpretations sought to suggest that *any* maternal figure, even of the opposite sex (say, a father), could be the caregiver of note. Feminist criticism of the maternal deprivation thesis pointed to Bowlby's overemphasis on mothers and the ways that social arrangements reaffirmed women's familial obligations, including not working outside the home.

Anthropologists Margaret Mead and Sarah Blaffer Hrdy weighed in on maternal deprivation too, each suggesting that while a caregiver is important, it need not be the mother. Mead offered abundant evidence from the non-Western cultures she studied, though in the United States, such ideas were not taken up until later feminist works appeared.

Another figure from the early era known for his experimentalism was psychologist Harry Harlow. Working with rhesus monkeys, he conducted most of his research at the University of Wisconsin, Madison. Harlow's infamous—and cruel—experiments included removing infant monkeys from their mothers and replacing the mothers with surrogates or leaving the babies isolated. The non-isolated caged infants could "choose" between a wire surrogate or a softer surrogate covered in cloth that was warmed, with milk provision alternating between the two: "But the milk seemed to make little difference. The monkeys spent most of their time with the soft mother, *regardless of which mother provided milk*" (emphasis added). Monkeys raised with *only* the wire surrogate, even if milk was provided, suffered more dire health and behavioral consequences than those who selected the cloth surrogate.

Accounts of Harlow's research are harrowing—more so than Spitz's sad foundlings—in that Harlow *purposefully* separated the infant monkeys from their mothers. In a review of Deborah Blum's *Love at Goon Park*, written about Harlow's research, Barbara Smuts writes in the *New York Times*, "Blum presents the puzzle of a man who legitimated a science of love while failing those who most loved him, and the paradox of work that made baby monkeys suffer in order to sensitize people to the needs of children. Was his research justifiable?"

And in her brilliant cultural study of primatology, Donna Haraway notes, "It was in this context that one must see the TV scientists talking calmly in the camera about love, while the visual field behind and around them is full of self-clutching, autistic infant monkeys, experimentally produced to show the 'touching' adequacy of a mother surrogate engaged in a liberal, rational society. Sadism demands a story."

Harlow knew of Spitz's work, and indeed the two men enjoyed steady communication, likely influencing each other. Bowlby, Spitz, Harlow, and others produced research and documentary films that led to greater knowledge about "the effects of separation and deprivation on young children." Their research soon made its way into the popular imagination, reaffirming certain cultural practices. To this day, women's role in the workforce is undercut by assumptions about threats to children's health and well-being from not enjoying the benefits of a stay-at-home mother. At the same time, the evidence bears witnessing: emotional deprivation is costly to infants.

Sadly, we do not learn from *any* of these studies the costs to *the mothers* of having their babies taken away. What fate awaited Harlow's mother monkeys after losing their babies? There is no archive of their grief or their lives and deaths.

Research on maternal deprivation mirrors other studies that attest to the importance of touch—reinforcing that the infant monkeys in Harlow's study who chose cloth surrogates were likely seeking physical contact and comfort and not merely nutrition. One study found that lack of touch, or inappropriate touch, resulted in developmental delays: "Organisms need sensory stimulation for normal development. . . . To paraphrase, a kiss may just be a kiss, a sigh may just be a sigh, but a touch can change your life (or at least your nervous system)!"

A biologist and adoptive mother writes, "I am well acquainted with the vast body of research that shows the physical and psychological harms of deprived environments. Orphanages can arguably be placed under this category along with other places such as refugee camps and some hospitals where children lack close contact and attention. Deprivation comes in many shapes and forms: lack of food, diseases, maltreatment, and child abuse are some of the harms that come to mind. However, I would argue that deprivation of love can be just as deadly."

Developmental psychologist Ann Bigelow, in an interview about the importance of physical contact and responsive parenting, remarked, "I don't want to give the impression that if babies don't get this they're marked for life. This early understanding of self and early understanding of other is developed through interaction. It teaches babies basic lessons that they have some agency in the world, so that allows them to explore the world and feel like they can affect their environment as opposed to just being helpless to whatever happens to them. We're basically a social species, and we learn those things through interacting with others."

More recently, scholars have investigated the relationship between *social* deprivation and infant death. Studies in the United States have focused on cities with high infant mortality rates, like Detroit. One epidemiological study found that segregation based on inequality contributed to higher rates of infant death: "Efforts to support equitable community investments may reduce incidents of death and the disproportionate experience of loss among [non-Hispanic] Black women."

An article in the *Guardian* chronicling Detroit's high rate of infant death among African Americans notes, "According to the National Institutes of Health, women residing in economically deprived areas—Detroit qualifies with more than 50% of children living below poverty level and an unemployment rate more than double the national average—are at increased risk of preterm birth. But in Detroit, the deprivation is even more extreme. Black mothers also face water shut-offs, hospital deserts and stress from economic racism."

Deprivation of all sorts is rampant, with devastating consequences.

To *intentionally* deprive of love, shelter, health, and safety is morally corrupt and wicked.

Even more offensive and disturbing are the same high infant mortality rates in communities of color we have seen for decades. Health disparities are chronic, have been chronic, and will remain chronic without intervention, signaling forms and patterns of deprivation that could be minimized if we created different, better, more just social arrangements.

That is, Detroit, Memphis, Milwaukee, and other cities need not be full of premature babies at risk of dying or Black women on the bleeding edge of death from pregnancy and birth. We need not be separating families at the U.S.-Mexico border, subjecting "tender age" children to a lifetime of trauma. Child detention centers are an especially cruel version of Harlow's despair pits, and in many of these there are no surrogate mothers, wire or cloth or otherwise.

The evidence has long shown us what is needed: consistent, quality, responsive parental (and not just maternal) care—love, in other words—and also institutions and structures that facilitate survival. Food, water, clean air, health care, shelter, and safety. Love of one's offspring may be smothered or sustained given the right set of conditions.

We have built the wrong conditions, over and over again, both inside and outside laboratories. And neither love nor survival is sustainable in zones of deprivation.

DISABILITY

Several years ago, in the early days of this project, I shared my ideas with a colleague in sociology who also studies health and medicine. She declared, "Oh, it's a book about disability!" I thought this was a strange response, slightly off-topic and not at all my focus. Yet as I dove into the literature and spoke with clinicians and advocates across a range of settings, disability showed up again and again. It turns out my colleague had insightfully presaged a thorny set of issues that emerge when thinking about disability in relation to infant mortality. Chief among these is the moral valuation: *What (and whose) lives are worth saving?*

According to the International Classification of Functioning, Disability and Health (ICF), disability is "an umbrella term for impairments, activity limitations and participation restrictions. Disability is the interaction between individuals with a health condition (e.g. cerebral palsy, Down syndrome [or] depression) and personal and environmental factors (e.g. negative attitudes), inaccessible transportation and public buildings and limited social supports."

More than one billion people globally, or about 15 percent of the world's population, live with some form of disability.

Critical disability studies perspectives have taught us that "disability" as a condition or label is produced through interaction between individuals and their environments. One's nonnormative body becomes "disabled" through attempts to navigate social, cultural, and physical spaces designed for normative, presumed-able bodies. For example, a person in a wheelchair or a temporarily injured person in a leg cast who is reliant on crutches will be unable to access the upper floors in a building if there is no elevator or lift. A person who struggles with dyslexia might be ill-served by normative teaching methods, classrooms, and assumptions about how people learn. A person who is unable to hear must learn to lip-read or use sign language to move through and understand a predominantly vocal soundscape. Somebody with limited hearing encounters a world where conference speakers refuse to use microphones and hearing devices are considered "cosmetic" and thus are not covered by most insurance policies.

The disability rights movement has challenged barriers and limitations facing people with disabilities and sought to change policies and physical environments to better accommodate a diverse range of human bodies and their needs. In many places, sidewalks now have curb cuts, facilitating greater freedom of movement; most buildings, especially newer ones, have elevators or lifts and accessible doorways; public events often include sign language interpretation; visual media include closed-captioning and accessible color schemes; service animals are welcome in many more spaces; and, perhaps most significantly, it is illegal to discriminate against any person on the basis of disability. Workplaces can be held legally accountable for treating people with disabilities differently than they do presumed-able-bodied people.

And yet, blatant discrimination and profound stigma persist, as do barriers to full participation for people with disabilities. Disability is ubiquitous in American life, especially visible through inequalities based on embodiment, impacting everything from education to employment to health care. Reproduction is a particularly fertile space for difficulties and challenges related to disability.

For example, pregnant people may in many instances elect to terminate a pregnancy if fetal impairment is identified through prenatal testing. A comprehensive study from 2012 that combined quantitative and qualitative data analysis found that nearly 70 percent of pregnancies were terminated following a diagnosis of Down syndrome. The study also found that the rate of termination on the basis of a Down syndrome or trisomy 21 diagnosis has *decreased* in the United States in recent years. Also, termination rates vary by maternal and gestational age; older women were less likely to abort an affected fetus. Comparatively, in Iceland, the termination rate for Down syndrome is nearly 100 percent. Abortion after sixteen weeks in that country is legal if the fetus has a "deformity," and more than 80 percent of women in Iceland undergo prenatal testing. In Denmark, the termination rate for Down syndrome is 98 percent and in France, 77 percent.

Sadly, it would seem that Down syndrome babies are deemed particularly undesirable, although prenatal diagnosis of other conditions, particularly those that are life-threatening, may also lead to a decision to terminate.

In the United States, where the right to abortion is increasingly threatened and the issue has long been politically vexed, abortion of a "disabled" fetus is especially contentious. Many, but not all, disability rights advocates oppose such terminations. In 2017, Ohio legislators introduced a bill to ban abortions on the basis of a Down syndrome diagnosis; doctors who perform such abortions would be charged with committing a felony. Arkansas followed suit, with one senator proclaiming, "I decided to push the bill forward to protect those that were born differently. Through the disastrous procedure of abortion, we lose valuable and special people from society." Several states also have legislation in place that restricts the information doctors can share with their patients about genetic testing and abortion.

These developments unfold against a backdrop of considerable erosion of the legal right to abortion and actual ability to access abortions, rendering disability rights and pro-life advocates somewhat strange occasional bedfellows. Ongoing challenges to abortion access and provision call into question the sincerity of antiabortion measures, including those allegedly championing disability. In many states where such legislation is enacted, infant mortality rates are high, funding for children's health is limited, and people with disabilities and their caregivers struggle to survive with vastly inadequate support.

To be sure, not all disability rights advocates support bans on abortion following prenatal diagnosis, but many do. Scholars have drawn attention to the challenges that come from placing disability rights alongside reproductive justice. D. A. Caeton writes, "If we are to choose wisely when presented with choice, then we must continue to labor to make disability recognizable as a valid mode of being. We, along with those feminists who will join us, must strive for fewer barriers and less pernicious stigmas."

Approximately 20 percent of all pregnancies end in miscarriage, also called spontaneous abortion, without external intervention. In half of these, chromosomal (genetic) abnormalities are the cause. Likewise, "birth defects," including chromosomal abnormalities and congenital malformations, can subsequently become primary drivers of infant mortality. Two decades ago, one in every five infant deaths was caused by a birth defect. In 2016, the CDC classified birth defects as the leading cause of infant mortality, with one notable exception. Among African Americans, the leading cause of infant death was and continues to be low birthweight related to prematurity. Some, but not all, birth defects may be preventable through interventions, such as pregnant people taking folic acid or early diagnosis and treatment—where these are available. Alas, other conditions are neither preventable nor treatable.

I want to pause a moment to discuss the fraught language of birth defects, and how this connects to disability rights. Naming bodily conditions as "defects" carries a negative connotation; to be defective means to be flawed, imperfect, broken, crippled, damaged, blemished, marred, spoiled, disfigured, deficient, inadequate, and/or incomplete. It is true that chromosomal and congenital circumstances that cause death are unfortunate and preferably avoided. Yet the current discourse about defects can negatively shape perceptions of surviving babies and adults, and even whole categories of people ("the mentally ill," "the disabled"). It is not much of a leap to go from "birth defects" to "defective babies," reflecting social discomfort and even revulsion related to disability, both real and imagined. Such discomfort and parental fears that a disabled child will struggle in life may translate into prenatal interventions, pregnancy termination, and even, in extreme cases, infanticide.

Indeed, acclaimed ethicist Peter Singer landed himself in scalding water by suggesting that it is ethically appropriate to kill an infant with disabilities, invoking harmful eugenics practices that should remain in the dustbin of history. He suggested that disability "comes with intrinsic suffering" of such magnitude that it might be more compassionate to kill those suffering than to force them to continue living in pain. He was not terribly specific about what constitutes pain and suffering and who gets to decide and/or for whom.

Writer Katie Booth notes that Singer's "ideas still ache in the disability world, like a wound that won't heal." She goes on, "His arguments are built intricately and beautifully, like a perfect mathematics equation, but at their core beats a single assertion, one that is still too difficult to concede: that this group of human beings aren't really *people*. That's the pain that obscures the rest."

And here, cloaked in the cold arithmetic of utilitarian philosophy, is the crux of the matter: *Who counts as a person, as human?*

Efforts to prevent infant death and reduce elevated infant mortality rates can obscure underlying antidisability motivations, or what we might call "the eugenic impulse." These efforts include, among others, admonitions to pregnant women to "commit to healthy choices to prevent birth defects." The CDC recommends that pregnant women plan ahead, avoid harmful substances (e.g., alcohol, cigarettes, drugs), choose a healthy lifestyle ("keep diabetes under control" and "strive to reach and maintain a healthy weight"), and talk with their health care provider. It is curious that the CDC does not recommend, for example, avoiding industrial waste and environmental toxins proven to cause anomalies. The focus is very much on *individual* behavior rather than the *broader social, political, and environmental situations* in which pregnancies and births occur.

And yet, a recent study suggests that climate change may bring about increases in congenital heart defects related to maternal heat exposure. The study authors note, "As global temperatures continue to rise, more intense, frequent, and longer-lasting heat events are expected. . . . In addition, the U.S. Census Bureau has projected a continuous increase in births across the nation through 2030. It is estimated that the number of pregnant women may increase nationwide by 5%, meaning 4.2 million would be affected annually. The potential increases in both the number of pregnant women and maternal heat exposure suggest an alarming effect that climate change may have on reproductive health."

Thus we might pose a new question: Exactly what can individual pregnant people do to prevent negative birth outcomes on a rapidly overheating planet? In such an apocalyptic context, expectant parents may well desire a surplus of alcohol or drugs to numb their anxiety about the world into which they are birthing their children, "defects" be damned. Others are choosing not to have children at all in such a world.

I want to return to my earlier point about the production of disability at the intersection of bodies and environments. There is an additional way disability is produced: through medical interventions on developing embryos and fetuses. The advent of fetal medicine and neonatal intensive care has resulted in saving babies who previously would have died. I believe this is what my colleague was alluding to regarding disability: if we can lower infant mortality rates by placing more premature infants in neonatal care, are we simultaneously producing more babies and children with disabilities? And if so, how might we ethically calibrate when and how to intervene, and with what consequences? Without defending Peter Singer, it is well worth asking the question, Are all lives actually *livable*? This question is at the heart of contemporary debates about some abortions, where termination of a fatally malformed baby results in a gut-wrenching decision.

Ana Todorović's essay "Nadia's Story" captures the emotional complexity of wrestling with the decision at thirty-seven weeks to deliver her daughter, who had a serious heart problem, or not: "A disengaged, calculating inner voice told me that a newborn doesn't need much more than a brainstem in order to be absolutely adorable. It would yawn and sneeze and blink and we would melt, forever tied to this creature that might leave us. But what would it be like if she didn't walk at four? Or talk at six? Or learn to control her bowels at 14? Or what if she was cognitive and functionally intact, but her heart could stop beating at any point during childhood?"

Ultimately, Todorović and her partner consulted a palliative care team and decided against immediate delivery. When Nadia eventually arrived, she was stillborn. Todorović writes, "People don't envy me for the position I was in, having to decide without warning while going on not much information and in a state of shock, but I don't envy those doctors who sat across from me either. It must be so hard, to have the technology to keep someone's body working, but to let them die instead."

Social work scholar Erica Goldblatt Hyatt faced a similar situation:

> Door Number One: wait for baby to die of heart failure in the womb.
> Door Number Two: give birth, if he lives, to a brain-dead fetus. Surgery to establish an airway will likely fail but if not he will live caged in a body that cannot speak, cry, or move with purpose. Those minutes without air while fingers fumble will ensure his death in a NICU either due to infection or withdrawal of supportive care.
> Door Number Three: termination.

Goldblatt Hyatt has written extensively on TOPFA (termination of pregnancy due to fetal anomaly), drawing from her own experiences and those of her clients. She innovated the ACCEPT model for addressing grief from babyloss, which includes "acknowledging disenfranchised grief, connecting emotions to the loss, continuing bonds, exploring distortions, practicing new skills, and telling the story."

She has also written and spoken publicly about the ways TOPFA intersects with reproductive politics, often placing women in deeply uncomfortable, if not impossible, situations. In a 2020 op-ed, she writes, "Women whose fetuses are diagnosed with severe anomalies or disabilities in-utero may be forced to carry to term. . . . I might have been forced to carry my son until his death in the womb or birth. Had he survived to term, he would have been born brain-dead but in compliance with 'Born Alive,' doctors would have to treat him. The moral and ethical implications of this are frightening."

The nexus of disability and reproduction brings no easy solutions to anyone. I certainly have no answer to the question of how we might reconcile the aims of reproductive justice, including women's right to seek abortion *and* the right to birth a baby who will survive past her first year, with the aims of disability rights. Sometimes, maybe often, these politics will clash. What is clear is that the political move to "protect" the disabled through abortion bans must be viewed alongside nationwide efforts to defund exactly the health and social services that parents—especially the most marginalized—require to birth and raise children with unique needs and challenges. It is also clear that preventive efforts targeting individual women are unlikely to transcend massive environmental threats to all human health but especially to the fragile unborn.

This section cannot end with simple solutions to "the problem of disability," which is in my view largely a social and political problem. That is, context—the situations of pregnant people—matters. But so too do bodies. As a number of disability studies scholars have noted, we must include the body, including pain and suffering, in our analyses and recommendations for care—not in the fleshless manner of utilitarian philosophy but rather in the messy, visceral, affective spaces in which people live, love, laugh, reproduce, and die. Or watch their babies die.

Disability is, in many respects, about loss: loss of function, loss of unmet expectations for a "healthy" baby, loss of life, loss of futurity. Of course, it does not have to be this way, but our social arrangements all but guarantee that disability comes with at least some degree of suffering. Rather than attachment to binaries of health and illness, normal and abnormal, imperfect and perfect, perhaps we would do better to think and act in terms of the complexities of surviving in a world that unequally values bodies and lives. In this broader context, much of it beyond any individual's control, birth outcomes are both foretold and foreclosed.

There is plenty of loss to go around.

DOULAS

In May 2019, Meghan Markle, the Los Angeles–born Duchess of Sussex, gave birth to baby Archie, who is seventh in the line of succession to the British throne. When it was reported that she was intending a home birth with midwives and a doula, a prominent obstetrician quipped, "Meghan Markle has decided she's going to have a doula and a willow tree . . . let's see how that goes. . . . She's 37, first birth. . . . I don't know. We'll have to see." His comments garnered "raucous laughter" at a conference of obstetricians/gynecologists who were meeting in Nashville.

This backlash reveals a long-standing divide between professional, expert birth attendance—deemed the province of doctors—and lay support for laboring women, including doulas and midwives. This chasm is as old as the professionalization of obstetrics, which marginalized women caregivers, especially midwives, and during the early twentieth century moved birth from homes into hospitals. The decline of midwifery and ascendance of obstetrics was no accident of history; it was an orchestrated effort, one steeped in misogyny and racism, to supplant traditional healers for "modern" medicine.

The obstetrician's joke is layered with racism and a hefty "scientific" distrust of women. Meghan Markle is a Black woman—and surely must be aware of the alarming statistics about Black maternal and infant mortality in the United States. Friend Serena Williams, who herself almost died giving birth, cohosted Markle's baby shower. The Duchess may be married to a handsome prince and have high-quality resources at her elegant fingertips, but she is still at high risk, statistically speaking. To joke about her informed efforts to improve her own birth outcome evidences how far obstetrics as a field has yet to travel to fully embrace women's lived experiences and reproductive choices.

In Rewire News, doula Samantha Griffin writes that

> by taking an active role in the process, Markle was combating what can frequently be a disempowering experience. Her desire for a doula may have been born purely out of fear. . . . As a new mother in her 30s, Meghan Markle . . . is a grown woman. She has every right to arrange her own health care, and that of

her child, without commentary from providers who've never met her. . . . Rather than paternalistically laughing about birth plans, ACOG members should concern themselves with the growing sense among many health-care workers and families that many OB-GYNs are out of step with patients' needs. The time spent laughing would be better spent finding out why people are making choices that make doctors uncomfortable.

It is worth noting here that Nashville, where the American Council of Obstetricians and Gynecologists (ACOG) conference was held, has an infant mortality rate of about 7.5 deaths out of 1,000 live births—well above the national average. The Black infant mortality rate in Davidson County, in which Nashville is located, was a staggering 12.4 deaths out of 1,000 live births at the time of this writing. And a review of maternal deaths in Tennessee based on 2017 data found that *85 percent of these were preventable*. Certainly, these statistics are no laughing matter.

And yet, a quick online search of the 2019 ACOG conference program reveals just three talks related to infant death and only one focused specifically on Black women. Hilarity wasn't listed on the agenda either.

Following the media storm that greeted the obstetrician's characterization of Markle, an ACOG official issued a statement: "While I was not in the room during this talk and I understand that the comment drew laughter, it was not someone in ACOG leadership who made the comment." Indeed, ACOG's clinical guidelines offer some support for doulas (though make no mention of willow trees): "Evidence suggests that, in addition to regular nursing care, continuous one-to-one emotional support provided by support personnel, such as a doula, is associated with improved outcomes for women in labor. Benefits described in randomized trials include shortened labor, decreased need for analgesia, fewer operative deliveries, and fewer reports of dissatisfaction with the experience of labor."

The word *doula* comes from the Greek, for handmaiden, servant, or slave, which makes for a somewhat complex origin story. It was first introduced in North America in the 1970s by Dana Raphael, a student of anthropologist Margaret Mead and author of *The Tender Gift: Breastfeeding*. She used the term to describe someone, usually a woman, who helped a new mother with breastfeeding. In 1992, a group of maternal-child health workers—Penny Simkin, Phyllis Klaus, Annie Kennedy, Marshall Klaus, and John H. Kennell—together formed Doulas of North America (DONA), later renamed DONA International. Drawing from Raphael's work, they chose "doula" to describe those who serve laboring women.

Given the origin of the word doula as "slave," its use—especially in Greece—has been somewhat contentious. One commentator wrote,

When the word traveled the continents and arrived in Greece, there were strong negative reactions. . . . When a word is already in use in modern language (as the word "doula"), we cannot ignore its current meaning. . . . Despite all this, I think it is important to keep something from this remote linguistic knowledge and connection: The ancient Greek "doula" was there to listen and follow the wishes of the mother, offering her services and life experience, but also aware of the humbleness her position asked for. . . . Often "specialists" overwhelm the mother with tons of information and in the end make her feel even more dependent and inexperienced, instead of empowering her to find her own ways to bring life and raise her children.

The popular women's health "bible," *Our Bodies, Ourselves*, describes doulas as a "nurturing and caring presence," noting that they perform no medical or clinical tasks. Doulas provide continuous care and support, often remaining in the laboring woman's presence even when busy caregivers, such as obstetricians, move on to other patients. *Labor doulas* care for women during labor and birth, while *postpartum doulas* support new mothers and their families after birth. There are also *breastfeeding doulas*. Sometimes, these are the same people; one doula might stay with a pregnant woman through her birth and well beyond (as mine did).

Unlike other health care professionals, doulas "mother the mother."

Often, doulas and midwives are seen as interchangeable, and they may be lumped together as "not scientific" by some medical professionals. Yet midwives are typically highly trained health care professionals who deliver babies. Doulas do not deliver babies; they provide support and may be present alongside midwives or other health care providers. Importantly, doulas can serve as translators between laboring women and health care providers, ensuring that birth plans are followed, women's needs are expressed and met, and women feel supported during and after their labor.

In some instances, doulas may be literal translators, helping bridge language differences between laboring women and health care providers. In Sweden, where nearly 30 percent of women who deliver babies were born in another country, doulas can save lives: "Research shows that immigrants from low-income countries are six times more likely to die of pregnancy-related illnesses or complications than their Sweden-born counterparts and more than twice as likely to have a serious childbirth-related problem." Doula culture interpreters fill gaps in communication, helping women who may well be unfamiliar with the medical system and birth practices. In 2015, 160,000 refugees and asylum seekers from conflict zones entered Sweden; "the language barrier was the biggest hurdle."

Doulas may foster cultural survival in other ways too.

Tewa Women United (TWU), in Española, New Mexico, has incorporated doula training into its work. Recognizing that Native Americans have the second-highest rates of maternal mortality after Black women, the Tewa Birthing Project is tackling health disparities head-on. Doula training is free, but students agree to assist with births in the community. Doulas are especially important in communities fearful of government and distrustful of Western medical care. The toxic legacy of the Indian Child Welfare Act of 1978, which allowed the U.S. government to remove Native children from their families, runs deep.

As Rebecca Moss reports, "Learning how to heal, not just the wounds of birth—but those carried by Indigenous culture more broadly—is an imperative of this space." TWU's executive director, Dr. Corinne Sanchez, remarked, "It was really a back and forth and fluidity of coming to our center to uncover the strength we had as women and girls—and also our ties with Mother Earth. We knew we had our strength. . . . It's not just work for me, it is my life journey."

The Manitoba Indigenous Doula Initiative in Canada also confronts histories of colonialism and genocide. In Manitoba, 90 percent of the children in foster care are Indigenous. Doula Dawn Lavand believes this is due to racism: "The stereotype is that Indigenous women are disposable, their families are being raised in horrible poverty, they're not capable of raising healthy robust children." Doulas can minimize systemic bias in health care and also reverse stereotypes, helping Indigenous women "connect with the spiritual traditions of being a 'life-giver.'" At the same time, doula care can help prevent child abduction by the state. A family advocate recalls, "I was at the hospital one day, and in a matter of an hour and a half, they took five newborn babies. . . . Our elders say the most violent act you can commit to a woman is to steal her child." Doulas can interrupt this practice, challenging the settler colonialist system, empowering women, and keeping families together.

Doulas and midwives are also helping fill a gap in care for queer, gender non-conforming, and trans people. Self-identified Cuban American doula Miriam Zoila Pérez, who lives in Washington, D.C., works at the intersection of reproductive justice, birth activism, LGBTQ issues, immigrant rights, and racial justice—issues not often brought together. Founder of Radical Doula, Pérez's popular TED talk takes up issues of racism and birth, including barriers to positive outcomes. Building on the pioneering work of midwife Jennie Joseph, founder of Commonsense Childbirth, Pérez contributes to public conversations about doulas, advocating for a more inclusive, intersectional view of reproduction, one that takes seriously structural barriers to health and well-being.

There is ample, even overwhelming, evidence that doulas improve birth outcomes. Julia Chinyere Oparah and the other authors of *Battling over Birth: Black Women and the Maternal Health Care Crisis* report that doula-assisted births led to a 31 percent decrease in the use of Pitocin (a drug used to stimulate uterine contractions), a 28 percent decrease in the risk for cesarean section, a 9 percent decrease in the use of pain medications, a 14 percent decrease in the risk of newborns being admitted to special care, and a 34 percent decrease in the risk of being dissatisfied with the birth experience. They also report shorter labors when doulas are present.

A 2018 study described doulas as "agents of reproductive justice because their work advances maternal health and women's empowerment through three means: improving health outcomes, promoting women's control over their health, and reducing cost-related health disparities." And a maternity blog titled "Doulas Are Unicorns" wrote, "OK, doulas are not actually unicorns, but doesn't the job title itself sound pretty mythical? And when you think about the fact that they support people who are literally creating and bringing life into this world, it's hard to refute the apparent magic of it all! But let's not get carried away: doulas are not anymore fantastical than the next person, they are just really good at what they do."

Doulas are *so* effective they have been tapped to help resolve high rates of infant mortality, particularly in Black communities. Yet doula care is not widely available, nor is it free. The authors of *Battling over Birth* note "significant barriers to access to doula-care for black women. . . . The high cost of doula training is a barrier for many low-income women of color [and] many of the opportunities for doulas of color wishing to serve women in their communities are voluntary [unpaid]."

This is indeed a conundrum: doulas, especially doulas of color, have been positioned as an ideal solution to improve poor birth outcomes, and yet the women most in need of their support are the least likely to have access to doula care. Consider these headlines: "Are Doulas the Key to Save Black Mothers' Lives?"; "To Reduce Infant Mortality, Cities Enlist Doulas for Black Moms"; "Milwaukee ZIP Code with Highest Infant Mortality Rate to Get 100 Doulas"; "Researchers Say Affordable Doula Services Might Lower Infant Mortality Rate"; "Do Black Women Need Doulas More Than Anyone?"; "Baltimore Enlists Doulas to Help Bring Infant Mortality Rate Down"; and "Why We Need More Black Doulas."

From Baltimore to Milwaukee, doulas are the answer to a question that, for too long, few were asking: How can we reduce infant mortality and poor birth outcomes for infants and mothers? Doulas are, if not unicorns, at the very least superheroes. They are tasked with eliminating persistent racial disparities in reproductive health care—and many are truly up to the challenges of doing so.

In Cleveland, Ohio, Christin Farmer, the founder of Birthing Beautiful Communities, is "fighting back" against the racism that harms Black women and babies. This collective of community-based doulas offers free support to women during pregnancy, in childbirth, and for the first year of an infant's life. Farmer is interested in more than healthy pregnancies and babies; she is also working to heal community trauma. She states, "For African Americans, we're dealing with at least three types of traumas at any given time," including generational trauma and "issues that have been born out of slavery." Farmer, like many community-based doulas, understands that "we have to get to the root and address these problems."

Uzazi Village in Kansas City, Missouri, also centers community, describing its vision as "born out of the community itself, by the community, for the people of the community." The organization focuses specifically on families of color and targets what founders call "the crisis" of Black infant mortality and prematurity. Services include doula care (through a collective of "Sister Doulas"), a walk-in breastfeeding clinic, childbirth education, birth worker training, and more. Cofounder and Executive Director Hakima Tafunzi Payne, a nurse educator and midwife, innovated the Black Infant Mortality Awareness Walk and Uzazi Village, both borne from her "frustration with the maternity care world." In a 2015 interview, she stated, "We need a new model of prenatal care in this country as the current one does not serve its most vulnerable citizens. . . . We [at Uzazi Village] serve as a beacon of light to those who wish to join us to transform society through radical maternity care, and of course to those that will be transformed by that care."

Yet as Christin Farmer and others note, doulas and related birth workers are not free (not even at Uzazi Village). Costs can range from a few hundred dollars to $3,500, and many insurance plans do not cover doula care. In 2020, only two states—Minnesota and Oregon—allowed reimbursement for doula services.

Indiana passed legislation for third-party doula reimbursement but provided no funding, "calling into doubt whether programming will be implemented." As one expectant mom remarked, "We need a policy change that makes doula support a covered birth expense so that more women can reap the benefits of having a strong support system throughout pregnancy and during birth. This is paramount for black women, especially, to ensure our survival."

The founder of a Milwaukee-based reproductive justice organization stated, "Black doulas have a bleeding heart. . . . And so our rates are very low compared to the work that we are doing." She notes that policy shifts requiring certification of doulas disadvantage doulas of color, who may not have the kind of training insurers and others demand. Such doulas may find themselves in the same boat as lay midwives, who encounter professional tensions with certified nurse-midwives.

Cities may thus be enlisting doulas to fight infant mortality, but they are doing so without compensating them. In Baltimore, resources are used to *train* doulas, but the city is not paying them for their work; "any money they make will have to come from clients." According to *Stateline*, "The architects of the Baltimore program said they warned trainees from the start that they would not be able to make a living from their doula work. Many of their patients cannot afford to pay." A government official described the doulas as "giving back to the community," with compensation allegedly not a motive. New York has a pilot doula program under Medicaid, but critics have identified "low reimbursement rates and lack of attention to racial equity."

In short, while community-based doulas are a promising solution to high infant mortality rates, insurance won't cover their work, cities and states that rely on them may not be paying them, and the women who need them the most may not be able to access them. If we really cared about improved birth outcomes and reducing our appalling maternal and infant mortality rates, then doulas would be as well-compensated as obstetricians, who make on average more than two hundred thousand dollars annually according to *U.S. News and World Report*. One might be forgiven for thinking that doula compensation, or lack thereof, has something to do with the populations they serve: laboring women and especially women of color.

Despite these barriers, which are significant, doulas improve birth outcomes. The evidence is clear. But sometimes, still too often, pregnancies end in miscarriage. Newborns and mothers may die during or after childbirth. Doulas can help here too.

Bereavement or grief doulas serve women and families suffering from pregnancy and babyloss. The founder of doula training network Still Birth Day, Heidi Faith, remarks, "I am here to bridge the gap where birth and death meet. I am here to provide comfort." She notes that bereavement doulas can help someone move forward "while they're crumbling." They can help families to complete death certificates, assist with funeral arrangements, and provide support when babylost mothers' milk comes in despite being unnecessary, and can brief them on how to react when people ask about the baby. Doula Heather Bradley, describing a friend's miscarriage, states, "It was awful. Hearing what other people said to her and how other people abandoned her. I couldn't believe the suffering. . . . We can't not support these families."

Women who lose babies may not be aware of the support a grief doula can provide, believing them to serve only laboring women or new mothers. Writer Emily Thompson recalls, "Hiring a bereavement doula was one of the best decisions I made in the days after we learned our baby would never be coming home with us as we had imagined. When someone made the suggestion to me, I remember thinking, 'What would they be doing?' In my head, a doula is supposed to hold your hand through your birth experience, advocate for your needs when necessary, and help guide you through the mental, emotional, and physical journey you are embarking on. And that's precisely what she did."

One of the most important things a bereavement doula can do for a babylost mom is encouraging her to feel like a mother. No matter what age a baby is when he dies—in utero, stillbirth, or later—babylost women may struggle with their identity. How is it possible, they may wonder, to be "Mom" to a dead child? Doula Alisa Blackwood, based in Minnesota, wants women who lose babies to know they are mothers "no matter what." She says, "Her tender heart needs love and support. . . . I feel incredibly honored to hold space for a woman and her partner during what may be a time of deep and unspeakable grief." Blackwood believes that "mothers deserve to be nurtured, cared for and listened to, whether they're birthing a full-term healthy baby or a baby who isn't going to live."

After Meghan Markle was criticized for her reproductive choices, U.K. charity Birthrights cofounder Rebecca Schiller attempted to describe what doulas actually do, including bereavement work: "A doula is someone who knows you and who knows birth, who will not tell you what to do, but who will let you work it out for yourself. . . . A doula helps you navigate a system that can be unfriendly to women. . . . Perhaps she is someone who was there with you and your partner when you birthed your stillborn baby. She took the photos of him that you keep in a memory box, and she cried with you and for you. Through that experience, she is someone who has a glimpse into the complex tangle of feelings you have for this child you are giving birth to today."

Doulas may not, as Miriam Zoila Pérez rightly notes, fix racism. Nor should they be tasked with doing so; why expect people who did not cause a problem to fix it? That said, doulas sure can go a long way toward minimizing the impacts of racism and other "isms" on birth outcomes and reducing health disparities.

Now if only we could get foundations, governments, and insurance companies to value doulas enough to adequately pay them for their work. This would ensure that all pregnant people everywhere, but especially those most at risk, have access to life- and baby-saving doula care.

Their futures depend on it.

E

EMPTINESS

"There's not a word in the dictionary that exists to describe the pain when you've lost your child. I kept saying I don't know what to do with my arms. My arms are empty. He was always in them."

Babylost parents speak of empty arms, empty wombs, and empty cradles. Life itself may feel empty. Books with titles such as *Empty Cradle, Broken Heart* and *Empty Arms: Hope and Support for Those Who Have Suffered a Miscarriage, Stillbirth or Tubal Pregnancy* fill grief and bereavement shelves. Indeed, so common is the experience and sensation of emptiness that clinicians write about "empty arms syndrome."

An infant's death leaves a baby-shaped imprint where a child should be, ghost-like, a life not realized.

Emptiness implies loss, nothingness, a vacancy. A list of *empty*'s synonyms illustrates that being empty is not a desirable state: unoccupied, bare, desolate, deserted, abandoned, meaningless, aimless, worthless.

The opposite of empty? Full, meaningful, worthwhile.

When a baby dies, the resulting emptiness creates a void. Here, the cup is neither half-empty nor half-full; it is not only empty but shattered.

As we saw earlier, barbershops display empty baby shoes to signify loss. In Greensboro, North Carolina, empty baby strollers served as "a stark reminder" of infant death during a community event. A coordinator with the Guilford County Coalition on Infant Mortality noted, "It's really about raising awareness. When we talk about a rate or statistic with infant mortality, people tend not to assign a face, a family, or a relationship with the baby that has died. We want to say it's here happening in our community and it could happen to anyone." The event also featured empty, formless baby hats.

What comes after the emptiness?

For some babylost parents, it is unending grief. For others, there are rainbow babies (babies born after a reproductive loss) and the fullness—even if partial—of family life. For many, it is acts of remembrance, tender memorials to their lost, but not forgotten, children. Families visit their graves, for example.

Empty stroller. Photo credit: Lukas Gächter / Unsplash.

But the sensation of emptiness may remain, sometimes forever. The feeling that there once was or could have been a beloved baby in one's arms; the grasping for something, someone not there; the echo of existence, however fleeting.

As one babylost mom wrote, "Twenty-seven days after Cayden's death, I opened that door. But I wasn't ready for it. I went in to iron my skirt on the ironing board but everything froze, including me. My eyes scanned the room making mental notes of the crib that wasn't put together, the empty car seat, his belongings, and the changing table. I quickly shut the door and accepted my wrinkly clothes. Empty, messy, unfinished . . . and wrinkly, that's me."

ENVY

When other people possess things we desire, we may envy them. We may covet their fancier cars, better jobs, sexier spouses, bigger houses. Envy, Aristotle noted, is tantamount to pain at the good fortune of others.

When people desire to be parents, reproductive loss—miscarriage, stillbirth, infant death, even termination—fuels a range of emotions, including envy. "Sometimes 'child envy'—the feeling of being envious of other people's children—can be an issue for those who have been through perinatal loss," writes one clinician. Consider the experience of this babylost woman:

I thought I was done. Thought I was OK, that I had achieved full acceptance. That is one of the so-called steps of grief, after all. . . . Instead, I find that I am jealous of first-time mothers and fathers. Whatever rocky or smooth road they may have traveled since they saw that positive pregnancy test to the crowning, groaning joy of birth, *they have a living baby in their arms.* Death did not rip their firstborn and their own innocence away. Fear does not now shadow their family, or their future pregnancies, or their children's lives. They have not learned how easily, how silently catastrophe can shatter all that is sacred.

While envy may be rooted in desire and want, it is clearly not a desirable or pleasant emotion to experience. It leaves us wanting, sad, regretful, and can even make us sick. In the Japanese comic *Fullmetal Alchemist*, for example, Envy is aptly cast as a sadistic, evil shapeshifter who torments humanity.

Envy is considered one of the seven deadly sins in Roman Catholicism. In the book of Genesis, Cain kills his brother, Abel, because God allegedly prefers Abel's sacrifice. God punishes Cain with a life of wandering.

For many people, especially those who believe in biblical sin, envy can foster shame and self-loathing. Indeed, some psychologists consider envy a "hidden dragon," a secret emotion whose expression is often muted because it reveals something about one's own perceived shortcomings.

The internet, in which many of us marinate daily, amplifies envy, so much so that "social media envy" has become a diagnostic category in social science and popular culture. Facebook posts and Instagram feeds show (allegedly) happy, rich, fulfilling lives that may often be inaccessible to others, promoting unhappiness, jealousy, and even anger. FOMO (fear of missing out) has entered our lexicon.

And baby pictures are everywhere online.

One babylost woman wrote to a friend,

I find myself crying after many of our interactions, angry at myself for allowing the hot tears to roll down my face, wishing with all my heart I could just stop feeling the heartache and envy. How can I tell you, the friend I hold so dear, that your happiness is hard for me to see? How do I tell you that the thought of entering your happy, blessed home brings me pain? I never thought it was possible to feel genuine gladness and crippling jealousy toward someone at the same time. In my sad existence, it happens all the time. It hurts. I yearn for my own version of what you have; I just want what's normal, like you. I detest myself every time I feel the grip of that jealousy take hold of me, but I can't stop it.

For those who suffer babyloss, to grieve without envy may be impossible. Because to envy, *to feel*, is to be fully human. Surely, we do not expect babylost parents to become fugitives from their own emotions?

EPIGENETICS

Imagine that our genetic makeup, our DNA, can be negatively or positively affected by outside forces, such as maternal trauma or exposure to environmental toxins. Imagine further that one key mechanism for such genetic change is reproduction;

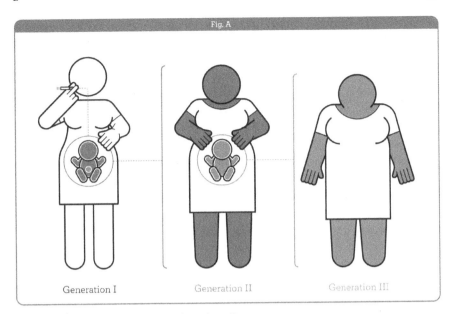

Fig. A

Generation I   Generation II   Generation III

Epigenetics. Photo credit: Illustration by Jude Buffum.
Epigenetic impact of behavior across three generations.

that is, pregnant people can "transmit" such trauma or environmental illness directly to their offspring in the womb.

This may sound like the realm of science fiction, an Octavia Butler novel perhaps. But the burgeoning field of epigenetics is exploring precisely these kinds of biological developments, appealing "to many because it seems to have a wide range of potential applications."

The term *epigenetics*, from the Greek *over*, *outside of*, or *around*, means "in addition to changes in genetic sequence" that may occur *within* a body's DNA. It was coined by developmental biologist Conrad Waddington in 1956. Waddington worked in the field of embryology, the study of embryos or babies-in-formation. This field was shaped by the idea of *epigenesis*, or development of an organism from a seed. In his 1956 paper, Waddington "succeeded in demonstrating the inheritance of a characteristic acquired in a population in response to an environmental stimulus."

Epigenetics suggests that the gene—and possibly the whole genome itself—can be altered *and these changes can even be inherited*. And though this field is still in formation, and somewhat controversial, these ideas have enormous implications for how we understand reproductive health, including infant mortality.

Some scholars have found evidence of transgenerational transmission of risk for preterm birth—one of the leading causes of infant death. Others have explored health disparities, including higher rates of infant death among African Americans. Intriguingly, if preterm birth *is* linked to transgenerational effects, the "epigenetic profile" of a pregnant woman may have been created by "the pregnant mother's own in-utero environment, when she was a fetus decades prior to her [current] pregnancy."

A study of thirty-eight women who were pregnant during the events of 9/11 and near the World Trade Center found that the children of women who developed PTSD subsequently had an increased stress response, measured by cortisol levels in their blood. This was especially the case for the children of women who were more advanced in their pregnancies, in the second or third trimesters during the crisis. This data, coupled with studies of children of Holocaust survivors, suggests "that children who inherited the nightmare of the World Trade Centre attack from their mothers while in the womb may in turn pass it on to their own children."

Thus epigenetics may be helpful in better mapping the causes of infant mortality, especially in populations affected by transgenerational trauma or exposure to environmental toxins. In the United States, these populations are far more likely to be poor communities of color. Consider, for example, the long-term impact on Native Americans of the vicious Indian Removal Act or the embodied legacy of chattel slavery among African Americans.

The environmental justice movement has revealed that low-income communities of color tend to be burdened with businesses that pollute more than most, including hazardous waste dumps, chemical production facilities, smoke-belching factories, fracking, and industries that poison the water supply. Fetuses and infants are especially vulnerable to direct exposure and also may be impacted epigenetically, across generations, when pregnant women themselves are exposed.

One commentator suggests that epigenetics has a "radical edge" in its focus on "social disasters," like pollution, poverty, and climate change. These, she writes, "leave much deeper and demographically more significant traces on children's neurobiological development than the stupid stuff that some women do when they're expecting."

"Epigenetics," writes scholar Susan Squier, "seems to reach from the body to society, holding out hope to illuminate issues as diverse as the development of gender identity; the intergenerational impact of slavery, war, or starvation; the range of factors that make us more vulnerable to depression or psychosis; or even the many variables that shape the health or illness of an ecosystem and the human beings dwelling within it."

I wonder, though: *How* does it help us to know that infant mortality may, sometimes or perhaps or always, be an epigenetic phenomenon? Does scientific knowledge inevitably lead to the necessary social changes that will improve maternal and infant health? If environmental exposure and trauma *are* causal agents of infant death, how might we begin to address their impacts on current and future generations? Or even prevent them? If epigenetics can result in negative consequences, such as illness and premature death, might these mechanisms also result in positive outcomes?

Of critical importance in this contemporary political moment, when women's health is highly embattled and politicized, where do we draw the line at interventions in and on pregnant bodies to improve fetal and newborn health? After all, it is one thing to encourage women to eat well and to avoid stress and toxins. It would be quite another thing to *require* certain behaviors and *forbid* others, especially as healthy "lifestyles" may be out of reach for many socially, economically, and geographically disadvantaged women.

Noted anthropologist Margaret Lock cautions, "If the intergenerational transmission of unwanted traits is to be modulated, then the habits and behaviour of pregnant women and young mothers is likely to be targeted and subjected to increased monitoring." Where, she asks, do we locate *responsibility* for ill health—that is, blaming or wanting to improve—when there are so many possible vectors of genetic variance?

The "lure of the epigenome" should not overshadow our commitment to pregnant women's autonomy. Nor should it capitalize on women's fervent wishes for healthy, living babies to shape maternal behavior. Improving infant survival—though urgent, especially in communities of color—should not be synonymous with monitoring and punishing pregnant people.

After all, many if not most pregnant women are *already* doing all they possibly can to birth healthy babies, from routinely taking folic acid supplements to regular prenatal checkups to ceasing harmful "lifestyle" behaviors. And they do so within a scientific and political context that views women at best as mere incubators, the physiological means to an end, and at worst as criminals, especially when birth outcomes are bad.

If we truly want to improve infant survival, we need to value *all* pregnant people as much as, *if not more than*, we value new scientific theories and cutting-edge clinical practices.

F

FOLIC ACID

When I was pregnant with each of my daughters, I faithfully ingested folic acid supplements, along with a daily prenatal vitamin that hardened my nails, glossed my hair, and allegedly marinated healthy babies in my womb. Though an expert on reproduction, I had not really considered *why* folic acid, other than the vague knowledge that it prevented neural tube disorders. Like so many women, I trusted the small chalky disks, along with the speckled, horse-size prenatal pills, to thwart negative birth outcomes. As an "older" mother-to-be (I was thirty-five when I birthed my first daughter), if I could do something as simple as swallow a few pills each day to prevent harm, I was all in.

Folate is one of the B vitamins: B_9. It is found naturally in many foods, including eggs, legumes, fruits, vegetables, and beef liver. Though water-soluble, it is not stable enough for food storage and lasting nutrition, so a synthetic version, folic acid, was developed in the early twentieth century. Concerned about anemia—a deficiency of red blood cells—in women and babies, researchers began exploring clinical solutions. In 1931, British physician Lucy Wills established a link between insufficient B vitamins and anemia, fostering interest in better understanding the role of folate in human health. Later research extending Wills's body of work demonstrated a robust relationship between folate, women's health, and fetal development.

Folate has especially been used to target neural tube defects (NTDs) in infants, "congenital malformations of the brain and spinal cord caused by failure of the neural tube to close between 21 and 28 days following conception." Ranging from anencephaly (missing part of the brain) to spina bifida (the spine and spinal cord don't form properly), NTDs may result in stillbirth, neonatal and infant mortality, or a significant degree of lifelong impairment and disability. More recently, evidence has grown that folate may help prevent congenital heart disease, oral cleft palate, and preterm birth, including inhibiting premature uterine contractions: "In observational studies, a shorter duration of pregnancy has been associated with low serum folate levels and with the absence of folic acid supplementation during pregnancy."

Folic acid was initially synthetically derived from yeast and other foods containing folate; it "received its name in 1941, when it was isolated from spinach (folium = leaf [in Latin]). . . . The compound was subsequently synthesized in pure crystalline form in 1943." With chemical synthesis came the ability to add folate, in the new form of folic acid, to all sorts of foods, thus "enriching" them with vital nutrients, which are often lost during food processing and storage. Food fortification, both voluntary and mandatory, proliferated globally: "Regulations for mandatory fortification of wheat flour with folic acid are currently in place in 53 countries although in many places these regulations have not been implemented. . . . Although mandatory flour fortification programs increase folic acid uptake, research has shown that they do not reach all women of reproductive age adequately."

Mandatory food fortification is somewhat controversial, especially where it has *not* been taken up. For example, one study of the United Kingdom measured how many NTDs would have been prevented had the government adopted mandatory rather than voluntary fortification. The study concluded, "Failure to implement folic acid fortification in the UK has caused, and continues to cause, avoidable terminations of pregnancy, stillbirths, neonatal deaths and permanent serious disability in surviving children." The National Health Service was compelled to respond to resulting media coverage, including reportage that "failure to fortify flour with folic acid 'led to 2,000 birth defects.'" Reviewing both the original research and cultural responses, the NHS concluded, "It is not yet known whether policy around flour fortification will change as a result of this study, but it will undoubtedly need to be reconsidered."

One British physician lamented, "What remains disappointing is that Britain has failed to introduce mandatory fortification of flour with folic acid. . . . There may be a systematic failure in the ability to translate research in preventive medicine into public health practice."

This failure of translation is not limited just to the U.K.

Fortification is important, in part, because not all pregnant people have access to the kinds of healthy, fresh, vitamin-rich food necessary to their own well-being, much less healthy fetal development during pregnancy. These foods include asparagus, leafy greens, broccoli, Brussels sprouts, beets, citrus fruits, legumes (beans, lentils, peas), nuts and seeds, bananas, and avocados, among others. While the "bible" of prenatal preparedness, *What to Expect When You're Expecting*, may recommend heaping piles of spinach or kale daily alongside multiple grams of fruits, fish, and grains, many pregnant people are lucky to find even canned spinach and enriched cereal on the shelf, much less the abundant, colorful, glistening rows of organic produce one enjoys at, say, farmers markets and good grocers.

Food insecurity is a serious problem globally and in the United States as well. Poor communities of color are less likely to have enough nutrient-abundant food for all household members to lead active lives. In 2017, nearly 12 percent of households in the United States were food-insecure, with 4.5 percent experiencing "very low food security." Middle- and upper-class families benefit from close proximity to well-stocked groceries and farmers markets—sometimes all in the same neighborhood. But "more than half (55 percent) of all ZIP codes with a median income below $25,000 fit the definition of food deserts."

There is simply no access to good, healthy food in these communities.

Food justice activist Karen Washington describes such inequalities as "food apartheid," which "looks at the whole food system, along with race, geography, faith, and economics. . . . It brings in hunger and poverty. It brings us to the more important question: What are some of the social inequalities that you see, and what are you doing to erase some of the injustices?" In 2016, CNBC described hunger as "America's dirty little secret," noting that forty-two million people, *including sixteen million children*, do not have enough to eat. Vulnerable populations—pregnant people, children, the elderly, the disabled, poor people—are especially hard-hit by food apartheid.

In this situation, and in the absence of quick, easy solutions to food deserts and a lack of government will to end hunger in the United States, fortified grains and prenatal supplements may provide critical support for healthier pregnancies and birth outcomes. The WIC program, administered by the United States Department of Agriculture, is supposed to ensure access to prenatal care for pregnant women, including nutritional assistance. According to the USDA, "WIC saves lives and improves the health of nutritionally at-risk women, infants and children. . . . Since its beginning in 1974, the WIC Program has earned the reputation of being one of the most successful Federally-funded nutrition programs in the United States."

Yet government programs often come with surveillance and judgment built in, especially for poor women and women of color. For example, use of food stamps (Supplemental Nutrition Assistance Program, or SNAP) is often heavily stigmatized, with recipients carrying the brunt of social moralizing about being on public assistance or "welfare." One need only conjure the racist trope of the "welfare queen," which served (and still serves) as a potent symbol for what one scholar describes as the shift "from eliminating poverty to eliminating the poor." Fears of such stigma and surveillance may prevent eligible people from seeking out much-needed benefits. This may especially harm children, and school-based lunch programs are inadequate to the task of filling the gaps.

In 2016, the USDA announced the use of EBTs (Electronic Benefit Transfers) rather than checks or vouchers, a change designed to reduce the stigma of welfare: "The transition from paper benefits to EBT systems allows WIC participants to shop for items as needed rather than requiring them to purchase all items in one trip or lose the remaining benefits. Implementing EBT will also reduce checkout times and potential stigma associated with using food benefits." Using a debit-type card rather than a paper form of payment may improve the quality of transactions, which is beneficial, but it does little to amend widespread inequality and the kinds of bigotry that categorize some people as "deserving" of aid or not.

Folic acid is a core component not only of public assistance around pregnancy. It is also now a part of *preconception care*, a series of public health and clinical interventions geared toward any woman who may eventually become pregnant. This is largely because neural tube defects occur so early in pregnancy, possibly even before women realize they are pregnant, "leaving a short window for women to benefit from supplementation." Another reason offered for such early interventions is that so many U.S. pregnancies—more than half—are unplanned.

On the one hand, the idea that all women of reproductive age, beginning in the preteen and teenage years, should prepare their bodies early for pregnancy makes good clinical sense. On the other hand, preconception care reduces focus on girls' and women's general health to *solely* their reproductive health—and frames girls and women as always potentially pregnant. As I have written elsewhere, "In current articulations of U.S. government policy, infant mortality may be a growing *social* problem, but the solutions target women's *individual* bodies and practices." In these frameworks, women become "containers of blame," held solely responsible for all birth outcomes despite the lack of social structural supports that might lead to better outcomes and do so through other means.

The CDC recommends that "all women of reproductive age should get 400 mcg of folic acid each day to get enough folic acid to help prevent some birth defects." And yet, a 2018 study of low-income women in Boston revealed that "fewer than 5 percent of them started folic acid supplementation and used it almost daily before pregnancy." Thus while "prevention in a pill" may be a catchy and marketable phrase, no nutritional supplement, nor fortified diet, nor access to leafy greens and legumes can fully undo the structural damage, including racism and poverty, that leads to premature birth and infant death for the most disadvantaged.

Magical elixir though folate may be, it is not quite magical enough to overcome systemic neglect.

Fracking

Fracking is shorthand for hydraulic fracturing, an extractive process of mining that releases gas and oil from shale rock: "Water, sand and chemicals are injected into the rock at high pressure which allows the gas to flow out to the head of the well." Vertical and/or horizontal mining may be used. Fracking reportedly contributes to lower electricity costs and potentially fewer greenhouse gas emissions; it also may reduce coal mining and other more harmful forms of resource extraction.

But fracking comes with a very steep price: threats to health and life, especially to fetuses, newborns, the elderly, the chronically ill, and other vulnerable populations, both human and nonhuman.

"How many dead infants does it take before you'll accept that there's a problem?" So asked a *Rolling Stone* reporter in a 2015 investigation of the relationship between fracking and infant mortality in Vernal, Utah.

The article followed midwife Donna Young, who reported carrying a weapon because of threats made to her life and family after she posed questions about the high number of miscarriages and infant deaths she was seeing in her practice. A "fiftysomething, heart-faced woman with a story-time lilt of a voice . . . she's the mother of six, a grandmother of 14 and an object of reverence among the women

Fracking. Photo credit: Jim West / Alamy Stock Photo.
Youngstown, Ohio—Activists protest hydraulic fracturing (fracking) by energy companies drilling for natural gas. They say the practice pollutes drinking water and results in the release of toxic fracking fluids.

she's helped, many of whom she's guided through three and four home births with blissfully short labors and zero pain meds."

Young noted ten infant deaths in 2013 alone, "a shockingly high infant mortality rate for such a small town." After raising the alarm with appropriate officials, the threats and accusations began, and her midwifery practice declined. A subsequent study commissioned by the county that Young had advocated for determined that the infant deaths were "not statistically insignificant." Meaning, the findings *were* significant, but local officials blamed the "health problems of mothers, citing smoking, diabetes, and prenatal neglect."

When four women in her practice suffered miscarriages in a span of two weeks, Young herself had their water tested: "Most of the batches tested were positive for extreme toxicity from hydrogen sulfide . . . one of the most deadly of the gases released by drilling. Exposure to it has killed a number of rig workers over the past few decades. In high enough concentration, just one breath is enough. In much smaller amounts, H_2S can cause miscarriages—and the amounts Young says she found were more than 7,000 times the EPA threshold for safety."

Counter to much of the community's response to Young's concerns, the *Salt Lake Tribune* later ran a story headlined "Midwife Was Right."

In 2016, the Center for Environmental Health released data showing that "fracking poses unacceptable and unignorable health risks to nearby communities." The Center also referred to an earlier article that "would have supported Donna Young's suspicion that fracking-induced air pollution impairs fetal health."

More than 750 chemicals have been identified for use in fracking; when these are injected as "slickwater" into the ground at high pressure, the chemicals themselves may be released back into the environment, along with radioactive materials discharged from the shale when it is drilled. Wastewater treatment does not remove all or even many of the chemicals, which are then deposited into landfills and evaporation pits from which they seep into and contaminate aquifers, groundwater, and surface water.

Fracking's dangers, despite the silver lining of cheaper electricity, have led to bans across the United States and globally. It is one of the most contested environmental issues of our time. As journalist Rachel Maddow writes, "The oil and gas industry is essentially a big casino that can produce both power and triumphant great gobs of cash, often with little regard for merit. . . . In the past twenty years, a technology-driven accelerant has been poured onto the fires of an industry that was already pretty good at burning up whole national economies and hopes of democratic governance."

Still, despite such criticism and community pushback, there are more than 150,000 injection wells in the United States, creating pollution and potentially causing untold harm.

According to the *Rolling Stone* article, "It's a desperately dirty job, marked by horrors of all kinds: blowouts of oil wells near houses and farms; badly managed gas wells flaring uncapped methane, one of the planet's most climate-wrecking pollutants. . . . Workers found dead atop separator tanks from exposure to wastewater fumes. Cows birthing stillborn calves on ranches near well-pad clusters. Children with cancers—leukemia, lymphoma—in places with no known clusters."

And always, it affects the babies: "A girl with a shredded epiglottis, choking her when she tried to feed; a boy born tongue-tied and with a clubfoot; a girl born tongue-tied and lip-tied as well, preventing her from latching on to her mother's breast. All required surgeries days after birth. Still others were born tiny and with mangled placentas—but at least they were alive and intact."

Minimizing health effects, including maimed and dead babies, the petroleum industry labors to make fracking palatable, emphasizing its economic potential rather than the colossal harm left in its wake. But with increasing attention to the damage of fracking and extractive practices writ large, public relations has become more and more challenging for those who seek to profit.

A game-changing study in 2017 offered further proof that fracking is detrimental to infant health. Based on analysis of 1.1 *million* births in Pennsylvania from 2004 to 2013, the study "found evidence for negative health effects of in utero exposure to fracking sites within 3 km of a mother's residence, with the largest health impacts seen for in utero exposure within 1 km of fracking sites. Negative health impacts include a greater incidence of low birth-weight babies as well as significant declines in average birth weight and in several other measures of infant health."

A 2019 study similarly reported, "The closer the mothers' residence at birth to fracking wells, the more negative are the effects on the infants' birth health."

Authors of the study suggest that "priority should be the prevention of public health costs, before considering any potential benefits associated with other dimensions of the economy. . . . A stronger regulatory environment is a high priority."

Unsurprisingly, such studies have spurred major media coverage with headlines such as "New, Major Evidence That Fracking Harms Human Health"; "Babies Born Closer to Fracking Sites Are More Likely to Be Underweight"; "Toxic Chemicals Used in Fracking Shown to Cause Miscarriage, Birth Defects, and Infant Mortality"; "Babies Born to Moms Who Lived near Fracking Wells Faced Host of Health Risks, Study Says"; and "Living near Fracking during Pregnancy Linked to Poorer Newborn Health." Fracking is big news, especially in communities and states with an abundance of mining.

Sadly, whose babies get sick and die, near fracking sites as elsewhere, is a matter of enduring inequality. A recent study found high levels of uranium in Navajo women and babies—many decades *after* the Manhattan Project detonated practice nuclear bombs nearby. Like other environmental contaminants, fracking injection wells are typically located in poor, often rural regions, bringing grief and heartache along with jobs to the area. People and local economies may benefit from fracking and other extractive processes, but they lose massively when their babies die or are born with profound physical limitations, need special medical help and specialized education, and cannot lead normal lives.

Hydraulic fracturing splinters far more than shale. It splinters bodies and lives for generations.

The question remains: *How many dead infants does it take before you'll accept that there's a problem?*

FRANKENSTEIN

Philosopher feminist Mary Wollstonecraft, who penned *A Vindication of the Rights of Woman*, died on September 10, 1797, just days after giving birth to her second daughter, Mary. Raised primarily by her father, political philosopher and anarchist William Godwin, Mary the younger would later marry Romantic poet Percy Bysshe Shelley, after his first wife's suicide. More famously, Mary Wollstonecraft Godwin Shelley would come to write *Frankenstein: Or, the Modern Prometheus*, a "ghost story" she conceived while traveling in Switzerland.

It is nigh impossible in the contemporary world to avoid reference to Frankenstein, so thoroughly has the story been interpreted and reproduced in films, television, plays, musicals, graphic novels, and other adaptations. The novel is considered "one of the world's most visionary works of literature, strewn with abiding philosophical questions about creativity and responsibility, the limits and liabilities of science, and the moral dimensions of technological progress." It is also a spellbinding, pleasurable, thoroughly spooky read, whether for the first time or after numerous readings.

Less well known than the story itself is that Mary Shelley composed her masterpiece *after* she lost her own first child, a daughter, who died a few days following a premature birth. Though she later birthed three other children, two of them also died quite young. William was three and Clara Everina only one year old. Only Mary's last son, Percy Florence Shelley, survived childhood. Mary was not yet twenty when she created Victor and his legendary monster, and she had already birthed and lost a baby, with more grief to come.

In 1815, Mary Shelley confided in her journal: "Dream that my little baby came to life again; that it had only been cold, and that we rubbed it before the fire, and it lives." What is a young woman to do with such maternal grief? In writerly Mary's case, craft a chilling tale about a mad scientist versed in alchemy and electricity who creates new life in a laboratory. The nameless monster, often mistakenly referred to as "Frankenstein" after his fictional father, is a motherless man-child, birthed on the page by a sad woman whose own baby had perished.

One wonders, Is Frankenstein a story about childbirth, as many critics have suggested? Is it about technology and invention and the dangers therein, as others opine? Or is it, perhaps, about child death and a babylost mother's enduring grief?

According to historian Jill Lepore, "'Nurse the baby, read,' [Mary] had written in her diary, day after day, until the eleventh day: 'I awoke in the night to give it suck it appeared to be sleeping so quietly that I would not awake it.' And then, in the morning, 'Find my baby dead.'"

Brilliant, tragic Mary Shelley, who fashioned life from death; a literary alchemist in her own right, vindicated.

G

GRIEF

A history of the word *grief* travels through Old French by way of Latin: *grever* (afflict, burden, oppress), *gravare* (make heavy, cause grief), and *gravis* (weighty). *Gravis* is also connected to *grave* (noun, verb, and adjective), which is multiply rooted and meaningful: heavy, weighty, and oppressive, as well as ditch, trench, and tomb for reception of a dead body. Grief is thus intimately connected to death. It is unsurprising that so many narratives of infant loss are saturated with the language of grief. Grief is the haunting familiar of parents with dead children; it is often unbearable, sometimes inexpressible, and seemingly unending.

Historian Elizabeth Heineman beautifully, terribly captures the experience of grief in her memoir *Ghostbelly*. Documenting the stillbirth of her son in 2008, she struggles to mark his existence in some way: "What is a baby who dies an hour before he is born? . . . How do you make sure your baby who died an hour before he was born is not nothing?" Heineman and her partner, Glenn, are not sure what to call the baby—Thor, which is the name his big brother bestowed prenatally, or Max, the name he would have been given had he lived. They settle on Thor.

After Thor's birth/death, they spend time with him in the hospital; they also bring his autopsied, embalmed body home with them: "Thor will not change during those six hours. He will not be freshly born when I get him, then six hours old when I give him back. He will not be awake, then asleep. . . . He will be exactly the same at the end of the six hours as he was at the beginning. Just a little cooler, a little stiffer, but we aren't thinking about that."

Heineman's interpretive skills allow her occasionally to move outside of her sadness, to make some intellectual sense of Thor's death. But her grief remains ponderous, ceaseless. No matter how much she tries to contain it with theories about what happened, it seeps into everything and shades her life with mourning.

Her grief is deeply embodied too: "Now the pregnant belly is there again. Ghost-belly. The ghost of an amputated limb hurts. My ghostbelly is solid, reassuring. . . . Suddenly the ghostbelly dissolves. Its invisible particles scatter into the air and vanish without a sound, without the slightest tug at the inner belly that remains.

Grief angel. Photo credit: Cathy Baird / Flickr.
"Angel of Grief," Cypress Lawn Cemetery, September 13, 2014.

Stomach and bladder and kidney wonder at the silence next door. . . . But the ghostbelly returns periodically."

Ghostbelly is a kind of phantom limb; a corporeal haunting; a lingering scar, folded inside the body's interior; a sign of profound and utter loss.

The organization "Faces of Loss, Faces of Hope" invites parents to share their stories of loss and grief due to fetal and infant mortality. Founder Kristin describes her own loneliness after learning, at twenty-six weeks gestation, that her baby girl no longer had a heartbeat; she was later delivered stillborn. Kristin created the group to provide support for members of what she calls the "babyloss club." The site features stories and pictures of women (there seem to be no men) with captions that begin "*I am the face of . . .*"

Torie laments, "I replay every detail in my head of Aaron's story over and over again. I lay in bed at night and relive it. I long and ache for my little one. . . . Nothing fills the void. Nothing makes the pain go away."

Zita, whose baby Amelie died two weeks after birth, writes, "9 months on, the shock of it is still unbearable as we struggle to be in the world without her in it."

Mokgadi's son, Ethan, was stillborn: "He was beautiful and peaceful. He was all that a mother could want in a son, but he was gone. I can't have him, I can't feed him, bathe him, clothe him, comfort him, or put him to sleep. Ethan was born sleeping. . . . He is our guardian angel looking over our family. This pain does not go away and it does not get any better even with time."

A 2020 study of transmasculine and nonbinary people's experiences of pregnancy loss found that a majority of study participants found the losses "devastating." While some received care after pregnancy loss, others "noted that they received little or no support from hospital staff." Even more reported a lack of understanding from family members. One participant, Will, described the pregnancy loss as "heartbreaking," while Charlie reported that he went "off the rails, absolutely nuts." As journalist Sarah Prager writes, "From healthcare response to planning a rainbow baby, trans people who miscarry have specific concerns that cisgender women don't, but in the end, the pain of losing a pregnancy is universal regardless of the parents' genders."

Grief, unending.

Unfortunately, grieving parents, rather than being allowed to "get bogged down in mourning," are often expected to cope, to recover, to seek closure, to carry on.

Feminist scholar bell hooks writes, "Just as the dying are often carted off so that the process of dying will be witnessed by only a select few, grieving individuals are encouraged to let themselves go only in private, in appropriate settings away from the rest of us. Sustained grief is particularly disturbing in a culture that offers a quick fix for any pain. . . . We are taught to feel shame about grief that lingers. Like a stain on our clothes, it marks us as flawed, imperfect."

Closure is the idea that grief can be processed, as in stages, and moved through in some sequential, organized fashion. Sociologist Nancy Berns, among others, troubles this idea: "Closure involves a tangled story of experiences and emotions. . . . People define the concept in so many ways, and apply it in so many varied contexts, that it is hard to summarize what is meant by the word. Some people become angry about the idea of closure and what it seems to imply about grief and losing loved ones."

It seems people do not overcome grief so much as find ways to live with or inside it.

For Berns, grief is not merely theoretical: "I have always been drawn to broken worlds. However, my interest in grief and death became quite personal after our son, Zachariah, was stillborn in 2001. My world was devastated and in some ways I am still picking up the pieces." Like the women quoted above, for Berns, grief remains palpable long after the actual loss. And while grief may evolve into or be masked by something else—anger, action, commemoration, theorization—its texture and hue can fundamentally remake, or profoundly *unmake*, a parent's life.

Babylost mom Jamie writes poignantly in *Still Standing,*

> Our society is broken in the way it handles grief and those deep within its trenches. . . . Our culture "accepts" grief to a point, but after that [variable] threshold is crossed, it is deemed excessive, over the top, or even unhealthy. . . . *Our grief is not something to cure.* It is not an illness. It is not a disease. We are not an epidemic and we need to stop being treated as such. . . . It's time to stop being uncomfortable with grief and shying away from the unknown. . . . And lastly, this is my whisper to you, broken friend of mine, sitting all alone in that

dark and messy place, with a heart seeping countless tears and a mind wondering if the pain will ever relent. . . . *It's okay that you are not ok. PERIOD.* . . . Tell your story. Share your pain. Only then can we—the broken—break the stigma of this "sickness" called grief.

Clearly, grief—including chronic grief—is elemental to lived experiences of babyloss. And yet, it is largely invisible in the public sphere save for remembrance days, support groups, spaces such as *Still Standing*, and a handful of books and films. Infant death is, on the whole, understood arithmetically, bureaucratically, and clinically in an abstract language of rates and numbers, charts and graphs, maps and diagrams. These abstractions seep emotions from infant death, transforming tender, visceral experiences of acute loss into a standardized object: infant mortality.

But in the end, grief cannot be measured by the volume of tears shed, nor the hours, days, or years of suffering, nor the number of characters typed onto a computer screen in a shared Facebook group. It exerts an ever-present, ghostly tug, inside bodies and lives and in shared understandings of infant death. We know death is about loss; and because it hurts, we sanitize, quantify, and reframe it. It is so much easier to speak of numbers than to speak of babies' deaths.

I wonder, sometimes, whose lives, and how many lives, we might save if we could capture parental grief in a bottle and sprinkle it on Congress, like fairy dust. Maybe only then would policymakers understand that reducing infant mortality—and minimizing other preventable deaths—is a matter not of numbers but of experiences and emotions.

Grief is felt, not counted.

Guilt

A blog post reads, "19 months on and the guilt of losing my girls still chews me up. Everyday I question what I did to cause my body to fail me, to fail my girls. . . . I just wish that a doctor could tell me why we lost our girls, so I can stop questioning myself, I wish that they could assure me that it is not my fault. Nothing will ever bring my girls back but living with the guilt of thinking that it may have been my fault that we lost our precious daughters is just too much to bear at times."

Guilt, an emotion that anyone with a conscience experiences at one time or another, stems from the Old English *gylt*, meaning "sin, moral defect, or failure of duty." It is considered a negative emotion, one that typically makes people feel bad about themselves. Though all emotions are social, in that they are shaped by our relations with others, "guilt is something you can experience alone. It is a feeling that you have done (or even thought) something wrong; it is your sense that you have committed a moral transgression."

When their babies die, babylost parents often feel tremendous, overwhelming, and persistent guilt. One study found that fifteen months after the loss of a child, most of the 311 mothers who responded to the survey reported guilt or self-blame. Though babylost mothers *and* fathers may feel guilty after a miscarriage, stillbirth, or a child's death, guilt seems especially resonant with women. This should not be surprising: the parent invested with the greatest responsibility—mothers—is weighted with the most crushing guilt when babies die.

Indeed, "maternal guilt" is a ubiquitous enough phenomenon that searching for it on Google (including on Google Scholar) brings up numerous pages of links. On the other hand, when one attempts to search for "paternal guilt," the search engine wants to know if *parental* guilt is meant instead. There seems to be no legible framework for understanding paternal guilt, outside of a few articles about men returning to work (if they left at all) after parental leave. Paternal guilt is so little discussed that one article asks, "Is 'Dad Guilt' Even a Thing?" (Turns out, it is.)

A 2018 article in the *Guardian* welcomes new mothers to "a world of guilt." The author writes, "When a foetus starts living in a woman's body, the woman moves into the house of guilt. It's quite a big house. Actually, it's more like a church, with pamphlets about breastfeeding and folic acid and child developmental psychology along the pews, and the latest parenting bibles in those slots on the back [where hymnals usually are], and a choir composed of crooning, straight-backed members of the many institutions invested in her success and wellbeing, such as the World Health Organization and the Royal College of Midwives."

Make no mistake: they are invested in a woman's reproductive success *because of* the baby inside her, not because of the woman. These institutions will not *feel guilty* when babies die, as the mothers will, though they may make policy recommendations in response.

Guilt may be further compounded by the circumstances of a baby's death.

Scientific and public discourse about sudden infant death syndrome (SIDS) and sudden unexpected infant death (SUID) emphasize the dangers of cosleeping and placing infants on their tummies. One study reports, "The potential hazard of an infant cosleeping with an adult has been recognized since Biblical times." And another, from 2000, notes, "During the past decade, the prone sleeping position has been identified as an important factor in SIDS, prompting a worldwide effort to promote placing infants on their backs to sleep."

The headline of one article reads, "This woman's baby died in his crib, and now she has a warning for other parents." The article notes that grieving mom Jordan shared the following on her Facebook page: "This is the face of immense, unfathomable grief, the face of longing, of heartbreak, of self-inflicted guilt. . . . I will never stop feeling responsible. . . . Please learn from my world-shattering mistake."

In other words, parents—especially moms—whose babies die preventable deaths really should have known better. The information is out there. They failed to pay attention.

No wonder there is an abundance of guilt.

Another mom, Elisha, writes of her three-month-old son's death: "He was completely healthy. He just went down for a nap and didn't wake up. There was nothing that would have been a red flag. *We did everything we were supposed to do*" [emphasis added]. But when she learned about a high-tech baby monitor that keeps track of a baby's heart rate and oxygen level, she wished she had purchased one to prevent her son's death: "I carry that guilt of why didn't we get one. I feel like if he had one there is such a good chance he would be here with us and so our ultimate goal is that no baby goes without this device."

Of course, there is little evidence that such monitors actually *prevent* infant death. Nor, at $299 per unit, can every family or even most families afford one, though manufacturer Owlet's marketing targets anxious parents' fears with the tagline "Know your baby is okay." In fact, the technology is better positioned to decrease parental anxiety than to reduce infant mortality rates; the company reports from its own study of nearly forty-eight thousand users that "96% of parents using Owlet feel *less* anxious," calling this "evidence for peace of mind."

Parental anxiety is good for business. If parents, especially mothers, don't get it right, so much can go terribly wrong, including the death of a baby. Guilt waits in the wings for its cue, poised to take center stage opposite grief.

So we have circled back to *gylt* and the failure of duty. Whose duty, we might ask, and whose failure? With so many infant deaths due to structural causes, especially racism and poverty, it is not mothers and fathers who should be wracked with guilt. It is instead governments and social institutions that are culpable, for failing to build and sustain the kinds of social conditions that foster survival.

It is unfortunate they are so unfeeling.

H

HOPE

Hope, as both emotion and idea, easily lends itself to the saccharine and cliché: Hope springs eternal. Hoping against hope. Hope for the best and prepare for the worst. Where there's life, there's hope. Hope is a good breakfast but a bad supper.

And yet, no matter if so overused it's virtually meaningless, still people hope. We desire, aspire, anticipate, expect, want, and dream. Hope runs counter to persistent cynicism and pessimism. It may also be an antidote to the persistent grief that comes from loss.

"Hope is the thing with feathers," penned Emily Dickinson, "that perches in the soul."

Babylost parents understand hope. Indeed, they cultivate hope as a technology of survival.

Jennifer lost her daughter at twenty-six weeks: "I delivered our baby girl by C-section . . . it was surreal, my worst nightmare. . . . We cradled her in our arms the way you would a living baby. She was perfect in every way. . . . Perfect, but dead. We named her Hope." Writing to inspire, she goes on: "As profound as our loss was, I came out on the other side with deeper friendships, a greater appreciation for family and a new perspective on life. As we mark Infant Loss Awareness Month . . . I want to encourage families suffering through a loss to never lose Hope."

The website Faces of Loss, Faces of Hope shares women's personal stories. In launching the site in 2010, founder Kristin wrote, "Loss has a FACE, shouldn't HOPE? . . . Hope is often what we loose [*sic*] when a baby dies. . . . Faces of Loss, Faces of Hope is boldly taking the next step with a weekly feature spotlighting Hope. You can now share how you've chosen to embrace Hope and mold it into something that inspires others. No matter what your story, we would like to hear it. . . . The pain doesn't end, but hope can still be found."

Stories of hope include women who have, from their grief, launched fundraisers, donated breast milk, founded nonprofits, created artworks, gone back to school, volunteered their time, built a wishing tree, organized walks and rallies, opened businesses, become doulas and careworkers, and pursued long-held dreams and passions.

Bears of Hope. Photo credit: Bears of Hope Pregnancy and Infant Loss Support.
Bears of Hope are donated to grieving families to show they are not alone.

Beryl, a photographer, writes, "Hiding behind the camera lens allowed me to begin to interact and socialize again. . . . It gave me a way to express my range of emotions and sparked an amazing opportunity to explore a new found hidden talent."

Tiffany shared, "Loosing Genesis has given me inspiration to do all the projects that I would have never attempted before. I have grown as a person and a mother. I have made some good come out of this horrible tragedy . . . which has made me feel that her death was not in vain."

Groups that support babylost parents and their families have capitalized on both grief and hope. One such organization, dedicated to pregnancy and infant loss, is called Bears of Hope. Grieving families receive a teddy bear donated by other babylost families, to show they are not alone. *Beyond the Bear Support* includes counseling services, grief workshops and wellness groups, a hope and healing library, and private online support groups.

The website Silent Grief promises "a message of hope for the grieving heart." Weekly emails offer a "Hope for the Day," sent every Monday, with notes of encouragement and inspiration. B'More for Healthy Babies sponsors the HOPE (Healing Ourselves through Peer Empowerment) project, offering resources and support, including home visits. Baltimore also hosts a Walk for Hope "to raise awareness for SIDS and infant loss."

In 2016, the newspaper *Richland Source* in Ohio launched "a nationally recognized series on infant mortality" called Healing Hope. Articles have focused on community baby showers, food insecurity, Black infant health, socioeconomic stressors, baby boxes (boxes of baby clothing and supplies that can double, when empty, as sleep environments), health care workers, and high infant mortality rates in Ohio. The newspaper notes, "Healing Hope started with a question: Why are so many babies dying in Richland County? After studying the complex problem of infant mortality for months, we were able to help bring Baby Boxes to the area, as well as connect families with local health professionals by hosting a groundbreaking community baby shower."

Hope manifests in relation to infant death in another way too—when talking about elevated rates and the problem of infant mortality writ large. Consider the title of an article in the journal *Pediatrics*: "Addressing High Infant Mortality in the Developing World: A Glimmer of Hope." Or, "Study Could Provide Sudden Infant Death Syndrome Hope" and "Why Do Babies Die? ZIP Code Study Hopes to Find the Answers." Another headline reads, "Seeking Hope for the Nation's Slipping Health." Here, as in many other conditions and diseases, hope is embodied in research. The quest for new knowledge may help resolve high infant mortality rates.

Yet hope without action is just . . . hope. While research *may* help reduce rates, more studies alone will not remedy the problem of infant mortality. Beyond hope, a problem as entrenched and persistent as infant death—especially Black and Indigenous infant death—requires institutional change, community buy-in, committed political leadership, and adjustments to birthing practices.

A clue might be found in this headline: "The Doula Who Delivers Hope for Puget Sound's Marginalized Mothers." The doula profiled, Erika Davis, suffered a pregnancy loss, experiencing a traumatic procedure (a dilation and curettage, or D&C) to remove her dead fetus. She describes that time as "the worst month of my life." Davis, who is Black, Jewish, and queer, finds statistics on race, infant death, and maternal mortality "unacceptable." Instead, "she wants to center her work around helping other black women bring babies into the world safely and respectfully." She remarks, "It's so nice to hold a fresh baby."

Hope, materialized.

I

Infant Mortality Rate

"Having been struck by lightning twice now, I derived no comfort from statistics."

So writes Kelly Kittel in *Breathe*, her poignant memoir of serial child loss. Statistics are of little aid to those who lose their babies before or after birth. Inside the cloud of sorrow after a mother has buried her child, it makes little difference if the risk was one in three, or two out of seven, or 6 percent. Dead babies have names, imagined futures, familial relationships, brightly decorated rooms they will no longer occupy, siblings who will mourn them forever.

Babies are not numbers.

Babylost parents do not bury statistics; they bury small bodies.

Yet the dominant discourse of infant death is numeric. We largely speak of such losses publicly through the infant mortality rate, a quantification of death rates relative to live birth rates. Fashioned from demography, epidemiology, and the history of vital statistics, the infant mortality rate is how we collectively and globally make sense of infant loss. But this sense-making happens at the level of populations, not individuals. The IMR is not concerned with the deaths of Kalisa, Javier, and Marcus; it is concerned with *how many* Kalisas, Javiers, and Marcuses there are across time and space. And what these collated deaths can tell us about the health of populations in counties, cities, and nations.

The infant mortality rate is how we have come to officially recognize and respond to baby death. It is the mechanism through which infant mortality itself has been shaped as a biomedical and political object. As sociologist David Armstrong framed it, "The 'problem' of infant mortality was not . . . a historical constant; it did not lurk on the underside of society waiting to be discovered by an enlightened public, but was invented by an analysis which established its existence both at that moment and, by extension, in the past." In other words, infant mortality was an invention, one deeply intertwined with the history of counting.

The abacus was one of the earliest counting devices (after fingers and toes), originating with the Babylonians in 300 BCE. A Latin word derived from the Greek *abax* or *abakon*, the word *abacus* means table or tablet. It is also likely related to the

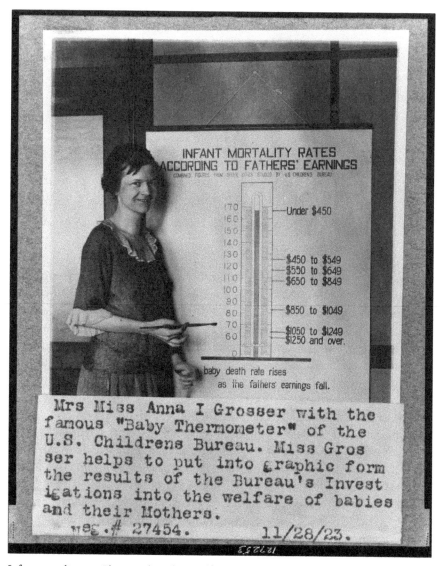

INFANT MORTALITY RATES
ACCORDING TO FATHERS' EARNINGS

COMBINED FIGURES FROM SEVEN CITIES STUDIED BY U.S. CHILDRENS BUREAU.

170
160 ——Under $450
150
140
130 ——$450 to $549
120 ——$550 to $649
110 ——$650 to $849
100
90
80 ——$850 to $1049
70
60 ——$1050 to $1249
——$1250 and over.
0

baby death rate rises
as the fathers' earnings fall.

Mrs Miss Anna I Grosser with the
famous "Baby Thermometer" of the
U.S. Childrens Bureau. Miss Gros
ser helps to put into graphic form
the results of the Bureau's Invest
igations into the welfare of babies
and their Mothers.
reg.# 27454.   11/28/23.

Infant mortality rate. Photo credit: Library of Congress Prints and Photographs Division, Washington, D.C.
Ms. Anna I. Grosser with famous "Baby Thermometer" of the U.S. Children's Bureau, 1923.

Semitic word *abq*, or sand; often, counting was done by drawing lines or shapes in the sand.

An abacus is a frame of wood, metal, or synthetic material on which beads, kernels, or other small objects slide back and forth. Some abacuses are layered, offering more complex calculations. Despite the development of slide rules, computers, and cell phones, abacuses are still used today in markets around the world.

The abacus is also a common child's toy.

Though many abacuses were and are portable—small enough to carry—I have coined the sociological term *portable abacus* to refer to quantification systems that travel. The infant mortality rate is one such portable abacus. Here, the histories of counting, "big numbers," and vital statistics converge to keep track of and manage people's lives, births, illnesses, migrations, and deaths.

A portable abacus, in my framing, must be mobile, translatable, recognizable, and standardized. That is, everyone who uses it must understand what it means, and these meanings are shared across time and space. They may be acted on locally in varying ways, including in differing languages, but the uniformity of the technology itself—the thing it names—sustains communication, relationships, and practices.

The infant mortality rate is a globally recognized object, a portable abacus whose "beads" recognizably mark death. The United Nations, the World Health Organization, the CIA, public health officials, and clinicians comprehend the infant mortality rate in much the same way, as the death of a child in the first year of life. Defining the infant mortality rate as a portable abacus—as a social technology for counting—draws attention to the governed quantification of life and death and the ways in which bodies are of keen interest to states.

It is this common understanding of the IMR that has led to a proliferation of studies attempting to account for death rates. Over the past several years, I have received hundreds of links to articles through Google Scholar alerts. These articles have titles such as "Air Pollution and Infant Mortality: Evidence from Saharan Dust"; "Toxic Air Discharge and Infant Mortality: Effects of Community Size and Socioeconomics"; "Associations between Breastfeeding Initiation and Infant Mortality in an Urban Population"; "U.S. Infant and Maternal Mortality Rates: Shamefully (and Unnecessarily) Bad and Getting Worse"; and "The Long-Run Effects of Tropical Cyclones on Infant Mortality."

All these articles share important data on factors that appear to cause infant death or to increase risk for death. This is valuable research linking infant mortality to everything from nutritional practices to income, air pollution to war. Taken as a whole, this archive offers useful data and often clear pathways to action. For example, if air pollution causes infant death, then perhaps we should reduce air pollution. If infant harm is linked to domestic violence, then perhaps we should work to eradicate violence against women. If Black mothers and babies are at higher risk for morbidity and death, then perhaps we should eliminate racism in prenatal care and childbirth practices.

Yet the proffered solutions do *not* always map to known causes of infant death. Sadly, just because there are clear pathways to action does not mean policymakers will follow them. Though the IMR may be standardized across time and place, responses to it are not. At national and local levels in the United States, infant mortality is typically, but not always, recorded in vital statistics registries, allowing bureaucrats to track and respond to population changes. Some states and municipalities respond more assertively, and with better outcomes, than others.

Woefully, some states simply ignore high rates of infant death, especially among marginalized populations. Elevated infant mortality rates among African Americans, Native Americans, and refugee populations, to name a few, are not, have not yet been, considered a national emergency. These rates register as a crisis only in certain parts of the country and by organizations and communities *that already care about racial and reproductive justice.*

If the infant mortality rate allows us to count—to make numeric sense—of infant deaths, it does not necessarily allow us to ask the vital question, *Who counts?* Knowing how many deaths there are is valuable information; infant mortality data enables communication across borders of all kinds. The IMR allows governments and NGOs and scholars to talk to each other. But it begs the larger, more political questions of whose deaths are tracked *and responded to.* I have long theorized that infant mortality is not considered a national emergency because it is disproportionately Black and Indigenous babies who are dying. Knowing how many babies die in a given year is not the same thing as knowing why they are dying and *what we intend to do about it.*

I suspect, too, that the numeric register of the IMR is partly responsible for why we tend not to frame infant death in the singular and why the issue fails to resonate emotionally. When I give talks, for example, I deliberately alternate between the terms *infant mortality* and *dead babies.* It is quite obvious which term punches people in the gut and which allows us to dialogue in a sanitized, technical, academic way. While the IMR facilitates research, communication, and policymaking, and allows me to talk to a variety of people about infant death, it does not stimulate emotion. It is an abstraction that bleeds feeling and loss out of death.

Of course, we need the infant mortality rate—and we need research that helps us better understand why babies die. I am immensely grateful for demographers and epidemiologists. But we also need people to care *and to be moved to action.* A portable abacus is highly useful, but it cannot do this; numbers alone will not generate caring and concern. Indeed, body counts can be mind-numbing in their endless listing of rates, and statistics can overwhelm with their magnitude. How are people to make sense of reports such as the WHO's figures: "Annual infant deaths have declined from 8.8 million in 1990 to 4.1 million in 2017"? Clearly, this reduction is good news, and yet 8.8 and 4.1 million are *staggering* numbers. They make little sense in terms of actual babies and families, or in terms of the lived experiences of babyloss.

We need to count so that we can learn.

Yet we need to feel so that we can act.

Dead babies are not abstractions. Their losses cannot be solely expressed in the language of numbers.

Who counts may be a demographic imperative, but it also must be a moral one.

Token. Photo credit: © The Foundling Museum, London.
Brass heart-shaped token left with child.

INFANTICIDE

When I began describing this project to colleagues, especially anthropologists, they would often ask if the book was about infanticide, or the deliberate killing of babies. Though I understood the intellectual concern behind the question and the topic's importance in anthropology, frankly, I was horrified. Why, I thought, would a project centering on premature death, racism, and grief, a project that I wanted babylost parents themselves to read, take up baby murder, which I see as grotesque?

As I began to investigate more thoroughly and to think through conditions and circumstances under which infant death is or is not grievable, I realized I could not neglect infanticide, no matter how horrible and viscerally disturbing the topic. Infanticide offers a lens through which we can view crucial issues related to infant death, including unwanted pregnancy, the history of foundlings, gender inequity, and the contemporary politics of late-term abortion.

More, infanticide reveals that our collective assumptions about motherhood and the so-called maternal instinct are highly suspect. This is because we have learned something deeply unsettling about infanticide: mothers kill their babies. Of course, so do fathers. But "mothers who kill" make for far more alluring headlines. "Fathers who kill" is an idea so ordinary in the context of widespread male violence that such headlines may fail to shock.

Scholarly and popular works on "mothers who kill" range from those that seek to situate maternal violence in a broader context, to those that refocus such violence on underlying causal factors, to those that privilege women's emotional lives and experiences as relevant to infant death. Even a cursory review of the literature, however, makes clear there are far more treatments of "mothers who kill"—maternal filicide—than those focused on men who murder their offspring. As framed in one study, "No crime is more difficult to comprehend than the killing of children by their own parents. But this kind of murder has always existed in history. Women rarely kill, and when they do, they often kill their husband. However, the second most frequent target for women killers is other family members, including their children."

Psychiatrist Margaret Spinelli writes, "Maternal infanticide, or the murder of a child in the first year of life by its mother, is a subject both compelling and repulsive." She suggests that many such killings are rooted in perinatal illness, including postpartum mental health issues: "The victim is innocent, but the perpetrator may be a victim too." Because the psychiatric community was slow to recognize perinatal illness—including postpartum depression or "baby blues"—with "a formal diagnosis," new mothers who kill their babies have been judged especially harshly legally. Unlike many other countries, Spinelli argues, the United States does not have infanticide clauses that may result in "more humane treatment and psychiatric care for mentally ill mothers who kill."

Anthropologist Laury Oaks studies safe haven laws in the United States, which decriminalize the leaving of unharmed infants in specific places, such as hospitals and fire stations. She writes, "Social science, criminal justice, and medical scholars seek to determine patterns in the age of infants' deaths, who kills infants, and with what life circumstances." Drawing on reproductive justice frameworks, her research highlights critical gaps in the study of safe haven legislation, including a lack of attention to women's mental health and "the lived experiences of women that drive them to unsafe infant abandonment, or infanticide."

In *Murder, Medicine, and Motherhood*, Canadian legal scholar Emma Cunliffe analyzes the sensational trial of Kathleen Folbigg, an Australian woman convicted in 2003 of killing her four infants over a decade. Folbigg has been described as "Australia's worst female serial killer" and the country's "most hated woman." Cunliffe argues *against* the conviction, suggesting that the trial was shaped by gendered cultural assumptions and improperly applied medical knowledge in the courtroom. She writes, "In some ways, the *Folbigg* case has the potential to tell us far more about our cultural expectations of motherhood and the faith we place in the twinned institutions of criminal trials and forensic science than about Folbigg herself. The case symbolises an obsession with the need to understand how and why infants die, a persistent sense that malevolent mothering is at the heart of the problem of unexplained infant death."

American legal scholar Dorothy Roberts recounts another such trial, this one centered on Jane, a Missouri slave convicted of murdering her infant daughter in 1831. The baby, Angeline, was allegedly poisoned, wrapped in bedclothes, choked, smothered, and suffocated. Roberts cites a former federal judge and historian, who suggests Jane may have killed Angeline "to protect her from slavery's brutality—to spare, rather than harm, her child." (This is the theme of Toni Morrison's searing, award-winning novel *Beloved*, which was based on the life of Margaret Garner.) Roberts raises a further question: "What if Jane sacrificed her child as an act of defiance, one small step in bringing about slavery's demise? . . . By bearing children, female slaves perpetuated the very system that enslaved them and their offspring. Perhaps Jane killed Angeline because she refused to take any part in that horrible institution."

Here, infant murder is a form of social justice or protest. Horrific, but perhaps justified. Who decides?

Anthropology, one of the few social sciences to attend to infanticide, offers much-needed complexity and nuance to discussions of the practice, challenging a narrow definition of infanticide as the crime of killing a child within a year of its birth. For example, Alexandra Brewis recognizes that infanticide may be difficult to distinguish from abortion, especially during later months of gestation. She also makes a distinction between "direct" infant killing and "deferred" infant death through neglect or chronic physical abuse. She writes, "Current anthropological definitions of infanticide emphasize perceptions of gestation, birth, and child development as intrinsicly [*sic*] related biocultural processes that do not have a definite start or end point in relation to each other." This means at-risk offspring may include embryos, fetuses, neonates, or children. Infanticide, in this framing, is relative.

It is also relatively disturbing and allowable, depending on the offspring's age, cultural meaning, recognized personhood status, circumstances of death, and local statutes and practices. This relational perspective is explored poignantly in anthropologist Nancy Scheper-Hughes's ethnography *Death without Weeping: The Violence of Everyday Life in Brazil*. Poor women in Northeast Brazil navigate extreme reproductive vulnerability, with very high rates of infant death in a setting where the average life expectancy is only forty years.

Scheper-Hughes writes, "What puzzled me was the seeming indifference of Alto women to the death of their infants, and their willingness to attribute to their own tiny offspring an aversion to life that made their death seem wholly natural, indeed all but anticipated." Coining the term *mortal selective neglect*, Scheper-Hughes explores what other scholars might call passive infanticide: "The survivors were nurtured, while stigmatized, doomed infants were left to die, as mothers say, *a mingua*, 'of neglect.' Mothers stepped back and allowed nature to take its course." She explores what mother love means in such an "inhospitable context," noting that "infant death becomes routine in an environment in which death is anticipated and bets are hedged." Death is not only routine but accelerated through lack of care and broader societal neglect of poor people, and not only in Brazil.

Brewis describes different models of infanticide, including what she calls "materialist" and "sociobiological." The former recognizes material reasons (e.g., lack of resources) why infanticide might be practiced, including fertility control and population regulation. Scheper-Hughes's study falls into this category. In sharp contrast, a sociobiological approach wades into troubling explanations of infanticide as "natural," either as innately pathological or as an adaptive response to, say, birthing a newborn with a significant disability. As scholars Glenn Hausfater and Sarah Blaffer Hrdy note in their comparative study, "In contrast to other primates, infanticide as practiced in traditional human societies appears to be primarily a form of parental manipulation of their progeny. . . . Infanticide may entail intentional destruction of the infant soon after birth, or take a less direct form."

Again in contrast, writer Sandra Newman explores infanticide through a cultural lens: "Evidence suggests that, while extreme protectiveness of children *is* hardwired in the human brain, it exists alongside a predilection for murdering them shortly after they are born." She goes on to describe a materialist understanding of infant murder: "Like infanticide in animals, infanticide in humans is mainly driven by survival concerns, and the children who are killed share the same qualities everywhere it has been practised. From ancient Greece to present-day Bolivia, newborns are at risk if the child is deformed or premature, if its mother already has other children, if it's illegitimate, and (with some exceptions) if it's female. These criteria remain the same regardless of whether fathers, mothers or even whole communities are responsible for deciding which children live and which die."

It is also the case that greater access to family planning and contraceptives has led to a decrease in infanticide as a form of fertility control. As Newman notes, "We stopped killing our babies when we started having fewer of them."

The establishment of foundling hospitals for abandoned infants also contributed to fewer infant deaths, providing a sanctuary (precursors to today's "safe havens") where desperate women might leave their babies, temporarily or, more often, permanently. Historian Julie Miller, investigating nineteenth-century New York, notes that foundlings typically resulted from poverty and single motherhood. She writes, "Infanticide was practiced more often than abandonment in rural American communities, since the murder and secret burial of an infant thoroughly, and tragically, eliminated all traces of the mother's sexual wrongdoing. Only when large cities developed in the United States did infant abandonment become common."

The Foundling Museum in London showcases the history of foundlings through a series of informative, heart-wrenching exhibits. Most striking and touching to me during our visit were the tokens and bits of fabric that were left with abandoned children, so that if and when their mothers (or other family members) returned, they could be matched. The children were adopted by the hospital and given new names; the fabric or tokens pinned to infants' clothing became the only means to identify their origins. While "literate parents could leave notes or letters as identifiers, keeping copies for themselves . . . those that could not write had to use something they could accurately describe when they came to reclaim their child." Again, we see the link between poverty and infant vulnerability. Significant here, foundling hospitals themselves had quite high rates of infant and child death.

Historically, it could be difficult to distinguish infanticide from natural causes of death. In the absence of forensic evidence (e.g., autopsy, toxicology, postmortem imaging, pathology), scholars hypothesize that some babies presumed to have died naturally were possibly murdered. And that many babies believed to have been killed deliberately or by neglect may have died from what we now understand to be sudden infant death syndrome or sudden unexpected infant death. The legal history is, in a word, murky. The American Academy of Pediatrics notes, "The failure to differentiate fatal child abuse from SIDS is costly . . . child maltreatment is missed, familial genetic diseases go unrecognized, public health threats are overlooked, inadequate medical care goes undetected, product safety issues remain unidentified, and progress in understanding the etiology of SIDS is delayed."

New technologies may be useful in solving some mysteries of infant death. X-ray microtomography (micro-CT) is a nondestructive method for examining bones, including bacterial bioerosion. The authors of a 2016 study in the *Journal of Archaeological Science* write, "The ability to differentiate between stillborn and short-lived infants would profoundly impact on the study of past human life courses and the study of infanticide in both archaeological and forensic contexts." A *Forbes* article reporting on this study was headlined, "Infanticide or Natural Death? New Method May Answer This Ancient Question."

Though infanticide is both ancient and of interest to historians, it is not simply a thing of the past. Indeed, it is vital to consider ongoing concerns and abuses, including the social inequalities underlying female infanticide. The murder of girl babies is, tragically, all too modern. Also called gender-selective killing or gendercide, female infanticide is the killing of girls *because they are girls*. Occurring largely but not only in India, Pakistan, and China, where girls tend to be viewed as less worthy economically and culturally, female infanticide is a human rights violation. In India, abandoned and murdered girl infants are called "trash bin babies" because they are often disposed of in garbage cans, like waste. In China, "female infanticide . . . stems from a deeply ingrained preference for sons." That country's one-child policy contributed to rapidly escalating rates of female infanticide over a period of decades.

The United Nations Population Fund estimates that globally, *more than 126 million girls* are "missing" as a result of female infanticide (and some gender-selective abortion), with some areas showing birth rates of male babies *25 percent higher* than the birth rates of female babies. Gender ratios in countries where female infanticide is practiced are heavily skewed, with many more men than women. This has lasting implications for, among other things, marriage and workforce development. While affected nations could outlaw gender-selective abortion and infanticide—a strategy that only works if laws are followed and prosecuted—a more lasting approach would be to change how girls and women are perceived culturally and to work toward greater gender parity. And this is needed not only in India and China but in *all* nations where "the female of the species" is seen as a second-class citizen, or worse, disposable.

While it would be easy to perceive female infanticide as something that happens only in countries viewed as "backward" or "third world," misogyny is universal. Women in the United States face a different type of reproductive violence, with abortion, contraception, and even basic women's health care under attack by fundamentalist politicians. Infanticide, in particular, became a major element in battles over abortion in 2019, with late-term abortion—typically performed only to save a pregnant woman's life—defined by conservatives as a form of infant murder. Congressional Republicans introduced H.R. 962, the "Born-Alive Abortion Survivors Protection Act," a measure doomed to fail but designed largely to portray Democrats who opposed it as "baby killers." Conservative media shifted its discourse from "partial-birth abortion," a term used previously to denote late-term abortions, to the more inflammatory "infanticide."

On February 25, 2019, President Trump tweeted, "Senate Democrats just voted against legislation to prevent the killing of newborn infant children. The Democrat position on abortion is now so extreme that they don't mind executing babies AFTER birth."

Of course, in the United States, infanticide is *already* illegal. And abortion remains *legal*, if not widely accessible, at least as of this writing.

The conservative playbook has been to again make abortion illegal, and Republican strategists believe that weaponizing late-term abortions is the means to do so. This is happening, despite polls continually showing most Americans are supportive of reproductive rights. Trump graphically depicted late-term abortions in stump speeches beginning in 2018, framing such procedures as "violence against newborns." At stake in this battle is the right to abortion but also the ability of doctors *to save pregnant women's lives* in the event of potentially disastrous birth outcomes. The Trump Administration sought to "Make Unborn Babies Great Again," as one sign declared. Yet actual policies on women's and children's health—from defunding clinics to scaling back public resources to promoting barriers to care—have achieved anything *but* healthy mothers and babies.

Infanticide, then, is both rooted in the past and current, both real and symbolic, both private and politicized. It is mundane and gruesome in equal measure. Its practice may devastate families and communities, while also starkly reflecting and sustaining gender relations in places where girl babies are unwanted and unloved. Infanticide reveals the dark, ugly underbelly of gender and culture, such as evidence that mothers kill, and not only because their mental health is compromised. Historically, killing their infants may have offered relief for poor single mothers, however offensive that may seem through our present-day lens. This is especially true when viewed comparatively alongside the devastating grief of unwanted babyloss.

There is no singular story of infanticide, just as there is no singular story of infant mortality. Yet as agonizing as it is to experience or witness an unwelcome infant death, it is also painful to comprehend deliberate infant death—especially in its cruelest forms of deprivation and murder.

J

Imagine a promised land where very few babies die from preventable causes, and the ones who do are preciously and publicly mourned.

Such a place exists: Japan.

The 2020 CIA's *World Factbook* identified Japan as having the third-lowest mortality rate in the world, just behind Monaco but slightly ahead of Iceland. Japan's rate was 1.9 deaths per 1,000 live births, an astonishingly low figure compared to the United States.

The rate for Asian/Pacific Islanders living in the United States is slightly higher, at 3.9 deaths per 1,000 live births; in 2014, one study showed that about 3.5 percent of Japanese American women received late or no prenatal care.

Japan's success in keeping babies alive past their first birthdays rests, in part, on near universal access to health care. Not only is the infant mortality rate low, but life expectancy also is among the highest in the world. Dr. Sanjay Gupta has called Japan "the Land of Immortals," noting that "nearly two-thirds [of 22 centenarians studied in Okinawa] are still functioning independently at age 97."

The low infant mortality rate is also attributed to use of the *Boshi Kenko Techo*, or *Maternal and Child Health Handbook*—"a long-standing fixture" of Japan's health care system. The *Handbook* was launched in 1947, just after World War II, when Japan's infant mortality rate was seventy-six infant deaths per one thousand live births, twice as high as that of the United States. Of course, hundreds of thousands of people, including infants, were killed instantly, or became severely ill and then died miserably, when the United States bombed Hiroshima and Nagasaki in 1945.

Infant mortality in Japan must be placed in the context of that war, including the Japanese Empire's devastating loss. A precursor to the *Maternal and Child Health Handbook* was the *Ninsanpu Techo*, issued during the war in 1942. This single-page document, folded into sections for recording health information, enabled pregnant women to "receive special rations of food and sanitation items, including cotton, gauze and soap."

Japanese shrine. Photo credit: John Steele / Alamy Stock Photo.
Mizuko shrine for abortion and stillborn children, Jizo Bosatsu statues and teddy bear offerings,
temple 31 Chikurinji, 88 temple Shikoku pilgrimage, Kochi, Japan.

The modern *Handbook*, comprised of two sections—one for record-keeping and one full of educational materials—serves as a communication technology between parents (primarily mothers) and health care providers. The record-keeping section includes data about the mother's health during pregnancy and infant and child health after birth: "Although the record book is only updated through age 6, many parents retain the [*Handbook*] well into the child's adult years."

The educational portion of the *Handbook* includes information regarding nutritional recommendations, what to look for in developmental milestones, vaccinations, and reminder cards for health and wellness visits: "Every resource in the book is intended to educate parents, allowing them to make informed decisions during the perinatal period and child development."

As a form of maternal surveillance, the *Handbook* has provoked questions about the reach of the nation-state and women's reproductive autonomy. Yet it has also, undeniably, contributed to lower rates of infant death in Japan, along with "the Japanese government's resources and funding, cultural emphasis on community involvement with child rearing, an impressive literacy rate, and high rates of residents with college and professional degrees."

More recently, fatherly interest in the *Handbook* prompted the introduction of the *Fushi Techo*: "Those issued by the Tokyo Metropolitan Government include advice from other fathers and mothers, a psychological test to find out what kind of dad a reader may be, an explanation about the physical changes a pregnant woman undergoes, the development of an infant and other basic information."

The *Handbook* has been deemed so successful it's been exported to other countries. The World Medical Association reports that "there are now 40-country versions of the *MCH Handbook*, all adapted to the local culture and socio-economic context." In Japan, it is available—for no cost—in at least eight other languages: English, Korean, Chinese, Thai, Tagalog, Portuguese, Indonesian, and Spanish. And "a digital handbook is spreading progressively . . . expected to be utilized in a way that protects confidentiality of the patient's health information."

The *Handbook* works because it is integrated into Japan's health care system, which offers primary care to the vast majority of its citizens. The Japanese government funds and regulates the Statutory Health Insurance System, which is considered a public good. Those covered pay 30 percent of costs, with the state picking up the remainder. By law, all levels of government are required to provide "good-quality medical care."

For pregnant women, quality care means "close care": regular checkups, accurate record-keeping, open communication with providers, access to interventions when needed, appropriate and sufficient nutrition, reliable and safe obstetric care, availability of midwifery, and timely postnatal and newborn care. While these are *routine* in Japan, they are sorely lacking across the United States, especially for poor women, African American and Native American women, and women without health insurance—accounting, in part, for the striking disparity between the infant mortality rates of the two countries.

Not only is Japan far more successful at fostering infant survival, but when babies are lost through miscarriage, stillbirth, or (more rarely) neonatal death, mourning rituals provide an outlet for grief and suffering. *Mizuko kuyō* is one relatively modern Buddhist practice of memorializing the dead, whether loss occurs through miscarriage, stillbirth, or abortion. *Mizuko*, meaning "water child," is the Japanese term for a stillborn baby or dead infant. *Kuyō*, meaning "to supply nourishment," refers to a memorial service.

The ritual of *mizuko kuyō* is used to make offerings to Jizō Bhodisattva, protector of women and children. It is, as one scholar notes, "A type of service for dead fetuses, designed to offer prayers and apologies, and to alleviate as much as possible the unfathomable pain of child loss. In the case of abortion, it may be viewed as a ceremony for the parent to offer a formal apology to the aborted child, as well as to recognize its life unlived or cut short. The numerous little stone figures with red bibs with peaceful faces, then, may represent the potentially angry spirits pacified, easing the minds of the mothers wrought with shame, guilt, and pain of loss of a life and what could have been."

Not all is benevolent, however. In *Marketing the Menacing Fetus in Japan*, scholar Helen Hardacre argues that *mizuko kuyō* is not only a ritual that recognizes the grief of babyloss but also a lucrative and potentially exploitable practice. The cost of apology rituals can be prohibitive, and Buddhist proscriptions against taking life contribute to feelings of guilt and women's desire for atonement. As poet Erica Goss writes in *Modern Loss*, "The priest told me that in some Buddhist temples, the ritual had become quite coercive, with priests frightening women into making large financial donations to prevent retribution from the angry spirits of their dead children."

Like the *Boshi Kenko Techo* baby book, *mizuko kuyō* is also being exported from Japan and taken up by women elsewhere—though often severed from its cultural roots. That is, while grounded in Buddhism, *mizuko kuyō* is done in more secular fashion by people unschooled in Buddhism. In 2015, NPR reported, "Like a growing number of American *mizuko kuyo* participants, Ali Smith . . . is not religious at all. But after her miscarriages, she was open to trying anything. . . . The American *mizuko kuyo*, at its heart, isn't about Jizo statues or chants. It's about compassion—for the losses we suffer, for everyone around us and for the lives all of us are living."

In 2017, Angela Elson wrote about her pregnancy loss and *mizuko kuyō* in the *New York Times*: "What *can't* one buy on the internet? Our statue of Jizo arrived a few days later. He was the height of a paperback and made of cement. His eyes were squinted in a mellow smile, hands folder in prayer." Elson describes fussing over the statue, talking to him, kissing him, and experiencing anxiety when he was out of her sight. She writes, "Without a prescribed course for mourning, I didn't know what else to do besides mother this lump of concrete as if he could actually transfer my love to the afterlife."

In 2017, the *Independent* also noticed the spread of *mizuko kuyō*: "For parents who experience the pain of a miscarriage, it can be difficult to know how to move on and where to seek solace and comfort. . . . However one Japanese tradition is starting to spread in the west, helping couples to cope after their heartbreak." Referencing Elson, the reporter goes on to say, "The comments below the article demonstrate that while many might not have heard of this Buddhist tradition, it is providing comfort to parents in similar situations."

With the *Maternal and Child Health Handbook* and *mizuko kuyō* finding purchase outside of Japan, including in the United States, I find myself wishing that we might also import other successes, including Japan's very low infant mortality rate. Rituals are important, to be sure, especially for babylost parents who are suffering. But also needed are structural reforms that would ensure quality health care for all, especially the most disadvantaged.

Only then might we consider ourselves enlightened.

K

Kangaroo Care

Named after the bouncing marsupial indigenous to Australia who gestates her joeys in a pouch, Kangaroo Care refers to skin-to-skin contact between a newborn and her mother or, less frequently, her father or other human. It is widely used in hospitals around the world to improve survival outcomes for premature babies.

In Bogotá, Colombia, at the Instituto Materno Infantil, large numbers of premature infants and a high infant mortality rate in the late 1970s led to the implementation of Kangaroo Mother Care by pediatrician Edgar Rey: "It was an idea born out of desperation." At Rey's overcrowded hospital, there were too few incubators to care for premature babies; more often than not, infants were dying.

The benefits of skin-to-skin contact were first described by clinicians in Sweden and the United States in the 1970s, in the context of improved infant health and maternal-infant bonding. Of course, mothers across cultures and species have long known the wisdom of close postnatal contact with their tiny offspring; they did not need scientific affirmation.

Skin-to-skin contact fosters temperature regulation in infants, assists in respiration, may reduce pain, and allows babies to sleep more soundly. Nestled between his mother's breasts, a newborn will benefit from her body heat, consistent breathing, and heartbeat. Clinical research shows that Kangaroo Care leads to healthier outcomes for infants and may also help the "human incubators"— primarily mothers—with stress reduction, emotional connection, and successful breastfeeding.

Kangaroo Care has, since its inception, been used in many settings, such as Malawi, where it is credited with a startling 40 percent drop in infant mortality rates. Because it is low-cost and requires no technology other than a warm body, it is especially useful in resource-poor environments or facilities with no incubators, which can be expensive.

As for kangaroos themselves, their unique (to marsupials) anatomy, with three vaginas and two uteri, means they can be fertilizing *and* gestating young at the same time. Or they are "perpetually pregnant." They also have the capacity to put their embryos "on hold," a useful reproductive strategy in times of scarcity, such as drought.

Humans should be so fortunate.

L

Life Expectancy

According to the U.S. Social Security Administration's life expectancy calculator, I can expect to live another 31.3 years, to the age of 85.5. This number is based on life expectancy tables for women my age (the calculator does not ask for race or ethnicity). My life expectancy estimate does not account for "lifestyle," current health status, family history, or chance. In other words, I might live longer than another three decades, or I might die sooner from causes unknown.

It's probably best not to dwell.

In 1966, the year I was born, life expectancy for women was much less, at 73.9 years. For men, it was 66.7 years. These numbers have improved dramatically—indeed since 1900, global life expectancy has more than *doubled*. But there are *new* wide disparities, even while rates fluctuate. For example, life expectancy in Afghanistan is only 52.8 years, compared to 89.3 years in top-ranked Monaco. The CIA's *World Factbook* ranks the United States forty-fifth in life expectancy—a rather unimpressive achievement.

If we consider disparities in the United States, we move from unimpressive to appalling, especially given the *preventability* of so many deaths. According to the CDC, in 2014, average life expectancy was 78.9 years. However, for Native Americans, it was just 75.06 years, and for African Americans, 75.54 years. Whites could expect to live to 79.12 years, with Hispanic Americans (82.89 years) and Asian Americans (86.67 years) living even longer. Asian Americans could expect to live up to a full *11 years longer* than Native Americans and African Americans.

A 2012 study found that "socioeconomic differences can account for 80 percent of the life-expectancy divide between black and white men, and for 70 percent of the imbalance between black and white women." Shaylyn Romney Garrett and Robert Putnam note that "the life expectancy gap between Black and white Americans narrowed most rapidly between about 1905 and 1947, after which the rate of improvement was much more modest. And by 1995 the life expectancy ratio was the same as it had been in 1961." They suggest white backlash as a key reason progress was stalled for African Americans after civil rights legislation.

As I have discussed elsewhere in this book, the languages of birth and loss are not the language of statistics; indeed, the two are antithetical. The dry, technical term *life expectancy* is largely the purview of demographers, actuaries, insurers, and other bureaucrats. When people birth babies, they do not immediately consult actuarial charts to determine how long their newborns might live. Even though I'm a sociologist, when my own daughters were born, in 2001 and 2004 respectively, I did not research "life expectancy at birth" for those years. Rather, I rejoiced in their arrival and wept with relief at having survived long, excruciating labors.

And yet, infant mortality can profoundly influence life expectancy rates: "Life expectancy at birth is very sensitive to reductions in the death rates of children, because each child that survives adds many years to the amount of life in the population. Thus, the dramatic declines in infant and child mortality in the twentieth century [in the United States] were accompanied by equally stunning increases in life expectancy."

Of course, the ways that we measure and understand life expectancy must be attentive to gross disparities, such as those highlighted above. We cannot focus solely on overall life expectancy rates without also examining *who* can expect to have a long life, and *under what conditions.*

Sociologist Jennifer Karas Montez and her colleagues report, "Life expectancy in the United States has increased little in previous decades, declined in recent years, and become more unequal across US states." This demonstrates how state policies significantly affect life expectancy. Conservative policies lead to reductions in life expectancy and more liberal policies—those that protect marginalized people—lead to increases in life expectancy. Montez et al. suggest that life expectancy could be improved for everyone "if all states enjoyed the health advantages of states with more liberal policies."

Well, yes.

I do know this:

Expectation is one of the singular experiences of pregnancy, so much so it appears twice in the title *What to Expect When You're Expecting.*

Pregnant people are *expecting, expectant,* existing in *a state of expectation.*

Expectation is anticipatory, future-oriented, often hopeful.

Yet situations, including racism, shape expectations—and may also ruin them.

Depending on the conditions of pregnant people's lives, they may expect to birth a healthy baby (or not). They may expect their baby to live (or not). They may expect to survive pregnancy (or not).

Life expectancy relies on calculating the odds of survival.

Unfortunately, the game is rigged.

M

The photographs that appear at the beginning of this section are from an installation and performance created by artist Michelle Hartney. Called "Mother's Right," the first performance took place on Labor Day in 2015, at Daley Plaza in Chicago. The installation is made up of 1,200 hospital gowns hand sewn by Hartney in her studio, each one representing an American woman who died in 2013 from maternal causes. The fabric was silk-screened with images of plant derivatives of the drugs that have been used on laboring women for 150 years. During the performance, paired women fold the gowns into triangles, as occurs after a military death. There are twelve folds, with the ninth fold symbolizing womanhood.

Hartney writes,

> I feel that good art can be very provocative and is often layered with meaning. . . . I am appropriating the flag folding ceremony as a model of respect and grief. Women are coming out of childbirth with the same psychological symptoms as soldiers who are fighting wars. PTSD is a serious issue, and a very personal issue for me. Few people know that it is estimated that one in three women suffers from some elements of PTSD after giving birth, and PTSD is diagnosed in 3–7% of laboring women. It is my mission to change that, and to bring awareness to this issue. Mother's Right is not about placing blame nor judgment on women in any way. It is not about options of cesarean section vs. epidurals vs. natural childbirth vs. home births. It is about human rights, informed consent, and respectful care.

The World Health Organization defines maternal mortality as the death of a woman while pregnant or within forty-two days of termination of a pregnancy by any means (e.g., live birth, stillbirth, natural or surgical abortion). Accidental deaths are not included. The maternal mortality rate (MMR) is defined as the number of maternal deaths per one hundred thousand live births. Though WHO describes the worldwide MMR as "unacceptably high," it also acknowledges difficulties in measuring maternal mortality. Not all nation-states keep vital statistics

Mother's Right, an installation and performance piece that addresses the United States' high rates of maternal mortality, postpartum PTSD, and obstetric abuse. Photo credit: Michelle Hartney.

on maternal deaths. And in many parts of the world, reticence about reporting abortion-related deaths may limit accurate data collection. For example, in the United States, "inconsistent death reports are a barrier to lowering the maternal mortality rate. . . . Without having good information on who is dying where and when, federal and state health officials as well as advocates can't determine how and where to focus their efforts."

Globally, we know that *more than three hundred thousand women die annually from largely preventable causes* related to pregnancy and childbirth, including post-partum hemorrhaging, infections, high blood pressure during pregnancy, delivery complications, and unsafe abortions. The vast majority of these deaths (94 percent) occur in countries with limited resources: "Poor women in remote areas are the least likely to receive adequate health care." Of course, the CIA's *World Factbook* maintains data on maternal mortality. In 2017, top-ranked Poland had the lowest rate, with just 2 reported maternal deaths per 100,000 births. South Sudan had the worst rate, with a staggering 1,150 maternal deaths per 100,000 births.

In the United States, pregnancy and childbirth are surprisingly deadly for a resource-rich country. The United States is the *only* industrialized nation where the maternal mortality rate is *rising*. In 2019, the CDC reported that the overall maternal mortality rate in the United States had increased to 17 pregnancy-related deaths per 100,000 births—well above the rates of every other developed nation. For African American and Native American women, the situation is even more dire. In 2019, the maternal mortality rate for Black women was *40.8 deaths per 100,000 births* and for Native American women, *29.7 deaths per 100,000 births.*

As the headline of a *New York Times* article by columnist Nicholas Kristoff queried, "If Americans Love Moms, Why Do We Let Them Die?"

For the most part, articles, studies, headlines, and policies focused on infant mortality—such as those I've drawn on for this book—make too little mention of maternal mortality. Headline after headline describes the rising or falling infant mortality rates in the United States and elsewhere *without also discussing maternal health and well-being.* It is as if infants die untethered to the people who birth them. Similarly, efforts to address maternal mortality often unfold in a vacuum in which the broader conditions of women's lives—including factors that may hamper infant survival—are rendered invisible. The terms *maternal mortality, infant mortality*, and *maternal-infant health* each frame the problem of dead mothers and babies differently, with a range of consequences.

Language matters.

Yet one cannot discuss infant mortality and babyloss without also considering maternal mortality and motherloss. These are deeply intertwined and consequential. If infant mortality has not been at the top of the public health agenda in the United States for more than a century, neither has maternal mortality. It is only recently that maternal death has begun to garner some of the attention that the noisier, more volatile politics of abortion attract. And it is only very recently that conversations about maternal death have taken center stage—generated in large part by the efforts of Black women.

Why? Because Black women die *at higher rates than all other women* from pregnancy-related causes. As *Harvard Public Health* accurately noted in the following headline, "America Is Failing Its Black Mothers." They are more likely to die from preventable causes than white women, and many complications are more likely to be fatal for Black women than for white women. Where women give birth matters too. Predominantly Black-serving hospitals have higher complication rates than those serving non-Black populations, and they are more likely to have serious complications, including higher rates of infection. African American women and those who care about them pay attention to maternal mortality because they are the most impacted by those losses.

For example, the Black Mamas Matter Alliance (BMMA) centers Black mothers "to advocate, drive research, build power, and shift culture for Black maternal health rights and justice." BMMA began in 2013 as a partnership between the Center for Reproductive Rights and SisterSong Women of Color Reproductive Justice Collective. This partnership submitted a report, "Reproductive Injustice: Gender and Racial Discrimination in U.S. Health Care," to the United Nations Committee on the Elimination of Racial Discrimination.

In 2016, BMMA became its own entity, committed to an alliance structure with numerous partners including, among others, Families for Equity, Feminist Women's Health Center, Mothering Justice, SisterReach, and the National Black Midwives Alliance. BMMA created and leads Black Maternal Health Week, which takes place April 11–17 during National Minority Health Month: "Activities during BMHW are rooted in human rights, reproductive justice, and birth justice frameworks."

Sometimes the vital, daily work of nonprofits and activists needs the boost that elevates an issue to the level of a cultural and political emergency. Megastars Beyoncé and Serena Williams provided such a boost when each experienced traumatic, potentially fatal pregnancy complications. Before the birth of her twins by emergency cesarean section in 2017, Beyoncé was on bedrest for preeclampsia. She writes, "I was in survival mode and did not grasp it all until months later. Today I have a connection to any parent who has been through such an experience."

Williams, obviously in excellent physical shape and deeply knowledgeable about her own body, gave birth to her daughter via emergency cesarean section in 2017, with problems escalating shortly after birth. She suffered a pulmonary embolism, her wound opened up, and she had a large blood clot in her abdomen. Her medical team failed to grasp the seriousness of her condition. She writes, "When I finally made it home to my family, I had to spend the first six weeks of motherhood in bed." Drawing attention to inequities and the lack of services for many women globally, she asks, "What if we lived in a world where every mother and newborn could receive affordable health care and thrive in life?"

But Serena Williams has done more than just pose these questions. She has invested her hard-won tennis dollars in a Black-owned start-up company called Mahmee (among many other enterprises), through Serena Ventures. The app connects clinicians and helpers of all kinds—physicians, midwives, doulas, lactation consultants, therapists—so they can "share care plans and stay on the same page about mom and baby's care options. . . . Mahmee is the glue that connects the care ecosystem and closes the gaps." Williams issued a statement about her support of the start-up: "Given the bleak data surrounding maternal death and injury rates, I believe that it is absolutely critical right now to invest in solutions that help protect the lives of moms and babies." Today, Mahmee is targeting cities with higher maternal morbidity and death rates.

Beyoncé and Serena Williams are not the only celebrities to turn their star power to social change. Supermodel Christy Turlington Burns founded Every Mother Counts after a harrowing birth experience with her daughter, Grace, in 2003: "I felt so well-prepared for everything, except for what occurred after she was born. My placenta was retained and could not expel itself so it had to be removed. As a result, I lost a few liters of blood. While the active management of this complication was painful, I never feared for my life because I had confidence in my midwife and others who worked together to stabilize me. Without access to this critical and timely care, I may not be here today. Many other women are not as lucky."

Every Mother Counts works to build awareness about maternal health issues, mobilize communities, and support local efforts. The organization has produced educational films, including the series "Giving Birth in America," and offers grants that center women, strengthen the maternal health care workforce, and are led by those most impacted: women and their communities. Since its inception, Every Mother Counts has invested more than sixteen million dollars in public education, community engagement, and grants, impacting more than seven hundred thousand people.

The Black Mamas Matter Alliance, SisterSong, Every Mother Counts, and other organizations clearly have taken an active role in shifting maternal health policy. A recent array of legislative initiatives has emerged directly from their important labor. For example, the MOMMIES Act (Maximizing Outcomes for Moms through Medicaid Improvement and Enhancement of Services) was introduced by Congresswoman Ayanna Pressley of Massachusetts and Senator Cory Booker of New Jersey, specifically to address high maternal mortality rates. Booker stated, "We live in a nation that spends more than any other country on health care, yet we still have the highest rate of pregnancy-related deaths of any country in the developed world."

Maternal health is, finally, again on the federal agenda as it was in the early twentieth century. Let it not again fade from concern.

There are global efforts, too, as there should be given that most maternal deaths are in resource-poor countries. More than half occur in sub-Saharan Africa and almost one-third in South Asia. The embarrassingly high maternal death rate in the United States should not distract us from understanding the widely international scope of the problem. As one WHO official noted, "It's hard to believe that in 2015, almost 6 million children and more than 300,000 mothers died from complications of childbirth."

U.N. Millennium Development Goal 5, improving maternal health, established clear targets, including a reduction in maternal mortality by 75 percent and achieving universal access to reproductive health. Obviously, these targets were not met. The World Health Organization noted, "Looking beyond 2015, the Sustainable Development Goals offer a renewed opportunity to see improvements in maternal health for all women, in all countries, under all circumstances."

In the meantime, until we can mend the problem at its roots, more than eight hundred women around the world will die *every day* from preventable causes related to pregnancy and childbirth.

Motherhood—and mothers—lost.

MEDICAID

Imagine if the federal government and states could do something relatively simple to improve infant survival. Perhaps something that is already built into existing programs, with a proven track record and a wealth of data showing its effectiveness. Surely, if such a "something" exists, policymakers would already be doing it, right?

Sadly, no.

That "something" is Medicaid.

Established in 1965 as Title XIX (an amendment) of the Social Security Act, "Medicaid is a public insurance program that provides health coverage to low-income families and individuals, including children, parents, pregnant women, seniors, and people with disabilities. Each state operates its own Medicaid program within federal guidelines." Eligibility and benefits vary widely across the United States, though the federal government mandates certain groups for coverage, including low-income pregnant women and children. Each state determines eligibility requirements and income limits, and in nineteen states, eligibility levels are quite low. In 2015, Medicaid helped ninety-seven million low-income people, including thirty-three million children, gain access to health care services.

In 2020, the Affordable Care Act (ACA) expanded Medicaid: "As of 2016, Medicaid covered 11.9 million newly eligible Americans in expansion states," dramatically increasing the number of people with some form of health insurance. In seventeen states, however, "lawmakers have blocked their constituents from sharing in these benefits. As of 2018, 18.4 percent of nonelderly adults in nonexpansion states lacked insurance."

Key here, Medicaid expansion increases maternal and infant survivability, especially for low-income women and babies. For example, it can help reduce mortality rates and racial inequities in mandatory newborn screening. Simply stated, Medicaid can help reduce the high infant mortality rates that the federal government and states purport to care about. It is difficult to ignore the data, which overwhelmingly support the expansion of Medicaid for improved coverage and better health outcomes.

One study published in *Social Science and Medicine* reported that "a 10 percent increase in infant-related spending leads to a 2.07 percent decrease in infant mortality rates in Florida. Black infant mortality rates are even more responsive to targeted public health spending, falling by 4.04 percent for each 10 percent increase in targeted spending." Another study, in the *American Journal of Public Health*, "found that states expanding Medicaid saw greater declines in their infant mortality rates between 2010 and 2016. . . . Medicaid expansion states reduced infant mortality rates *more than 50% greater* than non-Medicaid expansion states." The study authors suggested that "future research should explore what aspects of Medicaid expansion may improve infant survival."

One of the benefits to infants of increasing access to care is healthier pregnant women. An epidemiologist weighed in on the findings of one *Journal of the American Medical Association* study: "The benefits of consistent access to health insurance and health care may accrue across years to result in improvement in women's health generally. That would translate [in]to improved pregnancy outcomes but might not be apparent with only one or two years of expansion status. . . . In other words, it is critical we continue to evaluate the longer term impacts of Medicaid expansions."

The Center for American Progress estimates that expanding Medicaid in states that have been resistant to expansion would actually *save* fourteen thousand lives per year. From the report, "Medicaid is critical to women's health, including during pregnancy and childbirth. . . . Medicaid finances nearly half of all births in the United States. Unsurprisingly, Medicaid also plays a vital role in infants' health at birth. Infants whose mothers are uninsured or sporadically insured are more likely to experience adverse outcomes such as low birth weight in part because their mothers receive fewer prenatal care services."

The coauthor of a study in *BMJ* notes, "Our analysis indicates that these are literally life or death decisions." The study examined the impact on infant mortality rates of federal expenditures to states, including for Medicaid, between 2004 and 2013. The findings "strongly suggest that increases in federal transfers are associated with reductions in infant mortality rates," with "particularly robust" results for Black infants. The authors suggest that reductions in infant mortality could come about through *directly* reducing deaths by preventing low birthweight babies, illness and infection, and SIDS/SUID, among other benefits.

The authors also point to another possible outcome of increased transfers: greater availability of contraception, especially among higher-risk women. They conclude that "federal transfers can prevent the unnecessary deaths of thousands of children, and these benefits should be carefully considered when state officials are deciding whether to accept or reject federal funds."

The Kaiser Family Foundation created an interactive map of the United States showing which states have adopted and implemented Medicaid expansion, which have adopted expansion but not implemented it, and which have not adopted expansion. As of April 2019, the states *not* adopting expansion included Alabama, Florida, Georgia, Kansas, Mississippi, Missouri, North Carolina, Oklahoma, South Carolina, South Dakota, Tennessee, Texas, Wisconsin, and Wyoming. Idaho, Nebraska, and Utah are adopters but not implementers. What I find most striking about this map is that an overlay of states with high infant mortality rates would essentially match the Kaiser map. In 2017, states with the highest infant mortality rates—in order, beginning with the worst—were Mississippi, Arkansas, Oklahoma, South Dakota, Alabama, Tennessee, Indiana, Georgia, Ohio, Louisiana, and North Carolina.

Several of these states—Alabama, Georgia, Missouri, South Carolina, and Tennessee—are also on the leading edge of antiabortion legislation. Alabama and Georgia have proposed so-called heartbeat bills, which would give them the most restrictive laws in the country, including severe punishments for women who terminate pregnancies.

In signing the Life Act, Governor Brian Kemp remarked, "Georgia is a state that values life. . . . We stand up for those who are unable to speak for themselves." One wonders how many more lives would be saved if Georgia adopted Medicaid expansion. The data cited earlier tells us it would likely be a quite significant number.

Talk of Medicaid, expansions, waivers, and so on can be dry. Yet the implications and importance of the data I've cited are clear: *increased federal and state expenditures can help reduce infant death rates.* Full stop. Infant mortality is a chronic social problem that we could, in fact, address by throwing money at it. Not indiscriminately, of course, but targeted and strategic funding as part of existing programs already serving low-income pregnant people and children.

But of course, resistance to Medicaid expansion is not about the data. Because politics is never just about the data. It is about values, promises, power, and hierarchies. States that have opted out of Medicaid expansion reveal their profound disregard for low-income pregnant women and babies. It is no coincidence that many of the low-income residents of these states, especially in the South, are Black. And that infant mortality rates for Black babies in these states are perilously high.

When Governor Kemp asserted the value of fetal life, he was assuredly not talking about the lives of Black women and children, nor the poor. Because if he was, no doubt he and the Georgia legislature would have increased Medicaid eligibility and spending.

Resources matter to human thriving. People with empty pockets and pantries especially know this to be true. Scottish historian Thomas Carlyle coined the term *dismal science* in a racist essay about slavery, describing the negative outlook of economics in the nineteenth century. Infant mortality, the collective deaths of babies then and now, is indeed dismal.

Yet I prefer to look to New Zealand feminist economist Marilyn Waring, whose influential body of work has long proven that economic spaces, even—perhaps especially—when dismal, are *precisely* where we see who gets to count, who does not, and whose lives are valued.

MEMPHIS

Perched on the Eastern bank of the Mississippi River, Memphis, Tennessee is justly famous for barbecue, Beale Street, the Peabody Ducks, and Graceland, Elvis

Presley's estate. A city of 652,000 people, it is located in Shelby County, in the south-western corner of the state.

Memphis is also home to St. Jude Children's Research Hospital, founded in 1962 by Hollywood entertainer Danny Thomas, who believed that "no child should die in the dawn of life." Focused on childhood cancer and other diseases, St. Jude is a multibillion-dollar endeavor, among the country's largest health charities. Individual donations encouraged by celebrities on-screen are often dropped into buckets at cinemas around the country, sustaining the organization.

Despite its mission, there is little evidence St. Jude works directly to improve infant mortality rates, which in Memphis are *among the highest in the nation*. In 2003, nearly 15 babies died in Memphis for every 1,000 born—a rate "higher than that of Saudi Arabia and Venezuela." In 2015, the Shelby County infant mortality rate was 8.2 per 1,000 live births, compared to a statewide rate of 7 deaths, and a national rate of 5.8 deaths.

Unsurprisingly, African Americans comprise 63 percent of the city's population. In Memphis, infant mortality, like that in Detroit and Washington, D.C., is colored by race. In Shelby County, 60 percent of births are to African American women, but 80 percent of infant deaths are among African Americans: "An African-American baby born in Tennessee has a greater chance of dying than if that baby were born in any other state in the South."

But the infant mortality rate in Memphis did improve—a direct result of targeted interventions by the government, community groups, and hospitals. In 2006, Tennessee governor Phil Bredesen announced an initiative called "1 For All," and additional programs followed. That same year, Vanderbilt University and Meharry Medical College cosponsored a summit, "Why Our Babies Die," that brought together experts on infant health, racial disparities, and public policy—a conference that fostered my own research on infant death.

Early interventions focused attention on preterm birth, teen pregnancy, and smoking, all seen as public health crises. Preconception care was introduced as a promising solution targeting women's behavior even *before* they become pregnant. More recent efforts have promoted breastfeeding. Yet despite improvements, infant mortality rates in Memphis remain much higher than the national rate.

Nia, an early childhood advocate, told my research assistant, "When I came here [from Illinois] I was shocked to see that they were still dealing with these racial issues. Slavery ended a long time ago. For me coming here it was like the Twilight Zone. I came here with insurance and I see people without insurance, and I do see how they are treated differently. We have major problems with that, and work needs to be done. You know, educating our doctors. . . . They should take the time so that we can get this baby beyond their first birthday."

The 2008 documentary film *Babyland*, centered and filmed in Memphis, shows that a focus on improved medical care alone *cannot* overcome premature death in a context of racial injustice, especially by focusing on pregnant women's "behaviors." Late neonatologist Dr. Sheldon B. Korones, profiled in the film, defined infant mortality as "a manifestation of the accumulated social inadequacies that we have tolerated historically."

Faced with such persistent "inadequacies," babies die, parents grieve, and communities crumble.

MIDWIVES

Newspaper headlines from 2018 and 2019 read, "Call the Midwives: Addressing America's Black Maternal and Infant Mortality Crisis"; "To Lower Maternal and Infant Mortality Rates, We Need More Midwives"; "A Larger Role for Midwives Could Improve Deficient U.S. Care for Mothers and Babies"; and "Rural America Has a Maternal Mortality Problem. Midwives Might Help Solve It." As we saw earlier in the entry on doulas, today midwives also are increasingly repositioned as a solution to high maternal and infant death rates in the United States, especially among women of color and other underserved populations.

In 2018, the U.S. Joint Economic Committee Democrats wrote, "Increasing access to midwives could lead to improved health and economic outcomes for mothers and babies. New evidence suggests that the incorporation of midwives into state health care systems has significant health benefits, including lower rates of cesarean section, preterm and low birth weight infants, and infant mortality, as well as higher breastfeeding rates. Other research shows that greater access to midwifery could lower medical costs by reducing the likelihood of life-threatening complications that keep women and babies in the hospital."

And yet, a 2008 article in the *Journal of Perinatal Education* asked, "Where Have All the Midwives Gone?" This is an excellent question. As this article and numerous other studies have shown, it is not the case that we need more midwives now because we have *never* had them. Quite the contrary. Historically, *only* other women attended laboring women, and many of these were midwives and lay healers. Midwife means "with woman," and the history of labor and delivery is intimately connected to the history of midwifery. Today, midwifery needs reinvigoration and support, not invention.

With the development of obstetrics and the movement of birth from the home to the hospital, starting toward the end of the nineteenth century, American midwives were displaced. This was done deliberately—orchestrated by white male physicians interested in the professionalization of medicine and creating new markets for physicians. At the same time, women who could afford in-hospital medical care sought allegedly safer births. A significant body of work on the history of midwifery and the transition in childbirth attendance from midwives to obstetricians reveals clear gender and racial dynamics, most starkly in the United States. (Midwives are today and historically were more fully integrated into pregnancy and childbirth care in Europe, Canada, and the U.K.)

In contrast, among women of color, legal scholar Michele Goodwin writes, "In the wake of slavery's end, skilled Black midwives represented both real competition for white men who sought to enter the practice of child delivery, and a threat to how obstetricians viewed themselves. Male gynecologists claimed midwifery was a degrading means of obstetrical care. They viewed themselves as elite members of a trained profession with tools such as forceps and other technologies, which excluded Black and Indigenous women from practice within their institutions."

Black midwives were especially targeted by the nascent medical profession. A 1914 article in the *American Journal of Public Health* by C. C. Terry, Health Officer of Jacksonville, Florida, drew a blatantly racist link between Black midwives and infant mortality: "The classification of deaths, where the sole attendant was an ignorant negro midwife, is of course far from accurate. . . . That dangerous infections of any nature might be expected in the practice of these women, no one, familiar with their type, may doubt. They belong, for the most part, to the most ignorant class of negroes, many of them infirm through age and all governed by folklore and superstitions quite easily traceable to the East Coast of Africa."

Political scientist Annie Menzel has described the midwife's bag, which was subject to frequent mandatory inspection by physicians, as an object of gendered and racial surveillance. Contents of the bag, which could be any kind of sack, included "herbal remedies, vernacular and sometimes commercial medicines, and other tools of the trade." These were replaced by Southern health officials with "standard-issue bags: usually black leather 'medical' tote bags" containing "a small inventory of permitted items, including a safety razor, sterile gown, antiseptic, soap, scissors, and silver nitrate eyedrops." The distinction between an "untrained" and a "trained" midwife was symbolized by the bag she carried—though surveillance of midwives continued, even with the "medical" bags.

Situating her analysis in the context of the Sheppard-Towner Act of 1921, which was designed to improve birth outcomes, Menzel writes, "In practice, however, medical and societal racism largely prevented the act's programs from effectively addressing Black infant mortality, particularly in the South." There, she argues, officials "blamed not poverty—let alone racist terrorization—for high infant mortality rates but rather the alleged ignorance, unhygienic practices, and superstitions of Black midwives. 'Midwife control' was hence the primary thrust of Southern infant mortality prevention programs under Sheppard-Towner."

This history serves as an important backdrop to contemporary calls for increased midwifery to resolve infant and maternal mortality. Though the medical profession promised safe, successful birthing, that promise has been far from fully realized, especially in the United States. Beginning in the nineteenth century, with the rise of obstetrics, birth came to be understood as a pathological condition to be managed rather than as a natural occurrence in pregnant people's lives. The pregnant body became a site for medical and technological interventions of all kinds—from forceps and episiotomies to induced labor and cesarean sections—with significant consequences for women's health, birth outcomes, and reproductive futures and autonomy.

Current practices in the United States predominantly include hospital births (less than 2 percent of births are out of hospital) and a very high cesarean section rate—32 percent or nearly one-third of all births. These, along with documented obstetric racism and medical sexism, have contributed to a situation in which far too many mothers and babies are dying during pregnancy and childbirth. I do not mean to suggest here that doctors are uncaring individuals; I believe the vast majority seek the best care for their patients. However, *structurally speaking*, contemporary medicine in the United States has not lived up to its historic promise. This is especially true regarding pregnancy and birth outcomes. Our comparatively high infant and maternal mortality rates indicate that the vaunted "best care" is not forthcoming for all.

Enter the midwives, who are seemingly expected to save the day—with all the fanfare of a Marvel superhero movie.

The American College of Nurse-Midwives (ACNM) defines certified nurse-midwives (CNMs) and certified midwives (CMs) as trained and certified professionals "who offer a full range of primary health care services for women from adolescence [to] beyond menopause." They may be educated in nursing and/or midwifery (usually both), and their work may also include "health promotion, disease prevention, and individualized wellness education and counseling. These services are provided in partnership with women and families in diverse settings such as ambulatory care clinics, private offices, community and public health systems, homes, hospitals and birth centers."

The Midwives Alliance of North America (MANA) identifies additional kinds of midwives, including certified professional midwives (CPMs) who, like CMs above, are so-called direct entry professionals. They do not have nursing education and tend to provide care outside hospital settings. MANA also denotes *traditional midwives* as those who are not certified or licensed: "They believe that they are ultimately accountable to the communities they serve; or that midwifery is a social contract between the midwife and the client/patient, and should not be legislated at all; or that women have a right to choose qualified care providers regardless of their legal status."

A patchwork of regulations that varies by state means that where one is pregnant and gives birth has a great deal to do with the kinds of care a person can receive. Certified nurse-midwives can practice in all fifty states, whereas direct-entry certified midwives can practice in only a few states. Further, according to MANA, "As of October 1, 2019, CPMs are legally authorized to practice in 35 states." While all midwives face far greater surveillance than physicians, unlicensed midwives (e.g., traditional or "lay" midwives) are at the highest risk for legal interference in their practices. They may also fall through the cracks of regulation and operate under the radar of licensure and certification.

A 2019 article in the *Washington Post* observes, "In the 1970s and '80s, those in support of midwifery and home birth formed organizations, hired lobbyists, organized conferences and published newsletters to educate the public about out-of-hospital birth. The growing visibility and the increasing popularity of home birth triggered a regulatory backlash in many states, resulting in new and more restrictive licensure laws requiring education and certification that continue to restrict the practice of midwifery."

It is important to note that this "backlash" came largely from doctors. In 2008, the American Medical Association introduced three resolutions that sought "to limit the scope and practice of midwifery, insure physician and regulatory oversight of midwives, and promote legislation to ensure that all births take place in hospitals or birthing centers." In her astute 2020 essay "The Criminalization of the American Midwife," journalist Jennifer Block suggests that "politics and patriarchy" render midwives suspect and, in many places, illegal—"to the detriment of women and underserved communities."

Given the historic tensions between organized medicine and midwifery, many contemporary advocates support *integrated care*. Here, midwives are integrated into health care systems and recognized as full members of the health care team, including having hospital privileges for birthing patients. A 2018 study found that integrated midwives were associated with "significantly higher rates of spontaneous vaginal delivery, vaginal birth after cesarean, and breastfeeding, and significantly lower rates of cesarean, preterm birth, low birth weight infants, and neonatal death."

Of course, if hospitals are unwelcoming to midwives, integration is challenging if not impossible. As one Tennessee midwife reported, "Unfortunately, we walk into really hostile situations and respect isn't there for the provider or the client. . . . We want there to be mutual respect. It shouldn't be about us. It's about the families." Integrated care also assumes that midwives will be part of a *medicalized system* in which pregnant people are still expected to deliver babies in *medical institutions*.

The struggle over home birth—and who may legally deliver babies—is seemingly unending, with historical roots and contemporary shoots. On the one hand, MANA and other midwifery advocates invoke studies attesting to the safety of home birth. On the other, the ACOG in 2020—during COVID-19–reiterated that "even during this pandemic, hospitals and accredited birth centers remain the safest places to give birth." Thus the battle continues—doctor versus midwife, hospital versus home—with pregnant people caught in the middle.

Contrast this ACOG statement with the words of Tiana Hylton, a Los Angeles woman who delivered her baby girl at home in 2020. When asked why she wanted to have a home birth, Hylton, who is African American, responded, "The first reason was because of the pandemic. Everything was so chaotic and scary. The second reason was because I am a woman of color. That's what I was really afraid of. . . . Modern European medicine has always been against us. . . . A lot of (women of color) don't make it through childbirth." Hylton (and her daughter) did make it, with the help of a doula and a midwife.

According to *Cronkite News*, which profiled Hylton, "Concerns like Hylton's are well known at the Los Angeles County Department of Public Health, which reports that the disparity in Black infant mortality has remained static for decades. Even in typical [nonpandemic] years, Black women [in California] are most likely to consider a midwife at birth compared with other races." In the same story, Viergeni White, who is African American, remarked, "I think Black women seek the holistic approach because we want someone to see us, we want to learn, we want the full approach not the medical approach. We are not numbers, we are people. . . . Midwives do that. They see you."

We should likewise see—and support—midwives. And not only to reduce maternal and infant mortality rates but because midwifery care centers *the whole person*. It thus offers an important corrective to many medical practices that view humans as mere collections of body parts and diseases. Midwifery care views pregnancy and childbirth as normal processes—that may nonetheless be experienced differently by different groups of people. And yet, midwifery remains overwhelmingly white. According to the American Midwifery Certification Board's 2019 Demographic Report, 99 percent of certified nurse-midwives and certified midwives that year were women, but only 6.31 percent were African American and fewer than 10 percent were "other visible minorities."

The American College of Nurse-Midwives, in its fiscal year 2020 statement advocating for increased federal funding for midwifery, observed that the United States is facing "a severe shortage of trained maternity care providers," including obstetricians/gynecologists, family physicians, and midwives. Considered alongside rising mortality rates, the ACNM correctly notes that "maternal and infant health is in a state of crisis" and "collective action is needed." More than five million women live in a maternity care desert—zones where there is *no* maternity health care at all or limited access to existing services. The ACNM, like other advocates, deems midwives "essential to the provision of quality of care in all settings."

More than thirty years ago, I wrote a senior college thesis on midwifery's historical demise because I was horrified that an entire class of women professionals was systematically disenfranchised by organized medicine, then largely the province of white men. The misogyny and racism underlying those attacks in the nineteenth century were obvious, as they are now. Midwives may be our best hope for reproductive futures, but only if policymakers recognize that they are integral to reproductive health care. Not only does ongoing tension between midwives and doctors exhaust those struggling to provide patient- and community-centered care, but it also delays the urgent business of saving mothers and babies, especially in communities of color.

Midwife Rebecca Polston founded the Roots Community Birth Center in Minneapolis, where Black babies are twice as likely to die as white babies. According to the *Guardian*, "Polston trains midwives with an eye toward diversifying the profession—more than 90% of nurse midwives are white." As Polston herself says, "Why do we think that increased access to racist institutions will give us a non-racist outcome? The decision to open the birth center was very specifically to provide access." One of the center's clients remarked, "My first visit here, after talking to them, I cried because somebody actually cared." Another stated, "It feels like a revolution is happening."

Long live the revolution.

And long live mothers *and* babies.

MOTHER'S DAY

What we now recognize as the official anniversary celebrating mothers originated in the United States in the late 1800s, when suffragist, pacifist, and *Battle Hymn of the Republic* scribe Julia Ward Howe in 1872 suggested Mother's Day as a day focused on peace. Alas, Howe's antiwar campaign did not catch fire in a nation emotionally depleted and deeply riven by the Civil War.

The holiday finally took hold through the efforts of Philadelphian Anna Jarvis, who sought to honor her own mother, Ann Marie Reeves Jarvis, who founded Mother's Day Work Clubs in West Virginia in the 1850s. The elder Jarvis had lost eight of her twelve children, all of them dead before age seven; at that time, a not uncommon occurrence. She organized the clubs, later called Mother's Friendship Clubs, to address poverty, sanitation, and high children's mortality rates. Her daughter, Anna, wanted to honor this legacy.

Thanks to Anna Jarvis's efforts and that of her many supporters, by 1911, Mother's Day was celebrated in all the U.S. states. President Woodrow Wilson recognized it as an official holiday in 1914, and it has been celebrated since. But Anna Jarvis herself grew to loathe an annual event that quickly became commercialized in ways that eclipsed its radical roots in care for women, children, and social justice.

I am crafting this entry on May 13, 2019, sitting in my comfy writing chair, looking across to the file cabinet on which perch the three Mother's Day cards I received yesterday. My daughters and husband gifted me with beautiful, tear-inducing words of gratitude and love. I spent much of the day with them, and also with my own mother and sister, who live near me.

Last night, just before I slept, I contemplated my good fortune. Yet as I lay there in the dark, I also grew terribly sad. I knew that today I would return to this book manuscript and again immerse myself in stories of babyloss. Mother's Day had given me a brief reprieve from writing in a way that no amount of time can offer respite to the babylost. I could take a day off, emotionally, while some mothers cannot, ever. Quite literally, many women, especially those employed in retail and restaurant industries, likely worked on Mother's Day, away from their families.

Every year on Facebook, I have noticed that as we celebrate mothers, we are also more conscientious about recognizing that Mother's Day is deeply painful for many women, including those who have lost children or miscarried or been unable to have or adopt children at all. (It may also be painful for people who suffer from terrible, absent, or abusive mothers.) But I wonder whether we are really taking in just what it means for babylost moms to struggle through a day showcasing moms and motherhood.

Of course, some people who lose babies have other children, and there may be plenty of joy and celebration, gratitude and love, and cards and flowers. But for those who are still grieving, what is Mother's Day without living children?

Yesterday morning, I spent some time online, as I often do on Mother's Day, celebrating my own mom with old family photos and enjoying friends' posts and pictures. I also skimmed through my usual Sunday media, including newspapers and blogs. I noticed a promising trend: Mother's Day calls to action from a variety of outlets, organizations, and politicians. Several articles specifically drew attention to high maternal mortality rates. With major bills in Congress and significant media attention, especially to Black women's mortality, it seems the momentum around maternal health is building. More than a few Mother's Day op-eds were subtitled "Save Women's Lives."

Yet what I didn't see in my favored mainstream media was attention to infant death. Nor, outside of the more generous and inclusive Facebook messages in my friends network, did I notice any public attention to the grief and sorrow of babylost women. In the standard Mother's Day fare, it seemed there was little recognition of either infant death or maternal grief; the emphasis was almost entirely on *maternal death*. And I was glad to see it, of course; I have argued elsewhere that maternal mortality, and specifically Black maternal mortality, is one of the most pressing human rights issues of our time. But still, I wondered about the experiences of babylost mothers, who were still largely invisible.

I knew that International Bereaved Mother's Day had been observed the Sunday before Mother's Day, as it has been since 2010. Founded by Australian artist Carly Marie Dudley, International Bereaved Mother's Day (also known as International Babylost Mother's Day) is meant to provide witnessing and healing for babylost women. Dudley has written, "In 2010, I felt drawn to create International Bereaved Mother's Day to help heal hurting [mothers]. . . . [It] is a temporary movement . . . a heart centered attempt at healing the official Mother's Day. I believe that . . . sometime in the near future there will be no need for this day at all because all true [including babylost] mothers will be recognized, loved, supported and celebrated."

That is, Dudley founded International Bereaved Mother's Day *because* Mother's Day itself is *inadequate* for babylost moms. It fails to *see* them, and it typically excludes them—despite more capacious Facebook posts that try to name loss and grief alongside celebration. Yet one consequence of having a separate day for babylost mothers is that people who have both living and dead children may experience what sociologist Dorothy Smith called "bifurcated consciousness," expected to feel sad one Sunday and happy the next. Emotions are not so easily compartmentalized.

In *Still Standing Magazine*, mom Morgan McLaverty expresses this well, if sadly:

> I fight with these feelings every Mother's Day. I don't quite understand why it hurts me so much to live through this day without my son. I continually feel as if I sound 'ungrateful' for my living children who celebrate me, even when I behave like someone who is too sad to celebrate. . . . I rally my gumption and smile with my usual fervor and cry all the way home. Life isn't the same without one of my babies. Mother's Day highlights that for me, amplifies all the bad feelings that hide in the dark crevices of my mind during the majority of the year. . . . Once on the other side of Mother's Day, I can breathe again. And I do.

Even more, people with no living children may *still feel like mothers*. Hannah Rose Allen writes in *Still Standing Magazine*, "The only motherhood I've ever known is mothering a grave. A legacy. It makes me as a mom feel quite out of place, especially on Mother's Day. I hold my daughter in my heart, rather than my arms. I have no other living children on earth with me to help ease the pain. . . . My 'parenting decisions' are things like what sort of headstone will I pick out for Lily Katherine? . . . I think of how I can be a mom to her, without her here. . . . How many different ways can I say, *this is hard*? How many ways can I say, *I am thankful to be her mother still* . . ."

Here is my Mother's Day wish for all mothers, whether their children are living or dead:

You are a mother.

You deserve to celebrate Mother's Day.

You do not have to hide your joy or your sorrow.

I see you.

N

NEONATOLOGY

Jacqueline Bouvier Kennedy suffered a miscarriage in 1955. Just a year later, her daughter, Arabella, was stillborn while Senator John F. Kennedy was yachting in the Mediterranean with friends. Caroline Kennedy, the only surviving child of the Kennedys, was born in 1957 in Manhattan without complications. John Jr., who would later perish in a plane crash, was born three weeks prematurely in 1960. He experienced breathing difficulties, but a pediatric resident saved his life by inserting a tube into his tiny trachea and blowing into it. On August 7, 1963, Mrs. Kennedy, then First Lady, gave birth to son Patrick via emergency cesarean section; he died thirty-nine hours later of hyaline membrane disease (now called respiratory distress syndrome, or RDS). Three months later, President Kennedy was assassinated in Dallas.

The Kennedys serve as a grim reminder that even the wealthy and famous can experience incalculable tragedy and loss—and must also grieve under the microscope of public opinion. But high-profile loss can sometimes lead to action. Patrick Bouvier Kennedy's death spurred the development of neonatology, a medical specialty concerned with the care of newborns, especially those born prematurely or ill. ABC News reported, "The Kennedy baby's death put a new focus on diseases of the newborn and resulted in increased funding for research by the National Institutes of Health. . . . Millions of babies worldwide have been saved, largely because of the efforts to improve the first infant ventilators and the discovery of surfactant a decade later."

One of the physicians called by Patrick's doctors as he struggled to survive at Children's Hospital in Boston was Maria Delivoria-Papadopoulos. Considered the "mother of neonatology," in the 1960s, Delivoria-Papadopoulos was a resident at Toronto Children's Hospital. She had been using the Bird Mark 8 ventilator to save a handful of babies, learning through trial and error that earlier intervention was better. She stated, "By the time Patrick Bouvier had been born, we already had six survivors, because we had been intervening quicker and not waiting until their death bed." Patrick's doctors wanted the ventilator brought to Boston, but alas, this was not logistically possible.

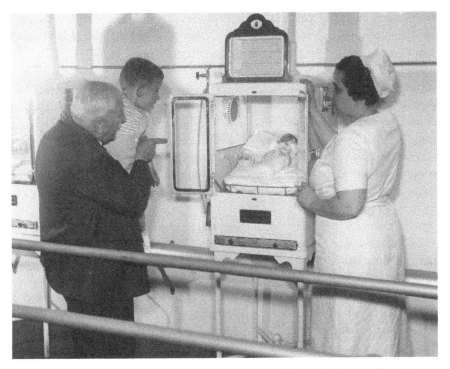

Infant incubator—Martin and Hildegarde Couney with boy looking at baby in incubator, New York World's Fair, 1939–1940. Photo credit: The New York Public Library Digital Collections.

Surfactant, or rather lack thereof, was also central to the development of neonatology. In healthy babies, pulmonary surfactant is essential to lung function. A mixture of lipids, proteins, and carbohydrates, surfactant reduces surface tension in the alveoli (air sacs in the lungs) where air and liquid meet. A deficiency of surfactant, such as when a baby is born prematurely, leads to higher surface tension and thus difficulty breathing. A premature infant can take one breath and exhale but cannot breathe in again as the lungs are likely to collapse. RDS ensues, sometimes fatally, as is very common historically. Lifesaving measures include mechanical ventilation, such as that pioneered by Delivoria-Papadopoulos, and artificial pulmonary surfactant, which appears on the World Health Organization Model Lists of Essential Medicines.

If Maria Delivoria-Papadopoulos was the "mother of neonatology," then perhaps pediatric researcher Mary Ellen Avery was the field's brilliant aunt for her role in understanding surfactant. Dr. Avery enjoyed many "firsts"—"the first woman to be appointed physician in chief at Children's Hospital; the first woman to head a clinical department at Harvard Medical School; the first woman to be chosen president of the Society for Pediatric Research; and the first pediatrician to lead the American Association for the Advancement of Science." She was also instrumental in revealing surfactant's role in RDS. Between 1959 and 1965, she published work that showed RDS stemmed from a *lack* of surfactant and not the *presence* of membranes. Her research was taken up by Japanese pediatrician Tetsuo Fujiwara, who helped develop a replacement surfactant using sheep lungs. In her *New York Times* obituary, Mary Ellen Avery is credited with saving eight hundred thousand lives.

The incubator was another early feature of efforts to save premature babies and was central to the rise of neonatology. Developed in France by obstetrician Stéphane Tarnier in the late nineteenth century, the incubator was a technical means of warming tiny newborns who often died of hypothermia in cold hospitals. Inspired by chicken incubators seen at the Paris Zoo, Tarnier's apparatus "was invented at an especially propitious moment in history," when the French government was "obsessed" with infant mortality and the declining birth rate. The incubator emerged alongside the increasingly political use of vital statistics in France and elsewhere.

In the United States, obstetrician Joseph DeLee set up the first incubator station at the Chicago Lying-In Hospital, which he founded in 1900. DeLee is considered a progenitor of so-called preventive obstetrics and professionalization of the field. He was technically proficient and innovative, including developing a portable incubator to collect premature babies during Chicago's harsh winters. Pediatrician and medical historian Jeffrey P. Baker writes, "For all of its promise, DeLee's station lasted [under] 10 years. It was a case of expectations far out of line [with] economic realities. . . . The main thrust of his career, moreover, was moving into interventionist obstetrics and leaving little time for the newborn." Yet Baker also notes that with the rise of eugenics, premature babies—especially the babies of immigrants—were considered "weaklings," and saving *all* babies became suspect.

In *The Strange Case of Dr. Couney: How a Mysterious European Showman Saved Thousands of American Babies*, author Dawn Raffel documents the fascinating story of Coney Island's "incubator babies." She traces the movements of Martin Couney from Europe to the United States, where he spent many years attempting to attract interest in his "sideshow" of preemies at carnivals across the country. He displayed the fragile infants for money to finance their care and ultimately helped inspire the first premature infant station at Cornell Hospital in 1943. Though criticized by many in the profession for commercializing infants, Couney had some champions, including Dr. Julius Hess in Chicago, who supported an incubator show at the Century of Progress in 1933. Raffel makes the important point that though criticism was directed toward Couney, at the time, few hospitals were taking seriously the need for neonatal care of premature babies. Couney filled a need and did so in spectacular fashion.

Contemporary neonatology, a now firmly established clinical specialty, often involves the Neonatal Intensive Care Unit (NICU). NICUs are high-tech wonderlands compared to the early days of mechanical ventilators and Coney Island incubators. Anyone who visits a NICU will see the tiniest of babies, some no larger than a hamster, attached to all sorts of monitors, wires, and dials. Many are encapsulated inside isolettes, making visibility and touch more challenging, especially for the most fragile babies. (Though some premature babies can and should be touched, given the importance of touch to development.) The NICU can and does save lives, but often, it may only prolong life temporarily. For some babies, death is as likely an outcome as survival.

In the NICU, as a number of scholars have noted, ethical decisions are made daily and lives hang in the balance. Sociologist Renee Anspach wrote, "Neonatal intensive care represents a triumph of sophisticated medical technology. At the same time, however, a number of difficult ethical dilemmas have appeared . . . [each posing] the hard question of whether what *can* be done *should* be done and [calling] into question the basic principle on which neonatal intensive care is premised: that of active, aggressive intervention." At the heart of these ethical conundrums are the kinds of questions that haunt infant mortality writ large: Which babies should live? Which should die? And perhaps most importantly, Who decides?

A study in 2011 of a ten-year period found that of the 414 babies who had died in NICUs, 61.6 percent of them had care withdrawn, 20.8 percent had care withheld, and 17.6 percent received resuscitative care. The authors conclude that the "significant increase [over time] in withholding of care suggests improved recognition of medical futility and desire to provide a peaceful death." A more recent study of a twenty-year period in one NICU documented a *reduction* in the neonatal mortality rate from 5.9 to 3.0 deaths per 100 admissions. While congenital anomalies were the leading cause of death, the authors found that 75 percent of infants died after care was withdrawn. In 92 percent of these cases, parents were involved in the decision to withdraw care.

It is heartening to read that in the majority of circumstances, parents were involved in decision-making. But what of the remaining 8 percent? Were these decisions made solely by clinicians? And if so, on what basis? Anspach and many others have drawn attention to how disability or imagined disability can influence clinical decisions. Underneath the question *who shall live* is a moral determination of what kinds of lives are *worth* living. Yes, neonatal intensive care and prenatal interventions can save lives that previously might have been lost. But at what point do parents and/or clinicians decide that an infant is better off dead? Conversely, at what point do parents and/or clinicians decide that a baby is better off alive, even if survival means a lifetime of physical and intellectual impairment?

Of course, these questions presume all parents have access to high-quality neonatal intensive care. But this is not the case. One study looked at the availability of NICUs vis-à-vis neonatal outcomes in the United States, hypothesizing that greater availability might lead to better outcomes. Not true. Further, they suggested some regions may have inadequate neonatal resources, whereas many others may have more resources than are needed. An important 2017 study in California showed that "large racial and/or ethnic differences in quality exist between and within NICUs." The authors expected some variability but found that "the difference between highest- and lowest-performing NICUs was extremely large."

Research on neonatal nursing found racial differences in satisfaction with care, reporting that "Black parents were most dissatisfied with how nurses supported them. . . . Nurses that incorporate racially sensitive behaviors into their daily practice will be able to better support families through a premature birth, engage parents in their child's care, and promote a more positive NICU experience."

Thus like all health care in the United States, neonatology is stratified and unequally distributed. But this does not mean there is no good care.

Babylost mom Megan Skaggs shared appreciation for her NICU nurse in a heartfelt letter published in *Still Standing Magazine*:

> You have no idea how much you mean to me, or how you will always hold a very special place in my heart. . . . You took care of my baby and you loved him. . . . I was thrust into the NICU hours after a c-section. The first time I saw my baby he was hooked up to more machines than I could count. . . . You taught me how to whisper in his ear and hold his hand without moving his chest tube. You let me change his diaper once and didn't get mad when I fumbled through three diapers. . . . When he needed his temperature taken, you let me do it. . . . You took picture after picture of my son and me. . . . You gave him, and me, every piece of your strength, day in and day out, for weeks. You did everything in your power and more to keep him alive. And then he died. And you gave me another gift that day. You told me how he was going to die, and you guided me through his death in a way so full of grace I couldn't explain it if I tried. . . . So from the bottom of my heart, thank you.

For some babies, then, the NICU is the golden ticket to survival and life beyond tubes and wires. For others, it is where they will draw their last breath. Sometimes babies come home; sometimes they don't. The NICU is thus a space of hope and despair, futurity and the present. It offers a chance for some parents to believe their babies will make it.

Terrified, sleep-deprived parents of three-pound newborns likely care little that the NICU is where moral decisions are made, even if they are making such decisions, or that it is stratified. They just want their beloved offspring to survive.

They want to believe in miracles, even when there are no more miracles.

Nurses

In 2014, I presented a talk to an audience of health care professionals, research scientists, and community members. The conference theme was sex and gender differences in women's health, with a directive from the organizers to discuss these through our own disciplinary lens. I focused on maternal and infant mortality as *sociological* problems of gender, race, and poverty. And I called out racism and sexism in health care as key contributors to poor birth outcomes.

The perplexed looks on the faces of some of my copanelists (one had described the thrilling prospects of personalized medicine and another his findings in lab rats), along with a few pointed questions from the audience, suggested that perhaps the doctors and clinical scientists in the room weren't quite on board with my argument. But one group of people seemed to completely get it: nurses. After the talk, I found myself beckoned over to a table of nursing faculty and nurses from the community. They thanked me, excitedly discussed implications, and asked that I follow up with them as my research progressed. (I did.)

All the women at that table—nursing remains a woman-dominated profession—encouraged me to include nursing in my book. I assured them I could not imagine writing about maternal and infant health without discussing the critical role of nurses. I also shared with them my special affinity for nurses; the doctoral program in sociology at the University of California, San Francisco, where I earned my PhD, lives in the School of Nursing. I became a sociologist alongside and in collaboration with nurses; I cannot recall a single class during my graduate studies that did not include at least one nursing student, and there were typically more.

What's more, as a sociologist of health and a bioethicist, I am acutely aware of the invaluable—and often invisible—role of nurses and nursing in securing our nation's health. Nurses are, in a word, indispensable. They are the heart, soul, and backbone of health care, with an emphasis on the word *care*. As the American Nurses Association (ANA) puts it, "A culture of caring is a culture of curing." Though nurses also engage in diagnosis, specialization, and high-tech treatment, and work across numerous diverse settings in and out of hospitals, they are universally "the glue that holds a patient's health care journey together." We are especially seeing this during the devastating COVID-19 pandemic.

Nursing has long been an important component of efforts to improve infant mortality in the United States. This was evident at the turn of the nineteenth century and into the first decades of the twentieth. The Sheppard-Towner Act—formally, the Promotion of the Welfare and Hygiene of Maternity and Infancy Act—of 1921 was a federal response to, among other problems, astronomically high infant mortality rates. In the early twentieth century, *30 percent* of babies died before their first birthdays in some parts of the country. Immigration and population growth brought major challenges to cities, especially in housing and sanitation. Tenements were notoriously small, cramped, and dirty, and close living fostered the spread of disease. Keeping babies alive, whether through preventing illness or maintaining a clean milk supply, was a herculean and often futile effort.

In line with other public health measures of the twentieth century, the Sheppard-Towner Act aimed to improve infant survival through direct interventions. With the guidance of Julia Lathrop and the U.S. Children's Bureau, the Act led to "the establishment of nearly 3,000 prenatal care clinics, 180,000 infant care seminars, over three million home visits by traveling nurses, and a national distribution of educational literature between 1921 and 1928."

Nursing scholars Mary Thompson and Arlene Keeling note that public health nurses "were dedicated to the cause of reducing infant mortality by teaching mothers the way to care and feed their children. They worked in families' homes, in milk stations, and other creative settings, to best meet the needs of the families they were caring for. . . . It is because of their ingenuity, courage, intelligence, and flexibility that they contributed so greatly to the reduction of infant mortality . . . a century ago."

Like the nurses I spoke to after my talk, today's nurses understand that infant mortality will not be solved by medical intervention alone or even educational campaigns. Nurses, far more than doctors and specialists who tend to compartmentalize illnesses, grasp that problems as entrenched as chronic infant death are as much about families, communities, and recalcitrant social structures, such as racism, as they are about the fragility of small bodies.

Though "nurses work tirelessly to identify and protect the needs of the individual," they try to do so within the broader contexts of their patients' lives. Nurses and midwives often go into communities and work directly with patients and their families—and this can make all the difference between life and death. Especially for society's most vulnerable, including pregnant people and newborns.

Nursing historian Patricia D'Antonio aims to flip the script on histories of nursing that emphasize invisibility and marginalization, showing that nursing practices across time and place reveal power and possibilities: "Nurses are indeed powerful and resourceful, and the illustration of their power stems less from the source of their training program than their ability to work within locations to shape their own practices." She identifies settings in which nurses have been quite powerful, including "in the clinical space where they interacted with patients; across institutions as they provided leadership and strategic thinking about their own welfare and the patients they served; and in political arenas where they negotiated the difficult path between the ideal and the real."

The patterns D'Antonio describes were on full display in the early twentieth century, as the Sheppard-Towner Act was rooted in the daily practices of public health nurses.

Describing preterm birth and high infant mortality rates as "a challenge for advocacy," nursing scholars Debra Brandon and Jacqueline McGrath call on their colleagues to engage in policy and advocacy work. Citing high infant death rates and efforts to combat these, they write, "As neonatal healthcare providers, we should be asking ourselves why does the United States continue to lag behind developed countries that spend less on healthcare . . . and how can we help the March of Dimes achieve this admirable goal" of reducing the premature birth rate to 5.5 percent by 2030. The rate was 9.8 percent in 2016. Noting that "infants cannot advocate for themselves," Brandon and McGrath declare, "Given our chosen professions and passions, we are stewards for at-risk and preterm infants and as such this stewardship must go beyond care at the bedside. We owe this to the infants and famil[ies] in our care."

An article at Nurse.com profiling nursing efforts to combat infant mortality acknowledges that maternal-child health care should reflect a team approach: "Some of the most innovative models of care have been pioneered by nurses. If we want to close the infant mortality gap, nurses need to play a strong leadership role." Addressing the needs of communities of color, the author highlights efforts in Racine, Wisconsin, where Black infant mortality is high; "a black baby born in Wisconsin is three times more likely to die in its first year of life than a white baby." The article features nurse practitioner Gwen Perry-Brye, with the Kenosha County Division of Health, who "says it is important for nurses to recognize the stress black women face in their lives and how that can lead to poor birth outcomes." The Black Health Coalition of Greater Kenosha, which Perry-Brye helped establish, addresses infant mortality in the region, along with other health disparities.

Maternal and infant health care for people of color can be very effectively addressed by nurses and nurse-midwives, many of whom are already active in the communities they serve. Recognizing this, *Minority Nurse* profiled three programs. In St. Louis, Missouri, Nurses for Newborns was founded by Sharon Rohrbach and "is on the front lines when it comes to saving the lives of minority infants." The program involves home visits by a wide network of pediatric nurses, a model Rohrbach borrowed from countries with lower infant mortality rates. Her evidence demonstrates that "one nurse can really make a difference."

In New Jersey, Camden Healthy Start aims to reduce that city's high infant mortality rate, consistently double that of the rest of the state. Focus is on changing systems and ensuring women and children can access necessary services that also help strengthen families. Camden's teen pregnancy rate is also significantly higher than the statewide rate.

April Lyons, a nurse involved with Camden Healthy Start, believes that "nurses need to be involved in initiatives like these. . . . If nursing is to continue to grow and thrive as a profession, we need to demonstrate through outcomes how nursing interventions impact the bottom line." She believes "minority nurses must help lead the charge, because many of the policymakers developing such programs have a limited knowledge of the cultural nuances of many vulnerable populations."

Minority Nurse discusses the Indian Health Service (IHS), including collaborations between Tribal Epidemiology Centers and IHS service areas to reduce SIDS. Infant mortality rates for American Indians/Alaska Natives (a federal designation) are generally one and a half to two times higher than those of whites. A public health nurse who works in the Billings, Montana, area reports, "Nurses are very involved in these initiatives. . . . Each project is positioned in a public health nursing environment or is working collaboratively with public health nurses, because [they can provide the services these projects need], including home visits to pregnant women and prenatal classes."

In targeting reproductive health issues in communities of color, nurses can be especially effective. In May 2019, the Center for American Progress issued "A Comprehensive Policy Blueprint" for eliminating racial disparities in maternal and infant mortality, noting that "efforts must be made to expand access to physicians, nurses, doulas . . . midwives, and perinatal support workers—with a special focus on recruitment, training, and certification of a workforce pipeline inclusive of people of color in order to meet the needs of the most affected communities." This blueprint echoed findings from a 2018 study which found that greater integration of nurses and nurse-midwives into reproductive health care resulted in "higher rates of physiologic [normal] birth, less obstetric interventions, and fewer adverse neonatal outcomes."

Nursing scholar Monica McLemore at the University of California, San Francisco writes and speaks frequently about Black women's reproductive health issues, including abortion, maternal mortality, and reproductive justice. Her research has found that prenatal health care for women of color is "largely disrespectful and stressful" and that women believe the discrimination, racism, and disrespect they experience "affects their health and that of their infants." McLemore has also written on the ethics of perinatal care for Black women, specifically the structural racism that contributes to poor birth outcomes.

McLemore demonstrates the professional intersection of history, experience, commitment, and passion. For her, nursing offers one path toward birth justice and equity, "ensuring quality care across the lifespan for Black birthing women." Her efforts involve translating the aims of the reproductive justice movement into clinical care to produce better birth outcomes—more Black mothers and babies who survive and even thrive. McLemore, herself born prematurely, writes, "I live as a Black American woman. The personal is always political and to believe that activism is separate from the core tenets of nursing and public health is to be both inaccurate and ahistorical."

Beyond a comprehensive understanding of structural causes of poor infant health and a commitment to advocacy for birthing people and their infants, nurses are critical to supporting experiences of babyloss. Several articles in the nursing literature explore how to care for patients after a reproductive loss. Nursing scholar Karen Kavanaugh notes, "Despite advances in obstetric and neonatal care, many parents will experience the birth of a stillborn infant or the death of a newborn. . . . Nurses who care for these parents must understand the [very wide] range and intensity of reactions that are unique to this type of loss."

Nurses and nurse-midwives must navigate loss and trauma while on the job, and their efforts can have a huge impact on their patients' lives. An essay, "To the Nurses Who Brought Me Back into Life," published by Rachel Whalen, a babylost mom, makes this touchingly clear: "Thank you for saving me. Your skills and your knowledge saved me from following my daughter into death, but it was your compassion that guided me back towards life. The humanity you demonstrated is what brought me back **into** life; you made it possible to think about living after death. For this, I owe you my love and deepest gratitude."

Another babylost mom, Amanda Ross-White, recounts her experience ordering copies of medical records after her babies (plural) died: "When the records arrived, I opened the envelope with some hesitation because I did not know exactly what I would find. When I looked at the nursing notes, my heart ached for what I saw. And not just because the nurses and social worker wrote down the details of [my babies'] birth. All those things I could not hope to remember in my shock and medication-induced confusion. No, my heart ached because the nursing care notes were [noticeably] stained with tears. Before I touched these pages, someone I didn't even know cried for my boys and me."

"Nurses grieve too"—as Amanda titled her poignant essay. Because they care.

O

Obstetric Violence

A wanted pregnancy can be a time of immense joy, hope, and connection. Yet even wanted pregnancies may be riddled with anxiety, fear, and sometimes stomach-heaving terror. Pregnancy can be deeply unpleasant and uncomfortable too. Both of mine were quite miserable, though I was thrilled to be pregnant.

In the United States, many people—especially those with access to good health care—presume their pregnancies will be uneventful, even pleasurable, and that outcomes will be positive. We are seduced by media images of smiling, glowing pregnant women (usually white women), hands on healthy round bellies while sitting lotus-style or wrapped in the loving arms of a generically handsome male partner in front of an attractive two-story home.

Most pregnant people do not anticipate serious problems, either during or after the pregnancy, except when they are deemed to be high risk. Infant death is shocking precisely because it is so unexpected, despite the alarming statistics. In sharp contrast, historically babies died at very high rates and women commonly suffered multiple losses. In many other parts of the world, child loss is still routine, though no less tragic.

What women tend *not* to expect during pregnancy, unless they are trapped in abusive relationships or living in a warzone, is violence. Most pregnant women will do everything in their power to protect their unborn babies and themselves, and so it is especially devastating when they are punched, kicked, knocked down, strangled, shot, knifed, starved, raped, or otherwise physically assailed, often to the point of miscarriage or their own deaths.

Pregnancy is, in a word, dangerous.

It is, in fact, far more dangerous than abortion.

When bodily violence against pregnant people happens in health care settings, which we usually assume to be safe (or safer) spaces, the sense of violation may be especially keen. The prevalence of obstetric violence illustrates just how often women are devalued and disregarded before, during, and after birth.

The term *obstetric violence* was coined in Venezuela in 2007 as part of the "Organic Law on the Right of Women to a Life Free of Violence." In the context of widespread violence against women and the urgent need for protections and remediation, the law defines obstetric violence as "the appropriation of the body and reproductive processes of women by health personnel, which is expressed as dehumanized treatment, an abuse of medication, and to convert the natural processes into pathological ones, bringing with it loss of autonomy and the ability to decide freely about their bodies and sexuality, negatively impacting the quality of life of women." All interventions should be "evidence-based." This last bit is critical, as Venezuela has one of the highest rates of cesarean section in the world.

Obstetric violence has since entered the maternity lexicon, appearing in clinical and legal literature, on patient care websites, and especially among birth advocates. Cristen Pascucci of Birth Monopoly describes such violence as "controlling women's choices." A 2019 story at Rewire News framed obstetric violence as traumatic and a violation, noting the term is in flux but that "usually it includes the use of threats or coercion to enforce medical opinion." Whimn, a now defunct online forum in Australia, wrote about "the threat facing women in the delivery room." And MadameNoire, an American magazine geared toward Black women, hosted a discussion entitled "How Can We Combat Obstetric Violence and Infant Mortality in Our Community" on its recurring "Listen to Black Women" feature.

Legal scholars have begun to clarify definitions of obstetric violence and to propose remedies. For example, Elizabeth Kakura, writing in the *Georgetown Law Journal*, claims that "maternity care in the United States is in a state of crisis" for several reasons, including "the extent to which women experience abuse, coercion, and disrespect while giving birth." Acknowledging that not enough is known about obstetric violence, in part "because there has been minimal research conducted in the United States on the subject," her work aims to identify what constitutes violence surrounding reproduction. Classifying different acts as abuse, coercion, and disrespect, she explores women's experiences ranging from dismissal of pain to physical restraint to forced cesarean sections and episiotomies. Obstetric violence, she notes, may also include sexual assault during clinical exams.

Human rights attorney Farah Diaz-Tello describes obstetric violence in terms of "invisible wounds," framing it as a form of gender-based violence. Drawing on a range of case studies, she reports that "obstetric violence is an infringement of women's human rights to non-discrimination, liberty and security of the person, reproductive health and autonomy, and freedom from cruel, inhuman, and degrading treatment. Such an attack on women's human dignity requires a more robust state response than access to civil courts—a remedy that itself remains elusive." Case studies include unconsented surgery, threats of arrest, and threats to remove children from mothers.

Kakura, Diaz-Tello, and other scholars have focused attention on the gendered aspects of obstetric violence. Women and transgender or nonbinary people with uteruses are the categories of people who usually can become pregnant, either willingly or not. Obstetric violence combines the gender-specificity of pregnancy, deep-seated distrust of female bodies, paternalistic medicine, and fetal harm mitigation in a combustible brew that targets women both unfairly and dangerously. As Diaz-Tello states, "The gender bias underpinning the use of threats and coercion to enforce medical advice is not subtle. It is axiomatic that a person of sound mind cannot be forced to undergo a medical procedure . . . even if the procedure would save the life of another person and even if that other person were their child. Pregnant women, however, are expected to sacrifice their health and dignity, and even potentially their lives, in the name of having a healthy baby."

Law student Maria T. R. Borges writes, "On its face 'obstetric violence' seems to be just a new term for the old problem of disrespect and abuse in obstetric and gynecological care. But the innovation introduced by this definition is an express recognition of how individual instances of obstetric abuse are part of the broader problem of gender-based violence." As she notes, this recognition is significant because "it highlights that [obstetric violence] is a type of structural violence and, therefore, needs to be addressed systemically."

Borges's article emphasizes the inadequacy of legal frameworks in the United States to address obstetric violence, either individually or collectively. Yet she advocates for use of the term, in part because it "problematizes coerced procedures not only in terms of a woman's right to choose her preferred delivery method; it inserts this right within the context of a woman's right to a life free of violence." From a policy perspective, Borges recommends embedding remedies for obstetric violence in broader legislation concerned with violence against women.

As philosopher and mother Sara Cohen Shabot writes in her phenomenology of obstetric violence, "My hope is that identifying violence in labor as part not just of the medical objectification of patients but of the general violence used to domesticate and silence women and their bodies under patriarchy will open new spaces for discussion, leading to real changes in obstetric practices and in how women can experience labor."

While any woman may be at risk for obstetric violence, some women are particularly vulnerable. In the United States, young women, poor women, Black women, incarcerated women, immigrant women, and women with disabilities are all more likely to experience coercion and abuse. The World Health Organization reports that globally, "adolescents, unmarried women, women of low socio-economic status, women from ethnic minorities, migrant women and women living with HIV are particularly likely to experience disrespectful and abusive treatment."

In many states, shackling pregnant women in jails and prisons is still allowed, even during labor and delivery. But "shackling a woman by the ankles, wrist, and/or waist during pregnancy and delivery is not only unnecessary for security reasons, it is also medically hazardous and emotionally traumatizing." Kimberly Mays, a formerly incarcerated woman and activist, described her own awful experience: "After the nurse covered my mouth, and scowled at me like I was an annoying animal who needed to be put down, instead of a mother who was about to give birth, I lost all sense of dignity and self-respect. I felt like I was an animal giving birth in front of its human masters—a worthless piece of trash."

Helping us make sense of such situations, anthropologist Dána-Ain Davis has coined the term *obstetric racism* to describe "the contours of racism that materialize during Black women's medical encounters." She states, "Obstetric racism is not new, but rather, it is entangled with histories that shadow contemporary expressions of medical racism deployed on Black women's bodies. The way that Black women have been demonized, stereotyped, violated, and policed in the past is consistent with contemporary medical interactions and operate as reminders of that past."

Too many women and babies die from obstetric violence. How many is unknown, given the dearth of research on the topic. This itself showcases just how little women and babies are valued. The United States has not kept comprehensive maternal morbidity and mortality statistics, so it is not entirely clear what is killing pregnant women and new mothers. While some states do maintain databases, these are incomplete. We can be assured from emerging research that racism has something to do with the tragic premature deaths of Black and Indigenous women and children.

The good news is that all this may be changing with new legislation targeting high maternal death rates in the United States. Maternal health, and specifically Black maternal health, even became a topic on the 2020 presidential campaign trail.

Yet until laws pass, cultures shift, and structures bend, women and babies will continue to be maimed and perish from forms of obstetric violence ranging from the subtle to the outrageous. These are more than human rights violations, though they are precisely that and should be adjudicated as such. These issues are also more than a breach of medical ethics or a deficiency in professional clinical training. Obstetric violence is fundamentally an expression of entrenched sexism, the belief that women are less than fully human. This can be coupled with the racist belief that some women are entitled to more humanity than others.

In the words of poet Adrienne Rich, "We need to understand the power and powerlessness embodied in motherhood in patriarchal culture." And I would add, white supremacist culture.

Mothers and babies deserve no less. They also deserve to live.

Birth may sometimes be painful, but it should never be degrading, damaging, or deadly.

Оню

The Percy Skuy Collection, housed at the Dittrick Medical History Center of Case Western Reserve University, is all about contraception. Percy Skuy, a pharmacist and executive with Ortho Pharmaceutical, assembled the world's largest collection of historic contraceptive devices. There are over 1,100 artifacts in the collection, which "depicts the social and cultural climate that influenced birth control decisions in this country." Offering a "multi-faceted look" at efforts to control reproduction, "the exhibit reveals a longstanding ignorance of essential facts of human conception." Some basic facts of life, such as when women ovulate, weren't discovered until the 1930s. Alongside the IUD and "The Pill," more dangerous methods of pregnancy prevention and termination, such as douching with Lysol and eating poisonous herbs, are also included in the exhibit.

As the exhibit reveals, desperate women take desperate measures.

Perhaps ironically, given this exhibit's message, Ohio is a stronghold of anti-abortion activity. For example, a "heartbeat bill" banning most abortions became law in 2019. Yet inconsistently given its alleged "pro-life" leadership, it is a state where far too many babies die. In 2017, Ohio was the ninth-worst state in the country for infant death, nestled between Georgia and Louisiana, with a rate of 7.2 deaths per 1,000 live births. (Neighboring Indiana, with a rate of 7.3 deaths, was the only other Midwestern state among the worst ten.)

In part, what makes Ohio distinctive is that *all* its major cities from Akron to Toledo have high infant mortality rates, as do rural pockets of Appalachia. This makes infant mortality in the Buckeye State, unlike many other states, both a Black *and* a white problem. And yet, the disparity between Black and white infant mortality rates persists, with one news outlet describing it as "a troubling trend." Nearly two-thirds of Ohio's infant deaths occur in nine urban counties, and demographics (and zip codes) matter. Black babies in the state are three times more likely than white babies to die before their first birthday. The title of a June 2019 article in the *Washington Post* was on point: "The surprisingly true comparison between infant mortality in Ohio and Iran."

Media coverage of Ohio's infant mortality problem is often confused and confusing, touting successes in reductions of overall rates and for white babies while also sounding the alarm on Black infant death. This headline from March 2019 captures this confusion perfectly: "Infant Mortality Rate Drops Overall, Racial Disparity Persists."

Let's look at the patterns.

Cincinnati, with approximately 301,000 people, 44.8 percent of them African American, had an infant mortality rate of 12.5 in 2017. The 2018 infant mortality rate in Hamilton County, in which Cincinnati is located, was 8.6 deaths per 1,000 live births. Among African Americans, it was a whopping 17 deaths per 1,000 births. Cradle Cincinnati, a coalition to reduce infant mortality, issued this statement: "A Black baby born in Hamilton County today has nearly the same chance of survival as a white baby born 50 years ago, despite five decades of technological advances."

Columbus, the state capital and largest city, has nearly 900,000 residents, 28 percent of them African American. Columbus is in Franklin County, which in 2018 registered an infant mortality rate of 8.2 deaths per 1,000 live births. But Black babies in Columbus are three times more likely to die than white babies in the city. An advocate for better birth outcomes remarked, "We have to embrace strategies that address structural racism, and the lived experiences of women who are pregnant who are non-Hispanic blacks, and the issues they face every day."

In Cleveland, with a population of 390,000, more than half African American, there are vast disparities. Cuyahoga County's overall infant mortality rate was 7.97 in 2017. For white babies, it was 2.54, and for Black babies, a staggering 15.6

deaths per 1,000 live births. Media coverage noted, "The improvement for white babies has widened an already shocking gap in the odds of survival for the county's smallest residents: For every white baby that died before reaching a first birthday in Cuyahoga County [in 2017], more than six black babies died, nearly double the gap in previous years." In 2016, the county also had the state's highest rate of low birthweight babies, at 11 percent.

Marjory Givens, a population scientist who worked on County Health Rankings and Roadmaps, noted, "This is a pattern that's not just playing out in Cuyahoga County and Ohio, but also the nation. It's really a very disturbing pattern and a poor start to life for children of color." A 2020 *National Geographic* article linked infant death in Cleveland's Black communities to "individual and structural racism," noting that "infant mortality, like economic security and educational achievement, is an example of 'the negative repercussions of historical racism.'"

Yet white babies are at risk too, especially if they are poor and rural. The Appalachian region of the United States extends into the southeastern edge of Ohio, encompassing the western hills of the Appalachian Mountains and the Appalachian Plateau. Thirty-two of Ohio's eighty-eight counties are included in Appalachia and some two million people live in Appalachian Ohio, most (but not all) white and with limited economic resources.

Health disparities abound between Appalachia and non-Appalachian parts of the United States. One study found infant mortality rates *16 percent higher* in Appalachia than elsewhere between 2009 and 2013, and there was a significantly higher association between poverty and life expectancy. High infant mortality was also connected to poverty. Another study found that poverty and rurality were linked to high infant mortality rates.

So what are the good folks of Ohio doing to reduce infant mortality rates, to stem the swelling tide of loss and grief, especially among Black and poor families? Besides, that is, passing "heartbeat bills" to "prevent" abortion, including one requiring doctors to reimplant ectopic pregnancies in the uterus (a physical impossibility). It turns out that *some* public health officials, community members, parents, clinicians, and policymakers are taking a surprisingly structural approach.

In April 2019, Cradle Cincinnati announced a new direction. The director of community strategies remarked, "Our strategy now is to focus squarely and unapologetically on Black women. . . . The problem here is not with individuals' behaviors, but rather with larger systems that are impacting Black families—*regardless of income*—in disproportionately negative ways." The organization's approach includes increasing the number of community health workers, expanding group prenatal care, advocating for policy-based solutions, and training health workers to recognize and remedy implicit bias.

Eschewing biological and genetic explanations for poor outcomes, health officials understand that social factors, including inequality, are a major factor in negative birth outcomes. The executive director of Cradle Cincinnati stated, "We need to think about the experience of being Black in America and why is that leading to poorer birth outcomes."

Bernadette Kerrigan with First Year Cleveland stated, "The three top reasons that we have a high infant mortality rate particularly among African American moms is structural racism, prematurity, and preventable sleep-related deaths. . . . We have to take a new approach to looking at decreasing African-American infant death." The mission of First Year Cleveland is specifically to reduce infant death by eliminating racial disparities. The organization runs a Safe Sleep Heroes training, a Centering Pregnancy initiative, and a Community Action Council, and also engages in public education and policy work. An explicit focus on social determinants of health is built into the programming. This framework includes enhancing transportation access, paid family and medical leave, access to improved housing, and criminal justice reform.

In Columbus, the executive director of CelebrateOne remarked, "The data show the need for programs that identify and reduce social barriers that many mothers and families face." In 2017, the organization's work was funded by city, county, and state funds, as well as corporate and individual giving—over six million dollars. Programs include the Community Connector Corps, Healthy Beginnings at Home, Step One for a Healthy Pregnancy, and sleep awareness campaigns involving personal stories—all designed to involve local communities and reach the most disadvantaged women and families. Columbus is also piloting an app for on-demand rides for pregnant women so they can better access health care. Funded by a Smart City grant and Medicaid, "The PTA [Prenatal Trip Assistance] project will enhance mobility and increase opportunity, efficiency and customer service for prenatal travelers."

The Toledo-Lucas County Health Department launched the Healthy Lucas County project, targeting that area's very high Black infant mortality rates. Efforts include a home visitation program by health workers and enlisting community organizations in the effort. One state health official remarked, "The most effective infant mortality reduction strategies are implemented at the local level." And a local project coordinator stated, "We really want to understand what these neighborhoods need to thrive, and that starts by getting input from our neighbors and truly listening to their concerns and suggestions."

All these efforts are important and inspiring. They target structural causes of health disparities and aim to "meet pregnant women where they are." Yet racial disparities continue, largely unabated. And though community groups and public health advocates have infant mortality firmly in their sights, they are not helped by elected officials who would rather "save" (white) embryos and fetuses from abortion than meet the needs of already living women and babies—especially African American and rural women and their babies.

What these officials seem not to understand, or perhaps choose not to understand, is that Black and poor babies have heartbeats too.

At least until they do not.

P

PLACENTA

Before my first daughter was born, I informed the care team that I wanted my placenta saved. Not because I wanted to eat it, as some women do. Rather, I wanted to bury it under a tree in our yard on Whidbey Island in Washington State, where I then lived.

My birthing experience was traumatic, and I left the hospital under a gray cloud of morphine and regret. None of us remembered to ask about the placenta. By the time I phoned the hospital a couple of days later, I was told it had been incinerated.

I cried, and it wasn't just the baby blues. I felt that a part of me—the part that had joined my daughter *to me*—was permanently lost.

Because it was.

Ashes to ashes.

Placentas (or *placentae*) are anatomical superheroes with breathtaking power and capabilities. Also called afterbirth, they are a testament to the magic, beauty, and incredible efficiency of the reproductive body. Though not every human mama eats her placenta—one commentator suggests no humans at all ate the placenta until about 1970—their imagined sorcery and anecdotal benefits contribute to their allure. If not engaging in outright placental eating (placentophagy), new mothers are often handling their placentas in other ways: burying, freeze-drying, banking, or creating artworks, such as jewelry and bloodprints. Others, of course, simply may not care if it ends up in the incinerator.

But the placenta is potent.

Part of its remarkability is that the placenta, unlike other organs, only forms during about the twelfth week of pregnancy with the *sole* purpose of nourishing and protecting the developing infant. Attaching itself to the uterine wall, the placenta generates the umbilical cord, through which oxygen and nutrients pass from mother to fetus and deoxygenated blood and waste pass from fetus to mother. Cotyledons (which sound to me like extinct dinosaurs) are the name of the tissues and blood vessels that connect the placenta to the uterus on the maternal side. The fetal side is wrapped in membranous layers, called the amnion and chorion.

Generally flat and roundish, like a big juicy patty, the placenta is etched with vessels, arteries, veins, and channels. It strongly resembles a branching tree and indeed is often referred to as the "tree of life." For a fee, placenta encapsulation companies turn placentas into pills. For example, one such company in the Pacific Northwest is called Tree of Life Placenta Services. And the phrase "tree of life" appears frequently on midwifery, doula, and birthing practice blogs, the obvious link being that the placenta is, quite literally, life-giving.

Except when it is not.

A variety of placental conditions, both common and rare, can lead to illness and death for mothers and their fetuses or newborns. Some result in preterm labor, which itself is a risk factor for premature infant death. Escalating attention to the scourge of maternal death in the United States is casting light on the placenta and its role in fostering (or impeding) healthy babies and mothers. This research is also revealing stark racial disparities, with Black women two to three times more likely to die from placental conditions than white women.

One such condition, *placenta accreta*, occurs when the placenta becomes too deeply attached to the uterine wall. In normal births, the placenta detaches from the uterine wall after birth. Hence the term *afterbirth*. But if it is too embedded, it cannot detach and may cause severe blood loss, requiring transfusion or hysterectomy. There are also more severe forms, and together, these various conditions are called the *placenta accreta spectrum*.

The rate of placenta accreta has quadrupled since the 1980s, now occurring in about 1 in 272 births, consistent with the rise in cesarean sections. Risk factors include prior uterine surgery, advanced maternal age, and previous childbirth. In the United States, about one in fourteen women die from placenta accreta, mostly from massive blood loss.

One article focused on California, where impressive strides have been made to reduce maternal death rates, describes a physician's early harrowing experience: "About seven months in, he saw a placenta accreta case at Long Beach Memorial that has haunted him since. 'It was just blood everywhere. . . . This lady ended up getting over 50 units of blood,' he recalls. The hospital didn't know how to handle the bleeding, and [the physician] watched the mother go limp and die on the operating room table."

In *placenta previa*, which affects about one in two hundred pregnancies in the third trimester, the placenta sits low in the uterus and may partially or fully cover the cervix. In so-called normal pregnancies and births, the placenta is higher up on the uterine wall, staying out of the cervix's way. During labor, when the placenta detaches, contractions help push the baby and the placenta down through the cervix, into the birth canal, and out into the world. But in a birth where placenta previa is happening, when the cervix thins and opens, the blood vessels may tear and cause excessive, even deadly, bleeding.

Risk factors for placenta previa include previous pregnancies, multiple births (i.e., carrying more than one baby), smoking and drug use, advanced maternal age, and prior uterine surgeries including cesarean sections. Previa is, as one study noted, "a recurrent pathology." That is, having a cesarean section means a greater likelihood of developing placenta previa (and other conditions), which then makes it more likely that a woman is at risk for another cesarean section, elevating her risk of previa. Thus intervention fosters a cycle of more intervention, which elevates the already very high cesarean section rate—32 percent of all births—in the United States.

In developed countries, placenta previa causes comparatively few maternal deaths. Yet it can be deadly in low-income or less-resourced countries, or in places in the United States with limited health care. And though risks to birthing moms of dying from placenta previa are statistically minimal, depending on geography and access to clinical intervention, placenta previa often leads to preterm birth, which in turn can lead to infant death. One study found that placenta previa "triples the rate of neonatal mortality, which is mediated mainly through preterm birth."

This finding is connected, in large part, to whether women receive adequate (or any) prenatal care, during which treatable conditions such as placenta previa might be diagnosed. Not all women in the United States receive appropriate or sufficient prenatal care. Black women are three times more likely than white women not to receive *any* prenatal care and only two-thirds of Native American women access prenatal care in the first trimester, thus escalating their risks for conditions that might otherwise be manageable and survivable.

A major risk factor for placental disorders, then, is lack of care.

Or, to use a more value-laden term, neglect.

We see similar dynamics in *placental abruption*, an uncommon circumstance with a high perinatal death rate. During placental abruption, the placenta detaches from the uterine wall before delivery. This can cause heavy bleeding for the mother and a lack of oxygen and nutrients for the baby. Abruption can happen suddenly, as described by its name. There may be little warning other than cramping, bleeding, and pain. Sadly, the quantity of blood lost is not a good predictor of how much the placenta has separated from the uterus.

One study reported a rate of about 6.5 abruptions per 1,000 births, but with *mortality* rates differing significantly. In births with placental abruption, the maternal mortality rate was 119 per 1,000, compared to 8.2 per 1,000 for all other births. Unsurprisingly, these statistics are further differentiated by race. A 2008 study found that "Black women have an increased risk of placental abruption compared to White women, even when controlling for known coexisting risk factors." The authors also reported a greater contribution of placental abruption to preterm birth for Black women than for white women.

Abruption can be life-threatening for both mother and baby, and there are a variety of risk factors, including race (and racism). Mild abruption can be monitored, whereas more severe abruption may require immediate delivery of the baby, most often via cesarean section. The mother may also need a blood transfusion depending on the amount and severity of blood lost. Babies born after abruption are also at higher risk for premature birth and stillbirth.

Supermodel Chrissy Teigen, whose son Jack was stillborn in 2020, suffered from abruption. In her unflinching Medium essay, she writes,

> My doctors diagnosed me with partial placenta abruption. I had always had placenta problems. I had to deliver Miles [her second child] a month early because his stomach wasn't getting enough food from my placenta. But this was my first abruption. We monitored it very closely, hoping for things to heal and stop. In bed, I bled and bled. . . . My bleeding was getting heavier and heavier. The fluid around Jack had become very low—he was barely able to float around. . . . After a couple nights at the hospital, my doctor told me exactly what I knew was coming—it was time to say goodbye. He just wouldn't survive this, and if it went on any longer, I might not either. . . . Utter and complete sadness.

The placenta is considered a "root cause" of yet another much more common condition, *preeclampsia*. This is a dangerous illness that presents with high blood pressure and protein in the urine. Affecting about 5 to 8 percent of all pregnancies in the United States, mothers may develop preeclampsia before or after birth. The Preeclampsia Foundation reports, "Globally, preeclampsia and other hypertensive disorders of pregnancy are a leading cause of maternal and infant illness and death. By conservative estimates, these disorders are responsible for 76,000 maternal and 500,000 infant deaths each year." These are terrifying numbers.

Preeclampsia *can* be prevented and treated. But as one study argues, in developing countries, "most of [the] maternal deaths and complications are due to lack of prenatal care, lack of access to hospital care, lack of resources, and inappropriate diagnosis and management of patients with preeclampsia-eclampsia." This is also the case in the United States, where preeclampsia causes about 15 percent of premature births and 8 percent of maternal deaths. Again, Black women are at higher risk for preeclampsia than white women: "African American women are more likely to have risk factors for preeclampsia and more likely to suffer an adverse outcome during peripartum care."

Clearly, the placenta is critical to maternal and infant health. And when things go wrong, they can go very wrong, very quickly. There is also another way in which placentas impact infant health—namely, through the transmission of environmental toxins.

Though scientists have long known that exposure to pollution can cause adverse birth outcomes, including prematurity and infant death, recent research locates transmission in and through the placenta. A 2018 study showed "that when pregnant women breathe polluted air, sooty particles are able to reach the placenta via the bloodstream." Focusing on placental macrophages (or cells), the research offered compelling evidence that inhaled pollution can move through a woman's circulatory system and then into the placenta.

According to the pediatrician who led the study, "We do not know whether the particles we found could also move across into the foetus, but our evidence suggests this is indeed possible. We also know that the particles do not need to get into the baby's body to have an adverse effect, because if they have an effect on the placenta, this will have a direct impact on the foetus." In other words, *because of* the significance of the placenta to the fetus, maternal exposure is highly likely to mean fetal exposure.

What remains unasked in this research, as in much research on fetal development, is the impact of toxins *on mothers themselves*. Surely, exposure to pollution—especially chronic exposure—is not good for *women's* health either. And as environmental justice advocates have long shown, exposure is stratified, with people of color and the poor more likely to be negatively affected.

Given the importance—indeed, the *indispensability*—of the placenta to maternal and infant health, it is somewhat shocking to learn it is "the least understood human organ." An article in *Science News* is headlined, "Though Often Forgotten, the Placenta Has a Huge Role in Baby's Health." Noting that some scientists underappreciate the placenta, the article's author writes, "I certainly thought much more about my little embryo turned fetus, growing from sesame seed to grape-sized, grapefruit and beyond, than I did about the disk of tissue supporting my baby-to-be. [Susan Fisher of UCSF] calls the placenta 'the forgotten organ.'" Another researcher describes it as "the Rodney Dangerfield of organs. Like the comedian, it gets no respect."

But change is afoot, including a federal initiative, the Human Placenta Project (HPP), through the Eunice Kennedy Shriver National Institute of Child Health and Human Development. The HPP has to date funded more than fifty million dollars in grants, with the objective to "revolutionize our understanding of the placenta and ultimately improve the health of mothers and children. . . . Ultimately, the success of the project relies on collaborations among creative thinkers from many different fields—from obstetrics and placental biology to bioengineering and data science."

The HPP website acknowledges, "The placenta is arguably one of the most important organs in the body. It influences not just the health of a woman and her fetus during pregnancy, but also the lifelong health of both mother and child. Despite its importance, we know little about this critical but temporary organ."

A major shift in contemporary placenta research is to focus on the organ *before* and *during* pregnancy rather than *after* delivery, as was common. The HPP states, "To fully understand the placenta and how it works, we need to be able to study it during pregnancy, while it's still doing its job. The Human Placenta Project aims to accelerate the development and application of innovative—and safe—technologies and approaches that will give researchers a new and dynamic picture of placental structure and function in real time. This information will help us better understand how the human placenta develops and how it works to ensure a successful pregnancy."

Focusing on the placenta during pregnancy—including early in pregnancy—may help identify which women are at risk for premature delivery or stillbirth. Once so informed, interventions may be possible.

Science News sees the HPP as beneficial, noting that "[fixing] the placenta could change the course for a dramatic number of babies who would otherwise be born too small or with birth defects. That's powerful stuff for would-be moms." Yet what "fixing" the placenta means is unclear.

Will placental research usher in a new wave of prenatal interventions? If so, who would have access to them? How might the HPP and scientists studying the placenta work to ensure that their findings are as widely accessible and implemented as possible, benefitting not only women with insurance and good access to care but *all* women? It is also worth asking, Should we "fix" placentas without also fixing the structures that surround pregnant people and shape birth outcomes?

Beyond the HPP, efforts to learn more about the placenta also include artificially growing them in laboratories. A team of researchers in the U.K. grew "mini placentas" from placental cells, describing them as "organoids." The team sought to do placental research without having to intrude into women's bodies during actual pregnancies. Their research questions focus on pregnancy disorders, such as preeclampsia and stillbirth, as well as viral infections (e.g., why do some viruses cross the placenta and others do not?), the role of hormones and proteins in pregnancy, and drug safety.

According to the study's lead researcher, a reproductive endocrinologist, "The placenta is the first organ that develops and it's the least understood." As for why lab-grown organoids are desirable, he says, "The human placenta is very different from any other species. . . . So animal models . . . and cell lines just don't really work."

Humans and nonhumans also differ in other important ways: most nonhuman animals consume their placentas after birth though few humans do, with the practice in humans originating only around the late 1960s or early 1970s, robust decades for social change.

Placentophagy is widespread, but not universal, among nonhuman species. Camels don't eat their placentas, for example. Possible scientific explanations range from postpartum shifts in food preferences, to ravenous hunger after delivering babies, to cleaning up the birth site to avoid attracting predators. Advocates of placentophagy in humans look to nature, and to China.

"Animals do it" is how the What to Expect website introduces placentophagy, going on to note that human proponents routinely cite animal behavior in their advocacy. They also cite Chinese medicine, specifically the sixteenth-century *Compendium of Materia Medica*, as justification for maternal placentophagy. However, in Chinese medicine, the placenta is more likely to appear in dried form to ostensibly heal humans who have *not* just given birth. As one study notes, "Although *Zi He Che*, the Chinese term for dried human placenta, has historically been used for treating various ailments . . . in non-postpartum humans, there is no clear evidence of postpartum women ingesting placenta."

Lack of clear evidence has not stopped sites such as What to Expect from pointing to nonhuman animals and Chinese medicine. It is worth noting here that *What to Expect When You're Expecting*, the book on which the website is based, is read by *90 percent* of pregnant women who read pregnancy books, and there are more than 18.5 *million* copies of the book in print. Obviously, it is highly influential. When the companion site says "animals do it" and "Chinese medicine has advocated it for centuries," many women listen. And when celebrities such as Kim Kardashian tout the benefits of placenta-eating on Instagram, where she is followed by *189 million* people, the potential reach is further magnified.

The seduction of placentophagy likely has more to do with an affinity for "natural" birth and parenting approaches, as well as the very reasonable desires of pregnant people to have healthy babies and to be as healthy as possible after giving birth. Postpartum depression and milk flow are among the major concerns placentophagy is meant to address. Of course, clever marketing also plays a role: "Positive placenta-eating anecdotes have flourished, and so have companies that charge hundreds [of dollars] to prepare a placenta for consumption, dehydrated like beef jerky or processed into smoothies and pills." One study found that it can cost between two hundred and four hundred dollars to steam, dehydrate, ground, and place the placenta into pills. This encapsulation ensures easier ingestion.

The "tree of life" messaging is also very compelling. Yet the practice of eating one's own placenta is neither evidence-based nor especially well researched among health care practitioners. While some find placentophagy relatively innocuous, in a "let them eat cake" kind of way, others believe it may be dangerous for both mothers and babies and thus discourage it.

In 2017, a newborn in Oregon became ill with group B *Streptococcus agalactiae* (GBS, a bacterium) after the mother consumed her placenta in encapsulated form. The CDC reported after much investigation that the newborn's illness could be attributed to "high maternal colonization [of bacterium] secondary to consumption of GBS-infected placental tissue." Fortunately, the infection was resolved with antibiotics. Another study linked breast budding and vaginal bleeding in a three-month-old baby girl to her mother's consumption of the placenta; when the mother stopped consuming encapsulated placenta, the budding and bleeding stopped too.

Given the placenta's function, it makes sense that a postpartum placenta would be full of nutrients, hormones, and cells. Yet it might also be brimming with waste, bacteria, and even metals. Today, the equation of "natural" with "healthy" may be dubious, but that hasn't stopped people from drying, chopping, mixing, encapsulating, and consuming placental tissue. A quick Amazon search reveals more than a handful of cookbooks devoted to placenta recipes. And many midwife, doula, and home birth sites offer an abundance of support for placenta eating, including recipes.

Other sites urge caution. At Lamaze International, a lactation educational consultant wrote, "How do we approach the topic of placentophagy in our classes? Keep it simple. As of today, consuming placenta is not an evidence-based practice. Therefore, we cannot recommend it directly to our students. However, to support our students' autonomy, I believe a mother should be able to take her placenta home and do with it as she will."

And why shouldn't parents be able to take their placentas home, even if they do not plan to eat them? Some may want to bury the placenta and plant something on that site; others may want to create a placental keepsake, such as an art print. Placentas offer a tangible connection to one's pregnancy, and they may have emotional value for some new parents. There is something beautiful and powerful about the many rituals that accompany birth.

But for babylost women, placentas may be more complicated objects. After a baby dies, do babylost women long for their missing placentas? For those who keep them, does the placenta serve as a kind of talisman or touchstone? Do the babylost resent or envy those parents whose babies survive and who also get to keep, consume, bury, or write about their placentas? The relationship between babylost parents and their placentas has been little explored, just like placenta research more broadly.

I do know this: I would take a living baby, any day, over all the placentas in the world. And I bet other parents would too. Mourning a placenta lost to an incinerator is but a splinter of grief compared to the weight of sorrow carried by the babylost.

Placentas may matter profoundly, but never more than the babies they have nurtured.

Prematurity

In her stunning volume *Reproductive Injustice: Racism, Pregnancy, and Premature Birth*, anthropologist Dána-Ain Davis traces the impact of medical racism on birth outcomes. Focusing on the problem of premature births, she writes that "Black women have higher rates of premature births than any other women in America, and these rates of prematurity go beyond class . . . being middle- or upper-class provides little protection from the precarity of prematurity, in ways that do not hold true for women of other racial backgrounds."

Precarity is an important keyword here; it signals a specific kind of structured or built-in vulnerability. Precarious lives, as philosopher Judith Butler argued, are not accidentally so. They are produced by the social situations in which people live their lives. Grounded in theories of economy and capitalism, precarity identifies social marginalization, vulnerability, and insecurity, conditions that move people away from livable lives. Butler described precarity as "the politically induced condition in which certain populations suffer from failing social and economic networks . . . becoming differentially exposed to injury, violence, and death."

Seen through the lens of precarity, premature births are produced, in part, by obstetric racism. Davis shows this eloquently. These are not "natural" occurrences, at least not most of the time. And they can be deadly.

A premature baby is one born before the thirty-seventh week of pregnancy. Globally, about fifteen million babies are born prematurely, or "preterm"—about one in ten births. An "extremely preterm" baby is one born earlier than twenty-eight weeks, a "very preterm baby" between twenty-eight and thirty-two weeks, and a "moderate to late preterm" baby between thirty-two and thirty-seven weeks.

Premature births are the leading cause of infant death, and yet, three-quarters of these deaths are *preventable*. The CDC claims that "reducing preterm birth is a national public health priority." But rather than dropping, the preterm birth rate *increased* in 2017. We seem to be getting worse, rather than better, at preventing prematurity. This is especially true among already marginalized populations.

Premature babies are very tiny and fragile. An extremely preterm baby may weigh less than two pounds. These babies are likely to end up in the NICU (Neonatal Intensive Care Unit), where their fates are both unknown and structured by the same conditions that resulted in their prematurity. The NICU too, as Davis reveals, is not immune from racism.

While some "preemies" survive—becoming "miracles of technology"—far too many die.

Like all diagnostic categories, prematurity has a history. Davis discusses the origins of the term *feeble*, linking it to racist and gendered assumptions of fragility and frailty as well as maternal blame. At the beginning of the twentieth century, premature babies (especially those of immigrants) were described as "weaklings"—another term that implies frailty. In both cases, fragility was seen as innate and survival uncertain. For babies diagnosed as already nearly dead, interventions were few and limited.

The term *premature* comes from the Latin *prae*, for "before," and *maturus*, for "ripe." In the reproductive context, premature means born too early. It is no coincidence that pregnancy is sometimes referred to as "ripening" a baby. But prematurity also means occurring before the usual time, in an untimely manner.

Ironically and sadly in the reproductive context, prematurity is about *both* premature birth *and* premature death. Not always, of course, but often enough to be considered a public health crisis, as the CDC does, though without effective action. What kind of emergency can it be, one wonders, if the situation is actually worsening?

For the past century, the story of prematurity has been a story of overcoming, at least for those babies with access to quality, high-tech care. But underneath the survival stories are other stories, of those babies who do not survive. Of clandestine journeys from the NICU to the hospital morgue. Of babylost moms and dads who will spend a lifetime grieving.

Thinking about—and through—*prematurity*, then, can help us understand how many of the same conditions that lead to premature births, including racism, also lead to premature deaths, and not just of infants. A significant body of literature has shown that African Americans are "at risk" for premature mortality from a variety of causes, ranging from cancer and heart disease to homicide. One study determined that "about 1 in every 1,000 black men can expect to be killed by police." Another shockingly found that "in utero exposure to police killings of unarmed blacks" resulted in substantially decreased birth weight and gestational age of Black infants living nearby.

Of course, African Americans are not the only population to suffer from premature debility and death. Other nonwhite populations also suffer, especially Native Americans, who survived genocide and displacement only to face a plague of social and health problems that impede cultural and biological survival. Not surprisingly, all groups of color in the United States are more likely to test positive for COVID-19 and to die from it. Marginalization of any type—racial, ethnic, economic, gendered, bodily, geographic—can lead to precarity that limits basic life, much less human flourishing.

Premature birth may be a public health emergency, but so too is premature death. Obstetric racism is but a subset of racism, an enduring social ill that kills systematically.

PRENATAL CARE

The word *prenatal* stems from the Latin word *pre*, which means "before," and the Latin word *natus*, which means "to be born." Prenatal has roughly the same etymology as pregnant, and both have come to mean *before birth*. The prenatal period is considered to be from the time of conception through birth. For much of human history, there was no such thing as formal "prenatal care"—women and their caregivers simply engaged in a variety of practices to achieve a healthy pregnancy and successful birth.

Prenatal care emerged as a specific sector and practice of medicine around the mid-nineteenth century, as medicine was becoming professionalized and midwifery was displaced, especially in the United States. The discovery in 1843 of a link between albuminuria (kidney disease) and edema (swelling) with convulsions and eclampsia during pregnancy paved the way for clinical intervention during the prenatal period. Around the same time, the first prenatal clinic was established, in Dublin, Ireland.

In the United States, Mary Mills West of the Children's Bureau in Washington, D.C. published an educational booklet in 1913, called *Prenatal Care*. West was commissioned to write the booklet by bureau chief Julia Lathrop, who selected West "because in addition to being an experienced, college educated writer, West was also a mother of five children." Topics included nutrition, exercise, hygiene, instructions for at-home births, and information about infection and miscarriages. West also penned a subsequent booklet entitled *Infant Care*.

When the Sheppard-Towner Act was repealed in 1929, a number of maternal-child health programs ended. Yet "*Prenatal Care* remained one of the Children's Bureau's most widely distributed publications. In 1929, the Children's Bureau estimated that the reach of the booklets was so wide that half the infants in the US at that time had been affected by the booklets' advice."

Comparatively, the more contemporary *What to Expect When You're Expecting* has been read by 90 percent of women who read pregnancy books, and there are 18.5 million copies in print.

The rise of prenatal care stems from a combination of factors: the medicalization of pregnancy and childbirth; increasing clinical specialization; women's own demands for safer, healthier births; the emergence of the fetal patient as an object of clinical interest; and expansion of practices and technologies designed to improve birth outcomes, from folic acid pills to ultrasounds to fetal monitoring. While in

1900 very few pregnant women had contact with a medical provider prior to birth, prenatal care is now *so* entrenched that its absence is seen as a public health crisis. Bluntly stated, deficient prenatal care is understood to be a key cause of declining infant mortality rates throughout the twentieth century.

How prenatal care works has remained relatively unchanged since its inception. Pregnant women undergo blood pressure, urine, and weight screening, and—increasingly often—ultrasound and prenatal testing to evaluate fetal health and development. They are also offered nutritional advice. The current model of care, endorsed by the American College of Obstetricians and Gynecologists, emphasizes prevention: "Prenatal care often consists of identifying fetal problems and arranging modified prenatal care to best manage the outcome via surveillance in an appropriate site, care by maternal-fetal medicine subspecialists with consultation by pediatric/fetal surgeons, and delivery in the best place and under the best circumstances so that newborn care specialists can give the baby the best chance of survival."

Unfortunately, as with so many beneficial health practices, prenatal care is unevenly available to pregnant people, despite Medicaid and other public programs. In 1990, an article in *Health Affairs* stated, "One of the most glaring failures of the American health care system has been its persistently high rates of infant and maternal mortality . . . [which] disproportionately burdens those groups already most disadvantaged." The authors critique the "micro-incrementalism" of U.S. health policy, which prioritizes cost-savings over caregiving. They offer policy solutions for expanding access beyond state-by-state Medicaid expansion. They conclude, "Certainly cost containment is important. But with current initiatives, the price of cost saving is counted in terms of death and disability among children who are already the most disadvantaged. This seems a price almost certainly too high for this country to pay."

Three decades after this article appeared, we are still paying that price.

A 2016 study reported eighteen million prenatal care visits in the United States in 2015, making it one of the most commonly used health services. Yet the authors note significant barriers: "Younger women, women with less education, women having a fourth or higher-order birth, and non-Hispanic NHOPI [Native Hawaiian or Other Pacific Islander], non-Hispanic AIAN [American Indian or Alaska Native], and non-Hispanic black women were the least likely to begin care in the first trimester of pregnancy or to have at least adequate PNC [prenatal care]."

Financial barriers are among the most significant: "Women with the greatest need for prenatal care do not seek it because they cannot pay for it." Even when pregnant people do access prenatal care, clinical encounters may range from uncomfortable and unhelpful to dangerous and disastrous. A number of studies have found that Black women especially are negatively impacted by such encounters, which can erode trust between providers and patients and deter these women from continuing care. As one study noted, "Women of color's experiences during pregnancy and birth were influenced by how they were treated by providers, particularly in how information was shared and withheld."

To me, one of the most striking things about prenatal care, having studied reproduction for thirty years, is its focus on the fetus. Though birth outcomes impact both mothers and newborns, prenatal care is less about ensuring healthy moms than it is about producing healthy babies. While midwives and doulas tend to center mothers *and* babies, medicine often seems to forget the people carrying the babies unless there is a problem. Fetal medicine, as I illustrated in my first book, *The Making of the Unborn Patient: A Social Anatomy of Fetal Surgery*, is an excellent example of this. When the fetus is the patient, pregnant women are, at most, technologies for gaining access to the unborn. Rarely is the care and feeding of mothers—maternal health outcomes—the point of prenatal care. This may be one of the reasons our maternal mortality rates are so high.

The other striking fact about prenatal care is that especially in the United States it is, or has been made to be, about responsibility—the pregnant woman's responsibility to be healthy and to do everything possible for her baby. *Or else.* Of course, most pregnant people do this anyway, to the best of their ability. And yet, prenatal care is increasingly framed as a kind of maternal imperative. And the "or else" hovers over women's lives, evoking caution and fear about what might happen if our babies are not born healthy, or if they die. Women are told in a hundred different ways, by doctors and *What to Expect When You're Expecting*, by vitamin manufacturers and public health campaigns, that it is their *individual responsibility* to birth healthy babies.

In the early twentieth century, the federal government took a robust interest in prenatal survival through the Sheppard-Towner Act and other initiatives. But currently, policymakers seem to pay attention only when things go wrong. Pregnant people are largely on their own to procure folate, buy organic produce, avoid workplace toxins, exercise regularly, say no to alcohol, drugs, sushi, and soft cheeses, and dodge violence in the home. There is little help from policymakers in producing healthy babies but plenty of judgment (and punishment) when women, especially, do not. The language of failure—as in, women "failing" to receive prenatal care—speaks volumes about whose responsibility it is to secure positive birth outcomes.

And if prenatal care was not already fraught for pregnant women who are positioned as moral agents and legal subjects whether we want to be or not, today *preconception* care deepens these complexities. Preconception care suggests that women and girls should focus on positioning themselves and their bodies optimally for their future reproductive lives. And they should do so from the moment they could potentially become pregnant—that is, from the onset of menstruation, or even earlier. Preconception care focuses on the period *before* pregnancy, which for many women might be quite a long period. According to the CDC, potentially reproductive girls and women should create a reproductive plan, see a doctor, ingest folic acid daily, avoid alcohol, smoking, and "street drugs," avoid toxic substances, maintain a healthy weight, "get help for violence," learn your family history, and "get mentally healthy."

But how many of these guidelines are, in fact, under girls' and women's control? Is it that easy for *potentially* pregnant women to simply avoid substances, especially if they're addicted? I wonder if the CDC will help with drug and alcohol treatment? What about avoiding toxins and environmental contaminants? Surely, this is simple for those women who live near fracking or work in industrial plants or beauty salons. My personal favorite is "avoiding violence in the home." In the United States, *every nine seconds* a woman is beaten *by a man*, making this guideline laughable if it were not so tragic. And "securing mental health" is increasingly challenging in a for-profit health care system, where most insurers do not cover mental health treatment.

The problem with making women personally responsible for pregnancy outcomes is that the kinds of things that make women and babies unhealthy involve other people, and indeed whole systems. Access to prenatal care cannot, for example, fix racism or misogyny. Nor will it reduce violence against women. Prenatal care is only as effective as the structures in which it is embedded.

Q

Quiet

Babylost parents understand the quiet spaces. They understand that a nursery that formerly sheltered a newborn is now heartbreakingly silent. They understand that often, they must quiet their own riotous emotions because there are few public spaces in which to express their anguish. They understand that their sorrow, while echoing loudly inside their own heads and hearts, must be quieted elsewhere so as not to alarm their partners, children, friends, coworkers, or new acquaintances.

On the many blogs devoted to babyloss—one of the few spaces where parents can scream and shout and cry if they need to—women (it is mostly women who post) remark on how often they censor themselves, not wanting to make others uncomfortable. Not wanting to frighten people away with their colossal grief and pain. This is a kind of emotional labor, and it is largely invisible.

On the *Still Standing* website, Marisa Michaud writes, "I want to always share my son with anyone who will listen or wants to know. But sometimes I am unsure how to bring him up in conversations, especially with people who don't already know. . . . Constant struggles on how many times to talk about him, the right time to bring him up or the times to possibly keep quiet. How much will scare others?"

Chloe describes her hurtful experiences of sharing her story online:

Hey you. Yes, *you*. The family members/friends who choose to ignore the posts I make about my sweet son. You know who you are; just know that your absence in support has been noted. I have stayed silent and tried to pretend it hasn't affected me in the least bit but—*I can't stay silent anymore.* I realize there may be many reasons for your social media silence, in regards to my son. Maybe it's as simple and innocent as not knowing what to say. Maybe it makes you uncomfortable because you're not good with the emotional stuff. That's okay. I get it. In that case though, just simply 'like' the post. . . . That simple gesture makes me feel a little less alone in this, and I really need that right now.

Such silencing is full of echoes of reproductive loss.

Anthropologist Linda Layne, in her richly layered 2003 study *Motherhood Lost*, describes a "culture of silence that shrouds pregnancy loss in the United States." She notes that while pregnancy loss *has* become more visible, "members of pregnancy loss support groups attest that the suppression and avoidance of these unhappy events remain the norm. . . . The cultural denial of pregnancy loss clearly has a profound effect on those who experience a loss." The book details various "silence-making" practices, from women's own pregnancy disclosure stories to reproductive technologies, while also foregrounding women's grief, experiences, and voices. Layne also attends to the material culture of pregnancy loss, including what remains after loss, such as empty nurseries and unworn baby clothes.

In *Death without Weeping*, anthropologist Nancy Scheper-Hughes's haunting ethnography of infant death in Brazil, she excavates the multiple silences of daily life in Bom Jesus de Mata, including the silences that accompany child loss. She situates silence inside the structural violences that render the powerless mute, noting that "silence and feigned ignorance serve as their cover." She observes that "two decades of military government have driven the point home and taken a toll on people who can now be depended on to police, silence, and check themselves. 'Silence is protection,' the people of the Alto are wont to say, often adding, 'Whoever says nothing has nothing to fear.'" The intensity of Scheper-Hughes's attention to structures of silence and grief captivated me when I read the book almost thirty years ago, and her work planted a fertile seed for my own.

But my entrée into the question of infant mortality hinged on another structural silence, different from Northeast Brazil, of course, but also consequential: that of U.S. policymakers who seemed to ignore high infant death rates, especially in Black and Indigenous communities. Why, I wondered, given that so many babies were dying, was there almost nothing happening at the federal level? The more I read and talked to people and learned, the more concerned—and angry—I became.

Outside of municipal and state initiatives, few in Washington, D.C., seemed to have infant death on their radar—which struck me as especially neglectful given the capital's appalling Black infant mortality rates. As a sociologist and reproductive justice advocate, I wanted to know *who cared about infant death, why, and how they planned to address these problems.* I also keenly wanted to know why infant mortality had not percolated up to the status of a legitimate social problem, though British physician George Newman had defined it in precisely those terms *as early as 1906.*

What I learned, surprisingly, is that not all spaces are quiet, and that the work of "fixing" infant mortality *is* happening in homes, neighborhoods, clinics, and statehouses around the country. I also learned that, with few exceptions and until very recently, at the federal level, there *has* been a deafening silence (at least since the Sheppard-Towner Act was repealed—in 1929!). Only those spaces already concerned about racial justice have been paying attention to Black and Indigenous infant death and, relatedly, Black and Indigenous maternal mortality. It has taken *a whole century* for policymakers to again focus attention on reproductive loss.

One thread that runs through this book is that the silence and ignorance about infant death are also about race and racism, and the ways that issues concerning

Black and Indigenous and undocumented and poor women are either hyper-magnified as *economic* problems for the state to address or thoroughly *invisibilized*. Pregnant women and babies in need are deemed burdens or epidemiological problems to solve or are missing entirely from the national agenda—except as objects of surveillance.

There is another way in which infant mortality politics are quiet, namely, in relation to other reproductive issues. In the United States, we fight loudly, openly, and violently about abortion, and we have done so for decades. Currently, *Roe v. Wade* hangs in the balance of an ideologically imbalanced Supreme Court. The flanks are clearly and aggressively drawn, though there is much variation between "pro" and "anti" in actual beliefs and practices.

Antiabortion rhetoric has escalated in recent decades, forcing women's health advocates to narrow their focus from a broad range of issues to just one, securing the precarious constitutional right to abortion. This means that other concerns, including reproductive loss, are marginalized. While noisy abortion politics rivet a divided nation, the quiet politics of infant mortality haunt from the sidelines.

If only we could listen better. Because here is what I know:

Babies still die—too many of them.

Women still die—too many of them.

Quiet is . . .

. . . an empty nursery.

. . . a hollow campaign speech.

. . . the underbelly of abortion politics.

. . . the erasure of pregnant women and children.

Silence really is deadly.

R

Racism

Black and Indigenous babies are far more likely to die in their first year of life than white babies, and Black and Indigenous mothers are more likely to suffer injury or die in childbirth than white mothers. This is, in part, because of the accrual of white privilege, including access to care.

These differences are not simply a matter of nature or an all-powerful deity sorting out who shall live and who shall die. Of course, there is a bit of the accidental, biological, and genetic (or some combination thereof) in determining who is fortunate enough to survive.

But when we use the term *race*, we're relying on a made-up category. It is a demographic variable that has been historically applied—often violently—to distinguish some groups of people from others. And it does not merely separate but orders in a hierarchical fashion, determining value and worth, or lack thereof.

Race becomes a shorthand for blame and attribution, on the one hand, or for the sort of false pity and sympathy that leads to paternalist, seemingly benevolent but actually dangerous interventions like "welfare" and "child removal."

In the arena of health disparities research, the category of "race" has been used to explain everything from African American hypertension to Hispanic diabetes to Native American alcoholism. So many studies have been done linking skin color to disease and DNA to survival rates and genetics to degeneration without ever digging below the surface of U.S. census categories.

Far more useful, as scholars such as sociologist David Williams and others have found, is the category of *racism*. It seems that understanding *the patterned accumulation of risks, stressors, and vulnerabilities that leads to premature illness and death* for some people is much more useful than simply knowing their "race." This is because race is an idea, an intangible fantasy, manifest only through layers and layers of *practices* that deepen what we have come to understand as skin color.

For example, we could talk about an entire group of people as a coherent category known as "white." Or we could instead track how some people with lighter skin have accrued the privileges of living inside of whiteness. These privileges translate into higher incomes, less risk for certain kinds of illnesses, greater proximity to cultural and economic resources that deepen privilege, better connections to other white people (e.g., in neighborhoods and businesses) that amplify racial benefits, and so on. White privilege can become so entrenched that we begin to see it as "the natural order"—unassailable, unchangeable, unmoving.

We could also track how some people with darker skin have accrued the disadvantages of living *outside of* whiteness. Good health, economic security, school choice, access to clean water and healthy food, home ownership—all are often *out of reach* for Blacks and other nonwhite people in the United States. Not because of skin color, but because of the historic layers of risk, vulnerability, and marginalization that quite literally keep people in their places. And these places are not, generally speaking, in proximity to or inside of privilege.

In speaking of race, then, we gloss over the *structural* ways in which "race" comes to stand in for living, breathing, nefarious racism. Race is a seemingly inert category, with a matter-of-fact thingness about it that hides all the work that goes into making it seem so natural. Race is just something that people are. This is, in part, why it is so insidious; if race is natural, a fact of life, then it becomes that much harder to challenge and dismantle.

Racism, on the other hand, is a far more dynamic concept, one that draws attention to and names the individual and social practices that go into sustaining inequalities. Racism helps us understand why women of color are more likely to encounter obstetric violence and to have limited access to high-quality pregnancy and childbirth care. It also helps us understand why women of color may be more likely to be blamed for causing negative birth outcomes. And it can provide a lens for making sense of the experiences of Black women like Beyoncé and Serena Williams, whose tremendous wealth, status, and proximity to privilege did not protect them from nearly dying in childbirth.

Race is a descriptor. Racism is an explanation.

Yet none of this knowledge helps when a parent is drowning in the shoals of babyloss. I do not believe most babylost parents spend the aching, tender moments during and after their child's death pondering racial dynamics, either their own relative privilege or lack thereof.

But for the rest of us, in a culture seemingly obsessed with race, the denial and ignorance of racism are unacceptable. Babies do not die from "race" any more than they die because the planets are aligned in a particular way. But they do die, frequently, because of racism.

Fixing infant mortality, then, cannot be simply about measuring race.

We must, and we can, do better. This means working to unravel *all the ways* racism tentacles its way in and through social structures, practices, and beliefs. This includes medicine as much as real estate practices, prenatal care as much as the tax code. Racism is everywhere around us and in us, and to pretend otherwise is both delusional and deadly. If not for our own child, then for somebody else's.

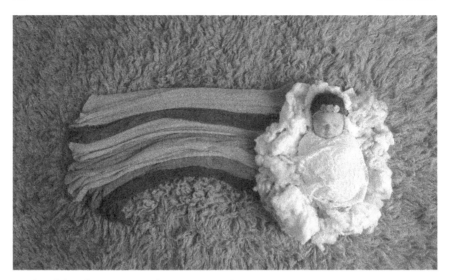

Rainbow baby. Photo credit: RealCreation / iStock.

Rainbow Baby

Sunlight passes through raindrops, tiny liquid prisms, creating rainbows, beautiful arcs of color that delight after a passing storm. In Greek mythology, Iris is the goddess of rainbows, a daughter of sea and sky, deemed to be loyal and faithful, but also a shape-shifter. In Irish lore, Leprechauns hide pots of gold at the end of rainbows, which are forever elusive as rainbows form and disappear—impermanent traces.

Rainbows are associated with goodness and light, with Dorothy in *The Wizard of Oz* singing of "dreams that you dare to dream," with hope and blue skies after trouble and strife, with an imagined rosier future.

A rainbow baby in the context of reproductive loss is another child born after a miscarriage, stillbirth, or infant death: "Like the miracle of a rainbow after a storm, many mamas refer to babies born after loss as their rainbow babies. The rainbow doesn't erase the storm, nor does the arrival of a new baby eclipse the tragedy of previous pregnancy loss."

And yet, as Kelly Kittel writes in her memoir, *Breathe*, "The promise of life so soon after Noah's death implied that maybe we had a future. I cradled my delicious secret, this glimpse of a rainbow."

As described by Emily Grorud in *Still Standing Magazine*, "Rainbow babies have a way of forcing you back to the land of the living—ready or not. . . . A rainbow baby doesn't heal all wounds, but they can give you that push to live in the land of the living and focus on the future again."

Victoria Denney writes, "As I watched my carefree rainbow daughter I thought of how she has taught us how to dance in the rain. She has given us a reason to smile through the tears, to dance through the pain, and has given us the strength to dance through the storm."

Rainbow babies bring light and promise, but they can also bring a range of emotions including guilt, fear, and dread. Catherine Ashe shared, "This pregnancy after loss hasn't been all rainbows. . . . Rainbow pregnancies aren't always filled with joy and laughter. They can be dark and lonely journeys filled with fear, insomnia, and doubts."

Some women may worry, as Kimberly Fain at Simply Baby writes, "that others will think they have gotten over their previous loss, or that they have moved on to replace their baby. They fear that having a rainbow baby after stillbirth in some way dishonors their baby who has passed, and that the joy of the next baby will prevent the mother from properly grieving."

Prak Pandiyan, whose newborn died and who later gave birth to a daughter reflected, "My husband and I always wondered what life would have been like if our son could be discharged and come home with us. . . . When we welcomed our rainbow baby into this world, our perspective as parents shifted. Whenever things get hard—feeding challenges, sleeping challenges, mild illnesses—we always make it a point to step back and remember that things could be so much worse."

Other parents, such as Ren Benson writing for The Motherload, may eschew the label of rainbow baby entirely: "I didn't want [my son] to be labelled before he had a chance to show me who he was, I didn't want to always look at him and be reminded that he was a sequel to a prequel that never was. He is not a rainbow baby, he is all colours, he is the Earth, the Sun, the stars and the Moon, he lives in no one's shadow and I'll be sure he knows that every day of my life."

The term *rainbow baby* speaks to the enduring power of babyloss and the ways that reproductive grief can shape subsequent meanings and experiences of parenting. Babyloss is so intense that babies born *before* such a loss may also be granted, ex post facto, a special term of their own—*sunshine babies*: "Just as a rainbow baby represents the hope after a storm, a sunshine baby represents the calm before."

Jessica Zucker, a clinical psychologist specializing in maternal health, appreciates the terms *sunshine* and *rainbow babies*, believing "they acknowledge the complexity of pregnancy and infant loss and the pregnancies that follow. . . . I think as a culture it behooves us to recognize just how challenging these losses can be for women and families, and these terms help ground us in that."

Yet one wonders about infants born before or after the dark cloud of babyloss. What does it feel like to be configured as a sunshine baby or rainbow baby? Are these terms that children and later adults actually use to describe *themselves*, or are they useful only temporarily in the context of a parent's grief? What are the lifelong consequences for surviving babies of being identified in relation to lost siblings?

Some clues are offered in the essay "I Was a Rainbow Baby," whose author, Katie Reed, was born three years after her brother died of SIDS at twelve weeks. She describes a childhood of hypervigilance, with parents who constantly soothed, praised, and adored her. She writes, "Jacob's memory was not mine. He died before I was born, and I didn't know him. But my whole life was spent in his shadow."

Her teen years involved episodes of depression and self-harm, leading her eventually to ask her parents if Jacob's death was her fault. They assured her it was not.

And yet, she laments in closing, "I was a rainbow baby. I was supposed to bring sunshine back into their lives. But when I look back on the last almost 34 years that I've been here, I wonder. Was it a fair trade?"

Sadly, even if a baby is not labeled "rainbow" or "sunshine," if there has been babyloss in the family, it may well be consequential in a wide variety of ways for surviving siblings—a topic about which we know far too little.

REPRODUCTIVE JUSTICE

I came of age politically in the 1980s, attending college as a white, working-class, first-generation student from 1984 to 1988. During that period, President Ronald Reagan and his supporters were pushing "trickle-down economics" and a conservative "pro-life" agenda with roots in Christian religious fundamentalism. The times were ripe for the publication of Margaret Atwood's 1985 dystopian novel, *The Handmaid's Tale*, which craftily embodied what was unfolding in U.S. politics and culture.

My burgeoning college activism mostly centered around reproductive rights and divestment from South Africa in protest against apartheid. Long interested in women's health and what, in the 1970s, I knew as "women's lib," I was frankly horrified at the realization that women could be told what to do with our bodies. A student of sociology and the history of medicine, I read *The Malleus Maleficarum* (Hammer of Witches) for the first time during college, understanding that historical assaults on women healers and midwives were connected to contemporary reproductive politics.

Then interested in attending law school, my focus was very much on securing legal rights for all women to safe, secure abortions and the right to bodily autonomy writ large. I read as much as I could about reproduction across fields as diverse as law, literature, and anthropology. Reproductive rights was the readily accessible framework I adopted in my studies, with "choice" as an already established discourse that centered (some) women. I did not realize, at the time, that there existed a body of work that could make better sense of my varied social justice commitments, including women's health, economic and racial justice, the deadly reach of global capital, and women's bodies as cultural and political battlefields.

That body of work later became called "reproductive justice," and I did not come to it until graduate school in the 1990s in San Francisco. There, studying sociology and women's health with Virginia Olesen and Adele Clarke, I began to read literature such as the Combahee River Collective's Statement, Evelyn C. White's *The Black Women's Health Book*, and a wealth of African American, Indigenous, Latina, Asian American, and transnational feminist scholarship on gender, race, sexuality, health, and inequality. I learned about intersectionality around the same time I discovered the lens of reproductive justice, cementing an intellectual and political perspective that has permeated my scholarship and activism ever since.

"Reproductive justice" as an alternative to "reproductive choice" was created in 1994 by Black women attending a pro-choice conference in Chicago. Adopting the name Women of African Descent for Reproductive Justice, the caucus coined the term *reproductive justice* to counter what founding mother Loretta Ross described as dissatisfaction "with the pro-choice language." She stated, "Perhaps because we were just returning from the International Conference on Population and Development in Cairo, Egypt in 1994, we began exploring the use of the human rights framework in our reproductive rights activism in the United States. . . . We sought a way to partner reproductive rights to social justice and came up with the term 'reproductive justice.'"

Legal scholar Dorothy Roberts also situates the emergence of reproductive justice: "For too long, the rhetoric of 'choice' has privileged predominantly white middle-class women who have the ability to choose from reproductive options that are unavailable to poor and low-income women, especially women of color. . . . The language of choice has proved useless for claiming public resources that most women need in order to maintain control over their bodies and their lives."

SisterSong, a reproductive justice organization founded in 1997 by a coalition of women-of-color-led organizations, describes the history of the term as embodying recognition that "the women's rights movement, led by and representing middle class and wealthy white women, could not defend the needs of women of color and other marginalized women and trans* people. We needed to lead our own national movement to uplift the needs of the most marginalized women, families, and communities."

In their 2017 primer, *Reproductive Justice: An Introduction*, Loretta Ross and historian Rickie Solinger define reproductive justice as characterized by three principles: "(1) the right *not* to have a child; (2) the right to *have* a child; and (3) the right to *parent* children in safe and healthy environments." They write, "At the heart of reproductive justice is this claim: all fertile persons and persons who reproduce and become parents require a safe and dignified context for these most fundamental human experiences. Achieving this goal depends on access to specific, community-based resources including high-quality health care, housing and education, a living wage, a healthy environment, and a safety net for times when these resources fail."

One of the main differences between reproductive choice and reproductive justice is scale. Though rights rely conceptually on universal notions of rights-bearing groups such as "human" and "women," in the United States, reproductive rights too often translate into *individual* choice. For example, women's constitutionally protected right to abortion has in practice become a woman's right to choose pregnancy termination. In contrast, reproductive justice is fundamentally about structure, power, and the collective; it includes recognition of the conditions under which people reproduce, or not. Individuals matter, but even more, social systems matter. As a framework, it necessarily includes gender, embodiment, race, ethnicity, class, ability, age, sexuality, geography, language, citizenship, and other dimensions of social life.

As SisterSong notes on its website, achieving reproductive justice means analyzing power systems, addressing intersecting oppressions, centering the most marginalized, and joining together across issues and identities. The contributors to *Undivided Rights: Women of Color Organize for Reproductive Justice* do precisely this, offering a range of examples of women of color and their allies actively working toward reproductive justice. Part of this work is about challenging the historic limitations of mainstream frameworks and rejecting the language of "choice," while also building on important early contributions that took up sterilization abuse, birth control, and population control, always with a critical eye toward how inequality shapes people's diverse reproductive experiences.

The reproductive justice framework is essential for understanding infant mortality and working to reduce infant mortality rates. Yet outside of reproductive justice organizations, the framework all too often has been ignored. In spaces that emphasize people's right *not* to bear children, such as courtrooms and mainstream choice organizations, there is little room for acknowledging infant death. Abortion is *so* highly embattled in the United States, it leaves limited space for other reproductive issues, especially those related to motherhood and parenting. It is as if people cannot hold in tension the various principles of reproductive justice, that one can advocate for the right and access to abortion *and* the right to bear and raise children.

In the United States, we rely on binaries to such a degree that we are unable to recognize that the very same person may terminate a pregnancy (or indeed multiple pregnancies) and also mourn a deeply wanted baby who dies in the first year of life. Indeed, across a unique woman's life course, she may have a range of reproductive experiences, including contraceptive use, unintended pregnancy, abortion, miscarriage, infertility, and babyloss. Her likelihood of experiencing (and surviving) these depends, in part, on her social location, including race, income level, access to health care and safety, and citizenship status, among other factors.

Our political and legal systems are not set up in such a way as to recognize the highly varied natures of people's reproductive lives. This is clear evidence that the reproductive justice framework has not yet fully materialized in our institutions and social processes. And in the United States today, where "choice" is ever more precarious, reproductive choice approaches are centered at the expense of comprehensive solutions to improving *all* people's reproductive lives.

Parents whose babies die before, during, or after birth, especially when these babies die from preventable causes, deserve much more attention. Reproductive justice is not the only answer to these horrors and our collective shame. But it is our current best hope for creating a more equitable future for all.

S

STILLBIRTH

The word *stillborn*, or still-born, first appeared in English around 1597. Its meaning is "dead at birth," and it was sometimes written as *deadborn*, though few use that term today. The word *still*, in this usage, does not refer to the temporal; it refers to the corporeal. A stillborn baby is one without movement or life.

In the United States, stillbirth affects 1 percent of all pregnancies, resulting in approximately twenty-four thousand deaths per year. Unlike miscarriage, which occurs *before* the twentieth week of pregnancy, stillbirth occurs *after* the twentieth week. Early stillbirth happens between weeks twenty and twenty-seven; late stillbirth between weeks twenty-eight and thirty-six; and term stillbirth at or beyond thirty-seven weeks. These different stages have implications for how families choose to memorialize their babies. A stillborn baby at thirty-nine weeks looks very different than a stillborn baby at twenty weeks.

Oddly, stillbirth is not statistically folded into infant mortality, which registers the death of a baby within the first year of life. Yet stillbirth is as common as infant death, and perhaps even more so. After many years of the reverse, a 2015 article reported that stillbirths had *exceeded* infant deaths. One obstetrician quoted said, "We've made very little progress in reducing stillbirth in the U.S.," noting the report "should get people to focus" on stillbirth. Public health scholar Ruth Fretts writes, "Globally, the progress toward counting each birth and making each birth count has been achingly slow; this has been particularly true of stillbirths. In some ways, stillbirth is where SIDS was thirty years ago."

Such concerns are echoed in a 2016 article titled "Stillbirth Is More Common Than You Think—and We're Doing Little about It." Journalist Sarah Muthler, whose daughter died in the thirty-sixth week of pregnancy, writes, "Stillbirth might seem like a tragic relic from a bygone era, but it's relatively common. . . . And the United States has made some of the slowest progress of any country in reducing stillbirths."

Noting that there is no national system for reporting stillbirths, Muthler says, "About half of stillbirths are unexplained. . . . If we don't know more about why they happen, we won't be able to prevent them. Stillbirth research is far behind that for infant death. . . . Stillbirth has not received the same interest because the public underestimates its devastating toll and also tends to view it as inevitable [rather than preventable]."

Muthler points to a significant aspect of stillbirth: "Black women in particular are vulnerable: One of every 87 pregnancies for this group ends in stillbirth, a rate *double that of white women*." Among risk factors for stillbirth, the CDC recognizes "being Black" as a top risk; we might reframe this as living while Black and thus experiencing racism. These racial disparities persist even when Black women have access to prenatal care, just as they do with infant and maternal mortality.

The United States is not alone in this: a 2019 study of fifteen million pregnancies in the United Kingdom found a twofold risk for Black women over white women. Jenny Douglas, founder of the Black Women's Health and Wellbeing Research Network at the Open University, stated, "The alarming feature is the persistence of this gap, and the fact we do not know what the causes are because we're not doing the research. . . . It's not just stillbirth, in terms of maternal mortality black women in the UK are five times more likely to die in pregnancy and childbirth than white women."

The lack of research on stillbirth is, in a word, shocking—particularly given how widespread it is and how dangerous it can be for women's health. A clinician in the U.K. reports that "stillbirth is hugely under-researched compared with other areas of medicine, and even other areas of baby loss—there are around 3,000 published research papers on stillbirth, 30,000 on preeclampsia and nearer 90,000 on ovarian cancer." According to a press release accompanying a landmark 2016 study, "more than 2.6 million stillbirths continue to occur globally every year with very slow progress made to tackle this 'silent problem.'"

More recent research in the United States, published in *Obstetrics and Gynecology*, found that "nearly 1 in 17 women who deliver a stillbirth in California experience severe maternal morbidity. Furthermore, the risk of severe maternal morbidity was more than fourfold higher for women undergoing stillbirth delivery than live birth delivery." The CDC defines severe maternal morbidity through eighteen indicators, ranging from having an acute myocardial infarction to the need for being on ventilation.

One of the study's authors, anesthesiologist Alex Butwick, found the results "appalling," noting "the dearth of previous research is part of the same trend that's given the United States one of the highest maternal mortality rates in developed countries—that is, a trend of undervaluing pregnant people's lives." He suggested that care might look different for women presenting at hospitals with stillbirths versus live births, suggesting perhaps those with stillbirths may not receive the "overall package of care" other women receive. This might especially be the case if women are from more marginalized communities. Butwick says, "I cannot imagine what the impact must be emotionally and psychologically incurring a morbidity on top of a stillbirth delivery. . . . There's obviously systems issues here."

In 2016, the *Lancet* published the series "Ending Preventable Stillbirths." This "call to action" declared that "the global health community, country leaders, and individual women and men must recognize stillbirth and its consequences as largely preventable, collaborating more effectively and raising their collective voices to break the silence and reduce stigma and taboo." Noting that stillbirth reduction was *not* included in the United Nations Millennium Development Goals, the series found that globally, the highest risk is among poor families; stigma, fatalism, and taboo must be challenged; bereavement care and social support must be expanded; and there are direct, indirect, and intangible costs of stillbirth to individuals and to society. The series recommended an integrated approach using the U.N. Sustainable Development Goals (SDGs) and the Global Strategy for Women's, Children's, and Adolescents' Health.

Yet a 2015 study published in the *British Medical Journal* points to limitations of the SDGs, which do not actually mention stillbirth, instead suggesting the World Health Organization's "Every Newborn Action Plan" as a possible better way forward. The authors note, "There are ethical and pragmatic reasons to give similar value to stillbirths and neonatal deaths." They identify challenges in counting stillbirths, including that vital statistics often rely on self-reporting from women and their families. Stillbirth may in many contexts be seen in terms of maternal fault (the stigma referred to in the *Lancet* series) and such deaths may be undercounted. The authors of the *BMJ* article conclude, "Counting stillbirths in health metrics is long overdue."

But how does one count a stillbirth? Is it a miscarriage? A not-live birth? A fetal outcome? Does gestational age matter? When public health research and interventions rely so heavily on having adequate data, what does it mean for stillbirth (and for parents) that it remains undercounted? According to a 2009 study, "Stillbirths need to count. They constitute the majority of the world's perinatal deaths and yet, they are largely invisible. . . . Only a fraction [of stillbirths] are registered in any health information system." The authors provide a guide to counting stillbirths, including targets, techniques, and systems, illustrating how knowledge of reproductive loss is intimately caught up with health surveillance systems. They conclude by reiterating that, "with careful collection and analysis of these data, the numbers will speak for themselves."

One of the ways births and deaths come to count—to matter, especially for the bereaved—is that certificates are issued. But stillborn babies present a category challenge. Should a birth certificate be issued for a stillborn baby? Or a death certificate? In the past several years, a movement has been spearheaded by those who have lost babies to recognize stillbirth with customized birth certificates. As Sari Edber lamented in a *New York Times* article about stillbirth, "The experience of giving birth and death at the exact same time is something you don't understand unless you've gone through it. . . . The day before I was released from the hospital, the doctor came in with the paperwork for a fetal death certificate and said, 'I'm sorry, but this is the only document you'll receive.' In my heart, it didn't make sense."

Joanne Cacciatore, a social work scholar in Arizona who led efforts to register stillbirths in that state, remarked, "It's dignity and validation." She founded the MISS Foundation to advance legislation related to stillbirth loss. Arizona then became the first state to offer certificates for stillbirth. When Cacciatore received a death certificate in the mail after her daughter, Cheyenne, was stillborn, she says, "I literally dropped it. When I called and asked for my daughter's birth certificate, the woman asked how she died, and when I told her, she said I didn't have a baby, I had a fetus, and I couldn't get a birth certificate." She founded a support group and then an organization dedicated to the formal recognition of stillbirth.

Most states now have Certificates of Birth Resulting in Stillbirth—a move that many babylost parents and their supporters applaud. Yet the certificates make some uncomfortable, particularly in the political context of the United States, in which fetuses are often afforded priority over pregnant women. Though some women's health organizations support recognition of reproductive losses, others believe stillbirth certificates advance fetal personhood at the expense of women. Antiabortion opponents have suggested that aborted fetuses be issued death certificates, for example.

In 2007, at the height of the certificate movement, National Organization for Women president Kim Gandy stated, "There's no question in my mind that the anti-abortion crowd will look for some way to use this." On the other hand, a lawyer for Planned Parenthood remarked, "At a level of great abstraction, there are probably some people who worry that recognizing a nonviable fetus as a person would in some way be a seed that could sprout into a threat to abortion. . . . But I don't think we see it that way. We recognize the tragedy and loss of stillbirth, and as long as these laws are medically accurate, and the certificates are optional and commemorative, they're a way to recognize that loss."

Or, as Cacciatore says, "The bottom line is, if these women want it, it should be their choice."

But what if there is no choice?

Increasingly in the United States, miscarriage and stillbirth are being criminalized. Women who lose babies and are devastated by grief might find themselves instead on the receiving end of an arrest warrant. Attorney Lynn Paltrow, founder of National Advocates for Pregnant Women, has written that "hundreds of laws designed to prevent women from accessing abortion services . . . are being used to justify the arrests of pregnant women. . . . Law enforcement officials have disproportionately targeted low-income women and women of color for these arrests and equivalent deprivations of liberty."

In one case, a woman who was thirty-four weeks pregnant and involved in an automobile accident was charged with manslaughter after her baby died. Another woman fell down the stairs in her home and was charged with attempted feticide. In Arkansas, a woman who delivered a stillborn baby was arrested after she brought the remains to a hospital. She was charged with "concealing a birth"—a crime with roots in the seventeenth century—and "abuse of a corpse."

In 2006 in Mississippi, sixteen-year-old Rennie Gibbs was indicted for "depraved heart murder" after her daughter, Samiya, was stillborn. Though medical examiners determined cause of death to have been the umbilical cord wrapped around the baby's neck, an autopsy revealed traces of cocaine in Samiya's blood. Her death was ruled a homicide. Gibbs, who is Black, faced a sentence of twenty years to life in prison. In 2014, after she had been imprisoned, the murder charges against her were dropped.

Writing in the *Guardian* in 2014, filmmaker Sadhbh Walshe posed an interesting comparison to the Gibbs case:

> Like many women of her time, and many women since, Jacqueline Kennedy Onassis smoked while she was pregnant. Jackie-O had a history of troubled pregnancies—at least one miscarriage, a stillborn daughter and baby Patrick, who barely survived two days. Those losses caused the Kennedy family enormous pain. Now imagine if an overzealous prosecutor decided that Jackie's smoking had harmed the babies and indicted the First Lady on murder charges. Such a scenario might seem far-fetched; indeed, for a woman in the Kennedy demographic, it is. But for poor women—especially poor black women suspected of drug use who fail to carry babies to term—criminalization is already a popular sport.

Race and class matter in stillbirth just as they do in all reproductive experiences.

This was evident in early 2019 when a twenty-four-year-old Honduran woman detained in an Immigration and Customs Enforcement detention center in Texas delivered a stillborn son. She was twenty-seven weeks pregnant and had been complaining of abdominal pain. A joint statement from ICE and Customs and Border Protection noted, "Although for investigative and reporting purposes, a stillbirth is not considered an in-custody death, ICE and CPB officials are proactively disclosing the details of this tragic event to be transparent with Congress, the media and the public."

One commentator remarked that the policy "seems at odds with the stance taken by President Trump, who has made clear that the administration's position is that 'life begins at conception. . . . One is left to wonder why the delivery of a stillborn baby by a migrant woman in ICE custody was not considered an in-custody death."

Indeed.

Stillbirth is a devastating loss, one with significant, long-term emotional and physical consequences: "Stillbirth stories are tragic tales too incomprehensible for the average person to wrap their heads around." And yet such tales increasingly appear in news media, online, and in visual commemorations such as photographs and videos. For example, the CDC maintains an archive of babyloss stories from women who are ambassadors for Count the Kicks, a public awareness campaign. The volume *They Were Still Born* includes a range of stories, including Joanne Cacciatore's account of stillbirth as a "traumatic contradiction" in which "birth and death collide."

Babylost parents are speaking up about their losses, and it is imperative that we listen.

Jill Wieber Lens, a law professor, writes, "We weren't in the room for long before the nurse put the monitor on my belly and couldn't find Caleb's heartbeat. The nurse called in another nurse to help, and she couldn't find it either. . . . Finally, around 5 am, the on-call doctor officially informed us that my placenta had detached and Caleb had died. . . . It's been over 10 months since his birth and death, and I'm still adjusting to this new normal—of being a parent to a child who died."

Kristine Jepsen, who also lost her baby in utero, writes, "I would need to birth a baby that was [already] dead." Her words evoke the confusion and horror of the moment: "There was no escalation of contractions, no hands rubbing my back, no gritting of teeth or wailing, knees apart. Instead, I jolted awake from drug-laced sleep directly into late labor, curled on my left side, clinging to the bedrail."

Lucy Biggs had "no words" for her loss, until she did: "Before we knew stillbirth, we too had no words for it. We knew it was possible. It had happened to people we knew. We were afraid of it. How could we find the right words? But as we took the weight of our baby into our arms, his beauty overwhelmed us and the fear that we felt fell silent. They say there are no words for stillbirth, because your baby has died, but there are many words for stillbirth, because your baby was here."

In the *New York Times*, there is a feature from 2015 called "Stillbirth: Your Stories," with accounts of hope and joy upended by loss and suffering. This archive, so painful to read, is both a dataset and also an accidental "how to" guide for surviving babyloss. In it, Megan writes, "Ever since losing my daughter when I was just 24 weeks pregnant, I've dreamed of becoming a superhero. When I read or hear about another family that's experienced a stillbirth, I want to don a disguise and fly to the mother's side. I want to guard her front door, answer her phone, manage her Facebook account, intercept her text messages, anything that can shield her from the well-meaning, but often thoughtless behavior of people."

A common thread across many such stories is the desire to memorialize the stillborn baby. Historically, it was often the case that women were not allowed to see or touch their dead infants—stillborn babies were whisked away to protect women's tender feelings. Yet today, in much of the United States, it has become routine for babylost parents to hold their child, spend time with her, and even in some cases take him home. Visual images of stillborn babies now appear in private and public collections, though such images also have a history, especially during the Victorian era when memento mori (memorabilia of the dead) were desirable.

Photographer Margaret Godel, writing in the *Journal of Visual Studies*, suggests that "contemporary stillbirth photographs . . . allow mothers and fathers to define themselves as parents [and] help to maintain the memory of the baby, continue the bond between the baby and the family and support this vulnerable social group."

Now I Lay Me Down to Sleep (NILMDTS), a nonprofit organization in Colorado, offers free photographic services to babylost parents. It was inspired by the death of Maddux Achilles Haggard in 2005. His mother, Cheryl, wanted to memorialize him with professional images rather than those taken with her own camera. She recalls, "Maddux deserved that space on our wall. I could not comfortably hang the pictures I had taken. The color images bring back the reality of that day. I wanted heirloom portraits as a way to remember and honor our son."

A story in *Narratively* reveals that "NILMDTS photographers typically spend between thirty minutes to an hour in their sessions. In cramped, busy hospital rooms, they balance professionalism and intimacy while assisting grieving families." One mother, who initially did not want photographic images, was persuaded by a crying nurse. She has no memory of the photographer, but she is now grateful: "Even now I cherish [the photos] and I can remember details that have started to fade with time. . . . I'm so thankful I had the photos done; they're all I have."

A Chicago-based medical photographer, Todd Hochberg, started his own service, Touching Souls, in 1997 to provide bereavement images. He considers himself a documentarian: "I thought I would do what I had seen in the Victorian photographs—portraits or photos with family. . . . But what I discovered was this incredible story of love and loss."

Stillbirth images are not limited to still photography—videography is also popular. A study in *OMEGA—Journal of Death and Dying*, researched fifty YouTube videos published since 2008. The authors found that 70 percent were posted by babylost mothers, with an average length of over five minutes and a mean viewing history of 2,429,576 views. They also, according to the investigators, follow a script: video footage followed by black and white still photos, background music, and religious references. They suggest that "the videos published on YouTube assume the function of an introduction to society—as baptism was once ago—a reception, a presentation of the child to the family and to the whole world."

As one article reports, "Today, parents are coming out of the shadows online, using the virtual world to evidence the reality of their children. They post photos of babies with blue lips and mournful family portraits on Facebook or Instagram under hashtags like #bornsleeping, #stillbornstilloved, #stillbornbutstillborn. They join groups for 'loss moms' or read magazines like *Still Standing*, devoted to exploring the feelings associated with stillbirth. They participate in documentaries like 'Don't Talk About the Baby,' breaking the silence surrounding stillbirth and miscarriage, discussing loss openly."

The article follows Aimee, whose husband, Tyson, began filming their birth story before they realized it would instead be a death story: "The camera shuts off and comes on again. Aimee is in her hospital gown crying. Beckett is dead. They keep filming, not sure at the time if it will be just for them or for a video blog, knowing as painful as the moment is, it needs to be remembered. Though Beckett died of a stroke in utero, Aimee will still have to give birth to him." Aimee's online stillbirth video is her most popular.

Memento mori are today reincarnated for the digital age. Or, as the French authors of the *OMEGA* study put it, "Our era seems to have become a technological Pangea, a place where everything is reachable and shared, including the grief." The title of their article? "Angels in the Clouds."

SURVIVAL

Survival of the fittest.

Who hasn't heard (or used) this pithy phrase? It was coined not by Charles Darwin—as often mistakenly assumed—but by English philosopher Herbert Spencer in 1864. Having read Darwin's *On the Origin of the Species: Or the Preservation of Favoured Races in the Struggle for Life*, Spencer wrote in his own *Principles of Biology*, "Rejecting metaphor we see that the process called Natural Selection is literally a survival of the fittest."

For Darwin, the naturalist and biologist, natural selection was understood largely if not exclusively in reproductive terms. He wrote, "I should premise that I use the term Struggle for Existence in a large and metaphorical sense, including dependence of one being or another, and including (which is more important) not only the life of the individual, but success in leaving progeny."

Survival of the fittest has had a long shelf life.

For one thing, it formed the ideological foundation of Social Darwinism, which framed social inequality in terms of natural selection. This perspective, heavily inspired by Victorian-era statistician and scientist Sir Francis Galton, helped usher in the late nineteenth- and early twentieth-century eugenics movement, a broad effort to foster reproduction of the "fit" and to discourage reproduction of the "unfit." Practices with roots in eugenics include compulsory sterilization, Nazism including euthanasia, unethical human experimentation, racial segregation, and genocide.

Though "eugenics" as a term is no longer stylish—it fell out of favor after revelations of Hitler's atrocities in World War II—eugenic ideas are alive and well. We see them constantly and vividly in racist population control practices, public policies that breed inequality, and segregated reproductive health care in the United States and beyond. For example, the urging of young women of color to use LARCs (long-acting [supposedly] reversible contraceptives) is an especially eugenic practice as their reproductive futures may be placed in jeopardy.

The persistent belief that some people are better—more "fit"—than others and thus should be encouraged to reproduce is potent. It is also dangerous and deadly for those deemed "unfit."

Survival is different from being alive; one is a status (I am alive), whereas the other is an action (I am surviving). Survival is also a project, freighted with emotion and the work of self-care. Sometimes, we must survive others, including our children and parents and other loved ones. There is a legal sense in which survival matters too, especially where economic resources, such as estates, are involved.

Survival is not to be confused with viability; a viable fetus is that which could potentially live outside the womb with the right set of conditions, technologies, and politics. Viability is a chronobiological artifact, a time stamp, one with significant influence as definitions of fetal viability undergird *Roe v. Wade* and prenatal care, impacting reproductive autonomy.

Viability may shape abortion debates and limit reproductive options, but it offers no guarantee of fetal or infant survival. It is a technical term, though one heavily fraught politically.

In the #MeToo moment in which gender-based violence is very much on the public radar, survival has taken on an entirely different valence. To be a survivor—and not just a victim—means that one has come through the gauntlet of assault and out the other side. Damaged, perhaps, but alive. And statistically speaking, "one" here is most likely to be a female "one."

Survival, then, is intimately braided with gender, trauma, and risk, and with having to navigate the natural and man-made hazards of our time.

To survive, in many contexts, is a badge of courage and resilience. It is fortitude embodied. One is alive but also living. Continuing to live. Living on. Living through.

Several fields—economics, public health, sociology, medicine—use *survival analysis* to statistically predict when an event or series of events will happen. For example, when will deaths from a certain disease happen? (An especially urgent question during a pandemic.) Such prognostic data are useful for clinicians, insurers, and lawyers, especially when attributing blame for adverse outcomes.

Survival analysis is one of the few places in the scientific literature where "survival" is discussed in relation to infant mortality. (Indeed, a Google search of "infant survival" first displays information about infant self-rescue and swimming lessons.) This, to me, is both fascinating and puzzling. So much ink has been spilled on infant mortality and infant death for more than a century. Yet relatively few interventions focus on *survival* itself.

I wonder: How might our efforts to reduce infant mortality look if we centered *infant survival* rather than death? What if clinical research was focused on *fostering* infant survival rather than (or in addition to) *preventing* premature death? How would this slight adjustment of the lens affect our understanding and responses to "excess" infant death? Could it clarify our understanding of preventable death, for whom, and under what conditions? Can peering at infant death through a survival lens bring into sharper focus the eugenics principles still operating, quietly and in the shadows, in contemporary reproductive politics?

I want to suggest that thinking with and through survival might open up new and better ways to see and ameliorate infant death. We can start by asking, who gets to survive, and how? That is, what accumulation of privilege, resources, and care factors into the more favorable survival rates for white babies? What kinds of health care practices facilitate better survival rates, and for whom? What should we stop doing that currently impedes survival for some groups of women and babies?

Survival implies continuity. The goal should be not only to improve birth outcomes but also to foster survival *across the life course*. It is not enough to "fix" the sky-high infant mortality rates through preconception care schemes and other measures, although it would be excellent to reduce the rates without undue prying into people's lives. Doing so would translate into less grief and pain for babylost moms and dads, though this is not easily measurable.

But what about *after* the first year of life? Surely, we want all children to survive not only their first year but their entire childhood and adolescence. Many children do, of course; but too many children do not. That those children are more likely to be Black and brown should trouble us profoundly.

Stopping premature death is crisis management, the jurisdiction of doctors and public health experts. Fostering survival, on the other hand, is a collective strategy or community issue, within the jurisdiction of us all. If infant mortality is an epidemiological problem to be fixed, infant survival conjures hope and planning for the future.

Thinking in terms of survival allows us to make connections to other forms of survival: cultural survival, planetary survival, economic survival, social survival. The antithesis of social death. This expands our focus from intervening primarily in and on pregnant bodies—as in preconception, prenatal, and childbirth care—to different kinds of interventions, such as reversing the climate crisis and supporting the vitality and sustainability of all communities, most especially those of the marginalized and at-risk.

A survival lens encourages us to consider premature infant death in Black, Indigenous, and poor communities alongside other premature death in these spaces. The crisis of Missing and Murdered Indigenous Women (MMIW), lethal police violence in Black communities, detention of migrants including children in filthy, crowded cages—these must be addressed along with the shame of allowing too many babies to die from preventable causes. This is the shame of not caring enough.

Evolution has long been interpreted as survival of the fittest. Equal opportunity survival seems a better goal today.

T

On July 24, 2018, an orca known as J-35 birthed a calf in the Salish Sea: "A whale watch operator, staring through binoculars, had caught sight of a healthy calf swimming beside its mother—a rare beacon for a population that had not seen a healthy infant in years."

Sadly, the baby cetacean did not survive.

Orcas are vulnerable to human harm, including pollutants, ocean noise, ship traffic, habitat loss, a dwindling food supply, and capture for entertainment.

The baby's death might have been the end of the story, since nature unfolds all around us and often humans are not present to witness it. Even, perhaps especially, when we are the causal agents.

But J-35, nicknamed Tahlequah, could not let go of her dead calf. She carried her baby for nearly three weeks, across one thousand miles of ocean, exhausting herself and astonishing the people who study whales who had never seen anything quite like it: "She was forever picking up the body as it sank, hoisting it out of the water to take a breath, and repeating."

It was clear to anyone paying attention, to anyone with a heart, that Tahlequah was mourning her loss, grieving deeply just as human mothers do.

Some went so far as to call J-35's behavior a "tour of grief."

One expert said, "You cannot interpret it any other way."

The images of Tahlequah and her dead baby were difficult to witness. A beautiful, graceful, sad creature carrying her slowly disintegrating, inert infant whose body parts—fin, nose, tail—would occasionally surface, to be photographed and shared by those watching and studying.

Babylost women were watching too, and they were grieving in whale song.

Cori McKenzie of Fort Wayne, Indiana, said, "Our middle daughter was stillborn six years ago. . . . I think every baby-loss parent I have ever met relates to Tahlequah. We all wish that our society and culture would recognize how deep this loss is felt and how it changes you down to your core."

A babylost friend wrote on my Facebook page, "This story wrecked me."

"SEE ME"
Tahlequah J35   Lori Christopher

Tahlequah. Photo credit: Lori Christopher.

Other people wrote poems, built shrines, and crafted stunning artwork.

Tahlequah's loss was achingly individual, but the "morbid weight" of her calf was also a tremendous loss to the J-pod. As of this writing, there are just seventy-four members left in the Southern Resident killer whale population, a thirty-year low, and their reproductive prospects are grim.

So dire is the situation that members of the Lummi Nation, whose culture has long been intimately intertwined with that of the orca, have begun to hand-feed the declining pod buckets of Chinook salmon. Sle-lh'x elten Jeremiah Julius, elected chair of the 6,500-member nation, remarked, "The bottom line is the Salish Sea and the whales and the tribes need more salmon. We're at the point now where we don't have much time. We are possibly the last generation that can do anything about it."

The death of Tahlequah's calf figured heavily into the tribe's decision to feed the whales directly, though some researchers believe the orca cannot be saved "one whale at a time." Still, master totem pole carver Tse-Sealth Jewell James, who lost two children, conjured Tahlequah's suffering in validating the tribe's efforts: "She showed the world, 'Look at what you did to my baby.' I look at the whale, and I say, 'Yeah, I understand. You can't just let them go."

Like the Lummi, many observers saw in the whale's behavior a political statement broadcasting their own fate: "It's terribly upsetting and yet at the same time uplifting. I think the orca family is doing this to bring attention to their plight. They are very intelligent. I hope humans care enough and find a way to restore their natural wild salmon resource. It's the right thing to do."

Ken Balcomb, founder of the Center for Whale Research, stated, "She's telling the story far better than I can that these whales are in trouble. It's a message. These are pretty amazing animals. They know they're being watched, they know what's going on and they know that there's not enough food. And maybe they know that we have something to do with it."

Tahlequah may have been trying to send a message to those watching. Certainly, those whose life's work it is to study and save whales from human harm, as well as the Lummi people whose culture is braided with theirs, believe this to be true.

There is little doubt that Tahlequah's behavior was an arduous, shattering display of mourning, and of motherhood: "The strength it takes for a killer whale to bear the weight of even a lifeless baby for a short time while battling currents and waves, and having to continually surface to breathe is remarkable."

Then, on September 23, 2020, good news: the Center for Whale Research announced that Tahlequah had again given birth, to J-57, a male calf. Researchers estimate his birthdate was around September 4, noting that "he was photographed rolling, spyhopping, and swimming alongside his mother, who was actively foraging for food."

Regarding J-57's birth, British Columbia-based wildlife photographer Alena Ebeling-Schuld remarked, "Tahlequah in particular means a great deal to me. Her tour of grief was beyond impactful, telling the story to a wide audience not only of the plight of the Southern Residents, but also of the complexity of animals' emotions—something humans are so quick to disregard."

While researchers and whale-lovers alike rejoiced in the calf's birth, the center soberly reminded supporters of the high fatality rate for young whales: "Regrettably, with the whales having so much nutritional stress in recent years, a large percentage of pregnancies fail, and there is about a 40% mortality for young calves. We hope this calf is a success story."

Grief, love, and hope, intertwined.

TRAUMA

Earthquakes. Hurricanes. Floods. Tsunamis.

The Twin Towers collapsing. School shootings. Subway bombs.

A train, derailed. A minivan, crushed. A plane, falling.

Vietnam. Sarajevo. Rwanda. Police killings.

Rape. Murder. Suicide. Torture.

These are the many kinds of events that most of us tend to think of as *traumatic*. They are both large-scale and intimate, local and global, violent and shocking, and they evoke horror and disbelief.

Why me? Why us? Why now? Why?

These events may bring (some) people together as survivors are attended to, communities are rebuilt, and bodies and psyches are healed. But they may drive people apart too, as certain events reproduce conflict, terror, and social schisms. This especially may be the case when catastrophic events become opportunities for political intervention, as happened after 9/11 when President Bush used the occasion to advance anti-Muslim propaganda, warfare, and surveillance activities that violated many people's civil liberties.

There are some traumas, such as the Holocaust, that most everyone knows about.

Still other traumas are ignored, forgotten, erased, or buried.

Like babyloss.

The death of a child may be devastating, but it is rarely a spectacle worthy of headlines or declarations of war or marbled memorials in urban parks. There are few opportunities for public mourning or memorialization of babyloss, which is perceived by many others—though assuredly those not suffering—as a relatively minor trauma in the broad scheme of things. After all, a dead baby is not a crashed plane, a rubbled building, an entire town swept away by floods, a genocide, or climate collapse.

Babyloss is but one small death among so many. An intimate, often private occasion for grief.

Yet this is the problem with often unrecognized or at least unacknowledged trauma. Understanding disruptive events as "trauma"—both a diagnostic and political category—does not get us any closer to understanding why some events are deemed "traumatic" and others are not. Why some people are allowed and expected to mourn and others are not. Why some deaths are memorialized across an entire city block and others barely garner a tiny gravestone if any at all. Why the psychological literature focuses on some causes of post-traumatic stress disorder (PTSD) while overlooking others. Why so much suffering is silent, clandestine, unseen. Counted statistically, perhaps, but not witnessed *as loss or harm*.

Trauma is, generally speaking, a somatic and emotional response to a shocking event. It is a disruption in the normal order of things, and it is often unspeakable. That is, we are so impacted by the event that we are unable to articulate what has happened. People who suffer trauma often lose the capacity for speech; their memories may be fuzzy; they become confused, disoriented, unclear about the details. They may experience bodily symptoms, such as nausea, headaches, stomach cramps, joint pain. They may develop psychological distress in the form of anxiety, depression, flashbacks, sleeplessness, and suicidal thoughts.

As experts—and survivors—have noted, trauma lives on in the mind and the body, often long after the initial event has passed, too often in the quiet hours of the night. The "post" in PTSD signifies a temporal component to suffering; traumatized people speak of "before" and "after." For some survivors, although trauma can be "managed" through therapy and other tools, it is never-ending. I have come to speak of trauma as a trajectory rather than an event, an identity rather than a condition, a lived experience rather than something that happened to you in the past. Trauma is an emotional shapeshifter, but it is no less real for its many facets and forms.

The half-life of trauma can be a lifetime.

One babylost woman writes, "Since my daughter, Blake, died, I've heard the word 'trauma' a lot. . . . I guess I reserved that word for something horrific; I hadn't considered trauma when it came to my family. I've come to realize, as parents who lost a child, we have been through so much trauma and it pops up all the time." Describing her panicked reaction when her three-month-old developed a tummy bug, she admits, "I constantly worry about my two living daughters and my husband. Not in the typical way that a mother worries, it's worry on steroids. Many mothers in the loss community tell me they are overcome with anxiety too. . . . I'm trying to function while living with a broken heart and a truckload of trauma."

Priscilla Blossom shares a similar story, narrating how PTSD stemming from the death of her daughter manifested during her next pregnancy. Her anxiety skyrocketed. She writes, "I abused Google searches, fixating over the cesarean rates at all my local hospitals, my fears growing as I imagined the same loss of control I'd experienced during my first labor. All I could think about was how awful my daughter's birth had been—the way the doctors pulled her away before I even got a chance to touch her or see her face. How I never got to hold her while she was alive." It did not help that physicians were judgmental about Priscilla's choices during both pregnancies. She writes, "Once at the hospital, with my husband and doula at either side and a visibly angry doctor between my legs, I gave birth to my rainbow baby."

Arica Carlson describes "living in a swamp" after babyloss, with panic attacks triggered by other women's crying babies and terrible, haunting nightmares. She writes, "One dream I was stepping out of a car when my feet were gnawed off by a wild animal. Another, all my hens were murdered, and I was finding their bodies in the morning. I saw birds take flight and crush their skulls into windows; I saw animals and people being struck by cars and trains." She suffered for more than a year after her son's death, until she was diagnosed with PTSD. She writes, "I began treatment and began to heal. But while I was living it, I had no idea what to call it. Now I know. PTSD comes in all forms, just as trauma comes in all ways. You don't have to be a war veteran or a rape victim to have experienced trauma. Losing a loved one can be traumatic, and it can leave a lasting mental mark."

Trauma offers a new vocabulary for babylost parents to help make sense of their experiences. Understanding there is a diagnosis for their pain and suffering can bring some relief and open a pathway toward healing. But only recently has science come to understand the scope of PTSD among the babylost. *Haaretz* published the results of a study in 2017 that found that "more than a third of the women who took part in the study were found to be suffering from full-blown PTSD." The study's author, Danny Horesh of Bar-Ilan University, an expert in trauma among soldiers, remarked, "To someone who researches trauma, a 32.7 percent rate of full PTSD is a horrifying figure. Percentage-wise, it's akin to soldiers who have just returned from the worst battle. The hardest traumas of all."

When Horesh began the study, there had been very little research in Israel, or anywhere else, on the trauma of women's experiences of reproductive loss. Nightmares and flashbacks were among the most common symptoms found among women in his study: "This didn't surprise us very much, considering the 'graphic' nature of the trauma of pregnancy loss. It may be called a 'still' birth, but when you really look at it, a lot of the women in our study experienced sights and sounds and smells and sensations of a traumatic nature." He believes reproductive loss has been understudied because "this kind of trauma is 'not heroic'. . . . Israel lives on heroic traumas. And I'm not belittling that. It is truly the tragedy of our country. But it doesn't justify the lack of attention to other traumas."

"Trauma" does appear in research on infant mortality; however, it is usually present in the context of the traumatic deaths of infants. For example, abusive head trauma (shaken baby syndrome) is the leading cause of death in child abuse cases in the United States, with most victims under one year old. Babies may also die from harm inflicted during birth, either accidentally or through negligence. Such iatrogenic ("brought forth by the healer") injuries have spawned a thriving wrongful death industry in the legal profession. Fetuses may die, too, when their mothers are injured through accidents, domestic violence, illness, or other assaults. We are thus accustomed to talking about "trauma" in the context of fetal and infant death.

We are much less accustomed to considering *women's experiences of loss as traumatic*. Consider women's lives a century ago in the United States, when there were multiple pregnancies with few living children. In such a context, the death of each baby may have been routine, expected, and thus barely a disruption of the normal order of things. (Though no less sad.) With the advent of "modern medicine," smaller families (for some; this is culturally specific), and pregnancy as a site of intervention, each pregnancy—each baby—has become that much rarer and more precious. This is not to suggest that historically women did not grieve, nor that dead babies were unmourned. I know that in my own family, in earlier generations, babyloss was heavily grieved.

It is to suggest that trauma denotes a particular kind of event; an interruption in the expected. And what is more expected, when one is willfully and happily pregnant, than a baby? It is right there in the name: *expecting*. (Consider the popular book *What to Expect When You're Expecting*.) To have that cherished expectation upended is to experience a most profound sense of shock and dismay. Babyloss is, for the most part, *un*expected; losing a baby before or after birth undoes the existential, embodied state of expectation. Babylost people are no longer expecting; they are hollowed out, undone, have lost their expectations.

The word *trauma* comes from the Greek; it means "wound."

A wound. To wound. Wounded. Wounding.

How are so many babylost parents among the walking wounded, grieving their missing children, and yet we fail to see them? How might we enliven our vocabularies of concern and action to acknowledge their invisible losses? And how might we ensure that maternal and paternal suffering is part of the public agenda as well as ostensibly more "heroic" losses, such as those sustained in warfare?

Babylost parents may be haunted, but they are not themselves ghosts. They are simply missing from the public conversation about what it means to be traumatized.

It is time to bring them in.

U

URGENCY

I began collecting data for this project around 2004, though I've been researching reproductive health since the late 1980s. This means that for several decades, I have amassed thousands of articles, news stories, and interviews that point to the urgency of the appallingly high United States infant mortality rate, alongside ongoing (and intensifying) threats to reproductive health and justice. Headlines scream distress with their near-hysterical attention to climbing infant mortality rates, punctuated occasionally by headlines expressing profound relief when the rates drop.

Of course, in most of these stories, infant mortality is merely a proxy for overall national health, as it is in governmental and public health frameworks. Few stories in mainstream media center dead babies themselves or lived experiences of babyloss. The rate *is* the story—and so, any urgency called forth by bold headlines focused on escalating rates tends to dissipate once these rates recede. There has long been significant movement of rates across time and place. But despite predictable panic when rates increase, with terms such as *spike, troubling, crisis,* and *alarming* peppering the headlines, there has been no serious and *consistent* sense of urgency about the problem of dead babies.

A 1910 article in *Publications of the American Statistical Association* was titled "A Statistical Survey of Infant Mortality's Urgent Call for Action." In 2018, UNICEF issued a report titled "Every Child Alive: The Urgent Need to End Newborn Deaths." In between these declarations of urgency, *across more than a century,* untold millions of babies around the world died before reaching their first birthdays. And with the exception of the Sheppard-Towner Act in place from 1921 to 1929, there has been no federal effort in the United States to reduce infant mortality rates. It would seem that urgency is more a Pavlovian rhetorical response triggered by large, frightening numbers than provocative of a measured, long-term strategy for saving lives.

Something *urgent* is, according to the dictionary, acute, grave, pressing, dire, desperate, critical, drastic, serious, and vital. One could argue, as I do in this book, that high rates of preventable infant death constitute a social, political, and public health emergency. Indeed, a *disaster* of epic proportions. Yet the achievement of lower rates, no matter how fleeting, diverts attention from the persistent, the structural, the epidemic, the ubiquitous. We stop noticing—at least until the next panicked headline about climbing rates.

But urgency should require immediate action, not complacency. It should require that problems become priorities, that solutions are sought, that resources are mobilized. Who in the United States today considers chronic, daily infant mortality an urgent problem? Do we not care enough to act because babies dying from preventable causes of death are predominantly Black, Indigenous, and poor? Do we not care enough to act because the suffering of babylost parents is largely private, invisible, and individualized? Do we not care enough to act as a nation because we believe infant death to be a personal concern, the province of singular, isolated, possibly faulty women rather than whole communities?

What would it take to make all people across the United States—many of them deeply committed to prenatal life, as evidenced by their reported politics on abortion—believe in the urgency of infant death *as a social problem*?

In 1932, when Charles Augustus Lindbergh Jr.—the infamous Lindbergh Baby—was kidnapped from his crib, it was a national sensation, the "crime of the century," with headlines large and above the fold. When the boy's mutilated body was later found in the woods, many across the nation grieved. His death led very quickly to the passage of the Federal Kidnapping Act, known more parochially as the Lindbergh Law.

Just one dead white and privileged baby, with an aviator father and writerly mother. And his murder, after a desperate and highly publicized hunt, led to lasting political change.

In the United States, since I began this project, *hundreds of thousands* of babies have died, bringing grief and sorrow to many babylost parents and their families, but alas very little public recognition. Communities, especially Black and Indigenous and poor and rural communities, are being decimated by preventable deaths, and not only among infants. Mothers are dying in these communities too. And so are fathers and brothers and sisters and aunts and uncles and neighbors. At staggering rates, with devastating consequences, and largely outside public view.

You might ask, as I do frequently, *Where is the urgency?*

Perhaps it is in Baltimore, Maryland, where six infants died in as many weeks in December 2018 and January 2019. The assistant commissioner of the local Bureau of Maternal and Child Health remarked, "We watch the trends really carefully and we know when there are any deaths. It obviously alarmed us and we wanted to do something immediately."

The city quickly expanded its B'More for Healthy Babies campaign focused on safe sleep practices. A senior program officer connected to the John Hopkins Center for Communication Programs, which helped the campaign with its messaging, noted, "The key to the campaign is the consistency. . . . The more often people hear a message consistently the better. And if they are hearing it from an established and trusted source, then that helps make the message more powerful."

The campaign also created a new hashtag, #NotOneMoreBaltimore, to further distribute its messaging and impact.

A sense of urgency may also be found in Milwaukee, Wisconsin, where "unacceptably high" infant death rates prompted swift municipal intervention. The Black infant mortality rate in Milwaukee is more than three times the rate for white infants—"one of the largest health disparities in the country." The Wisconsin Department of Health Services reports that "7.9 percent of African American women received either no prenatal care or no third trimester care."

A coalition of Milwaukee organizations received a five-million-dollar, five-year grant in 2019 to address the crisis. Firmly on board are the city's doulas, many of them African American. The doulas launched the "It Takes a Village: Community Baby Shower and Resource Fair" during World Doula Week. A related program compensates one hundred doulas for their work in zip code 53206, which in 2016 had an appalling infant mortality rate of *15.1 deaths per 1,000 live births*. The city's health commissioner commented about the program, "A doula is pretty much like a wing-woman."

Baltimore and Milwaukee offer two encouraging, if localized, examples of urgency in action. But so much more is needed or too many babies, and mothers, will continue to die from preventable causes.

History offers us this lesson:

In 1921, the infant mortality rate in the United States was a staggering seventy-six deaths per one thousand live births. In response, with persuasive advocacy from the newly formed Women's Joint Congressional Committee and the Children's Bureau, Congress passed the Sheppard-Towner Act. The government's first major foray into social security legislation, the act led to the creation of *more than three thousand* child and maternal health centers across the country, as well as educational materials, funding for prenatal care, and midwifery licensure. Along with helping to decrease infant mortality rates, the act also, unfortunately, contributed to the medicalization of pregnancy and birth and to the professionalization of midwifery and the elimination of traditional practitioners, mostly African American women, in the U.S. South.

The Sheppard-Towner Act was imperfect. But it was something. By the end of the 1920s, the infant mortality rate had dropped to 67.6 deaths per 1,000 births, and it continued to drop for the next many decades.

And yet, the United States infant mortality rate today is well above the rates of other Global North nations. Death rates for African American, Indigenous, and poor mothers and babies are embarrassingly, tragically high. Indeed, as Deirdre Cooper Owens and Sharla M. Fett write, "Although infant death rates overall have plummeted since the 19th century, the disparity between Black and White infant deaths today is actually greater than it was under antebellum slavery."

The situation is, in a word, urgent.

So where *is* the Sheppard-Towner Act for the twenty-first century?

Who cares enough to "save the babies"?

V

Vulnerability

Giraffe babies, called calves, can stand and walk on their spindly legs within thirty minutes of birth; they can run within the first day. Lizards have been known to "deposit their eggs, cover them, immediately forget they did that and move along." Baby elephants gestate for nearly two years, and yet—despite weighing up to two hundred pounds!—they too can stand and walk shortly after birth, though they may wobble a bit.

In the nonhuman animal world, locomotion and independence are critical to survival. Giraffe and elephant calves need to be able to dash quickly when predators (including humans) are near.

Human babies, by contrast, are far less independent and mobile.

The term *altricial* refers to young that require more care and have limited mobility. In contrast, *precocial* refers to young who can locomote right out of the gate, or rather, the womb or egg. Humans are the best-known (to us) altricial species, but many other mammals (e.g., dogs, cats, marsupials, rodents), birds, and insects also need care beyond birth.

Our cousins the chimpanzees are somewhere in-between on the altricial-precocial spectrum. Chimpanzee babies are less helpless than human babies—for example, they can cling to their mothers, which seems key to their survival. But like gorillas and humans, infant chimps require a great deal of hands-on care.

Being altricial necessarily leads to vulnerability in the big bad predatory world. In humans, this quality has been described in terms of "puppy-like floppiness and general uselessness." As neonates we are, in a word, helpless.

An article in *Scientific American* is aptly titled "Why Humans Give Birth to Helpless Babies." Reasons range from natural selection to maternal pelvis size, from birth timing to maternal metabolic rate.

One of the most astonishing things about human newborns, especially for brand-new parents, is just how utterly fragile and dependent they are. I carried my babies as if they were precious cargo. I was terrified to drop them, sit on them, or accidentally let go of them in the bathtub. Yet when my first baby was about five months old, she flipped herself right out of her carrier, which I had set down on the kitchen table, and onto the floor, headfirst. I was sure I had broken her and sobbed with relief when I realized she was okay.

Human babies' vulnerability is tied inextricably to their survival. Without abundant and appropriate care, they will die. Left unattended, injury and even death may well be inescapable. The word vulnerability stems from the Latin *vulnus*, "wound," and *vulnerare*, "to wound." This led to the use of "vulnerable" in the early seventeenth century. To be vulnerable is to be susceptible to harm, and also to be in danger, at risk, or unsafe. And to be in need of protection and care.

Drawing on the work of naturalist Charles Darwin and zoologist Konrad Lorenz, noted paleontologist and evolutionary biologist Stephen Jay Gould posited a theory of *neoteny*, or juvenilization, in which adults are attracted to juvenile or baby-like features as an evolutionary strategy. That is, cute babies are read as helpless and vulnerable and thus make us want to protect them. Theoretically, through our protecting them, they survive, and we thus perpetuate the species.

In the words of science writer Natalie Angier, "Cute cues are those that indicate extreme youth, vulnerability, harmlessness and need. . . . As a species whose youngest members are so pathetically helpless they can't lift their heads to suckle without adult supervision, human beings must be wired to respond quickly and gamely to any and all signs of infantile desire." Angier suggests the cuteness bar for humans is set quite low and includes not just our own babies but anything resembling one, including "the young of virtually every mammalian species, fuzzy-headed birds like Japanese cranes, woolly bear caterpillars," and so on.

Despite cuteness and its presumed evolutionary advantages, we do not always protect human newborns. In fact, we may accelerate their demise through practices that work against their survival and flourishing. Undernourishing female offspring as a means of "passive" infanticide, racism, abuse, and antichild policies are some examples.

I have been writing of vulnerability thus far as if it is solely an individual, biological characteristic of newborns. But there is also an important social component to their helplessness. The terms *social vulnerability* and *structural vulnerability* allow us to better understand the conditions under which we nurture some newborns while facilitating the premature deaths of others.

Social vulnerability refers to the idea that some people or groups are more susceptible to risk and harm than others, in part because they are (made to be) less resilient. Structural forces, such as chronic racism and poverty, render certain populations more vulnerable to disaster, illness, and premature death. While individuals may overcome systemic risks, the social, political, and economic nature of vulnerability keeps whole communities in harm's way. The *collective vulnerability hypothesis* describes the fragility of social connections among groups of people who suffer repeated traumatic events or violence and associated loss of resilience.

In fact, the U.S. Center for Disease Control and Prevention (CDC) maintains a *social vulnerability index* (SVI), which attempts to quantify community resilience when confronted with external stresses, such as disease outbreaks or natural disasters. The SVI uses census data to assist local governments in identifying communities that may be particularly at risk.

Structural vulnerability, like social vulnerability, focuses on systems. Drawing from anthropologist and physician Paul Farmer's work on structural violence, which addressed the impact of policies, institutional forces, and inequalities on human health, structural vulnerability is kin to the social determinants of health perspective. Here, various demographic factors and social arrangements, including racism, can influence health outcomes.

The Center for American Progress identifies ways that structural vulnerability negatively impacts maternal and infant health. Recognizing that Black maternal and infant death rates far surpass those of whites, the authors write, "Disparities in maternal and infant mortality are rooted in racism. Structural racism in health care and social service delivery means that African American women often receive poorer quality care than white women . . . it bears mentioning that significant underinvestment in family support and health care programs contribute to the alarming trends in maternal and infant health."

Vulnerability theories tell us that some people get sicker and die quicker because of their social locations. They are highly vulnerable due to conditions and arrangements that impede their survival. In the United States, such people tend to be nonwhite, poor, undocumented, and near the beginning and end of life. African Americans are especially vulnerable to premature debility and death. Babies and the elderly are also at significant risk, in large part because their biological fragility and social vulnerability intersect.

It is not enough, as some theorists argue, simply to be aware of structural vulnerability. Clinical and public health practices must be thoroughly transformed, based on the needs of the most vulnerable. It is also not enough to recognize that some groups are more vulnerable than others. We must shift resources and priorities so that entire communities are not decimated by disasters, such as hurricanes and disease outbreaks or the chronic loss of infants and other family members to *preventable* premature deaths.

A major problem with structures is that they are obdurate. Social change is possible, but it is challenging to transform institutions and societies. The United States is built on interlocking legacies of chattel slavery, genocide, settler colonialism, white supremacy, and patriarchy. These are woven into everything, from our for-profit health care system to a profound disregard for Black and brown lives and for women's bodies. Like poison, these legacies infuse our social structures, which in turn reproduce arrangements that allow some people to live and thrive while rendering others disposable.

No amount of cuteness in newborns can foster their survival if social systems have been set up to eliminate the neediest among us at birth or soon after. Under current arrangements, human evolution is merely partial, with differential survival across groups based on vulnerability. These deaths are not "natural." They are *patterned*. Indeed, one might suggest they are also *deliberate*, given that after more than a century of research we know enough about disparities to know how to save babies and mothers much if not most of the time.

Theories of human evolution may tell us something important about ourselves. But they fail to explain why we permit the deaths of more than four million babies globally each year. Surely, the magnitude of these losses warrants a different evolutionary story, one that foregrounds the human actions and inactions that cause them.

The irony, perhaps, is that everyone is vulnerable. Or, rather, vulnerability is a recognized, even desirable, part of the human condition. To be vulnerable, some say, is to be honest, open, and real. To be fully human. And to some degree, this is true. Vulnerability both requires and fosters human connection.

Yet it seems to me, only those with an abundance of privilege can afford to wrap themselves in vulnerability like a beautiful silk tapestry. The rest of the world is simply trying to stay alive.

The human condition is, like all social things, unequal.

W

Washington, D.C.

The headlines catalog catastrophe: "Poor D.C. Babies Are More Than 10 Times as Likely to Die as Rich Ones"; "Why Washington Is One of the Worst Places to Be Black and Pregnant"; "Washington, D.C. Has the Highest Infant Mortality Rate of 25 Rich World Capitals"; "D.C.'s Infant Mortality Rate: An 'International Embarrassment'?"

The official visitor website describes Washington, D.C., as "a place unlike any other." Of course, the site does not feature the city's terribly high infant mortality rate, which marks it as a city of distinction—but not the kind of distinction that bolsters tourism.

Seat of the federal government and home to foreign embassies, international NGOs, domestic nonprofits, and renowned cultural institutions, the District of Columbia can be a fascinating, delightful place to visit, a rich archive of and for "we, the people."

It is also an awful place to be born—especially if you are not wealthy, white, and living in one of the "better" wards. The city's glaring health disparities are shaped, in large part, by its history and geography.

Originally inhabited by the Indigenous Nacotchtank, colonization brought white settlement, development, and eventually the federal government. D.C. was not the original capital—that was Philadelphia: "The City of Brotherly Love became the ex-capital for several reasons, including a deal between Alexander Hamilton and Thomas Jefferson, and a compromise over slavery."

The United States Constitution authorized the fledgling Congress to create a new, permanent seat of government to be governed under the exclusive jurisdiction of Congress. James Madison, in *Federalist 43*, argued for a capital that was distinct from the states, for autonomy. The current location, nestled on the shores of the Potomac River, was chosen after much negotiation, with both Maryland and Virginia ceding land.

The capital was named after George Washington, the first duly elected president of the United States. In the mid-1800s, D.C. was torn by the issue of slavery, with

Midwife in D.C. Photo credit: Tyrone Turner / WAMU.
Midwife Ebony Marcelle reunites with ten-week-old Mercury, who she delivered.
The baby's mother, Mercedez Milling-Robinson, smiles in the background.

proslavery factions in Virginia demanding the return of Alexandria, a thriving crossroads of the slave trade. That city was retroceded (given back) to Virginia in 1847, leaving the District of Columbia geographically smaller but more favorable to emancipation and the Union. Indeed, "slaves owned in Washington were emancipated on April 16, 1862, nine months before the Emancipation Proclamation, and it therefore became a hub for freed slaves."

This act, plus the subsequent northern migration of freed slaves from the South, contributed to a relatively high percentage of African Americans in D.C.: "During the Civil War (1861–1865) and Reconstruction (1865–1877), more than 25,000 African Americans moved to Washington. . . . By 1900 Washington had the largest percentage of African Americans of any city in the nation." In 2019, African Americans made up 48.3 percent, or nearly half, of the district's total population of 713,244. As NPR noted in 2011, "For decades, Washington, D.C., was known affectionately as 'Chocolate City' to many black Americans, because it was predominantly African-American."

Racial segregation, demographics, and a legacy of federal neglect led to the passage of the District of Columbia Home Rule Act in 1973, which transferred some powers from Congress to local government. Though Washington, D.C., has a municipal government, including a mayor and district council, Congress retains the jurisdiction to veto laws enacted—making for frequent skirmishes between the district and Congress.

Residents of the district have repeatedly indicated their support for statehood, which would carry Congressional voting rights, greater autonomy, and the federal benefits of statehood. In 2017, Representative Eleanor Holmes Norton introduced H.R. 1291, the Washington, D.C. Admission Act, to Congress: "This bill provides for admission into the United States of the state of Washington, Douglass Commonwealth." The name, Douglass Commonwealth, honors abolitionist Frederick Douglass, a resident of the district from 1877 to 1895.

As of this writing, statehood remains aspirational. Most Democrats favor statehood for D.C., recognizing it as intimately connected to social, economic, and racial justice. Indeed, in 2020, then–presidential candidate Joe Biden tweeted, "DC should be a state. Pass it on." With Democrats gaining control of the White House and Congress with the 2020 elections, statehood seems increasingly likely.

African Americans have lived and worked in Washington, D.C., and shaped it for more than a century, but they have not always thrived. The city is becoming ever more prosperous, and yet that prosperity is not equally shared: "While the median income for white households has increased significantly over the last decade, the median income for Black households hasn't budged. . . . These are signs that the legacy of racism and current barriers facing residents of color—in our workforce, schools, housing, and more—continue to prevent too many residents from being part of our city's growing prosperity."

Racism and poverty are key contributors to extensive health disparities, including infant mortality. In 2014, D.C.'s infant mortality rate was 7.6—but this varies by ward. In Ward 8, which is 90 percent African American, the rate was 12.5 deaths per 1,000 live births. Comparatively, in Ward 3, the city's most affluent, where 72 percent of residents are white, the rate was 1.3. Here, we see the lethal effects of segregation compounding other, largely preventable causes of infant death.

Loss is sedimented.

Anthropologist Margaret Boone drew attention to D.C.'s infant mortality crisis in 1989, with the publication of *Capital Crime: Black Infant Mortality in America*. Blending qualitative and quantitative methods, she situated high rates of infant death in context, ethnographically attending to the local fabric of Black women's lives. In Boone's sample of women who gave birth to underweight babies, a common thread regardless of marital status and age was insufficient prenatal care. This led to specific constellations of risk and vulnerability.

Boone's book title plays on the tragic irony of Black babies dying in the nation's capital, the place where policy measures *could* be taken but often are not. A general lack of regard continues, with too many Black babies and mothers dying prematurely. Not only is the district's infant mortality rate "an international embarrassment," but the maternal mortality rate for African American women is *the highest in the nation*: "From 2005 to 2014, an average of about 39 women per 100,000 live births died in D.C. of causes related to pregnancies. . . . That's more than double the national average of about 17 women who died per 100,000 live births."

D.C. is home not only to people and institutions tasked with governing the United States but also to myriad nonprofits focused on a range of domestic issues and to transnational organizations committed to improving the world. These NGOs focus on health, poverty, economic security, peace, the environment, families, veterans, trade, immigration, and a plethora of related issues. Yet few focus exclusively or even tangentially on improving infant and maternal health.

Proximity to the Capitol may make for better communication and collaboration among nonprofits, NGOs, and policymakers, not to mention access for some constituents to key decision-makers. But for the mothers and babies dying in poorly funded D.C. hospitals, on the street, or in their own homes, the benefits of living in a vibrant, world-class district of social change and economic prosperity are negligible.

Myra Jones-Taylor, of the Washington, D.C.-based nonprofit ZERO TO THREE, writes, "To do better for our babies and our nation's future, we need Congress and state leaders to make babies a priority, through policies built on the science of brain development and budgets that put babies and families first. This includes providing child care for low- and moderate-income families; ensuring paid family leave and sick leave for all working families; expanding Medicaid; and ensuring that plans cover maternal depression screening and other services that support the emotional development and well-being of parents and children."

Such advances would be, in a word, capital—and they would save infant and maternal lives.

WEATHERING

To weather something is to come through safely, as in sailors weathering a storm. One can weather a divorce, a financial hit, or any other crisis and make it through. Even, sometimes, the loss of a loved one. Weathering also implies that something can become worn down or chipped away, as with stone exposed repeatedly to water flows or ice shelves melted by warm air.

Significantly, weathering is also meaningful in health disparities research, stemming from public health scholar Arline Geronimus's innovative work on Black women's health. Her focus is on *wearing down*.

Writing in 1992, Geronimus argued that the health of African American women deteriorates by early adulthood, largely as a consequence of *cumulative disadvantage*. The conventional wisdom then was that teen pregnancy was the dominant cause of maternal and infant death among young low-income Black women, but Geronimus believed differently. She recalls, "That's when I got the fire in my belly. . . . These young women had real immediate needs that those of us in the hallowed halls of Princeton could have helped address. But we weren't seeing those urgent needs. We just wanted to teach them about contraception."

Correlating infant mortality by maternal age, Geronimus found that among the African American women in her study, *older women* suffered greater maternal and newborn health complications and death than younger women. Her data told a surprisingly different story than anticipated: namely, that Black women "may be less healthy at 25 than at 17. . . . If young black women were already showing signs of weathering, how would that play out over the rest of their lives—and what could be done to stop it?"

An unfortunate outcome of this research was the suggestion that Black women should have babies earlier to avoid linking birthing to the weathering effects of aging and chronic exposure to disadvantage. Yet as Geronimus notes, "In our rush to see teen childbearing as a major social and public health problem we have succumbed to thinking that is overly simplistic or self-serving or outright wrong." She advocated instead for understanding maternal age—any maternal age, even teenagers—as a cumulative life course issue. Weathering could begin as early as conception.

The weathering thesis complicated long-held and often racist assumptions about "lifestyle" choices among low-income African American women and poor women of color generally—stereotypes that persist. Bad food, alcohol, drugs, smoking, single motherhood, promiscuity, poverty, obesity—as if these are ever simply a matter of choice and not also social location. In contrast, Geronimus says, "What I've seen over the years of my research and lifetime is that the stressors that impact people of color are chronic and repeated through their whole life course, and in fact may even be at their height in the young adult-through-middle-adult ages rather than in early life. And that increases a general health vulnerability—which is what weathering is."

Erica Garner, who died in 2017, is a tragic case in point.

A mother of two, Garner suffered a heart attack shortly after delivering her second child. Four months later, she suffered a second heart attack brought on by an asthma attack. Brain-damaged, she was placed into a medically induced coma, from which she never recovered.

Of course, this is not the entire story. To understand Erica Garner's death, we need to understand racism, including the 2014 murder of Garner's father, Eric Garner, by New York City police. His dying words—"I can't breathe"—were uttered *eleven times* and became a rallying cry for the Black Lives Matter movement and advocates for police reform.

The murder of Eric Garner pushed his daughter toward activism, though she was "initially apprehensive about becoming a face of the movement for police accountability." She later became outspoken—"a warrior," according to her mother—and even organized a "die-in" on the same corner where her father was placed in a chokehold.

Anti-racist author and activist Rachel Cargle writes, "The loss of Erica is not only a loss of a hero on the front lines of our fight against police brutality it is a blaring testament to an issue in the US healthcare system that is not addressed nearly enough: Mortality rates among black women during pregnancy and childbirth. . . . It is heartbreaking to consider that she didn't receive proper and sufficient healthcare upon the delivery of her child and the onset of these complications."

Arline Geronimus discussed Erica Garner's death on NPR:

I heard an interview with Emerald Snipes Garner, who was talking about the death of her beloved sister Erica. She used a metaphor that I think would also be a great description of weathering. She talked about the stresses that she felt led to Erica's death at age twenty-seven as being like if you're playing the game Jenga. They pull out one piece at a time . . . and another piece and another piece, until you sort of collapse. . . . I thought that Jenga metaphor was very apt because you start losing pieces of your health and well-being, but you still try to go on as long as you can. . . . But there's a point when enough pieces have been pulled out of you, that you can no longer withstand, and you collapse.

Subsequent research has largely supported the weathering data. A study published in the journal *Health and Place* found that "states with elevated levels of structural racism had higher relative risk of infant mortality for black mothers." Factors such as incarceration, unemployment, educational attainment, and poverty were used to measure structural racism. The study showed that "as the ratio of black to white unemployment rose, so too did infant mortality. The converse was not true. The authors found no effect on white infant mortality from any change in black to white unemployment." In other words, African Americans in the study were more likely to be negatively impacted by such structural shifts than white people.

A 2019 study focused on American Indian/Alaska Native (AI/AN) mothers, an understudied group in this country. The authors note, "AI/AN birth outcomes are often excluded from studies on the weathering hypothesis, likely because of their much smaller relative population size, making up only about 2% of the U.S. population." This research found that while AI/AN birth outcomes are generally similar to those of white mothers, "divisions by maternal age suggest modestly increasing unfavorable birth outcomes with advancing age. This population level evidence provides indications that weathering is present in this population." The study's authors conclude that while white women may benefit from a delay in childbearing, the contrary may hold true for women of color.

Though the weathering hypothesis eventually took hold, despite earlier pushback, and influenced later research on racism and health outcomes, the exact mechanisms of weathering remain somewhat elusive. Valerie Montgomery Rice, president and dean of the Morehouse School of Medicine, has suggested that "not only do bias and racism build up to affect the health of black women over time, but that stress from racism and poverty may have adverse effects as early as in utero or soon after a baby is born." Yet *how* the uterine environment is impacted remains woefully understudied. Does the placenta have a role? If so, what? And what of epigenetics?

Drawing on her weathering research, Geronimus has expressed caution about the broad influence of epigenetic research in public health, worried that the impacts of structural factors may be sidelined in favor of a shiny new science that ignores the situations in which people live their lives. She states, "To constructively apply epigenetic science to understanding and eliminating population health inequality requires deeply integrating social science theory, research, and techniques with molecular science. It is important to recognize that whatever pieces of the puzzle basic epigenetics research may supply, the study of social inequalities in health is first and always a matter of robust *social* research."

In other words, we need to attend not only to what's happening inside people's bodies but also to what's happening *outside* their bodies. Genetics matter, to be sure, but so too do structural foundations of good health. Every person, pregnant or not, deserves access to healthy food and clean water, adequate health care, sanitary housing, educational opportunities, safety, economic security, and an environment free of overt and subtle racism. Tackling so-called lifestyle factors or epigenetics without also attending to gaps that lead to cumulative structural disadvantage cannot remedy the problems of excess mortality rates.

All too often, for so many people, life is something to be weathered. And in its harshest forms, life is simultaneously weathering, an accretion of the body and spirit with layers of disregard and disadvantage, leading to premature death for so many.

What would it take to *unweather* the lives of the most disadvantaged? I hope we will find out.

Women's Health

You might ask, What does infant mortality have to do with women's health?

Everything. Or very nearly everything.

But you would not know it from the way we talk about the problem of infant mortality in the United States (and elsewhere). When we *do* talk about it, that is. Rarely do we see "women's health" centered; rather, the focus is primarily on "maternal health" or "maternal and infant health," as if women are only and always mothers or potential mothers. Incubators, as it were.

As if we exist only to birth and nurture and, all too often, grieve. As if we are not whole people outside of motherhood. As if we are secondary to the real problem at hand: too many dying babies. Never mind that mothers, especially women of color, are also dying at much-too-high rates.

Perhaps if we focused more on women's health and less on "infant mortality" or "maternal-infant health," we would see increased survival. Why? Because we would be focused on women *throughout their lives*, as people in the world navigating numerous challenges and opportunities, rather than viewing women's bodies merely as means to an end.

This is undeniably a feminist claim, grounded in three decades of studying and advocating for reproductive health care and justice. Yet it is also an embodied truth: healthy women will, for the most part, make healthy babies. Not all of the time, but most of the time.

We are missing the forest of women for the trees of maternity.

Centering women's health does not mean doing away with clinical and public health practices of infant health, maternal-infant health, maternal health, or trans health. These may be necessary to target and care for specific populations at risk. During pregnancy and childbirth, all pregnant people certainly deserve skilled attendants who understand maternal health and well-being.

Yet women also deserve an emphasis on women's health across their life course. Not because some women may eventually have babies, but because we are half the population. And we should matter to scientists, clinicians, policymakers, and funders.

In 1998, I published a book on fetal surgery. In it, I asked what would have to happen to make fetal surgery a practice that is good for women's health—ethically, scientifically, clinically, politically, and otherwise. I was not interested in banning fetal surgery or suggesting that I knew better than the women choosing it. But I was (and am) interested in ensuring that a clinical focus on the fetus did not, and does not, displace a clinical focus on the pregnant woman.

A comprehensive women's health agenda—as many scholars and advocates have suggested for decades—*would center women's health across the life course*. It would first be fully attentive to diversity and equity, including the unique needs of marginalized women: women of color, young women, queer women, trans women, immigrant women, older women, and women with disabilities.

It would emphasize inclusion and integrity in clinical research trials and in all studies of devices and pharmaceuticals, many of which have harmed women unnecessarily. Women would not be second thoughts to research done on mostly male bodies but would be the primary foci of research and potentially beneficial interventions.

Diverse women would also be at the health care table: as researchers, ethicists, *informed and consenting* research subjects, clinicians, funders, and policymakers. This means we need to continue the challenging work of supporting diverse women's leadership and participation across all fields and sectors in the United States, and well beyond.

Additionally, we would fund women's health research into all sorts of issues and diseases. This includes everything from heart disease, which has largely centered men, to cancer prevention to reproductive health care to aging. We would not *defund* basic women's health care because one political party believes women to be second-class citizens. As of this writing, for example, *nearly nine hundred women's health clinics in the United States have lost funding*. This is unacceptable. And frankly, it is death-dealing for many girls and women, especially those of color.

If we centered women's health, alongside efforts to empower women and foster equity, we would, without a doubt, have a world full of healthier women.

If we centered women's health, we would act on knowledge that *we already have* about what causes maternal morbidity and mortality. We would take seriously threats to women's survival, including lack of access to care, racism, poverty, violence, and other structural factors. We would work as hard to save women's lives as we do to protect the unborn, who (though some policymakers seem not to realize this) exist *only* inside the bodies of pregnant people, the vast majority of whom are women.

If we centered women's health, we would do everything in our collective power to ensure that all girls and women have access to care and technologies that prevent unwanted pregnancies. Because we know that more women die in childbirth than die from abortions—and if we cared about saving women's lives, we would pay attention to this statistic.

If we centered women's health, we would do everything in our collective power to care for women before, during, and after pregnancy. We would provide adequate maternal leave from employment as well as affordable childcare so that women may return to work. We would invest in children's and adolescent health, too, so that women who manage their family's health care are supported. And men *should* step up and do more; they *should* manage household well-being as much as women have long done.

If we centered women's health, we would increase the survival rates for newborns and infants. We would improve pregnancy outcomes by investing in women. Because if we make *all* girls and women healthier, then we also make those who (choose to) reproduce healthier. We should make girls and women healthier because they matter in and of themselves, not only because they *may* become mothers.

If we centered women's health, we would take seriously women's grief stemming from miscarriage, stillbirth, and infant loss. We would not isolate women in their own silence and pain but embrace them, collectively and lovingly. We would say their names and their lost children's names. We would honor their losses and recognize their motherhood and their fundamental humanity.

If all of this sounds like a political agenda, it is.

What could be more political—and more essential—than ensuring a world full of healthy girls and women? Than ensuring the survival, ultimately, of mothers and their babies?

Women's health matters because women matter.

It's about time we acted to center *all* women's health.

X

XENOPHOBIA

On the policy front, infant mortality may seem like a separate issue from the so-called border crisis. And yet, if we view baby loss through the lens of xenophobia (fear of "outsiders" or "others"), we see that the premature death of some babies and children—like the premature deaths of adults—is shaped by militarized border patrol and enforcement in the name of national security.

Fear and racism are foundational to current U.S. immigration policy, from a long-standing ban on Muslims entering the country, now reversed, to an actual if temporary government shutdown from partisan conflict surrounding a border wall. Donald Trump was elected president in 2016 in part on the basis of his inflammatory anti-immigration rhetoric and promises to offer immigration "reform."

Xenophobia is from the Greek root *xenos*, which can mean either "stranger" or "guest," and *phobia*, which means "fear of." In the United States, especially in the Sonoran Desert, where I lived during much of the writing of this book, there are competing notions of immigrants as either "strangers" or "guests." Tucson, Arizona, is the heart of the modern-day sanctuary movement. There, conservative local and national politicians work to build walls and keep out "unwanted" immigrants from Mexico and Central America, while more progressive folks with humanitarian impulses provide sanctuary, water, and support to migrants.

Immigration is both one of the key political issues of our time and a global human rights crisis. Because reproduction is an important component of human experience and of women's lives, it is entangled with all social processes, including migration. Indeed, historian Laura Briggs has argued that *all* politics are reproductive politics, echoing feminist scholars—including me—who have long understood reproduction and women's reproductive bodies (especially those of women of color) as political and politicized.

For example, the derogatory and rhetorically charged term *anchor baby* relocates rampant xenophobia inside migrating women's wombs. White fears of escalating birth rates among immigrants, especially but not only those from Mexico and Central

Photo credit: Leslie Ann Epperson
U.S.-Mexico border wall, Ambos Nogales.

America, are encapsulated in the fury around birthright citizenship, or the notion that having babies in the United States makes it easier for immigrants to remain.

Immigrant women's reproductive motivations are highly suspect in this framework, which rests on the belief that "illegal aliens" will hyperreproduce and take over the United States, displacing the culture and language of white people. (Never mind that white people are far from homogenous.) Rather than seeing immigrant pregnant women as vulnerable and deserving of care and protection, "anchor baby" discourse reframes them as politically savvy, instrumental operators keen on draining resources away from more "deserving" (white, native-born) citizens.

It is not surprising that a sizable body of demographic and epidemiological research links immigration and infant mortality rates. What is surprising, perhaps—given what we know about the relationship between poverty, access to care, and insufficient health care—is that some immigrants to the United States have *lower* infant mortality rates than white native-born populations.

One study found that "despite a lower socio-economic status, children of first-generation immigrants of Hispanic origin have better birth outcomes than children of US born white women." Later generations, though benefiting from socioeconomic integration, face an *increase* in negative health outcomes. This is sometimes referred to as the Latina (or Hispanic) Paradox, an idea that has been challenged by, among others, sociologist Airín Martinez, especially around supposed nutritional differences.

In 2016, one study of immigrants living in California and Florida, key migration destinations, found that second-generation children of immigrants from Mexico and Cuba retain this advantage. In contrast, the children of Puerto Rican immigrants have *worse* birth outcomes than those of U.S.-born white women. By the third generation, all Hispanic outcomes begin to decline, except among Mexican Americans.

The advantage in birth outcomes for certain groups of immigrant women likely stems from "informal systems of prenatal care" that provide "a behavioral context for healthy births." In other words, from strong community ties that unfortunately begin to erode the longer families live in the United States: "This loss of advantage in birth outcomes is caused in part by the process of acculturation to the norms of mainstream American society."

It may also be caused by the disintegration of *informal* networks of care and a corresponding lack of *formal* prenatal care—leaving Hispanic women, like many other women of color and poor women, at risk for preterm birth and other structural causes of infant death.

Studying infant mortality in relation to immigration is extremely useful for determining causes of death and charting pathways for intervention. However, while much of this research examines race and ethnicity in relation to mobility, it rarely—like health disparities research writ large—examines *racism*. And in failing to attend to racism alongside mobility, this literature offers only part of the story.

As Raj S. Bhopal, the chairman of the executive committee of the World Congress on Migration, Ethnicity, Race, and Health, notes, "Racism and xenophobia are among the most dangerous threats to public health, with death rates that cannot be equaled even by the deadliest contagion. . . . Bridging the gap between work on racism, migration, race, and ethnicity is difficult but necessary. In these efforts, we should not forget the emigration of white Europeans, displacing and decimating indigenous people, with consequences still cascading across the centuries."

Bringing in critical race and ethnicity perspectives poses some challenges to the concept of acculturation: "Research on acculturation and health has not paid sufficient attention to the possibility that proxy indices of acculturation—such as length of time living in the United States—might be measuring exposure to discrimination." This body of work shows that racial and ethnic discrimination (racism) has a negative effect on the physical and mental health of immigrants.

And so, we come full circle, right back to xenophobia, to U.S. immigration policy—which is increasingly punitive and exclusionary—to debates about "anchor babies" and deservingness.

In short, some women born in the United States, especially African American and Indigenous women, experience terrible birth outcomes, including high infant and maternal death rates. Some women who migrate to the United States have better birth outcomes initially, but these worsen generationally with time and exposure to discrimination. In both instances, racism is a key influence, alongside and amplifying poverty, violence, and lack of access to health care.

We would be remiss to think that the act of people moving to and fro between borders *causes* morbidity and mortality—though the migratory trail itself is dangerous especially for women and children in all sorts of ways, not least reproductively.

Women with babies and small children are more likely to die in the desert, just as women with children are more at risk in natural and man-made disasters everywhere.

Also hazardous are the many public and private detention facilities across the American Southwest, where people of all ages, including pregnant women and infants, are detained in appalling conditions. In 2019, as discussed earlier, a young Honduran woman delivered a stillborn baby at a Texas facility after complaining of abdominal pain. A stillbirth "is not considered an in-custody death," meaning customs and border patrol officials do not need to count—and thus be held accountable for—the baby's death as directly related to detention.

Perhaps even more shocking, in 2020, a nurse employed at the Irwin County Detention Center in Georgia reported extreme medical neglect and human rights violations, including sterilization abuse. A protected whistleblower, Dawn Wooten described conditions in which women did not understand what had been done to them or why. In her testimony regarding a particular gynecologist, she reported, "That's his specialty, he's the uterus collector. . . . Everybody he sees, he's taking all their uteruses out or he's taken their tubes out." In a subsequent interview about why she spoke out, Wooten stated, "Enough is enough."

Sadly, such harms are nothing new in the United States, which has a long history of sterilization abuse, especially but not only of women of color. A vicious form of reproductive violence, such abuse is defined as sterilizing people (including through tubal ligation, hysterectomy, removal of ovaries, or medical experimentation) against their will or without their knowledge or consent. A favorite of eugenicists, sterilization has often been used to prevent reproduction by those deemed "undesirable," targeting women of color, the mentally ill, those with disabilities, prisoners, foreigners, and others.

Rather than the act of migration itself, then, it is the racist institutional and cultural scaffolding in the United States (and elsewhere) that enfolds, challenges, and limits geographic mobility while reshaping migrating bodies and lives, often to their detriment. In the ongoing war on immigration, xenophobia trumps human thriving and even basic survival, especially for mothers and their babies.

Women and children are not first; they are casualties of a political order that refuses to see all lives as worthy.

Welcome to America.

Y

Yearning

The esteemed Black feminist scholar bell hooks describes yearning as "the depths of longing in many of us."

Beyond everyday desire, yearning is an intense craving, a hunger for something that has been lost or from which you have been separated. The word comes from the Old English *giernan*, by way of the Germanic root meaning "eager." To yearn is to wish deeply, tenderly, urgently, eagerly for something or someone, especially that which you may not have or once were.

Yearning is a symptom of what the Diagnostic and Statistical Manual of Mental Disorders (DSM-5) calls "complicated grief," or Persistent Complex Bereavement Disorder. This is a fancy clinical term for feeling your heart has been violently cleaved from your body.

Babylost parents yearn for their missing children.

One mother, with a Facebook page dedicated to her lost son, Beau, posted in 2017, "We're all yearning for our children. Let that grief out. Tell the world. Our hurt has been taboo for too long."

And this comes from a grief blog on dealing with the death and loss of a child: "*Yearning*: Many parents report praying obsessively to have even five more minutes with their child so they can tell them how much they love them."

In a 2012 study of perinatal loss, "mothers who had more invested in their pregnancy, for example those who had thought of a name or bought things for the baby, also showed a higher level of grief-related yearning for the loss of the infant."

Another study, from 2018, focused on grieving mothers whose babies had died unexpectedly, reporting that "daily, intrusive emotional pain or yearning was found in 68.1% of subjects; yearning was significantly associated with emotional pain." It was also linked to anger, desolation, emotional numbness, and "feeling stunned, dazed, or shocked by the loss."

Yearning hurts. It stuns. It dazes. It numbs.

What it does not do, cannot do, is resurrect lost babies.

It is an unquenchable need.

Z

Zip Code

Though much of the world has gone digital, with emails, mobile calls, and text messages replacing handwritten letters, most of us still receive some paper mail, largely but not only business-related correspondence. In the United States, in order for mail to arrive at its correct destination, an address must contain a five- to nine-digit zip code.

Sending or receiving mail is likely the extent to which most people living in the United States think about zip codes. Few would know that "zip" in the name refers to the Zone Improvement Plan, a mid-twentieth century effort to assist the United States Postal Service (USPS) in delivering increasing quantities of mail through automation.

Historically, postal delivery relied on hand-sorting. Between 1940 and 1965, mail use grew by 160 percent, prompting postal visionaries to explore mechanization. In the early 1960s, building on a sorting system developed during World War II when many postal employees had joined the war, a new five-digit system was launched: "By July 1963, a five-digit code had been assigned to every address throughout the country." Mr. Zip, a cartoon character also known as Zippy, was deployed to popularize the effort.

But zip codes have made possible more than just efficient mail delivery across the United States. They also have fostered demographic data collection, with the Census Bureau being an early and active customer; risk management for insurance and mortgage companies; marketing of all kinds; targeted military recruitment; epidemiological studies; utilities management; and more. The Office of the Inspector General estimates that the zip code, "an intangible asset," has a ten-year value of $16.8 billion.

As a technology, the zip code has been incredibly fecund, spawning the creation and formation of distinct geographic groups. Zip codes, especially in real estate, have taken on both positive and negative valences. In many large cities, zip codes were used to "redline" some neighborhoods as undesirable. Refusing mortgages to African American applicants in certain "white only" zip codes contributed to persistent racial segregation that even the Fair Housing Act of 1968 could not vanquish.

Zip code stamp, ca. 1970s. Photo credit: Delaney R. Casper.

It is no surprise that zip codes also figure prominently in health research. In 2014, the Harvard T. H. Chan School of Public Health reported new data with the provocative headline, "Zip Code Better Predictor of Health Than Genetic Code." The zip code has become a key variable in health disparities research, allowing scholars to better map geographic distributions of illness and death. If we know where people are more likely to become sick or die, the logic goes, then we can better direct our interventions.

Of course, zip codes are not merely descriptors. They are also numeric representations of neighborhood attributes, referencing illness-inducing structural factors such as poverty, violence, environmental toxins, lack of access to nutritious food, and deficient medical care. One zip code might have excellent health care and abundant fresh produce while a nearby zip code might be a blighted food desert with nary a health clinic in sight.

As one commentator remarks, "It's not supposed to happen here. We think we live in a meritocracy in which our fate depends on hard work, determination, and grit. Our circumstances of birth should not matter. Where we live should not matter. How much money our parents have should not matter. Our socioeconomic status should not matter, especially when it comes to health. And yet it does. We can predict your health and life expectancy from your zip code. The social determinants of health are profound."

In short, people live and die inside zip codes: "There are places where you pay a price in loss of life because of your address."

Unsurprisingly, certain zip codes may be highly injurious to the people who live inside their bounds. Qing Wai Wong, a public health scholar reporting on communities in Texas, identified "considerable variation in infant deaths based on zip code." Such variations show up in cities across the United States where mothers and babies, especially Black and Indigenous women and infants, die at significantly higher rates.

According to the *Atlantic*, "Researchers say that birth outcomes are not just a barometer of a mother's health, but the health of the community, and also a predictor of its next generations' health. In many places, adverse birth outcomes can be traced to a history of segregation and economic inequality."

In Ohio, where the state's major cities are negatively impacted by high infant mortality, some public health responses have also been geographic. According to one official with the Butler County Health District, "[The county] is among the top 10 worst urban areas for infant mortality, especially among our black babies. . . . Analysis tells us that we have too many babies born too small and too early.'"

In 2016, the infant mortality rate in zip code 44128, in the Cleveland area, was 14.8 out of 1,000 births, double that of the state overall, and babies there were 50 percent more likely to be premature. Yet the "44128: One Community" initiative celebrated zero deaths in 2018, in large part by engaging the neighborhood, building a coalition of stakeholders including faith groups, and recognizing the physiological impact of weathering.

Zip codes, then, are not simply groupings of people. They are zones of natural and built environments shaped by long histories sometimes of great inequality, with bounded health disparities produced and reproduced across generations. And while people do relocate, geographic mobility has slowed in the United States; between 2015 and 2016, only 1.5 percent of the population moved to a different state.

Significant here, poor people in all regions of the country have far less capacity to move, especially during periods of economic recession: "This has enormous implications for the country as a whole, leading to a stratification of America, in which the wealthy and skilled live in certain amenity-rich cities and low-income people are stuck in places with few opportunities." This also makes *local* interventions all the more critical.

If the zip code has evolved "from finding *where* we are to defining *who* we are," then we as a nation are seemingly comfortable with vast inequality, with people in some neighborhoods more likely to become sick and die than those in "better" neighborhoods. We have organized ourselves—or been organized by powerful others—into zones of extreme wealth and of deprivation, where some babies receive sufficient prenatal care and survive to their first birthdays and beyond while others wither and die in the shadows of abandoned buildings.

The USPS mechanization campaign of the 1960s, personified by Zippy, suggested that "only you can put ZIP in your postal system." And yet in many neighborhoods, dual meanings of the word *zip* are tragically relevant: these zones are devoid of energy and vigor, of life—and some mothers and babies within them have zip chance of survival.

In the twenty-first century United States, geography is still destiny for too many mothers and babies.

ACKNOWLEDGMENTS

When a book takes many years to write, there are many people to thank.

First and foremost, immense gratitude to all the babylost parents and their advocates who shared stories, information, and resources, either directly or through their own published writing. This includes memoirs, blog posts, articles, and other media. For all such stories in the public domain, I have attempted to adhere as closely as possible to original context and meaning. Unfortunately, some of these stories proved ephemeral and were no longer available online when I returned to properly cite them. This saddened me and underscored the importance of witnessing babyloss, including providing ample and lasting spaces for storytelling.

For nearly three decades, I have shared intellectual community with feminist scholars of reproduction and advocates. Their work has indelibly shaped mine, and I am forever grateful. Rayna Rapp's appreciation of the "portable abacus" came at just the right moment. Jeanne Flavin answered questions via Facebook when I needed data. An interview with Hakima Tafunzi Payne for *The Feminist Wire* steered me in a different direction. Donna Haraway, Anne Fausto-Sterling, Elise Lopez, Patricia MacCorquodale, and others tried to help me track down the fate of Harry Harlow's maternal subjects. Lisa Jean Moore has long been my sociological partner in crime. And many more folks—over coffee, at conferences, via email, by phone, on social media—served as sounding boards for ideas and/or tried to help me locate bits and bobs of information. I wish I could remember and acknowledge every instance of help and support.

Dan Morrison and Black Hawk Hancock organized an invited session on my research at the 2017 meetings of the Pacific Sociological Association. Not only was it lovely to be feted; the project benefitted from the thoughtful, critical engagement of Dan, Black Hawk, Alyasah Ali Sewell, and Bryan Sykes. The idea for a "Dads" entry emerged directly from that panel.

I have presented this project at numerous other conferences and seminars through the years, as well as given invited talks around the country and internationally. I am appreciative of *all* the folks—too many to name individually—who invited me to share this work, engaged my ideas and words, and sent me on my way with kindness, helpful criticism, and encouragement.

On the rare occasions when criticism has been less than helpful or lacking in intellectual generosity, I have noted with keen interest two things: some academics are (still) deeply uncomfortable with a capacious definition of what counts as scholarship; and some academics are (still) deeply uncomfortable with women, bodies, emotions, and/or reproduction.

Of course, I will be further writing about this.

I am grateful to former undergraduate and graduate students Dan Morrison, Erin Rehel, Haley Swenson, Heather Laine Talley, and Kalen Young, each of whom provided important labor and insights for this project at various stages along the way. I am so proud of each of these fine people and who they have become in the world, both in and out of academia.

Much gratitude to Erica Goldblatt Hyatt for sharing her work, reading mine, and witnessing the kinds of reproductive silences (and silencing) of which we both speak and write. Sometimes, people come into your life at precisely the right moment, and so it was with Erica.

Judith McCoyd provided helpful feedback on an earlier version of the manuscript and affirmed the value of "crossover scholarship." And a number of exchanges with Christine Morton, across the many years we've known each other, have helped me to think outside the box about maternity care.

Sociologist Terrence Hill, whose move to the University of Texas at San Antonio was the University of Arizona's great loss, read the manuscript through the lens of quantitative medical sociology, finding "no red flags." Thank you, Terrence, especially for the Berkeley joke.

A special shout-out to the wildly talented poet Monica Ong, whose brilliant book, *Silent Anatomies*, inspired me to change forms. Sometimes, all it takes is an example and tacit permission to color outside the lines.

My cousin Kelly Sandidge kindly clarified details of her brother's heartbreaking death.

This work benefited tremendously from a sabbatical taken during academic year 2018–2019; my first since 2008. And during the "dry spell" between sabbaticals, I was largely a full-time administrator (director, department head, associate dean). My leave from the University of Arizona was thus a precious gift—earned with time served, but still a gift. I am deeply grateful to my friend and colleague John Paul Jones III, dean of the College of Social and Behavioral Sciences, for supporting my sabbatical, and also for signing off on many work-from-home Fridays so I could write. I am also infinitely appreciative of the entire dean's office staff—especially my top-notch team November Prentiss and Mika Galilee-Belfer—for stitching things together in my absence.

At San Diego State University, much gratitude to Provost Salvador Hector Ochoa and the College of Arts and Letters dean's office staff for recognizing my urgent need to finish the book. With their kind support, I managed to find some "free" hours to write and edit.

Abundant thanks to Peter Mickulas and the good folks at Rutgers University Press for bringing me back into the fold. From *The Making of the Unborn Patient* to *Babylost* feels like a most appropriate homecoming.

Dána-Ain Davis and Annie Menzel provided the most generous, insightful reader reviews I've had the pleasure to receive. This book emerged in conversation with their brilliant works, and it is all the richer for it. For an earlier incarnation of the book, then with a different press, I received thoughtful reader reports from Julia Chinyere Oparah and an anonymous reviewer. Though that version of the book morphed into this one, much of the feedback in those earlier reviews found its way into *Babylost*.

An early conversation with the wonderful Ilene Kalish at New York University Press, with whom I have worked a great deal, provided a helpful perspective on tone and the need to balance a fraught topic with the absence of sentimentalism.

In 2019, I was fortunate to participate in a writing retreat on Whidbey Island—my former home and a place I dearly love—with writers Sonya Lea and Laurie Wagner. I learned a great deal about the lyric essay and how to give and receive feedback with a keen eye and an open heart. When I read a few entries to Sonya, she responded with warmth and generosity—and I am grateful.

Since I began this project, I divorced and remarried; relocated from Nashville to Phoenix to Tucson to Southern California; raised two daughters, for a time as single mom and sole breadwinner; and lost my beloved stepfather to a preventable hospital infection. It is safe to say that the period during which *Babylost* came into being was, in a word, dynamic. To wit: the devastating COVID-19 pandemic was the grim backdrop to finalizing this manuscript. It is obvious to me, if not to others, that this book would not be finished, nor would I be the reasonably sane and successful human that I am, without my loved ones—family and friends and colleagues and canines alike.

Two people did more than anyone to push me across the finish line:

Adele Clarke, mentor extraordinaire and chosen family for more than three decades, read the manuscript(s) and offered her customary generous copyedits and suggestions. It takes tremendous trust, on both sides, to give and receive this kind of loving criticism. And it takes someone truly special to follow and support an intellectual work through nonlinear twists and turns, entirely new conceptual-izations, and authorial crises of confidence. Fortunately, Adele knows *how* I think better than most, and she gracefully kept pace.

Linda Van Leuven ("LVL")—Southern Californian, clear-eyed sociologist, and sage friend—has been my touchstone, in more ways than one. She provided encouragement and support for this book every step of the way and then some. She read entries, shared her thoughts, and sent emails saying, "You're doing great, buddy!" and "Keep going!" From the heart: Thank *you*, friend! I couldn't have done it without you—our near-daily check-ins are a feminist lifeline. I look forward to another Santa Monica seafood adventure, postpandemic.

To my other dear friends, who know my secrets and faults but love me anyway: thanks for having my six! You know who you are.

My mom and sister—Pat Struck and Tanya Casper—are simply the best. If they were disappointed when "I need to work on the book" got in the way of quality time together, they never complained. (To me, at least.) Their love and support have shaped who I am in so many ways, and I am both fortunate and grateful.

My husband, William Paul Simmons, read every word of this manuscript. His lens—human rights—offered an important refraction for the kinds of issues I study, helping me see them differently. But even more than his intellectual expertise, which is vast, I value how often he tells me I'm the best writer he knows, even if he is stretching the truth. And I appreciate how often he runs to Starbucks for my flat white and puppuccinos for Bao and Beaumont. He's a keeper, as our youngest child once quipped.

Finally, I am profoundly, eternally, humbly grateful for my daughters, Mason and Delaney. Researching reproductive loss has thrown into sharp relief the infinite ways my life has been enriched and expanded by their beautiful, living presence in it. Though "mom" is only one of my many identities, it is that which patterns all the others.

REFERENCES

BOOK EPIGRAPHS

Abbott, Grace. 1931. "The Washington Traffic Jam." In *The Grace Abbott Reader*, edited by John Sorensen with Judith Sealander. Lincoln: University of Nebraska Press.

Gibney, Shannon, and Kao Kalia Yang. 2019. "Introduction: Reclaiming Life." In *What God Is Honored Here? Writings on Miscarriage and Infant Loss by and for Native Women and Women of Color*, edited by Shannon Gibney and Kao Kalia Yang. Minneapolis: University of Minnesota Press.

Inglis, Kate. 2018. *Notes for the Everlost: A Field Guide to Grief.* Boulder, Colo.: Shambhala.

McCracken, Elizabeth. 2008. *An Exact Replica of a Figment of My Imagination.* New York: Little, Brown.

Teigen, Chrissy. 2020. "Hi." Medium, October 27, 2020. https://chrissyteigen.medium.com/hi-2e45e6faf764.

Yuknavitch, Lidia. 2015. *The Small Backs of Children.* New York: HarperCollins.

INTRODUCTION

Barbero, Guilio J., and Eleanor Shaheen. 1967. "Environmental Failure to Thrive: A Clinical View." *Journal of Pediatrics* 71 (5): 639–644.

Brosco, Jeffrey P. 1999. "The Early History of the Infant Mortality Rate in America: 'A Reflection upon the Past and a Prophecy of the Future.'" *Pediatrics* 103 (2): 478–485.

Cacciatore, Joanne. 2013. "Psychological Effects of Perinatal Death." *Seminars in Fetal and Neonatal Medicine* 18 (2): 76–82.

Cacciatore, Joanne, and Suzanne Bushfield. 2008. "Stillbirth: A Sociopolitical Issue." *Affilia: Journal of Women and Social Work* 23 (4): 378–387.

Colen, Shellee. 1995. "'Like a Mother to Them': Stratified Reproduction and West Indian Childcare Workers and Employers in New York." In *Conceiving the New World Order: The Global Politics of Reproduction*, edited by Faye D. Ginsburg and Rayna Rapp, 78–102. Berkeley: University of California Press.

Freidenfelds, Lara. 2020. *The Myth of the Perfect Pregnancy: A History of Miscarriage in America.* New York: Oxford University Press.

Goldblatt Hyatt, Erica. n.d. "Termination." Unpublished manuscript, last accessed September 26, 2021. PDF.

Layne, Linda. 2003. *Motherhood Lost: A Feminist Account of Pregnancy Loss in America*. New York: Routledge.

Mead, George Herbert. 1938. *The Philosophy of the Act*. Chicago: University of Chicago Press.

Meckel, Richard A. (1990) 2015. *Save the Babies: American Public Health Reform and the Prevention of Infant Mortality, 1850–1929*. Illustrated ed. Rochester, N.Y.: University of Rochester Press.

Menzel, Annie. 2014. "The Political Life of Black Infant Mortality." PhD diss., University of Washington.

Newman, George. 1906. *Infant Mortality: A Social Problem*. London: Methuen.

Pernick, Martin S. 1996. *The Black Stork: Eugenics and the Death of "Defective" Babies in American Medicine and Motion Pictures since 1915*. New York: Oxford University Press.

Russell, Tonya. 2021. "Mortality Rate for Black Babies Is Cut Dramatically When Black Doctors Care for Them after Birth, Researchers Say." *Washington Post*, January 13, 2021. https://www.washingtonpost.com/health/black-baby-death-rate-cut-by-black-doctors/2021/01/08/e9f0f850-238a-11eb-952e-0c475972cfc0_story.html.

Strauss, Anselm L. 1978. *Negotiations: Varieties, Contexts, and Social Order*. San Francisco: Jossey-Bass.

ABSENCE

Casper, Monica J., and Lisa Jean Moore. 2009. *Missing Bodies: The Politics of Visibility*. New York: New York University Press.

Centers for Disease Control and Prevention. 2020. "What Is Stillbirth?" Last modified November 16, 2020. https://www.cdc.gov/ncbddd/stillbirth/facts.html.

Heineman, Elizabeth. 2014. *Ghostbelly: A Memoir*, 105. New York: Feminist Press.

Kittel, Kelly. 2014. *Breathe: A Memoir of Motherhood, Grief, and Family Conflict*, 190. Berkeley, Calif.: She Writes Press.

McCracken, Elizabeth. 2008. *An Exact Replica of a Figment of My Imagination*. New York: Little, Brown.

Todorović, Ana. 2016. "Nadia's Story." Aeon, July 21, 2016. https://aeon.co/essays/my-daughter-came-out-they-handed-her-to-me-she-was-dead.

ABUSE

Centers for Disease Control and Prevention. 2020. "Infant Homicides within the Context of Safe Haven Laws, 2008–2017." *Morbidity and Mortality Weekly Report* 69 (39): 1385–1390. https://www.cdc.gov/mmwr/volumes/69/wr/mm6939a1.htm.

———. 2020. "Infant Mortality: What Is CDC Doing?" Last modified September 30, 2020. https://www.cdc.gov/reproductivehealth/maternalinfanthealth/infantmortality-cdcdoing.htm.

Child Trends. 2015. "Infant Homicide." https://www.childtrends.org/indicators/infant-child-and-teen-mortality.

Mayo Clinic. 2017. "Shaken Baby Syndrome." October 28, 2017. https://www.mayoclinic.org/diseases-conditions/shaken-baby-syndrome/symptoms-causes/syc-20366619.

National Children's Alliance. n.d. "National Statistics on Child Abuse." Last accessed September 26, 2021. https://www.nationalchildrensalliance.org/media-room/national-statistics-on-child-abuse/.

Reijneveld, Sijmen A., Marcel F. Van der Wal, Emily Brugman, Remy A. Hira Sing, and S. Pauline Verloove-Vanhorick. 2004. "Infant Crying and Abuse." *Lancet* 364 (9442): 1340–1342.

Thompson, Andy. 2017. "Crying Infants Can Be Target of Severe Abuse." *Post-Crescent*, May 21, 2017.

ANGEL BABIES

Angel Babies. n.d. "Practical Information for Parents Coping with Late Pregnancy and Infant Loss." Last accessed September 26, 2021. https://angelbabiesinfo.com/.

Angel Babies: Angel Gowns and Memorial Events. n.d. "Home." Facebook. Last accessed September 26, 2021. https://www.facebook.com/AngelBabies1217.

Flam, Lisa. 2016. "'Somebody Cares': Donated Wedding Dresses Become 'Angel Gowns' for Babies Who Die." *Today*, October 14, 2016. https://www.today.com/parents/somebody-cares-donated-wedding-dresses-become-angel-gowns-babies-who-2D79476642.

Leonard, David J. 2014. "When All the Angels Are White." Gawker, September 13, 2014. https://gawker.com/when-all-the-angels-are-white-1634298232.

National Desk Staff. 2018. "'She Is an Angel Now': Woman Creates Infant Burial Gowns from Wedding Dresses." KCRA3, August 17, 2018. https://www.kcra.com/article/she-is-an-angel-now-woman-creates-infant-burial-gowns-from-wedding-dresses/22761954#.

Phillips, Trevor. 1997. "Black Angels? It's a Hope in Heaven." *The Independent*, November 15, 1997. https://www.independent.co.uk/voices/black-angels-it-s-hope-heaven-1294167.html.

AWARENESS

Glaser, Barney G., and Anselm L. Strauss. 1965. *Awareness of Dying*. Piscataway, N.J.: Transaction Publishers.

October 15th. n.d. "The Official Site of Pregnancy and Infant Loss Remembrance Day." Last accessed September 26, 2021. https://www.october15th.com/.

Purtle, Jonathan, and Leah H. Roman. 2015. "Health Awareness Days: Sufficient Evidence to Support the Craze?" *American Journal of Public Health* 105 (6): 1061–1065.

Reagan, Ronald. 1988. "Pregnancy and Infant Loss Awareness Month." Proclamation No. 5890. October 25, 1988. https://www.govinfo.gov/content/pkg/STATUTE-103/pdf/STATUTE-103-Pg2593.pdf.

U.S. House of Representatives. 2005. *Supporting the Goals and Ideals of National Pregnancy and Infant Loss Remembrance Day*. H. Con. Res. 222, 109th Cong., 1st sess. July 27, 2005. https://www.govinfo.gov/content/pkg/BILLS-109hconres222ih/html/BILLS-109hconres222ih.htm.

Willer, Erin K., Emily Krebs, Nivea Castaneda, Kate Drazner Hoyt, Veronica A. Droser, Jessica A. Johnson, and Jenni Hunniecutt. 2019. "Our Babies['] Count[er Story]: A Narrative Ethnography of a Baby Loss Remembrance Walk Ritual." *Communication Monographs* 87 (2): 179–199.

BABYLAND

Ashoka. 2007. "Kathryn Hall-Trujillo: Ashoka Fellow." https://www.ashoka.org/en-us/fellow/kathryn-hall-trujillo.

Atruj. 2008. "Babyland." YouTube video, 2:28. January 21, 2008. https://www.youtube.com/watch?v=KFIw5-PHvhs.

Berger, Danielle. 2010. "Birthing Project Provides Mentors for At-Risk Mothers-to-Be." CNN, July 23, 2010. http://edition.cnn.com/2010/HEALTH/07/22/cnnheroes.birthing.project/index.html.

Birthing Project USA. n.d. "Home." Last accessed September 26, 2021. https://www.birthing projectusa.org/.

Chrisien, Sarah. 2016. "Evergreen Cemetery Works to Mark Anonymous Infant Graves." WUFT News, February 24, 2016. https://www.wuft.org/news/2016/02/24/evergreen-cemetery -works-to-mark-anonymous-infant-graves/.

Edgette, J. Joseph. 1999. "'Now I Lay Me Down to Sleep': Symbols and Their Meaning on Children's Gravemarkers." *Children's Folklore Review* 22 (1): 7–24.

Ferri, Jessica. 2019. "7 Forest Lawn Cemetery Graves That Are Downright Haunting." Lineup, April 23, 2019. https://the-line-up.com/forest-lawn-cemetery.

Greenfield, Rebecca. 2011. "Our First Public Parks: The Forgotten History of Cemeteries." *Atlantic*, March 16, 2011. https://www.theatlantic.com/national/archive/2011/03/our-first -public-parks-the-forgotten-history-of-cemeteries/71818/.

Hinckley, David. 2008. "Infant Death Haunts Grim 'Babyland' on ABC's '20/20' Special." *New York Daily News*, August 21, 2008.

Kragen, Pam. 2019. "Cemetery for Forgotten Babies Commemorates Its 200th Burial." *San Diego Union-Tribune*, September 30, 2019.

Leake, Craig, and David Appleby, dirs. 2008. *Babyland*. ABC News, Documentary Group. First broadcast August 22, 2008, on ABC.

Marlowe, Bob. n.d. "Forest Lawn: Glendale." Last accessed September 26, 2021. https://bobsaw .smugmug.com/Cemeteries/Forest-Lawn-Glendale-1/i-jwHMzFR.

Mortice, Zach. 2017. "Perpetual Neglect: The Preservation Crisis of African-American Cemeter-ies." *Places*, May 2017. https://placesjournal.org/article/perpetual-neglect-the-preservation -crisis-of-african-american-cemeteries/.

Park Triangle Productions. 2012. "Kathryn Hall-Trujillo: Birthing Project USA." YouTube video, 3:00. June 11, 2012. https://www.ashoka.org/en-us/media/36232.

Petrella, Christopher. 2019. "Gentrification Is Erasing Black Cemeteries and, with It, Black History." *Guardian*, April 27, 2019.

Witmer, Emma. 2018. "Remembering the Forgotten Children of Babyland." WUFT News, April 25, 2018. https://www.wuft.org/news/2018/04/25/remembering-the-forgotten-children -of-babyland/.

BLACK INFANT MORTALITY

Armstrong, David. 1986. "The Invention of Infant Mortality." *Sociology of Health and Illness* 8 (3): 211–232.

Berlant, Lauren. 2007. "Slow Death (Sovereignty, Obesity, Lateral Agency)." *Critical Inquiry* 33 (4): 754–780.

Duke University. 2018. "Why the Black-White Infant Mortality Gap Exists and How to Eradicate It." Phys.org, March 29, 2018. https://phys.org/news/2018-03-black-white-infant -mortality-gap-eradicate.html.

Dyson, Tauren. 2019. "Death Rates for Black Infants More Than Double Rate for White Infants." *United Press International*, August 1, 2019.

Galvin, Gaby. 2019. "Black Babies Face Double the Risk of Dying before Their First Birth-day." *U.S. News and World Report*, August 1, 2019.

Greenwood, Brad N., Rachel R. Hardeman, Laura Huang, and Aaron Sojourner. 2020. "Physician-Patient Racial Concordance and Disparities in Birthing Mortality for Newborns." *Proceedings of the National Academy of Sciences* 117 (35): 21194–21200.

Hale, Christiane B. 1990. "Infant Mortality: An American Tragedy." *Black Scholar* 21 (1): 17–26.

Hayes, Chris. 2019. "Remembering Why Black Lives Matter with Alicia Garza: Podcast and Transcript." In *Why Is This Happening?*, podcast, MP3 audio. NBC News, June 11, 2019. https://www.nbcnews.com/think/opinion/remembering-why-black-lives-matter-alicia-garza-podcast-transcript-ncna1013901.

Kahn-Cullors, Patrisse, and Asha Bandele. 2018. *When They Call You a Terrorist: A Black Lives Matter Memoir*. New York: St. Martin's.

Menzel, Annie. 2014. "The Political Life of Black Infant Mortality." PhD diss., University of Washington.

Neely, Priska. 2018. "America's Black Babies Are Paying for Society's Ills. What Will We Do to Fix It?" LAist, June 28, 2018.

———. 2018. "Black Babies Die at Twice the Rate of White Babies. My Family Is Part of This Statistic." LAist, June 21, 2018.

Owens, Deirdre Cooper, and Sharla M. Fett. 2019. "Black Maternal and Infant Health: Historical Legacies of Slavery." *American Journal of Public Health* 109 (10): 1342–1355.

Singe, Gopal K. 2019. "Infant Mortality in the United States, 1915–2107: Large Social Inequalities Have Persisted for over a Century." *International Journal of Maternal and Child Health and AIDS* 8 (1): 19–31.

Vilda, Dovile, Rachel Hardeman, Lauren Dyer, Katherine P. Theall, and Maeve Wallace. 2021. "Structural Racism, Racial Inequities and Urban-Rural Differences in Infant Mortality in the U.S." *Journal of Epidemiology and Community Health* 75 (8): 788–793. https://pubmed.ncbi.nlm.nih.gov/33504545/.

Wise, Paul H. 2003. "The Anatomy of a Disparity in Infant Mortality." *Annual Review of Public Health* 24:341–362.

Wisner, Wendy. 2019. "Infant Mortality Rates Are Twice as High for Black Babies, and That Is a Big F*cking Deal." *Scary Mommy*, August 5, 2019. https://www.scarymommy.com/infant-mortality-is-higher-black-babies/.

Griffin, Samantha. 2017. "The Ina May Gaskin Racial Gaffe Heard 'Round the Midwifery World." Rewire News Group, April 26, 2017.

Human, Melanie, Sulina Green, Coen Groenewald, Richard D. Goldstein, Hannah C. Kinney, and Hein J. Odendaal. 2014. "Psychosocial Implications of Stillbirth for the Mother and Her Family: A Crisis-Support Approach." *Social Work (Stellenbosch)* 50 (4): 392.

Kittel, Kelly. 2014. *Breathe: A Memoir of Motherhood, Grief, and Family Conflict*, 233. Berkeley, Calif.: She Writes Press.

Meadows-Fernandez, Rochaun. 2017. "Just So We're Clear: Black Mothers Aren't to Blame for High Infant Mortality." *Yes!*, May 4, 2017.

National Advocates for Pregnant Women. 2018. "NAPW Demands Indiana Prosecutor Drop Murder Charge against Woman Who Had a Stillbirth at Home." August 2, 2018. https://www.nationaladvocatesforpregnantwomen.org/napw-demands-indiana-prosecutor-drop-murder-charge-woman-stillbirth-home/.

Villarosa, Linda. 2018. "Why America's Black Mothers and Babies Are in a Life-or-Death Crisis." *New York Times Magazine*, April 11, 2018.

BREASTFEEDING

Adams, Jermone M. 2017. "Breastfeeding and Infant Mortality in Indiana: Changing the Culture and Saving Lives: A Model for Other States." *Breastfeeding Medicine* 12 (8): 456–458.

Allers, Kimberly Seals. 2018. "Presenting Breastfeeding as a Choice Is Contributing to Black Infant Deaths." *HuffPost*, August 1, 2018; updated August 8, 2018.

American Academy of Pediatrics. 2012. "Policy Statement: Breastfeeding and the Use of Human Milk." *Pediatrics* 129, no. 3 (March 2012). https://publications.aap.org/pediatrics/article/129/3/e827/31785/Breastfeeding-and-the-Use-of-Human-Milk?autologincheck=redirected.

Biks, Gashaw Andargie, Yemane Berhane, Alemayehu Worku, and Yigzaw Kebede Gete. 2015. "Exclusive Breast Feeding Is the Strongest Predictor of Infant Survival in Northwest Ethiopia: A Longitudinal Study." *Journal of Health, Population and Nutrition* 34, no. 9 (May 2015). https://pubmed.ncbi.nlm.nih.gov/26825334/.

Bristow, Jennie. 2013. "'I've Been Likened to a Holocaust Denier.'" *Spiked*, January 28, 2013.

Centers for Disease Control and Prevention. 2020. "Breastfeeding Report Card: United States 2020." Last modified September 17, 2020. https://www.cdc.gov/breastfeeding/data/reportcard.htm.

Dieterich, Christine M., Julia P. Felice, Elizabeth O'Sullivan, and Kathleen M. Rasmussen. 2013. "Breastfeeding and Health Outcomes for the Mother-Infant Dyad." *Pediatric Clinics of North America* 60 (1): 31–48.

Edmond, Karen M., Charles Zandoh, Maria A. Quigley, Seeba Amenga-Etego, Seth Owusu-Agyei, and Betty R. Kirkwood. 2006. "Delayed Breastfeeding Initiation Increases Risk of Neonatal Mortality." *Pediatrics* 117 (3): e380–e386.

Glass, Kelly. 2017. "How Our Conversation around Breastfeeding Hurts Black Infants." Medium, August 21, 2017. https://medium.com/the-establishment/how-our-conversation-around-breastfeeding-hurts-black-infants-ee1ed1c318c.

Jacobs, Andrew. 2018. "Opposition to Breast-Feeding Resolution by U.S. Stuns World Health Officials." *New York Times*, July 8, 2018.

James, Regina Smith. 2017. "Breastfeeding Disparities in African American Women." *NIMHD Insights* (blog), August 8, 2017. https://nimhd.blogs.govdelivery.com/2017/08/08/breastfeeding-disparities-in-african-american-women/.

Jeltsen, Melissa. 2018. "Mother Accused of Killing Baby with Her Own Breast Milk." *HuffPost*, July 18, 2018; updated July 19, 2018.

Kendall-Tackett, Kathleen A. 2015. "Infant Mortality: Narrowing the Gap." *The SES Indicator*, American Psychological Association, January 2015. https://www.apa.org/pi/ses/resources/indicator/2015/01/infant-mortality.

Morton, Christine H., and Elayne Clift. 2014. *Birth Ambassadors: Doulas and the Re-emergence of Woman-Supported Birth in America*. Amarillo, Tex.: Praeclarus.

Office of Disease Prevention and Health Promotion. n.d. "Healthy People 2030: Building a Healthier Future for All." https://health.gov/healthypeople.

Ombuor, Rael. 2018. "Kenya Banks on Human Milk to Reduce Newborn Mortality." *Voice of America*, August 9, 2018.

Savage, Luiza Ch. 2011. "Why Breastfeeding Is Overrated: Author Joan B. Wolf in Conversation." *Maclean's*, January 10, 2011.

Timsit, Annabelle. 2018. "The Simple Post-birth Step That Dramatically Increases Babies' Chances of Survival." Quartz, July 31, 2018.

Wolf, Joan. 2010. *Is Breast Best? Taking on the Breastfeeding Experts and the New High Stakes of Motherhood*, xii. New York: New York University Press.

World Health Organization. n.d. "Breastfeeding." Last accessed September 26, 2021. https://www.who.int/health-topics/breastfeeding#tab=tab_1.

CHILDREN'S RIGHTS

Central Intelligence Agency. n.d. "Infant Mortality Rate." *The World Factbook*. Last accessed September 26, 2021. https://www.cia.gov/the-world-factbook/field/infant-mortality-rate/.

Christopher, Andrea S., and Dominic Caruso. 2015. "Promoting Health as a Human Right in the Post-ACA United States." *AMA Journal of Ethics* 17 (10): 958–965.

Commonwealth Fund. 2017. "New 11-Country Study: U.S. Health Care System Has Widest Gap between People with Higher and Lower Incomes." Press release, July 13, 2107.

Embassy of Monaco in Washington, D.C. 2017. "Key Facts." https://monacodc.org/keyfacts .html.

Fox, Maggie. 2017. "Infant Mortality Rates Fall 15 Percent in U.S." NBC News, March 21, 2017.

Ghani, Faras. 2018. "UNICEF: One Million Children Die the Day They Are Born." *Al Jazeera*, February 20, 2018.

Gruskin, Sofia, Jane Cottingham, Adriane Martin Hilber, Eszter Kismodi, Ornella Lincetto, and Mindy Jane Roseman. 2008. "Using Human Rights to Improve Maternal and Neonatal Health: History, Connections and a Proposed Practical Approach." *Bulletin of the World Health Organization* 86 (8): 577–656.

Haider, Mohammad Hakim, and Sumit Kumar. 2019. "Consequences of Poverty in Afghanistan." In *Poverty in Afghanistan: Causes, Consequences, and Coping Mechanisms*, edited by Mohammad Hakim Haider and Sumit Kumar, 127–144. Cham, Switzerland: Palgrave Pivot.

Human Rights Watch. 2014. "25th Anniversary of the Convention on the Rights of the Child." November 17, 2014.

Ingraham, Christopher. 2014. "Our Infant Mortality Rate Is a National Embarrassment." *Washington Post*, September 29, 2014.

Kumar, Sanjay. 1998. "Perinatal Mortality a Human-Rights Issue in India." *Lancet* 351 (9112): 1340.

Kurani, Nisha, Daniel McDermott, and Nicolas Shanosky. 2020. "How Does the Quality of the U.S. Healthcare System Compare to Other Countries?" Peterson-KFF Health System Tracker, Peterson Center on Health Care, August 20, 2020. https://www.healthsystemtracker.org/ chart-collection/quality-u-s-healthcare-system-compare-countries/#item-start.

Mehta, Sarah. 2015. "There's Only One Country That Hasn't Ratified the Convention on Children's Rights: US." ACLU, November 20, 2015. https://www.aclu.org/blog/human-rights/ treaty-ratification/theres-only-one-country-hasnt-ratified-convention-childrens.

Papanicolas, Irene, Liana R. Woskie, and Ashish K. Jah. 2018. "Health Care Spending in the United States and Other High-Income Countries." *JAMA* 319 (10): 1024–1039.

Rahimzai, Mirwais, Mirwais Amiri, Nadera Hayat Burhani, Sheila Leatherman, Simon Hiltebeitel, and Ahmed Javed Rahmanzai. 2013. "Afghanistan's National Strategy for Improving Quality in Health Care." *International Journal for Quality in Health Care* 25 (3): 270–276.

Schneider, Eric C., Dana O. Sarnak, David Squires, Arnav Shah, and Michelle M. Doty. 2017. "Mirror, Mirror 2017: International Comparison Reflects Flaws and Opportunities for Better U.S. Health Care." Commonwealth Fund. https://interactives.commonwealthfund .org/2017/july/mirror-mirror/.

Tibetan Centre for Human Rights and Democracy. 2015. "TCHRD Report Documents Crisis of Maternal and Child Health in Tibet." March 4, 2015.

United Nations Human Rights. 1989/1990. "Convention on the Rights of the Child." Office of the High Commissioner, United Nations. https://www.ohchr.org/en/professionalinterest/ pages/crc.aspx.

———. n.d. "Human Rights-Based Approach to Reduce and Eliminate Preventable Mortality and Morbidity of Children under 5 Years of Age: Technical Guidance." Office of the High Commissioner, United Nations.

World Health Organization. 2000. "World Health Organization Assesses the World's Health Systems." February 7, 2000.

CIA'S *WORLD FACTBOOK*

Buneman, Peter, Heiko Müller, and Chris Rusbridge. 2009. "Curating the CIA World Factbook." *International Journal of Digital Curation* 3 (4): 29–43.

Central Intelligence Agency. n.d. "Infant Mortality Rate." *The World Factbook.* Last accessed September 26, 2021. https://www.cia.gov/the-world-factbook/field/infant-mortality-rate/.

Federation of American Scientists. n.d. "Central Intelligence Agency." FAS.org. Last accessed September 26, 2021. https://irp.fas.org/cia/.

History.com Editors. 2017. "CIA." History.com, July 13, 2017; updated August 21, 2018. https://www.history.com/topics/us-government/history-of-the-cia.

National Security Act. 1947. Pub. L. No. 235, 61 Stat. 496. July 26, 1947.

Prasad, A. N. 2008. "War Affected Children in Afghanistan." *Medical Journal Armed Forces India* 64 (1): 65–66.

Rotberg, Robert I., ed. 2003. *State Failure and State Weakness in a Time of Terror.* Cambridge, Mass.: World Peace Foundation; Washington, D.C.: Brookings Institution Press.

Simmons, William Paul, and Monica J. Casper. 2012. "Culpability, Social Triage, and Structural Violence in the Aftermath of Katrina." *Perspectives on Politics* 10 (3): 675–686.

Truman, Harry. 1946. "Presidential Directive on Coordination of Foreign Intelligence Activities." Office of the Historian. January 22, 1946. https://www.trumanlibrary.gov/library/public-papers/19/directive-coordination-foreign-intelligence-activities.

Weiner, Tim. 2008. *Legacy of Ashes: The History of the CIA.* New York: Anchor.

Zegart, Amy B. 2007. "License to Fail." *Los Angeles Times*, September 23, 2007.

CONGRESSIONAL BLACK CAUCUS

African American Voices in Congress. n.d. "Anti-Apartheid." Last accessed September 26, 2021. http://www.avoiceonline.org/aam/history.html.

Barnett, Marguerite Ross. 1977. "The Congressional Black Caucus: Symbol, Myth, and Reality." *Black Scholar* 8 (4): 17–26.

Barrett, Katie Shea. 2020. "Black Maternal Mortality Rates and the Implicit Biases—How Can We Address Them?" *Hill*, September 15, 2020.

Black Maternal Health Caucus. n.d. "Black Maternal Health Momnibus." Last accessed September 26, 2021. https://blackmaternalhealthcaucus-underwood.house.gov/Momnibus.

Boone, Margaret. 1989. *Capital Crime: Black Infant Mortality in America.* Thousand Oaks, Calif.: SAGE.

Brown, Stacy M. 2018. "CBCF Aims to Lower Black Childbirth Mortality Rates." *Washington Informer*, September 25, 2018.

Congressional Black Caucus Foundation. n.d. "Vision & Mission." https://www.cbcfinc.org/learn-about-us/vision-mission/.

Congresswoman Robin Kelly. 2018. "New Bill Looks to Reduce Infant and Maternal Mortality Rates in the U.S." May 21, 2018. https://robinkelly.house.gov/media-center/in-the-news/new-bill-looks-reduce-infant-and-maternal-mortality-rates-us.

Dayen, David. 2016. "Has the Congressional Black Caucus Lost Its Conscience?" *New Republic*, March 2, 2016.

Du Bois, W. E. B. 1903. *The Souls of Black Folk: Essays and Sketches.* Chicago: A. C. McLurg.

Erhagbe, Edward O. 1995. "The Congressional Black Caucus and United States Policy toward Africa: 1971–1990." *Transafrican Journal of History* 24:84–96.

Gile, Roxanne L., and Charles E. Jones. 1995. "Congressional Racial Solidarity: Exploring Congressional Black Caucus Voting Cohesion, 1971–1990." *Journal of Black Studies* 25 (5): 622–641.

History, Art and Archives, United States House of Representatives. n.d. "Creation and Evolution of the Congressional Black Caucus." Last accessed September 26, 2021. https://history.house.gov/Exhibitions-and-Publications/BAIC/Historical-Essays/Permanent-Interest/Congressional-Black-Caucus/.

Hughes, Everett C. 1984. *The Sociological Eye: Selected Papers.* New Brunswick, N.J.: Transaction.

Johnson, Theodore R. 2016. "The Increasing Irrelevance of the Congressional Black Caucus." *Atlantic*, April 28, 2016.

Jones, LaMont. 2019. "Largest-Ever Congressional Black Caucus Sworn In." *Diverse Issues in Higher Education*, January 3, 2019.

King, Mae, Tyson King-Meadows, Elsie Scott, and Menna Demessie. 2011. "CBC Roundtable: The Conscience of Congress: The Congressional Black Caucus after 40 Years and Its Impact on Domestic and Foreign Policy." NCOBPS 43rd Meeting Paper, October 7, 2011. https://papers.ssrn.com/sol3/papers.cfm?abstract_id=1939872.

MOMMA's Act. 2017–2018. H.R. 5977. 115th Congress. https://www.congress.gov/bill/115th-congress/house-bill/5977/text.

Nelson, Alondra. 2011. *Body and Soul: The Black Panther Party and the Fight against Medical Discrimination.* Minneapolis: University of Minnesota Press.

Ruffin, Rachael. 2014. "The Village Lost a Child." Congressional Black Caucus Foundation, October 20, 2014. https://www.cbcfinc.org/village/the-village-lost-a-child/.

U.S. Senate. 1985. "Preventing Infant Mortality: Intergovernmental Dimensions of a National Problem: Joint Hearings before the Subcommittee on Intergovernmental Relations of the Committee on Governmental Affairs and the Committee on the Budget." 99th Cong., 1st sess. September 11, October 11, and October 31, 1985. https://eric.ed.gov/?q=mortality&ff1=pubLegal%2fLegislative%2fRegulatory+Materials&id=ED290537.

CUBA

Acosta, Lisandra Fariñas. 2019. "Cuba Closes 2018 with the Lowest Infant Mortality Rate in Its History." *Granma*, January 7, 2019.

Berdine, Gilbert, Vincent Geloso, and Benjamin Powell. 2018. "Cuban Infant Mortality and Longevity: Health Care or Repression?" *Health Policy and Planning* 33 (6): 755–757.

Bhardwaj, Nakul, and Daniel Skinner. 2019. "Primary Care in Cuba: Considerations for the U.S." *Journal of Health Care for the Poor and Underserved* 30 (2): 456–476.

Blizzard, Brittany, and Jeanne Batalova. 2020. "Cuban Immigrants in the United States." Immigration Policy Institute, June 11, 2020. https://www.migrationpolicy.org/article/cuban-immigrants-united-states-2018.

Blumenthal, David. 2016. "Fidel Castro's Health Care Legacy." *To the Point*, Commonwealth Fund, November 28, 2016. https://www.commonwealthfund.org/blog/2016/fidel-castros-health-care-legacy.

Borgen Magazine. 2019. "Success in Keeping Cuba's Infant Mortality Rate Low." February 13, 2019.

Bragg, Michelle, Taraneh R. Salke, Carol P. Cotton, and Debra Anne Jones. 2012. "No Child or Mother Left Behind: Implications for the U.S. from Cuba's Maternity Homes." *Health Promotion Perspectives* 2 (1): 9–19.

Bryan, Miles. 2017. "What Chicago Is Learning from Cuba When It Comes to Fighting Infant Mortality." *World*, December 22, 2017.

———. 2018. "A Poor Neighborhood in Chicago Looks to Cuba to Fight Infant Mortality." *Washington Post*, January 10, 2018.

Chomsky, Aviva, Barry Carr, and Pamela Maria Smokaloff, eds. 2003. *The Cuba Reader: History, Culture, Politics*. Durham, N.C.: Duke University Press.

Editors. 2014. "Sen. Harkin Falls for Cuba's Health Care Propaganda." *Investor's Business Daily*, February 4, 2014.

Ely, Danielle M., and Anne K. Driscoll. 2019. "Infant Mortality in the United States, 2017: Data from the Period Linked Birth/Infant Death File." *National Vital Statistics Reports* 68 (10): 1–20.

Evenson, Debra. 2005. "The Right to Health Care and the Law." *MEDICC Review* 7 (9): 8–9.

Farmer, Paul. 2003. *Pathologies of Power: Health, Human Rights, and the New War on the Poor*. Berkeley: University of California Press.

Feinsilver, Julie M. 1989. "Cuba as a 'World Medical Power': The Politics of Symbolism." *Latin American Research Review* 24 (2): 1–34.

Hamblin, James. 2016. "How Cubans Live as Long as Americans at a Tenth of the Cost." *Atlantic*, November 29, 2016.

Havana Times. 2016. "Cuba Receives 4 Million Tourists in 2016." December 31, 2016.

Howerton, Jason. 2014. "If You Missed Marco Rubio's Amazing Response to Dem Senator Who Praised Cuban Socialism, Fix That Right Now." *Blaze Media*, February 26, 2014.

Mercer, Mary Anne. 2015. "Preventing Infant Deaths: What Can We Learn from Cuba?" *HuffPost*, March 6, 2015; updated December 6, 2017.

Mesa-Lago, Carmelo. 2014. "Can Cuba's Economic Reforms Succeed?" *Americas Quarterly*, November 5, 2014.

National Network on Cuba. 2018. "Cuba Will End 2018 with the Lowest Infant Mortality Rate." December 22, 2018.

O'Hanlon, Clare E., and Melody Harvey. 2017. "Doing More with Less: Lessons from Cuba's Healthcare System." *Georgetown Journal of International Affairs*, October 2, 2017. https://www.georgetownjournalofinternationalaffairs.org/online-edition/2017/10/2/doing-more-with-less-lessons-from-cubas-healthcare-system.

Pérez, Louis A. Jr. 2011. *Cuba in the American Imagination: Metaphor and the Imperial Ethos*. Chapel Hill: University of North Carolina Press.

Warner, Rich. 2016. "Is the Cuban Healthcare System Really as Great as People Claim?" Conversation, November 30, 2016.

Wiser, Daniel. 2014. "Cuba Manipulating Health Care Statistics." *Washington Free Beacon*, March 5, 2014.

DADS

Bowenbank, Starr. 2020. "Chrissy Teigen and John Legend Shared How They Are Grieving the Loss of Their Son Jack." *Cosmopolitan*, November 25, 2020.

Chidgey, Steven. 2017. "Don't Bottle It Up: A Message from One Stillborn Dad to Another." Tommy's, May 31, 2017. https://www.tommys.org/baby-loss-support/stories/stillbirth/dont-bottle-it-message-one-stillborn-dad-another.

Compton, Julie. 2019. "Trans Dads Tell Doctors: 'You Can Be a Man and Have a Baby.'" NBC News, May 18, 2019; updated May 20, 2019.

Gaudino, J. A., Jr., B. Jenkins, and R. W. Rochat. 1999. "No Fathers' Names: A Risk Factor for Infant Mortality in the State of Georgia, USA." *Social Science and Medicine* 48 (2): 253–265.

Geary, Daniel. 2015. "The Moynihan Report: An Annotated Edition." *Atlantic*, September 14, 2015.

Halliwell, Rachel. 2014. "Miscarriage Report: 'Dads Grieve Too: Why Didn't Anyone Ask If I Was OK.'" *Telegraph*, July 22, 2014.

Healthline. n.d. "Transgender Pregnancy: Moving Past Misconceptions." Last modified October 22, 2020. https://www.healthline.com/health/pregnancy/transgender-pregnancy-moving-past-misconceptions.

Johnson, Reginald, Sr. 2011. "Spike Lee on Fathers and Infant Mortality." YouTube video, 1:53. July 8, 2011. https://www.youtube.com/watch?v=dYG_ITBuSO4.

Maslin, Sarah. 2014. "Facing Grim Infant Death Rates, Milwaukee Focuses on Black Fathers." *Journal Sentinel*, October 11, 2014.

Morris, Warren. 2018. "The Often Lonely Road: On Being an Angel Dad." *Still Standing Magazine*, August 30, 2018.

Moyer, Crystal. 2018. "Barbershops Display Empty Baby Shoes to Raise Infant Mortality Awareness." News 4 Jax, September 27, 2018.

Pearce, Ruth. 2019. "If a Man Gives Birth, He's the Father—the Experiences of Trans Parents." Conversation, September 25, 2019.

Raeburn, Daniel. 2016. *Vessels: A Love Story*. New York: W. W. Norton.

Ravitch, Michael. n.d. "The Neverknown." Reconceiving Loss, https://reconceivingloss.com/the-neverknown-by-michael-ravitch/.

Rutgers University. 2019. "Pregnant Transgender Men at Risk for Depression and Lack of Care, Rutgers Study Finds." *EurekAlert!*, August 15, 2019.

Schaaf, Mark. 2016. "Dads Big Part of Infant Mortality Issues, Officials Say." *Journal Times*, June 20, 2016.

Shafer, Tara. 2016. "Men Grieve Baby Loss Differently but No Less Acutely." *Psychology Today*, April 13, 2016.

Stroumsa, Daphna, Elizabeth F. S. Roberts, Hadrian Kinnear, and Lisa H. Harris. 2019. "The Power and Limits of Classification—A 32-Year-Old Man with Abdominal Pain." *New England Journal of Medicine* 380:1885–1888.

Teigen, Chrissy. 2020. "Hi." Medium. October 27, 2020. https://chrissyteigen.medium.com/hi-2e45e6faf764.

University of Leeds. n.d. "An International Exploration of Transmasculine Experiences of Reproduction." https://transpregnancy.leeds.ac.uk/.

USF Health. 2010. "Fathers' Involvement Tied to Infant Mortality Rate." June 17, 2010.

DEPRIVATION

Ardiel, Evan L., and Catharine H. Rankin. 2010. "The Importance of Touch in Development." *Paediatrics and Child Health* 15 (3): 153–156.

Blum, Deborah. 2002. *Love at Goon Park: Harry Harlow and the Science of Affection*. New York: Perseus.

Bowlby, John. 1951. "Maternal Care and Mental Health: A Report Prepared on Behalf of the World Health Organization as a Contribution to the United Nations Programme for the Welfare of Homeless Children." *Bulletin of the World Health Organization* 3:355–534.

Burns, Robert B. 1991. "Maternal Deprivation." In *Essential Psychology*, edited by Robert B. Burns, 148–161. Dordrecht, Netherlands: Springer.

Casper, Monica J. 2016. "When Cities Fail, Babies Die." *Metropolitics*, February 2, 2016. https://metropolitiques.eu/When-Cities-Fail-Babies-Die.html.

Guzman, Martina. 2019. "Welcome to Detroit, Where Black Babies Are at Higher Risk of Death." *Guardian*, January 31, 2019.

Hansen, Elaine Tuttle. 1997. *Mother without Child: Contemporary Fiction and the Crisis of Motherhood*. Berkeley: University of California Press.

Haraway, Donna. 1989. *Primate Visions: Gender, Race, and Nature in the World of Modern Science*. New York: Routledge.

Harlow, Harry F. 1958. "The Nature of Love." *American Psychologist* 13 (12): 673–685.

Harmon, Katherine. 2010. "How Important Is Physical Contact with Your Infant?" *Scientific American*, May 6, 2010.

Hrdy, Sarah Blaffer. 2000. *Mother Nature: Maternal Instincts and How They Shape the Human Species*. Illustrated ed. New York: Ballantine Books.

Mead, Margaret. 1962. "A Cultural Anthropologist's Approach to Maternal Deprivation." *Public Health Papers* 14:45–62.

ReStore National Centre for Research Methods. n.d. "Townsend Deprivation Index." Last accessed September 26, 2021. https://www.restore.ac.uk/geo-refer/36229dtuks00y19810000.php.

Robert Graham Center. n.d. "Social Deprivation Index (SDI)." Last accessed September 26, 2021. https://www.graham-center.org/rgc/maps-data-tools/sdi/social-deprivation-index.html.

Smuts, Barbara. 2003. "No More Wire Mothers, Ever." *New York Times*, February 2, 2003.

Spitz, Rene A. 1945. "Hospitalism: An Inquiry into the Genesis of Psychiatric Conditions in Early Childhood." *The Psychoanalytic Study of the Child* 1 (1): 53–74.

Townsend, Peter. 2009. "Deprivation." *Journal of Social Policy* 16 (2): 125–146.

van der Horst, Frank C. P., and René van der Veer. 2008. "Loneliness in Infancy: Harry Harlow, John Bowlby, and Issues of Separation." *Integrative Psychological and Behavioral Science* 42:325–335.

van Rosmalen, Lenny, Frank C. P. van der Horst, and René van der Veer. 2012. "Of Monkeys and Men: Spitz and Harlow on the Consequences of Maternal Deprivation." *Attachment and Human Development* 14 (4): 425–437.

Varela-Silva, Inês. 2016. "Can a Lack of Love Be Deadly?" Conversation, May 19, 2016.

Vicdeo, Marga. 2010. "The Evolution of Harry Harlow: From the Nature to the Nurture of Love." *History of Psychiatry* 21 (2): 1–16.

Wallace, Maeve E., Joia Crear-Perry, Carmen Green, Erica Felker-Kantor, and Katherine Theall. 2019. "Privilege and Deprivation in Detroit: Infant Mortality and the Index of Concentration at the Extremes." *International Journal of Epidemiology* 48 (1): 207–216.

DISABILITY

Booth, Katie. 2018. "What I Learned about Disability and Infanticide from Peter Singer." Aeon, January 10, 2018.

Caeton, D. A. 2011. "Choice of a Lifetime: Disability, Feminism, and Reproductive Rights." *Disability Studies Quarterly* 31 (1). https://dsq-sds.org/article/view/1369/1501.

Centers for Disease Control and Production. n.d. "Birth Defects." Last accessed September 26, 2021. https://www.cdc.gov/ncbddd/birthdefects/prevention.html.

———. n.d. "Infant Mortality." Last accessed September 26, 2021. https://www.cdc.gov/reproductivehealth/maternalinfanthealth/infantmortality.htm.

Comfort, Nathaniel. 2012. "The Eugenic Impulse." *Chronicle of Higher Education*, November 12, 2012.

Copeland, Shelby. 2019. "Arkansas Bill Pushes to Ban Abortion in Down Syndrome Cases." CNN Health, March 22, 2019.

Davis, Lennard J., ed. 2017. *The Disability Studies Reader.* 5th ed. New York: Routledge.

Ely, Danielle M., and Anne K. Driscoll. 2019. "Infant Mortality in the United States, 2017: Data from the Period Linked Birth/Infant Death File." *National Vital Statistics Reports* 68 (10): 1–20.

Fleischer, Doris, and Frieda Zames. 2011. *The Disability Rights Movement: From Charity to Confrontation.* Philadelphia: Temple University Press.

Goldblatt Hyatt, Erica. 2020. "Chrissy Teigen's Pain Reminds Us That Ours Is Silenced, Too." NJ.com, October 5, 2020.

———. 2021. "Counseling Women Who Have Terminated a Pregnancy Due to Fetal Anomaly (TOPFA): The ACCEPT Model." *Clinical Social Work Journal* 49:52–63. https://link .springer.com/article/10.1007/s10615-019-00732-0.

———. n.d. "Termination." Unpublished manuscript, last accessed September 26, 2021. PDF.

Griebel, Craig P., John Halvorsen, Thomas P. Golemon, and Anthony A. Day. 2005. "Management of Spontaneous Abortion." *American Family Physician* 72 (7): 1243–1250.

Guttmacher Institute. 2021. "Abortion Bans in Cases of Sex or Race Selection or Genetic Anomaly." Last modified August 1, 2021. https://www.guttmacher.org/state-policy/explore/abortion -bans-cases-sex-or-race-selection-or-genetic-anomaly#.

Hall, Kim Q., ed. 2011. *Feminist Disability Studies.* Bloomington: Indiana University Press.

McCammon, Sarah. 2017. "Down Syndrome Families Divided over Abortion Ban." NPR, *Morning Edition,* podcast, MP3 audio, 3:21, December 13, 2017. https://www.npr.org/2017/ 12/13/570173685/down-syndrome-families-divided-over-abortion-ban.

McRuer, Robert. 2006. *Crip Theory: Cultural Signs of Queerness and Disability.* New York: New York University Press.

Natoli, Jaime L., Deborah L. Ackerman, Suzanne McDermott, and Janice G. Edwards. 2012. "Prenatal Diagnosis of Down Syndrome: A Systematic Review of Termination Rates (1995–2011)." *Prenatal Diagnosis* 32 (2): 142–153.

Petrini, Joann, Karla Damus, Rebecca Russell, Karalee Poschman, Michael J. Davidoff, and Donald Mattison. 2002. "Contributions of Birth Defects to Infant Mortality in the United States." *Teratology* 66 (S1): S3–S6.

Piepzna-Samarasinha, Leah Lakshmi. 2018. *Care Work: Dreaming Disability Justice.* Vancouver, Canada: Arsenal Pulp.

Quinones, Julian, and Arijeta Lajka. 2017. "'What Kind of Society Do You Want to Live In?': Inside the Country Where Down Syndrome Is Disappearing." CBS News, August 14, 2017.

Shapiro, Joseph P. 1994. *No Pity: People with Disabilities Forging a New Civil Rights Movement.* New York: Random House.

Siebers, Tobin. 2008. *Disability Theory.* Ann Arbor: University of Michigan Press.

Singer, Peter. 2013. "Discussing Infanticide." *Journal of Medical Ethics* 39 (5): 260.

Thomson, Rosemarie Garland. 1997. *Extraordinary Bodies: Figuring Physical Disability in American Culture and Literature.* New York: Columbia University Press.

Todorović, Ana. 2016. "Nadia's Story." Aeon, July 21, 2016. https://aeon.co/essays/my-daughter -came-out-they-handed-her-to-me-she-was-dead.

World Health Organization. 2020. "Disability and Health." December 1, 2020. https://www .who.int/news-room/fact-sheets/detail/disability-and-health.

Zhang, Wangjian, Tanya L. Spero, Christopher G. Nolte, Valerie C. Garcia, Ziqiang Lin, Paul A. Romitti, Gary M. Shaw, Scott C. Sheridan, Marcia L. Feldkamp, Alison Woomert,

Syni-An Hwang, Sarah C. Fisher, Marily L. Browne, Yuantao Hao, Shao Lin, and the National Birth Defects Prevention Study. 2019. "Projected Changes in Maternal Heat Exposure during Early Pregnancy and the Associated Congenital Heart Defect Burden in the United States." *Journal of the American Heart Association* 8 (3). https://www.ahajournals.org/doi/10.1161/JAHA.118.010995.

DOULAS

American College of Obstetricians and Gynecologists. 2018. "Approaches to Limit Intervention during Labor and Birth." Committee on Obstetric Practice, Number 766, February 2019. https://www.acog.org/clinical/clinical-guidance/committee-opinion/articles/2019/02/approaches-to-limit-intervention-during-labor-and-birth.

American Pregnancy Association. n.d. "What Is a Doula?" Last accessed September 26, 2021. https://americanpregnancy.org/healthy-pregnancy/labor-and-birth/having-a-doula-616/.

Anderson, Christina. 2019. "Where Doulas Calm Nerves and Bridge Cultures during Childbirth." *New York Times*, January 2, 2019.

Bey, Asteir, Aimee Brill, Chanel Porcia-Albert, Melissa Gradilla, and Nan Strauss. 2019. "Advancing Birth Justice: Community-Based Doula Models as a Standard of Care for Ending Racial Disparities." Ancient Song Doula Services, Village Birth International, and Every Mother Counts, March 25, 2019. https://blackmamasmatter.org/wp-content/uploads/2019/03/Advancing-Birth-Justice-CBD-Models-as-Std-of-Care-3-25-19.pdf.

Block, Jennifer. 2008. *Pushed: The Painful Truth about Childbirth and Modern Maternity Care*. Boston: Da Capo.

Boden, Sarah. 2018. "Researchers Say Affordable Doula Services Might Lower Infant Mortality Rate." 90.5 WESA, May 23, 2018.

Carrasco, Jenn Aguilera. 2018. "Doulas Are Unicorns." Gentle Beginnings Birth Services, July 27, 2018. https://gentlebeginningsbirth.com/doulas-are-unicorns/.

Carter, Christine Michel. 2019. "Do Black Women Need Doulas More Than Anyone?" *Parents*, February 21, 2019.

Casper, Monica J. 2015. "An Interview with Sherry Payne: Nurse, Childbirth Educator, Womanist." *Feminist Wire*, January 15, 2015.

De Graaf, Mia. 2019. "World's Top Obstetricians Laugh about Meghan Markle's Home Birth Plan at Global Summit—but Others Say the Duchess Is Right to Confront Dangers of Childbirth for Black Women in the UK." *Daily Mail*, May 6, 2019.

DONA International. n.d. "DONA International History." Last accessed September 26, 2021. https://www.dona.org/the-dona-advantage/about/history/.

Dukehart, Coburn. 2011. "Doulas: Exploring a Tradition of Support." NPR, July 14, 2011.

Ehrenreich, Barbara, and Deirdre English. 2010. *Witches, Midwives, and Nurses: A History of Women Healers*. 2nd ed. New York: Feminist Press.

Gebel, Christina, and Sarah Hodin. 2020. "Expanding Access to Doula Care: State of the Union." *MHTF* (blog), Maternal Health Task Force at Harvard Chan School, January 8, 2020.

Griffin, Samantha. 2019. "If Meghan Markle Chose a Doula, An OB-GYN's Mocking Proved Her Right." Rewire News Group, May 7, 2019.

Holohan, Meghan. 2019. "Bereavement Doula Help Grieving Families with Pregnancy Loss." *Today*, August 12, 2019.

King-Miller, Lindsay. 2018. "How Doulas and Midwives around the Country Are Filling the Gaps in Birth Care for Queer Families." Rewire News Group, March 22, 2018.

Kusmer, Anna. 2018. "Manitoba Indigenous Doula Initiative Empowers Women, Helps Keep Kids Out of Welfare System." Rewire News Group, September 12, 2018.

Luke, Jenny M. 2018. *Delivered by Midwives: African American Midwifery in the Twentieth-Century South*. Jackson: University Press of Mississippi.

Mamana. 2013. "The Term 'Doula' in Modern Greece." *International Doula Journal* 21 (1). https://www.mamana.gr/en/articles/94-the-term-%E2%80%98doula%E2%80%99-in-modern-greece.

McDaniels, Andrea K. 2017. "Baltimore Enlists Doulas to Help Bring Down Infant Mortality Rate." *Washington Post*, August 7, 2017.

McGevna, Allison. 2019. "Are Doulas the Key to Help Save Black Mothers' Lives?" *Motherly*, June 6, 2019.

McGregor, Deborah Kuhn. 1998. *From Midwives to Medicine: The Birth of American Gynecology*. New Brunswick, N.J.: Rutgers University Press.

Mishkin, Kathryn, and Luisa Fernandes. 2018. "Doulas as Agents of Reproductive Justice Who Promote Women's International Human Rights: An Evidence-Based Review and Comparative Case Study between Brazil and the United States." In *Reproductive Ethics II: New Ideas and Innovations*, edited by Lisa Campo-Engelstein and Paul Burcher, 161–178. Cham, Switzerland: Springer.

Morton, Christine H., and Elayne Clift. 2014. *Birth Ambassadors: Doulas and the Re-emergence of Woman-Supported Birth in America*. Amarillo, Tex.: Praeclarus.

Moss, Rebecca. 2019. "Tewa Women United." *Vogue*, March 6, 2019.

New York State Doula Pilot Program. n.d. New York State, Department of Health. Last accessed September 26, 2021. https://www.health.ny.gov/health_care/medicaid/redesign/doulapilot/index.htm.

OBOS Pregnancy and Birth Contributors. 2010. "The Role of Doulas." *Our Bodies, Ourselves*, October 16, 2010; updated April 3, 2014. https://www.ourbodiesourselves.org/book-excerpts/health-article/doulas/.

Ollove, Michael. 2017. "To Reduce Infant Mortality, Cities Enlist Doulas for Black Moms." PEW *Stateline*, August 17, 2017.

Oparah, Julia Chinyere, Helen Arega, Dantia Hudson, Linda Jones, and Talita Oseguera. 2018. *Battling over Birth: Black Women and the Maternal Health Care Crisis*, 136–137. Amarillo, Tex.: Praeclarus.

Owens, Deirdre Cooper. 2017. *Medical Bondage: Race, Gender, and the Origins of American Gynecology*. Athens: University of Georgia Press.

Papagni, Karla, and Ellen Buckner. 2006. "Doula Support and Attitudes of Intrapartum Nurses: A Qualitative Study from the Patient's Perspective." *Journal of Perinatal Education* 15 (1): 11–18.

Pearson, Catherine, and Lena Jackson. 2019. "Why We Need More Black Doulas." *HuffPost*, February 28, 2019.

Pérez, Miriam Zoila. 2016. "How Racism Harms Pregnant Women—and What Can Help." TEDWomen, October 2016. https://www.ted.com/talks/miriam_zoila_perez_how_racism_harms_pregnant_women_and_what_can_help?language=en.

Rice, Ashley. 2019. "Milwaukee ZIP Code with Highest Infant Mortality Rate to Get 100 Doulas." WTMJ-TV, April 2, 2019.

Roberts, Sam. 2016. "Dana Raphael, Proponent of Breast-Feeding and Use of Doulas, Dies at 90." *New York Times*, February 19, 2016.

Sauer, Mary. 2017. "What Is a 'Bereavement Doula?'" *Romper*, April 19, 2017.

Schiller, Rebecca. 2019. "Birth Doulas Are Misunderstood. Here's What We Actually Do." *Week*, March 13, 2019.

Schwartz, Marie Jenkins. 2010. *Birthing a Slave: Motherhood and Medicine in the Antebellum South*. Cambridge, Mass.: Harvard University Press.

Tennessee Department of Health. 2019. "Tennessee Issues First Maternal Mortality Report." February 19, 2019. https://www.tn.gov/health/news/2019/2/19/tennessee-issues-first -maternal-mortality-report.html.

Thompson, Emily. 2019. "Why I Hired a Bereavement Doula for My Pregnancy Loss." *Blood + Milk*, May 7, 2019.

Truong, Kimberly. 2019. "Meghan Markle's Rumored Birth Plan Was Reportedly the Butt of a Joke for Some Top Doctors." *InStyle*, May 6, 2019.

Tulsa Family Doulas. 2017. "The Mystery of the Magical Doula Fairy Dust." January 28, 2017. http://www.tulsafamilydoulas.com/blog/2017/1/28/the-mystery-of-the-magical-doula -fairy-dust.

Uzazi Village. n.d. "About." Last accessed September 26, 2021. https://uzazivillage.org/about/.

Wertz, Richard W., and Dorothy C. Wertz. 1989. *Lying-In: A History of Childbirth in America*. Expanded ed. New Haven, Conn.: Yale University Press.

Wilder, Candice. 2018. "Racism Is Killing Black Babies, but This Doula Is Fighting Back." Vice, September 27, 2018.

EMPTINESS

Brown, Keri. 2013. "Empty Baby Strollers a Stark Reminder of Infant Mortality." WFDD, September 18, 2013.

Davis, Deborah L. 2016. *Empty Cradle, Broken Heart: Surviving the Death of Your Baby*. 3rd ed. Golden, Colo.: Fulcrum.

Martinez, Claudya. 2017. "What This Mom Did after Her Baby Died from SIDS Is Incredible." Mom.com, July 24, 2017.

Murphy, Eliza. n.d. "'When You (and Your Nursery) Are Left Empty, Messy and Unfinished': Mom's Anguish after Baby's Stillbirth." Love What Matters. Last accessed September 26, 2021. https://www.lovewhatmatters.com/when-you-and-your-nursery-are-left-empty -messy-and-unfinished-moms-anguish-after-babys-stillbirth/.

Ollstein, Alice Miranda. 2019. "Republicans Pound Abortion 'Infanticide' Message." Politico, March 2, 2019.

Rotkirch, A. 2007. "All That She Wants Is A(nother) Baby: Longing for Children as a Fertility Incentive of Growing Importance." *Journal of Evolutionary Psychology* 5 (1): 89–104.

Vredevelt, Pam. 2001. *Empty Arms: Hope and Support for Those Who Have Suffered a Miscarriage, Stillbirth or Tubal Pregnancy*. Colorado Springs, Colo.: Multnomah.

ENVY

Burton, Neel. 2014. "The Psychology and Philosophy of Envy." *Psychology Today*, August 21, 2014.

Fullmetal Alchemist Wiki. n.d. "Home." Last accessed September 26, 2021. https://fma.fandom .com/wiki/Main_Page.

Gurevich, Rachel. 2019. "How to Deal with Pregnancy Envy: Why We Feel Pregnancy Envy and Learning How to Let Go." Verywell Family, November 13, 2019.

Kersting, Anette, and Birgit Wagner. 2012. "Complicated Grief after Perinatal Loss." *Dialogues in Clinical Neuroscience* 14 (2): 187–194.

Lamia, Mary C. 2011. "Envy: The Emotion Kept Secret." *Psychology Today*, March 15, 2011.

Orlaske, Jessica. 2018. "An Open Letter to a Happy Mama from Her Bereaved Mama Friend." *Still Standing Magazine*, January 9, 2018. https://stillstandingmag.com/2018/01/09/open -letter-happy-mama-bereaved-mama-friend/.

Samuel, Alexandra. 2018. "What to Do When Social Media Inspires Envy." JSTOR Daily, February 6, 2018.

Stanford Encyclopedia of Philosophy. 2002. "Envy." December 8, 2002; updated December 22, 2016. https://plato.stanford.edu/entries/envy/.

"When a New Envy Rises." 2014. *Still Standing Magazine*, January 21, 2014. https://still standingmag.com/2014/01/21/new-envy-rises/.

Whitbourne, Susan Krauss. 2015. "What to Do When Social Media Makes You Miserable." *Psychology Today*, November 21, 2015.

EPIGENETICS

Burris, Heather H., Andrea A. Baccarelli, Robert O. Wright, and Rosalind J. Wright. 2016. "Epigenetics: Linking Social and Environmental Exposures to Preterm Birth." *Pediatric Research* 79 (1): 136–140.

Burris, Heather H., and James W. Collins. 2010. "Race and Preterm Birth—the Case for Epigenetic Inquiry." *Ethnicity and Disease* 20 (3): 296–299.

Chiapparino, Luca. 2018. "Epigenetics: Ethics, Politics, Biosociality." *British Medical Bulletin* 128 (1): 49–60.

Costandi, Mo. 2011. "Pregnant 9/11 Survivors Transmitted Trauma to Their Children." *Guardian*, September 9, 2011.

Dawson, Faith. 2018. "New Hope for a New Generation." *Tulanian: The Magazine of Tulane University*, December 2018.

Dupras, Charles, and Vardit Ravitsky. 2016. "The Ambiguous Nature of Epigenetic Responsibility." *Journal of Medical Ethics* 42:534–541.

Hamilton, Jon. 2013. "How a Pregnant Woman's Choices Can Shape a Child's Health." NPR, *Morning Edition*, podcast, MP3 audio, 4:38, September 23, 2013.

Kellermann, Natan Pf. 2013. "Epigenetic Transmission of Holocaust Trauma: Can Nightmares Be Inherited?" *Israel Journal of Psychiatry and Related Sciences* 50 (1): 33–39.

Kuzawa, Christopher W., and Elizabeth Sweet. 2009. "Epigenetics and the Embodiment of Race: Developmental Origins of US Racial Disparities in Cardiovascular Health." *American Journal of Human Biology* 21 (1): 2–15.

Lock, Margaret. 2013. "The Lure of the Epigenome." *Lancet* 381 (9881): P1896–P1897.

Noble, Denis. 2015. "Conrad Waddington and the Origin of Epigenetics." *Journal of Experimental Biology* 218:816–818.

Rothstein, Mark A., Yu Cai, and Gary E. Marchant. 2009. "Ethical Implications of Epigenetic Research." *Nature Reviews Genetics* 10:224.

Shulevitz, Judith. 2014. "Geneticists' New Obsession with Pregnancy Isn't Bad for Women." *New Republic*, August 17, 2014.

Skinner, Michael K., and Carlos Guerrero-Bosagna. 2009. "Environmental Signals and Transgenerational Epigenetics." *Epigenomics* 1 (1): 111–117.

Squier, Susan Merrill. 2017. *Epigenetic Landscapes: Drawings as Metaphor*, 1. Durham, N.C.: Duke University Press.

Stanford Encyclopedia of Philosophy 2005. "Epigenesis and Preformationism." October 11, 2005.

Sullivan, Shannon. 2013. "Inheriting Racist Disparities in Health." *Critical Philosophy of Race* 1 (2): 190–218.

Thayer, Zaneta M., and Christopher W. Kuzawa. 2011. "Biological Memories of Past Environments: Epigenetic Pathways to Health Disparities." *Epigenetics* 6 (7): 798–803.

Vick, Alexis D., and Heather H. Burris. 2017. "Epigenetics and Health Disparities." *Current Epidemiology Reports* 4 (1): 31–37.

Weinhold, Bob. 2006. "Epigenetics: The Science of Change." *Environmental Health Perspectives* 114 (3): A160–A167.

Yehuda, Rachel, Linda M. Bierer, James Schmeidler, Daniel H. Aferiat, Ilana Breslau, and Susan Dolan. 2000. "Low Cortisol and Risk for PTSD in Adult Offspring of Holocaust Survivors." *American Journal of Psychiatry* 157 (8): 1252–1259.

FOLIC ACID

Bixenstine, Paul J., Tina L. Cheng, Diane Cheng, Katherine A. Connor, and Kamila B. Mistry. 2015. "Folic Acid Supplementation before Pregnancy: Reasons for Non-use and Associations with Preconception Counseling." *Maternal and Child Health Journal* 19 (9): 1974–1984.

Blencowe, Hannah, Simon Cousens, Bernadette Model, and Joy Lawn. 2010. "Folic Acid to Reduce Neonatal Mortality from Neural Tube Disorders." *International Journal of Epidemiology* 39 (S1): i110–i120.

Brones, Anna. 2018. "Food Apartheid: The Root of the Problem with America's Groceries." *Guardian*, May 15, 2018.

Caminiti, Susan. 2016. "America's Dirty Little Secret: 42 Million People Are Suffering from Hunger." CNBC, December 13, 2016.

Casper, Monica J., and Lisa Jean Moore. 2009. *Missing Bodies: The Politics of Visibility*. New York: New York University Press.

Centers for Disease Control and Prevention. n.d. "Folic Acid." Last accessed September 26, 2021. https://www.cdc.gov/ncbddd/folicacid/about.html.

———. n.d. "Planning for Pregnancy." Last accessed September 26, 2021. https://www.cdc .gov/preconception/planning.html.

Champlin, Emily R. 2016. "The Myth of the 'Welfare Queen': Reproductive Oppression in the Welfare System." *Poverty Law Conference and Symposium* 6. https://digitalcommons .law.ggu.edu/povlaw/6/.

Cheng, Tina L., Kamila B. Mistry, Guoying Wang, Barry Zuckerman, and Xiaobin Wang. 2018. "Folate Nutrition Status in Mothers of the Boston Birth Cohort, Sample of a US Urban Low-Income Population." *American Journal of Public Health* 108 (6): 799–807.

Crider, Krista S., Lynn B. Bailey, and Robert J. Berry. 2011. "Folic Acid Food Fortification—Its History, Effect, Concerns, and Future Directions." *Nutrients* 3 (3): 370–384.

Florida, Richard. 2018. "It's Not the Food Deserts: It's the Inequality." *Bloomberg CityLab*, January 18, 2018.

Greenberg, James A., Stacey J. Bell, Yong Guan, and Yan-hong Yu. 2011. "Folic Acid Supplementation and Pregnancy: More Than Just Neural Tube Defects Prevention." *Reviews in Obstetrics and Gynecology* 4 (2): 52–59.

Harrison, Clancy Cash. 2017. "Challenging the Stigma of Food Assistance." *Food and Nutrition*, January 20, 2017.

Hibbard, Bryan. 1964. "The Role of Folic Acid in Pregnancy." *British Journal of Obstetrics and Gynaecology: An International Journal of Obstetrics and Gynaecology* 71:529–542.

Hobson, Katherine. 2017. "Women Still Need Folic Acid Supplements to Prevent Birth Defects." NPR, January 20, 2017.

Hoffbrand, A. V., and D. G. Weir. 2001. "The History of Folic Acid." *British Journal of Haematology* 113:579–589.

Iacobucci, Gareth. 2018. "Experts Urge Addition of Folic Acid to Flour to Halt 'Avoidable Tragedy' of Birth Defects." *British Medical Journal* 360:k477.

Kancherla, Vijaya, Hallie Averbach, and Godfrey P. Oakley Jr. 2019. "Nation-Wide Failure of Voluntary Folic Acid Fortification of Corn Masa Flour and Tortillas with Folic Acid." *Birth Defects Research* 111 (11): 672–675.

Kelland, Kate. 2018. "Scientists Urge UK to Fortify Flour with Folic Acid to Limit Birth Defects." *Reuters*, January 30, 2018.

Kogan, Rachel. 2019. "Rollback of Nutrition Standards Not Supported by Evidence." *Health Affairs*, March 13, 2019.

Lawrence, Mark. 2013. *Food Fortification: The Evidence, Ethics, and Politics of Adding Nutrients to Food*. Oxford, U.K.: Oxford University Press.

Lynch, Lauren. 2017. "Treatment of Anemia during Pregnancy (1931), by Lucy Wills." *Embryo Project Encyclopedia*, Arizona State University. April 20, 2017; updated July 4, 2018. https://embryo.asu.edu/pages/treatment-anemia-during-pregnancy-1931-lucy-wills.

Morris, J. K., J. Rankin, E. S. Draper, J. J. Kurinczuk, A. Springett, D. Tucker, D. Wellesley, B. Wreyford, and N. J. Wald. 2016. "Prevention of Neural Tube Defects in the UK: A Missed Opportunity." *Archives of Disease in Childhood* 101:604–607.

U.S. Department of Agriculture. 2013. "About WIC—How WIC Helps." USDA Food and Nutrition Service. https://www.fns.usda.gov/wic/about-wic-how-wic-helps.

———. 2016. "USDA Improves the WIC Shopping Experience to Better Serve Our Nation's Low-Income, New and Expecting Mothers and Their Young Children." Press release no. USDA 0053.16, February 29, 2016.

———. 2020. "Key Statistics and Graphics." USDA Economic Research Service. Last updated September 9, 2020. https://www.ers.usda.gov/topics/food-nutrition-assistance/food-security-in-the-us/key-statistics-graphics.aspx.

Wald, Nicholas J. 2011. "Commentary: A Brief History of Folic Acid in the Prevention of Neural Tube Defects." *International Journal of Epidemiology* 40 (5): 1154–1156.

FRACKING

Akpan, Nsikan. 2017. "Babies Born Closer to Fracking Sites Are More Likely to be Underweight." *PBS News Hour*, December 13, 2017.

Apergis, Nicholas, Tasawar Hayat, and Tareq Saeed. 2019. "Fracking and Infant Mortality: Fresh Evidence from Oklahoma." *Environmental Science and Pollution Research* 26:32360–32367.

Bienkowski, Brian. 2015. "Poor Communities Bear Greatest Burden from Fracking." *Scientific American*, May 6, 2015.

Bruederle, Anna, and Roland Hodler. 2019. "Effects of Oil Spills on Infant Mortality in Nigeria." *Proceedings of the National Academy of Sciences* 116 (12): 5467–5471.

Busby, Christopher, and Joseph J. Mangano. 2017. "There's a World Going on Underground—Infant Mortality and Fracking in Pennsylvania." *Journal of Environmental Protection* 8 (4): 381–393.

Casper, Monica J., ed. 2003. *Synthetic Planet: Chemical Politics and the Hazards of Modern Life*. New York: Routledge.

Clabots, Barbara. 2019. "The Darkest Side of Fossil-Fuel Extraction." *Scientific American*, October 14, 2019.

Clough, Emily, and Derek Bell. 2016. "Just Fracking: A Distributive Environmental Justice Analysis of Unconventional Gas Development in Pennsylvania, USA." *Environmental Research Letters* 11 (2). https://iopscience.iop.org/article/10.1088/1748-9326/11/2/025001.

Cotton, Matthew. 2016. "Fair Fracking? Ethics and Environmental Justice in United Kingdom Shale Gas Policy and Planning." *International Journal of Justice and Sustainability* 22 (2): 185–202. https://www.tandfonline.com/doi/full/10.1080/13549839.2016.1186613.

Currie, Janet, Michael Greenstone, and Katherine Meckel. 2017. "Hydraulic Fracturing and Infant Health: New Evidence from Pennsylvania." *Science Advances* 3 (12): e1603021. https://www.science.org/doi/10.1126/sciadv.1603021.

Enverus. 2012. "10 Reasons Fracking Improves American Lives." October 5, 2012. https://www.enverus.com/blog/10-reasons-fracking-improves-american-lives/.

EPIC News. 2017. "Hydraulic Fracturing Decreases Infant Health, Study Finds." Energy Policy Institute at the University of Chicago, December 13, 2017.

FracTracker Alliance. n.d. "Waste." Last accessed September 26, 2021. https://www.fractracker.org/topics/waste/.

Greenstone, Michael. 2018. "Fracking Has Its Costs and Benefits—the Trick Is Balancing Them." *Forbes*, February 20, 2018.

Haelle, Tara. 2017. "Living near Fracking during Pregnancy Linked to Poorer Newborn Health." *Forbes*, December 15, 2017.

Harvey, Fiona. 2019. "High Court Rules Government's Fracking Guidelines 'Unlawful.'" *Guardian*, March 6, 2019.

Healy, Melissa. 2017. "Babies Born to Moms Who Lived near Fracking Wells Faced Host of Health Risks, Study Suggests." *Los Angeles Times*, December 13, 2017.

Hudetz, Mary. 2019. "US Official: Research Finds Uranium in Navajo Women, Babies." Associated Press, October 7, 2019.

Kille, Leighton Walter. 2014. "Fracking, Shale Gas and Health Effects: Research Roundup." *Journalist's Resource*, November 14, 2014.

Knox, Annie, and Kristen Moulton. 2015. "Midwife Was Right: Uinta Basin Sees Spike in Infant Deaths." *Salt Lake Tribune*, March 18, 2015.

Koster, Hilda B. 2018. "Trafficked Lands/Fractured Bodies: Sexual Violence, Oil, and Structural Evil in the Dakotas (@theTable: Planetary Solidarity)." Feminist Studies in Religion, March 23, 2018.

Maddow, Rachel. 2019. *Blowout: Corrupted Democracy, Rogue State Russia, and the Richest, Most Destructive Industry on Earth*, xx–xxi. New York: Crown.

Mazur, Alan. 2014. "How Did the Fracking Controversy Emerge in the Period 2010–2012?" *Public Understanding of Science* 25 (2): 207–222.

McDermott-Levy, Ruth, Nina Kaktins, and Barbara Sattler. 2013. "Fracking, the Environment, and Health." *American Journal of Nursing* 113 (6): 45–51.

Meyer, Robinson. 2017. "New, Major Evidence That Fracking Harms Human Health." *Atlantic*, December 13, 2017.

Mischen, Pamela, and Stephanie Swim. 2018. "Social Equity and 'Fracking': Local Awareness and Responses." *Administration and Society* 52 (1): 138–165.

Paternoster, Tamsin. 2014. "Miscarriage and Stillbirth Linked to Fracking Chemical Exposure." *Ecologist*, December 15, 2014.

Richards, Martin, José Maria Sotomayor, and Rune Olsen. 2015. "The Key to Deciding the Fracking Debate?" Oil and Gas IQ, September 28, 2015.

Shukman, David. 2018. "What Is Fracking and Why Is It Controversial?" BBC News, October 15, 2018.

Solotaroff, Paul. 2015. "What's Killing the Babies of Vernal, Utah?" *Rolling Stone*, June 22, 2015.

Tickell, Oliver. 2017. "Fracking Kills Newborn Babies—Polluted Water Likely Cause." *Ecologist*, April 25, 2017.

Turner, Jim. 2019. "Florida Senate Considering Adding Everglades Protections to Controversial Anti-fracking Bill." *Sun Sentinel*, March 4, 2019.

Webb, Ellen, Sheila Bushkin-Bedient, Amanda Cheng, Christopher D. Kassotis, Victoria Balise, and Susan C. Nagel. 2014. "Developmental and Reproductive Effects of Chemicals Associated with Unconventional Oil and Natural Gas Operations." *Reviews on Environmental Health* 29 (4): 307–318.

FRANKENSTEIN

Bennett, Betty T., ed. 1980. *The Letters of Mary Wollstonecraft Shelley*. Baltimore, Md.: Johns Hopkins University Press.

Franklin, Ruth. 2012. "Was 'Frankenstein' Really about Childbirth?" *New Republic*, March 6, 2012.

Guston, David H., Ed Finn, and Jason Scott, eds. 2017. *Frankenstein: Annotated for Scientists, Engineers, and Creators of All Kinds*. Cambridge, Mass.: MIT Press.

Judge, Lita. 2018. *Mary's Monster: Love, Madness, and How Mary Shelley Created Frankenstein*. New York: Roaring Brook.

Lepore, Jill. 2018. "The Strange and Twisted Life of 'Frankenstein.'" *New Yorker*, February 5, 2018.

Popova, Maria. 2018. "200 Years of Frankenstein: Mary Shelley's Masterpiece as a Lens on Today's Most Pressing Questions of Science, Ethics, and Human Creativity." *Brain Pickings* (blog), June 14, 2018.

Ruston, Sharon. 2015. "The Science of Life and Death in Mary Shelley's Frankenstein." Public Domain Review, November 25, 2015.

Sampson, Fiona. 2018. *In Search of Mary Shelley: The Girl Who Wrote Frankenstein*. London: Profile Books.

Shelley, Mary. 1818. *Frankenstein: The 1818 Text*. Introduction by Charlotte Gordon. London: Penguin Classics.

GRIEF

Berns, Nancy. 2011. *Closure: The Rush to End Grief and What It Costs Us*, 18. Philadelphia: Temple University Press. See also: http://www.nancyberns.com/.

Heineman, Elizabeth. 2014. *Ghostbelly: A Memoir*, 26–27, 105, 237–238. New York: Feminist Press.

hooks, bell. 2000. *All about Love: New Visions*, 200. New York: HarperCollins.

Inglis, Kate. 2018. *Notes for the Everlost: A Field Guide to Grief*, 102. Boulder, Colo.: Shambhala.

Prager, Sarah. 2020. "Pregnancy Loss Is Lonely—Especially for Transgender People." Healthline, December 9, 2020.

Riggs, Damien W., Ruth Pearce, Carla A. Pfeffer, Sally Hines, Francis Ray White, and Elisabetta Ruspini. 2020. "Men, Trans/Masculine, and Non-binary People's Experiences of Pregnancy Loss: An International Qualitative Study." *BMC Pregnancy and Childbirth* 20 (482). https://doi.org/10.1186/s12884-020-03166-6.

Stewart, Jamie. 2019. "This 'Sickness' Called Grief." *Still Standing Magazine*, April 24, 2019.

GUILT

Alice's Mom. 2017. "What Most Loss Parents Won't Tell You: Loss and Guilt." *Alice and After*, May 4, 2017. https://www.aliceandafter.com/new-blog/2017/5/4/the-worst-thing-you-can-do-to-a-grieving-parent-loss-and-guilt.

Boudin, Michelle. 2017. "Grieving Mom Whose 3-Month-Old Baby Died in His Sleep Shares What Could Have Prevented His Death: 'I Carry Guilt.'" *People*, July 18, 2017.

Cameron. 2018. "One Complicated Conclusion." *Glow in the Woods* (blog), December 4, 2018. http://www.glowinthewoods.com/blog/2018/12/4/complicated-conclusion.

Davis, Deborah L. 2015. "Coping with Guilt after Your Baby Dies." *Psychology Today*, September 13, 2013.

Dubé, Dani-Elle. 2017. "This Woman's Baby Died in His Crib, and Now She Has a Warning for Other Parents." Global News, July 7, 2017.

Evans, Diana. 2018. "New Mothers, Welcome to a World of Guilt." *Guardian*, June 22, 2018.

Fish, Jefferson M. 2016. "Guilt and Shame." *Psychology Today*, September 20, 2016.

Gold, Katherine J., Ananda Sen, and Irving Leon. 2017. "Whose Fault Is It Anyway? Guilt, Blame, and Death Attribution by Mothers after Stillbirth or Infant Death." *Illness, Crisis and Loss* 26 (1): 40–57.

Heinig, M. Jane. 2000. "Bed Sharing and Infant Mortality: Guilt by Association?" *Journal of Human Lactation* 16 (3): 189–191.

Julia. 2010. "The Sum of All Fears." *Glow in the Woods* (blog), October 5, 2010. http://www.glowinthewoods.com/blog/?offset=1297103531000&category=guilt.

Justin. 2016. "17." *Glow in the Woods* (blog), April 9, 2016. http://www.glowinthewoods.com/blog/2016/4/9/17.html.

Narjala, Susan. 2017. "Is 'Dad Guilt' Even a Thing?" Parent.com, September 27, 2017.

Owlet. n.d. Last accessed September 26, 2021. https://owletcare.com/.

Person, Tiffany L. A., Wendy A. Lavezzi, and Barbara C. Wolf. 2002. "Cosleeping and Sudden Unexpected Death in Infancy." *Archives of Pathology and Laboratory Medicine* 126:343–345.

HOPE

Baltimore City Health Department. n.d. "B'More for Healthy Babies." Last accessed September 26, 2021. https://health.baltimorecity.gov/maternal-and-child-health/bmore-healthy-babies.

Baskerville, Jennifer. 2015. "The Lessons I Learned after Losing a Baby, and Finding Hope." *Washington Post*, October 15, 2015.

Bears of Hope. n.d. Last accessed September 26, 2021. https://www.bearsofhope.org.au/.

Beryl. 2010. "Mother of Bella: Stillborn 9/11/09." Faces of Loss, Faces of Hope, September 30, 2010. http://facesofloss.com/2010/09/340.html.

Conaughton, Gig. 2013. "Study Could Provide Sudden Infant Death Syndrome Hope." County News Center, November 18, 2013.

Dickinson, Emily. 1951. "'Hope' Is the Thing with Feathers." In *The Complete Poems of Emily Dickinson*, edited by Thomas H. Johnson. Cambridge, Mass.: Belknap.

Evans, Michelle. 2018. "Fourth Annual Walk for Hope Shines Light on SIDS Awareness Month." *Baltimore Magazine*, October 1, 2018.

Kattwinkel, John. 2013. "Addressing High Infant Mortality in the Developing World: A Glimmer of Hope." *Pediatrics* 131 (2): e579–e581.

Kristin. 2010. "The Beginning: Stories of Hope." Faces of Loss, Faces of Hope, September 28, 2010. http://facesofloss.com/2010/09/the-beginning-stories-of-hope.html#comments.

KUOW Staff. 2018. "The Doula Who Delivers Hope for Puget Sound's Marginalized Mothers." KUOW, September 3, 2018.

Lopez, Tiffany. 2010. "Mother of Genesis, 3/16/07." Faces of Loss, Faces of Hope, September 30, 2010. http://facesofloss.com/2010/09/story-of-hope.html#more-341.

Richland Source. 2018. "Healing Hope: A Nationally Recognized Series on Infant Mortality." August 10, 2018. https://www.richlandsource.com/solutions/healing-hope-a-nationally-recognized-series-on-infant-mortality/collection_98b2447e-9cc0-11e8-a31e-57c3a6116032.html.

Silent Grief. n.d. "Home." Last accessed September 26, 2021. http://www.silentgrief.com/.

Smith, Diane. 2018. "Why Do Babies Die? ZIP Code Study Hopes to Find the Answers." *Fort-Worth Star Telegram*, January 20, 2018; updated January 22, 2018.

Sternberg, Steve. 2018. "Seeking Hope for the Nation's Slipping Health." *U.S. News and World Report*, August 17, 2018.

INFANT MORTALITY RATE

Alonso, William, and Paul Starr, eds. 1989. *The Politics of Numbers*. New York: Russell Sage.

Armstrong, David. 1986. "The Invention of Infant Mortality." *Sociology of Health and Illness* 8 (3): 211–232.

Bauer, Raymond A., ed. 1966. *Social Indicators*. Cambridge, Mass.: MIT Press.

Berman, Elizabeth Popp, and Daniel Hirschman. 2018. "The Sociology of Quantification: Where Are We Now?" *Contemporary Sociology* 47 (3): 257–266.

Bhatia, Amiya, Nancy Krieger, and S. V. Subramanian. 2019. "Learning from History about Reducing Infant Mortality: Contrasting the Centrality of Structural Interventions to Early 20th-Century Successes in the United States to Their Neglect in Current Global Initiatives." *Milbank Quarterly* 97 (1): 284–345.

Bowker, Geoffrey C., and Susan Leigh Star. 1999. *Sorting Things Out: Classification and Its Consequences*. Cambridge, Mass.: MIT Press.

Brosco, Jeffrey P. 1999. "The Early History of the Infant Mortality Rate in America: 'A Reflection upon the Past and a Prophecy of the Future.'" *Pediatrics* 103 (2): 478–485.

Casper, Monica J. 2013. "Biopolitics of Infant Mortality." Anthropologies, March 15, 2013.

Casper, Monica J., and William Paul Simmons. 2014. "Accounting for Death: Infant Mortality, the MDGs, and Women's (Dis)Empowerment." In *Counting on Marilyn Waring: New Advances in Feminist Economics*, edited by Margunn Bjørnholt and Ailsa McKay. Bradford, Ontario: Demeter Press.

Combs-Orme, Terri. 1988. "Infant Mortality and Social Work: Legacy of Success." *Social Service Review* 62 (1): 83–102.

Desrosières, Alain. 2002. *The Politics of Large Numbers: A History of Statistical Reasoning*. Translated by Camille Naish. Cambridge, Mass.: Harvard University Press.

Foucault, Michel. 2007. *Security, Territory, Population: Lectures at the Collège de France, 1977–1978*. New York: Picador.

Garrett, Eilidh, Chris Galley, Nicola Shelton, and Robert Woods. 2006. *Infant Mortality: A Continuing Social Problem*. Hampshire, U.K.: Ashgate.

Ifrah, Georges. 2000. *The Universal History of Numbers: From Prehistory to the Invention of the Computer*. Hoboken, N.J.: John Wiley and Sons.

———. 2001. *The University History of Numbers: From the Abacus to the Quantum Computer*. Hoboken, N.J.: John Wiley and Sons.

Igo, Sarah E. 2007. *The Averaged American: Surveys, Citizens, and the Making of a Mass Public*. Cambridge, Mass.: Harvard University Press.

Kittel, Kelly. 2014. *Breathe: A Memoir of Motherhood, Grief, and Family Conflict*, 204. Berkeley, Calif.: She Writes Press.

Mennicken, Andrea, and Wendy Nelson Espeland. 2019. "What's New with Numbers? Sociological Approaches to the Study of Quantification." *Annual Review of Sociology* 45:223–245.

Murphy, Michelle. 2017. *The Economization of Life*. Durham, N.C.: Duke University Press.

Nelson, Diane M. 2015. *Who Counts? The Mathematics of Death and Life after Genocide*. Durham, N.C.: Duke University Press.

Porter, Theodore M. 1986. *The Rise of Statistical Thinking, 1820–1900*. Princeton, N.J.: Princeton University Press.

———. 1995. *Trust in Numbers: The Pursuit of Objectivity in Science and Public Life*. Princeton, N.J.: Princeton University Press.

Ryerson University. n.d. "The Abacus: A Brief History." Last accessed September 26, 2021. https://www.ee.ryerson.ca/~elf/abacus/history.html.

Scott, James C. 1999. *Seeing like a State: How Certain Schemes to Improve the Human Condition Have Failed*. New Haven, Conn.: Yale University Press.

Wong, Peter D., Murtala Abdurrahman, Anna Banerji, and Rosemary G. Moodie. 2021. "Canada's Infant Mortality: A Developing World within Its Borders." *University of Toronto Medical Journal* 98 (1). https://www.utmj.org/index.php/UTMJ/article/view/1282.

World Health Organization. n.d. "Child Health." Last accessed September 26, 2021. https://www.who.int/health-topics/child-health#tab=tab_1--.

INFANTICIDE

American Academy of Pediatrics, Committee on Child Abuse and Neglect. 1990. "Mortality of Abandoned Infants before and after the Appearance of Foundling Homes in the Thirteenth Century." *Pediatrics* 86 (3): A66.

———. 2001. "Distinguishing Sudden Infant Death Syndrome from Child Abuse Fatalities." *Pediatrics* 107 (2): 437–441.

Australian Story. 2018. "Australia's 'Most Hated Woman' Kathleen Folbigg Speaks for First Time." ABC, December 3, 2018. https://www.abc.net.au/news/2018-08-13/kathleen-folbigg-speaks-for-first-time-about-infants-death/9906008?nw=0.

Booth, Thomas J., Rebecca C. Redfern, and Rebecca L. Gowland. 2016. "Immaculate Conceptions: Micro-CT Analysis of Diagenesis in Romano-British Infant Skeletons." *Journal of Archaeological Science* 74:124–134.

Brewis, Alexandra A. 1992. "Anthropological Perspectives on Infanticide." *Arizona Anthropologist* 8:103–119.

Bright, Janette, and Gillian Clark. 2011. *An Introduction to the Tokens at the Foundling Museum*, 3. London: Foundling Museum.

Coale, A. J., and J. Banister. 1994. "Five Decades of Missing Females in China." *Demography* 31 (3): 459–479.

Cunliffe, Emma. 2011. *Murder, Medicine, and Motherhood*, 4. Oxford, U.K.: Hart.

Friedman, Susan Hatters, and Phillip J. Resnick. 2007. "Child Murder by Mothers: Patterns and Prevention." *World Psychiatry* 6 (3): 137–141.

Goodkind, Daniel M. 2004. "China's Missing Children: The 2000 Census Underreporting Surprise." *Population Studies* 58 (3): 281–295.

Gupta, Monica Das. 2005. "Explaining Asia's Missing Women: A New Look at the Data." *Population and Development Review* 31 (3): 529–535.

Hesketh, Therese, Li Lu, and Zhu Wei Xing. 2011. "The Consequences of Son Preference and Sex-Selective Abortion in China and Other Asian Countries." *Canadian Medical Association Journal* 183 (12): 1374–1377.

Hvistendahl, Mara. 2015. "China's New Birth Rule Can't Restore Missing Women and Fix a Population." *Scientific American*, November 2, 2015.

Kemkes, Ariane. 2009. "'Smothered' Infants—Neglect, Infanticide or SIDS? A Fresh Look at the 19th Century Mortality Schedules." *Human Ecology* 37 (393). https://link.springer.com/article/10.1007%2Fs10745-009-9265-y.

Kertzer, David I. and Michael J. White. 2009. "Cheating the Angel-Makers: Surviving Infant Abandonment in Nineteenth-Century Italy." *Continuity and Change* 9 (3): 451–480.

Killgrove, Kristina. 2016. "Infanticide or Natural Death? New Method May Answer This Ancient Question." *Forbes*, September 8, 2016.

LeTourneau, Nancy. 2019. "The GOP's Newest Make-Believe Wedge Issue: Infanticide." *Washington Monthly*, March 5, 2019.

Levene, Alysa. 2005. "The Estimation of Mortality at the London Foundling Hospital, 1741–99." *Population Studies* 59 (1): 87–97.

Miller, Julie. 2008. *Abandoned: Foundlings in Nineteenth-Century New York City*, 17–18. New York: New York University Press.

Mohanty, Ranjani Iyer. 2012. "Trash Bin Babies: India's Female Infanticide Crisis." *Atlantic*, May 25, 2012.

Newman, Sandra. 2017. "Infanticide." Aeon, November 27, 2017.

Oaks, Laury. 2015. *Giving up Baby: Safe Haven Laws, Motherhood, and Reproductive Justice*, 41–42. New York: New York University Press.

Ollstein, Alice Miranda. 2019. "Republicans Pound Abortion 'Infanticide' Message." Politico, March 2, 2019.

Roberts, Dorothy. 1997. *Killing the Black Body: Race, Reproduction, and the Meaning of Liberty*, 48. New York: Pantheon.

Rouge-Maillart, Clotilde, Nathalie Jousset, Arnaud Gaudin, Brigitte Bouju, and Michel Penneau. 2005. "Women Who Kill Their Children." *American Journal of Forensic Medicine and Pathology* 26 (4): 320–326.

Ruberti, Dani. 2016. "Mission: India, Trash Bin Babies." WVLT, May 3, 2016.

Scheper-Hughes, Nancy. 1993. *Death without Weeping: The Violence of Everyday Life in Brazil.* Berkeley: University of California Press.

———. 2013. "No More Angel Babies on the Alto do Cruzeiro." *Natural History.*

Spinelli, Margaret. 2018. "Infanticide and American Criminal Justice (1980–2018)." *Archives of Women's Mental Health* 22:173–177.

United Nations Population Fund. n.d. "Gender-Biased Sex Selection." Last accessed September 26, 2021. https://www.unfpa.org/gender-biased-sex-selection.

JAPAN

Aoki, Mizuho. 2010. "The Mother-Child Health Log." *Japan Times*, July 27, 2010.

Blair, Olivia. 2017. "Jizo Statues: The Japanese Statues Giving Closure to Women Who Have Miscarried." *Independent*, January 10, 2017.

Brooks, Anne Page. 1981. "*Mizuko Kuyō* and Japanese Buddhism." *Japanese Journal of Religious Studies* 8 (3–4): 119–147.

Brown, Hannah Jean. 2019. "Key Tenets of Classical Buddhist *Dharma* Leave Space for the Practice of Abortion and Are Upheld by Contemporary Japanese Buddhist *Mizuko Kuyo* Remembrance Rituals." *Journal of Religion and Health* 58:476–489.

Central Intelligence Agency. 2021. "Japan." *The World Factbook*, updated January 29, 2021. https://www.cia.gov/the-world-factbook/countries/japan/.

Elson, Angela. 2017. "The Japanese Art of Grieving a Miscarriage." *New York Times*, January 6, 2017.

Goss, Erica. n.d. "Mizuko Kuyo: Japan's Powerful Pregnancy Loss Ritual." Modern Loss. Last accessed September 26, 2021. https://modernloss.com/mizuko-kuyo-japans-powerful -pregnancy-loss-ritual/.

Gupta, Sanjay. 2019. "The Land of Immortals: How and What Japan's Oldest Population Eats." CNN Health, May 21, 2019.

Hardacre, Helen. 1999. *Marketing the Menacing Fetus in Japan*. Berkeley: University of California Press.

Leppert, P. C. 1993. "An Analysis of the Reasons for Japan's Low Infant Mortality Rate." *Journal of Nurse Midwifery* 38 (6): 353–357.

Miyaji, Naoko T., and Margaret Lock. 1994. "Monitoring Motherhood: Sociocultural and Historical Aspects of Maternal and Child Health in Japan." *Daedalus* 123 (4): 87–112.

Moto-Sanchez, Milla Micka. 2016. "Jizō, Healing Rituals, and Women in Japan." *Japanese Journal of Religious Studies* 43 (2): 307–331.

Nakamura, Yasuhide. 2010. "Maternal and Child Health Handbook in Japan." *Japan Medical Association Journal* 53 (4): 259–265.

Nippon.com. 2019. "Close Care Keeps Japan's Infant Mortality Low." March 13, 2019.

Office of Minority Health, U.S. Department of Health and Human Services. n.d. "Infant Mortality and Asian Americans." Last accessed September 26, 2021. https://minorityhealth .hhs.gov/omh/browse.aspx?lvl=4&lvlid=53.

Prichep, Deena. 2015. "Adopting a Buddhist Ritual to Mourn Miscarriage, Abortion." NPR, *All Things Considered*, podcast, MP3 audio, 7:08, April 15, 2015.

Takeuchi, Jiro, Yu Sakagami, and Romana C. Perez. 2016. "The Mother and Child Health Handbook in Japan as a Health Promotion Tool: An Overview of Its History, Contents, Use, Benefits, and Global Influence." *Global Pediatric Health* 3:1–9.

Tikkanen, Roosa, Robin Osborn, Elias Mossialos, Ana Djordjevic, and George A. Wharton. 2020. "Japan." International Health Care System Profiles, Commonwealth Fund, June 5, 2020.

Willcox, D. Craig, Bradley J. Willcox, Sanae Shimajiri, Sayuri Kurechi, and Makoto Suzuki. 2007. "Aging Gracefully: A Retrospective Analysis of Functional Status in Okinawan Centenarians." *American Journal of Geriatric Psychiatry* 15 (3): 252–256.

Wilson, Jeff. 2009. *Mourning the Unborn Dead: A Buddhist Ritual Comes to America*. Oxford, U.K.: Oxford University Press.

World Medical Association. 2018. "WMA Statement on the Development and Promotion of a Maternal and Child Health Handbook." Adopted by the 69th WMA General Assembly, Reykjavik, Iceland, October 2018.

KANGAROO CARE

Association for Women's Health, Obstetric and Neonatal Nurses. 2016. "Immediate and Sustained Skin-to-Skin Contact for the Healthy Term Newborn after Birth: AWHONN Practice Brief Number 5." *AWHONN Practice Brief* 45 (6): 842–844.

Cleveland Clinic. n.d. "Kangaroo Care." Last accessed September 26, 2021. https://my .clevelandclinic.org/health/treatments/12578-kangaroo-care.

Corner, Lena. 2017. "Saving Babies' Lives by Carrying Them like Kangaroos." *Atlantic*, February 7, 2017.

Dawson, Terence J. 1995. *Kangaroos: Biology of the Largest Marsupials*. Ithaca, N.Y.: Cornell University Press.

Frevele, Jamie. 2012. "Kangaroos Have Three Vaginas, So Here Is How That Works." Mary Sue, April 17, 2012.

Graham, Jack. 2017. "The Secret to Malawi's Drop in Infant Mortality? Kangaroos." Apolitical, October 10, 2017.

Jefferies, Ann L. 2012. "Kangaroo Care for the Preterm Infant and Family." *Pediatrics and Child Health* 17 (3): 141–143.

Martínez, G. H., S. E. Rey, and C. M. Marquette. 1992. "The Mother Kangaroo Programme." *International Child Health* 3:55–67.

Rey, S. E., and G. H. Martínez. 1983. "Rational Management of the Premature Child." Fetal Medicine Course, National University, Bogotá, Colombia, 137–151.

Rosenberg, Tina. 2010. "The Human Incubator." *New York Times*, December 13, 2010.

Sharma, Deepak, Srinivas Murki, and Tejo Pratap Oleti. 2016. "To Compare Cost Effectiveness of 'Kangaroo Ward Care' with 'Intermediate Intensive Care' in Stable Very Low Birth Weight Infants (Birth Weight < 1100 Grams): A Randomized Control Trial." *Italian Journal of Pediatrics* 42:64.

LIFE EXPECTANCY

Carlson, Rosemary. 2020. "The Racial Life Expectancy Gap in the U.S." Balance, December 20, 2020.

Centers for Disease Control and Prevention. 2020. "Life Expectancy." Last modified October 30, 2020. https://www.cdc.gov/nchs/fastats/life-expectancy.htm.

Central Intelligence Agency. 2021. "Afghanistan." *The World Factbook*, updated February 1, 2021. https://www.cia.gov/the-world-factbook/countries/afghanistan/.

———. 2021. "Monaco." *The World Factbook*, updated February 3, 2021. https://www.cia .gov/the-world-factbook/countries/monaco/.

Garrett, Shaylyn Romney, and Robert D. Putnam. 2020. "Why Did Racial Progress Stall in America?" *New York Times*, December 6, 2020.

Montez, Jennifer Karas, Jason Beckfield, Julene Kemp Cooney, Jacob M. Grumbach, Mark D. Hayward, Huseyin Zeyd Koytak, Steven H. Woolf, and Anna Zajacova. 2020. "US State Policies, Politics, and Life Expectancy." *Milbank Quarterly* 98 (3): 668–699.

Murray, C. J. 1998. "The Infant Mortality Rate, Life Expectancy at Birth, and a Linear Index of Mortality as Measures of General Health Status." *International Journal of Epidemiology* 17 (1): 122–128.

PBS. n.d. "Infant Mortality and Life Expectancy." First Measured Century, PBS. https:// www.pbs.org/fmc/timeline/dmortality.htm.

MATERNAL MORTALITY

Associated Press. 2019. "Report: 85 Percent of Tennessee Maternal Deaths Preventable." WREG Memphis, February 20, 2019.

Belluz, Julia. 2017. "California Decided It Was Tired of Women Bleeding to Death in Childbirth." Vox, December 4, 2017.

Beyoncé. 2018. "Beyoncé in Her Own Words: Her Life, Her Body, Her Heritage." *Vogue*, August 6, 2018.

Black Mamas Matter Alliance. n.d. "About." Last accessed September 26, 2021. https://black mamasmatter.org/about/.

———. n.d. "Black Maternal Health Week." Last accessed September 26, 2021. https:// blackmamasmatter.org/bmhw/.

Blodgett, Sequoia. 2019. "Serena Williams, Mark Cuban Invest in Black-Owned Maternal Healthcare Startup." Black Enterprise, July 16, 2019.

Branigin, Anna. 2019. "Cory Booker and Ayanna Pressley Introduce Sweeping Bill to Prevent Pregnancy-Related Deaths among Black Women." Root, May 8, 2019.

Burns, Christy Turlington. n.d. "A Letter from Our Founder." Every Mother Counts. Last accessed September 26, 2021. https://everymothercounts.org/our-story/our-birth-story/.

Centers for Disease Control and Prevention. 2019. "Racial and Ethnic Disparities Continue in Pregnancy-Related Deaths." Press release, September 5, 2019. https://www.cdc.gov/media/releases/2019/p0905-racial-ethnic-disparities-pregnancy-deaths.html.

Central Intelligence Agency. n.d. "Maternal Mortality." The World Factbook. Last accessed September 26, 2021. https://www.cia.gov/the-world-factbook/field/maternal-mortality-rate/country-comparison.

Chicago Crusader. 2019. "Part of Collins' and Flowers' Plan to Fight Maternal, Infant Mortality Becomes Law." August 1, 2019.

Cirruzzo, Chelsea. 2021. "Lawmakers to Reintroduce Sweeping Maternal Health Bill." U.S. News and World Report, February 5, 2021.

Creanga, Andreea A., Brian T. Bateman, Jill M. Mhyre, Elena Kuklina, Alexander Shilkrut, and William M. Callaghan. 2014. "Performance of Racial and Ethnic Minority-Serving Hospitals on Delivery-Related Indicators." American Journal of Obstetrics and Gynecology 211 (6): 647.e1–647.e16.

Creanga, Andreea A., Carla Syverson, Kristi Seed, and William M. Callaghan. 2017. "Pregnancy-Related Mortality in the United States, 2011–2013." Obstetrics and Gynecology 130 (2): 366–373.

Every Mother Counts. 2018. "Help Us Get Maternal Mortality Review Legislation across the Finish Line." June 14, 2018.

———. n.d. "Policy and Advocacy." Last accessed September 26, 2021. https://everymothercounts.org/policy-and-advocacy/.

Guha, Auditi. 2017. "Black Mamas Sound Alarm on Maternal Death Rate." Rewire News Group, June 15, 2017.

———. 2018. "Some States Ignore Black Maternal and Infant Mortality Rates. Not New Jersey." Rewire News Group, August 1, 2018.

Hartney, Michelle. n.d. "Mother's Right." Last accessed September 26, 2021. https://www.michellehartney.com/mothers-right.

Hellmann, Jessie. 2018. "Maternal Deaths Keep Rising in US, Raising Scrutiny." Hill, April 19, 2018.

Hinchliffe, Emma. 2019. "Serena Williams and Mark Cuban Invest in Startup Fighting Maternal Mortality." Fortune, July 15, 2019.

Kozhimannil, Katy B. 2020. "Indigenous Maternal Health—a Crisis Demanding Attention." JAMA Health Forum. May 18, 2020.

Kristof, Nicholas. 2017. "If Americans Love Moms, Why Do We Let Them Die?" New York Times, July 29, 2017.

Lewis, Crystal. 2014. "U.S. Maternal Death Data Held Up by Nine States." Women's eNews, January 14, 2014.

Louis, J. M., M. K. Menard, and R. E. Gee. 2015. "Racial and Ethnic Disparities in Maternal Morbidity and Mortality." Obstetrics and Gynecology 125 (3): 690–694.

MacDonald, Margaret E. 2013. "The Biopolitics of Maternal Mortality: Anthropological Observations from the Women Deliver Conference in Kuala Lumpur." Somatosphere, July 25, 2013.

Martin, Nina, and Renee Montagne. 2017. "The Last Person You'd Expect to Die in Childbirth." ProPublica and NPR, May 12, 2017. https://www.propublica.org/article/die-in-childbirth-maternal-death-rate-health-care-system.

Maternal Health Task Force. 2015. "Call for Posts: Inequities in Maternal Mortality in the U.S." MHTF (blog), November 2, 2015.

———. n.d. "The Sustainable Development Goals and Maternal Mortality." Last accessed September 26, 2021. https://www.mhtf.org/topics/the-sustainable-development-goals-and-maternal-mortality/.

Roeder, Amy. 2019. "America Is Failing Its Black Mothers." *Harvard Public Health*, Winter 2019. https://www.hsph.harvard.edu/magazine/magazine_article/america-is-failing-its-black-mothers/.

Serena Ventures. n.d. "Home." Last accessed September 26, 2021. https://www.serenaventures.com/.

SisterReach. n.d. "Home." Last accessed September 26, 2021. https://www.sisterreach.org/.

Tucker, Myra J., Cynthia J. Berg, William M. Callaghan, and Jason Hsia. 2007. "The Black-White Disparity in Pregnancy-Related Mortality from 5 Conditions: Differences in Prevalence and Case-Fatality Rates." *American Journal of Public Health* 97 (2): 247–251.

Williams, Serena. 2018. "What My Life-Threatening Experience Taught Me about Giving Birth." CNN, February 20, 2018.

Women Deliver. 2019. Women Deliver 2019 Conference. https://wd2019.org/.

———. n.d. "Our History." Last accessed September 26, 2021. https://womendeliver.org/about/our-history/.

World Health Organization. 2006. *Reproductive Health Indicators: Guidelines for their Generation, Interpretation, and Analysis for Global Monitoring.* Geneva, Switzerland: WHO Press.

———. 2015. "10 Facts on Maternal Health." https://www.who.int/features/factfiles/maternal_health/en/.

———. 2019. "Maternal Mortality." September 19, 2019. https://www.who.int/news-room/fact-sheets/detail/maternal-mortality.

———. n.d. "Maternal Health." Last accessed September 26, 2021. https://www.who.int/health-topics/maternal-health#tab=tab_1.

———. n.d. "Maternal Mortality Ratio (Per 100,000 Live Births)." Last accessed September 26, 2021. https://www.who.int/data/gho/indicator-metadata-registry/imr-details/26.

WQAD Digital Team. 2019. "Lawmakers from Illinois Say 'MOMMA Act' Will Lower Infant Mortality, Call for More Spending." WQAD8, March 19, 2019.

MEDICAID

Bernet, Patrick M., Gulcin Gumus, and Sharmila Vishwasrao. 2018. "Effectiveness of Public Health Spending on Infant Mortality in Florida, 2001–2014." *Social Science and Medicine* 211:31–38.

Bhatt, Chintan B., and Consuelo M. Beck-Sagué. 2018. "Medicaid Expansion and Infant Mortality in the United States." *American Journal of Public Health* 108 (4): 565–567.

Bridges, Khiara. 2011. *Reproducing Race: An Ethnography of Pregnancy as a Site of Racialization.* Berkeley: University of California Press.

Brown, Clare C., Jennifer E. Moore, and Holly C. Felix. 2019. "Association of State Medicaid Expansion with Low Birth Weight and Preterm Birth." *JAMA* 321 (16): 1598–1609.

Center on Budget and Policy Priorities. 2020. "Policy Basics: Introduction to Medicaid." Last modified April 14, 2020. https://www.cbpp.org/research/health/policy-basics-introduction-to-medicaid.

Centers for Disease Control and Prevention. n.d. "Infant Mortality Rates by State." National Center for Health Statistics. Last modified April 24, 2020.

Guth, Madeline, Rachel Garfield, and Robin Rudowitz. 2020. "The Effects of Medicaid Expansion under the ACA: Findings from a Literature Review." Kaiser Family Foundation, March 17, 2020.

Howard, Jacqueline. 2019. "Medicaid Expansion Tied to Positive Gains for Black Babies." CNN Health, April 23, 2019.

Kaiser Family Foundation. 2021. "Status of State Medicaid Expansion Decisions: Interactive Map." August 10, 2021. https://www.kff.org/medicaid/issue-brief/status-of-state-medicaid-expansion-decisions-interactive-map/.

McLaughlin, Michael, and Mark R. Rank. 2018. "Impact of Federal Transfers upon US Infant Mortality Rates: A Secondary Analysis Using a Fixed Effects Regression Approach." *BMJ Open* 8:e021533.

Rothman, Barbara Katz. 1982. *In Labor: Women and Power in the Birthplace.* New York: W. W. Norton.

Sohn, Heeju, and Stefan Timmermans. 2019. "Inequities in Newborn Screening: Race and the Role of Medicaid." *SSM—Population Health* 9:100496. https://www.sciencedirect.com/science/article/pii/S2352827319301351?via%3Dihub.

Wax-Thibodeaux, Emily, and Ariana Eunjung Cha. 2019. "Georgia Governor Signs 'Heartbeat Bill,' Giving the State One of the Most Restrictive Abortion Laws in the Nation." *Washington Post*, May 7, 2019.

West, Rachel. 2018. "Expanding Medicaid in All States Would Save 14,000 Lives per Year." Center for American Progress, October 24, 2018.

MEMPHIS

Associated Press. 2016. "Infant Mortality Rate in Memphis Hits a Record Low." *Chattanooga Times Free Press*, November 21, 2016.

Brantley, Ashley. 2017. "Health Brief: Infant Mortality in Tennessee." Better Tennessee, April 17, 2017; updated September 8, 2017. https://bettertennessee.com/infant-mortality-in-tennessee-health-brief/.

Leake, Craig, and David Appleby, dirs. 2008. *Babyland.* ABC News, Documentary Group. First broadcast August 22, 2008, on ABC.

Lee, Tonya Lewis, exec. prod. 2009. *Crisis in the Crib: Saving Our Nation's Babies.* U.S. Department of Health and Human Services. 36 min. https://archive.org/details/crisisinthecrib.

Quinn, Mattie. 2017. "The Tragic Struggle to Prevent Infant Mortality." *Governing*, July 10, 2017.

Sainz, Adrian. 2016. "Fewer Babies Dying in Memphis, but Rate Still Higher Than US." *Washington Times*, November 21, 2016.

St. Jude Children's Research Hospital. 2017. "ALSAC/St. Jude Annual Report."

———. n.d. "About Us." Last accessed September 26, 2021. https://www.stjude.org/about-st-jude.html?sc_icid=us-mm-missionstatement#mission.

Tennessee Commission on Children and Youth. 2012. "Tennessee Efforts to Reduce Infant Mortality." *Advocate* (Infant Mortality Edition) 22 (4): 1–3.

Walton, Anna. 2018. "New Policy Brief Asks: 'Why Are Tennessee Moms and Babies Dying at Such a High Rate?'" Georgetown University Health Policy Institute, November 14, 2018.

MIDWIVES

American College of Nurse-Midwives. 2012. "Definition of Midwifery and Scope of Practice of Certified Nurse-Midwives and Certified Midwives." ACNM Division of Standards and Practice, updated February 6, 2012.

———. 2019. "Funding for Midwifery Education Programs Included in Federal Budget Bill." Press release, December 19, 2019. https://www.midwife.org/default.aspx?bid=3129.

———. n.d. "ACNM Justification Statement for Increased Federal Funding for Midwifery Education Programs."

American College of Obstetricians and Gynecologists. 2020. "ACOG Statement on Birth Settings." April 20, 2020. https://www.acog.org/news/news-releases/2020/04/acog-statement-on-birth-settings.

American Medical Association House of Delegates. 2008. *Resolution: 204 (A-08). Introduced by: American College of Obstetricians and Gynecologists. Subject: Midwifery Scope of Practice and Licensure. Referred to: Reference Committee B.* April 28, 2008.

———. 2008. *Resolution: 205 (A-08). Introduced by: American College of Obstetricians and Gynecologists. Subject: Home Deliveries. Referred to: Reference Committee B.* April 28, 2008.

———. 2008. *Resolution: 239 (A-08). Introduced by: Resident and Fellow Section. Subject: Midwifery Scope of Practice and Licensure. Referred to: Reference Committee B.* April 28, 2008.

Block, Jennifer. 2020. "The Criminalization of the American Midwife." Longreads, March 2020.

Borst, Charlotte. 1995. *Catching Babies: The Professionalization of Childbirth, 1870–1920.* Cambridge, Mass.: Harvard University Press.

Brodsky, Phyllis L. 2008. "Where Have All the Midwives Gone?" *Journal of Perinatal Education* 17 (4): 48–51.

Centers for Disease Control and Prevention. 2021. "Births—Method of Delivery." Last updated March 2, 2021. https://www.cdc.gov/nchs/fastats/delivery.htm.

Cheyney, Melissa, Marit Bovbjerg, Courtney Everson, Wendy Gordon, Darcy Hannibal, and Vedam Saraswathi. 2014. "Outcomes of Care for 16,924 Planned Home Births in the United States: The Midwives Alliance of North America Statistics Project, 2004–2009." *Journal of Midwifery and Women's Health* 59 (1): 17–27.

Craven, Christa, and Mara Glatzel. 2010. "Downplaying Difference: Historical Accounts of African American Midwives and Contemporary Struggles for Midwifery." *Feminist Studies* 36 (2): 330–358.

Cutler, Alison. 2020. "Mothers, Midwives and Mortality: Why Some Black Women Seek a Holistic Approach." *Cronkite News*, October 1, 2020.

Goodwin, Michele. 2020. "The Racist History of Abortion and Midwifery Bans." ACLU, July 1, 2020.

Kline, Wendy. 2019. "To Lower Maternal and Infant Mortality Rates, We Need More Midwives." *Washington Post*, January 16, 2019.

Litman, Jill. 2019. "Call the Midwives: Addressing America's Black Maternal and Infant Mortality Crisis." *Public Health Advocate*, May 8, 2019.

MacDorman, Marian F., and Eugene Declercq. 2019. "Trends and State Variations in Out-of-Hospital Births in the United States, 2004–2017." *Birth* 46 (2): 279–288.

MacDorman, Marian F., T. J. Mathews, and Eugene Declercq. 2014. "Trends in Out-of-Hospital Births in the United States, 1990–2012." *NCHS Data Brief* 144 (March). https://www.cdc.gov/nchs/products/databriefs/db144.htm.

Martin, Nina. 2018. "A Larger Role for Midwives Could Improve Deficient U.S. Care for Mothers and Babies." ProPublica, February 22, 2018.

Menzel, Annie. 2021. "The Midwife's Bag, or, the Objects of Black Infant Mortality Prevention." *Signs* 46 (2): 283–309.

Midwives Alliance of North America. n.d. "About Us." Last accessed September 26, 2021. https://mana.org/about-midwives.

Proujansky, Alice. 2019. "The Black Midwives Changing Care for Women of Color—Photo Essay." *Guardian*, July 25, 2019.

Rooks, Judith P. 2012. "The History of Midwifery." *Our Bodies, Ourselves,* May 30, 2012; updated May 22, 2014. https://www.ourbodiesourselves.org/book-excerpts/health-article/history-of-midwifery/.

Simpson, April. 2019. "Rural America Has a Maternal Mortality Problem. Midwives Might Help Solve It." PEW *Stateline,* August 16, 2019.

Terry, C. C. 1914. "Midwives: Their Influence on Early Infant Mortality." *American Journal of Public Health* (December): 695–699.

U.S. Senate Joint Economic Committee Democrats. 2018. "The Value of Midwifery in Maternal and Infant Care." September 21, 2018. https://www.jec.senate.gov/public/index.cfm/democrats/2018/9/the-value-of-midwifery-in-maternal-and-infant-care.

Vedam, Saraswathi, Kathrin Stoll, Marian MacDorman, Eugene Declercq, Renee Cramer, Melissa Cheyney, Timothy Fisher, Emma Butt, Y. Tony Yang, and Holly Powell Kennedy. 2018. "Mapping Integration of Midwives across the United States: Impact on Access, Equity, and Outcomes." *PLoS One* 13 (2): e0192523.

Wertz, Richard W., and Dorothy C. Wertz. 1989. *Lying-In: A History of Childbirth in America.* Expanded ed. New Haven, Conn.: Yale University Press.

MOTHER'S DAY

Allen, Hannah Rose. 2013. "Motherhood and Tears." *Still Standing Magazine,* June 5, 2013.

Devine, Megan. 2016. "International Bereaved Mother's Day and Project Heal." Mothering, May 1, 2016.

History.com Editors. n.d. "Woodrow Wilson Proclaims the First Mother's Day Holiday." Last accessed September 26, 2021. https://www.history.com/this-day-in-history/woodrow-wilson-proclaims-the-first-mothers-day-holiday.

Leonard, Teresa. 2016. "Mother's Day Has a Complicated History." *News and Observer,* May 3, 2016.

McLaverty, Morgan. 2019. "The Impossible Days." *Still Standing Magazine,* May 12, 2019.

Oliphint, Joel. 2015. "Anna Jarvis Was Sorry She Ever Invented Mother's Day." BuzzFeed, May 8, 2015.

Ross, Philip. 2015. "Mother's Day History and Traditions: 5 Surprising Facts You May Not Know about the Holiday's Dark Origins." *International Business Times,* May 9, 2015.

NEONATOLOGY

Adriel, Evan L., and Catharine H. Rankin. 2010. "The Importance of Touch in Development." *Paediatrics and Child Health* 15 (3): 153–156.

Anday, Endla K. 2020. "Obituary: Maria Delivoria-Papadopoulos, M.D." *Neonatology* 117:663–664.

Anspach, Renee R. 1997. *Deciding Who Lives: Fateful Choices in the Intensive-Care Nursery,* 3–4. Berkeley: University of California Press.

Baker, Jeffrey P. 1996. *The Machine in the Nursery: Incubator Technology and the Origins of Newborn Intensive Care.* Baltimore, Md.: Johns Hopkins University Press.

———. 2000. "The Incubator and the Medical Discovery of the Premature Infant." *Journal of Perinatology* 20:321–328.

Barry, Rebecca Rego. 2018. "Coney Island's Incubator Babies." JSTOR Daily, August 15, 2018.

Beck, Andrew F., Erika M. Edwards, Jeffrey D. Horbar, Elizabeth A. Howell, Marie C. McCormick, and DeWayne M. Pursley. 2019. "The Color of Health: How Racism, Segregation, and Inequality Affect the Health and Well-Being of Preterm Infants and Their Families." *Pediatric Research* 87:227–234.

Center for the History of Medicine. n.d. "The Story of Surfactant." Last accessed September 26, 2021. https://collections.countway.harvard.edu/onview/exhibits/show/avery/the-story-of-surfactant.

Chakraborty, Mallinath, and Sailesh Kotecha. 2013. "Pulmonary Surfactant in Newborn Infants and Children." *Breathe* 9:476–488.

Cook, Bonnie L. 2020. "Maria Delivoria-Papadopoulos, Scientist Who Saved Thousands of Infants, Dies at 90." *Philadelphia Inquirer*, September 22, 2020.

Davis, Dána-Ain. 2019. *Reproductive Injustice: Racism, Pregnancy, and Premature Birth*. New York: New York University Press.

DiGregorio, Sarah. 2020. *Early: An Intimate History of Premature Birth and What It Teaches Us about Being Human*. New York: Harper.

Goodman, David C., Elliott S. Fisher, George A. Little, Thérèse A. Stukel, Chiang-hua Chang, and Kenneth S. Schoendorf. 2002. "The Relation Between the Availability of Neonatal Intensive Care and Neonatal Mortality." *New England Journal of Medicine* 346:1538–1544.

James, Susan Donaldson. 2013. "JFK Baby Death in 1963 Sparked Medical Race to Save Preemies." ABC News, August 6, 2013.

Leavitt, Judith Walzer. 1988. "Joseph B. DeLee and the Practice of Preventive Obstetrics." *American Journal of Public Health* 78 (10): 1353–1361.

Livingston, Steven. 2013. "For John and Jackie Kennedy, the Death of a Son May Have Brought Them Closer." *Washington Post*, October 24, 2013.

———. 2013. "Jackie Kennedy's Five Pregnancies—the Tragic and the Successful." *HuffPost*, November 18, 2013; updated January 23, 2014.

Martin, Ashley E., Jo Ann D'Agostino, Molly Passarella, and Scott A. Lorch. 2016. "Racial Differences in Parental Satisfaction with Neonatal Intensive Care Unit Nursing Care." *Journal of Perinatology* 36 (11): 1001–1007.

Martin, Douglas. 2012. "Mary Ellen Avery, Premature Babies' Savior, Dies at 84." *New York Times*, January 11, 2012.

Michel, Marissa C., Tarah T. Colaizy, Jonathan M. Klein, Jeffrey L. Segar, and Edward F. Bell. 2018. "Causes and Circumstances of Death in a Neonatal Unit Over 20 Years." *Pediatric Research* 83 (4): 829–833.

National Academy of Sciences. n.d. "Mary Ellen Avery." Last accessed September 26, 2021. http://www.nasonline.org/member-directory/deceased-members/58112.html.

New York Times. 1956. "Mrs. Kennedy Loses Her Baby." August 24, 1956.

Polin, Richard A., Waldemar A. Carlo, and Committee on Fetus and Newborn. 2014. "Surfactant Replacement Therapy for Preterm and Term Neonates with Respiratory Distress." *Pediatrics* 133 (1): 156–163.

Profit, Jochen, Jeffrey P. Gould, Mihoko Bennett, Benjamin A. Goldstein, David Draper, Ciaran S. Phibbs, and Henry C. Lee. 2017. "Racial/Ethnic Disparity in NICU Quality of Care Delivery." *Pediatrics* 140 (3): e20170918.

Raffel, Dawn. 2018. *The Strange Case of Dr. Couney: How a Mysterious European Showman Saved Thousands of American Babies*. New York: Blue Rider.

Skaggs, Megan. 2014. "Dear NICU Nurse." *Still Standing Magazine*, August 20, 2014.

Taussig, Karen-Sue, Klaus Hoeyer, and Stefan Helmreich. 2013. "The Anthropology of Potentiality in Biomedicine: An Introduction to Supplement 7." *Current Anthropology* 54 (S7): S3–S14.

te Pas, Arjan B. 2017. "Improving Neonatal Care with Technology." *Frontiers in Pediatrics* 5:110.

Weiner, Julie, Jotishna Sharma, John Lantos, and Howard Kilbride. 2011. "How Infants Die in the Neonatal Intensive Care Unit." *Archives of Pediatric and Adolescent Medicine* 165 (7): 630–634.

World Health Organization. n.d. "WHO Model Lists of Essential Medicines." Last accessed September 26, 2021. https://www.who.int/groups/expert-committee-on-selection-and-use-of-essential-medicines/essential-medicines-lists.

NURSES

American Nurses Association. n.d. "What Is Nursing?" Last accessed September 27, 2021. https://www.nursingworld.org/practice-policy/workforce/what-is-nursing/.

Boggan, Lori. 2015. "Dealing with the Loss of a Tiny Patient." *AWHONN*, November 12, 2015.

Boivin, Janet. 2009. "Nurses Work to Prevent Infant Mortality in U.S." Nurse.com, December 7, 2009.

Brandon, Debra, and Jacqueline M. McGrath. 2016. "Infant Mortality Rates and Preterm Birth: A Challenge for Advocacy." *Advances in Neonatal Care* 16 (5): 323–324.

Centers for Disease Control and Prevention. n.d. "Achievements in Public Health, 1900–1999: Healthier Mothers and Babies." *MMWR Weekly* 48 (38): 849–858.

Dantonio, Patricia. 2020. "Histories of Nursing: The Power and the Possibilities." *Nursing Outlook* 58 (4): 207–213.

Foreman, Suzan. 2014. "Developing a Process to Support Perinatal Nurses after a Critical Event." *Nursing for Women's Health* 18 (1): 61–65.

Gelinas, Lillee. 2015. "A Culture of Caring Is a Culture of Curing." *American Nurse*, November 10, 2015.

Kavanaugh, Karen, and Teresa Moro. 2006. "Supporting Parents after Stillbirth or Newborn Death." *American Journal of Nursing* 106 (9): 74–79.

Lady Parts Justice League. n.d. "Black History Month Interview: Monica McLemore." Abortion Access Front. Last accessed September 27, 2021. https://www.aafront.org/black-history-month-interview-monica-mclemore/.

Madgett, Katherine. 2017. "Sheppard-Towner Maternity and Infancy Protection Act (1921)." *Embryo Project Encyclopedia*, Arizona State University. May 18, 2017; updated July 4, 2018.

McKinley, Tammi L. 2011. "Stillbirth—a Journey in Birth." *Midwifery Today*, https://midwiferytoday.com/mt-articles/stillbirth-series-stillbirth-a-journey-in-birth/.

McLemore, Monica R. 2015. "Toward a New Narrative of Black Women, Birthing and Prematurity." Black Women Birthing Justice, November 20, 2015.

McLemore, Monica R., Molly R. Altman, Norlissa Cooper, Shanell Williams, Larry Rand, and Linda Franck. 2018. "Health Care Experiences of Pregnant, Birthing and Postnatal Women of Color at Risk for Preterm Birth." *Social Science and Medicine* 201:127–135.

Neely, Priska. 2018. "These People Have Dedicated Their Lives to Keeping Black Babies Alive." LAist, July 6, 2018.

Puia, Denise M., Laura Lewis, and Cheryl Tatano Beck. 2013. "Experiences of Obstetric Nurses Who Are Present for a Perinatal Loss." *Journal of Obstetric, Gynecologic and Neonatal Nursing* 42 (3): 321–331.

Ross-White, Amanda. 2013. "Nurses Grieve Too." *Still Standing Magazine*, November 4, 2013.

Scott, Karen A., Laura Britton, and Monica R. McLemore. 2019. "The Ethics of Perinatal Care for Black Women: Dismantling the Structural Racism in 'Mother Blame' Narratives." *Journal of Perinatal and Neonatal Nursing* 33 (2): 108–115.

Taylor, Jamila, Cristina Novoa, Katie Hamm, and Shilpa Phadke. 2019. "Eliminating Racial Disparities in Maternal and Infant Mortality: A Comprehensive Policy Blueprint." Center for American Progress, May 2, 2019.

Thompson, Mary E., and Arlene A. Keeling. 2012. "Nurses' Role in Prevention of Infant Mortality in 1884–1925: Health Disparities Then and Now." *Journal of Pediatric Nursing* 27 (5): 471–478.

Vedam, Saraswathi, Kathrin Stoll, Marian MacDorman, Eugene Declercq, Renee Cramer, Melissa Cheyney, Timothy Fisher, Emma Butt, Y. Tony Yang, and Holly Powell Kennedy. 2018. "Mapping Integration of Midwives across the United States: Impact on Access, Equity, and Outcomes." *PLoS One* 13 (2): e0192523.

Wessling, Susan. 2013. "Closing the Infant Mortality Gap." *Minority Nurse*, March 30, 2013.

Whalen, Rachel. 2018. "To the Nurses Who Brought Me Back into Life." *Still Standing Magazine*, May 7, 2018.

OBSTETRIC VIOLENCE

Allers, Kimberly Seals. 2020. "Obstetric Violence Is a Real Problem. Evelyn Yang's Experience Is Just One Example." *Washington Post*, February 6, 2020.

Birth Monopoly. n.d. "Obstetric Violence." Last accessed September 27, 2021. https://birth monopoly.com/obstetric-violence/.

Boerma, Ties, Carine Ronsmans, Dessalegn Y. Melesse, Aluisio J. D. Barros, Fernando C. Barros, et al. 2018. "Global Epidemiology of Use of and Disparities in Caesearean Sections." *Lancet* 392 (10155): P1341–P1348.

Bohren, Meghan A., Joshua P. Vogel, Erin C. Hunter, et al. 2015. "The Mistreatment of Women during Childbirth in Health Facilities Globally: A Mixed-Method Systematic Review." *PLoS Med* 12 (6): e1001847.

Borges, Maria T. R. 2018. "A Violent Birth: Reframing Coerced Procedures during Childbirth as Obstetric Violence." *Duke Law Journal* 67:827–862.

Brink, Susan. 2019. "Why Are Health Care Providers Slapping and Yelling at Mothers during Childbirth?" NPR, October 14, 2019.

Castro, Arachu. 2019. "Witnessing Obstetric Violence during Fieldwork." *Health and Human Rights Journal* 21 (1): 103–111.

Chadwick, Rachelle. 2017. "Ambiguous Subjects: Obstetric Violence, Assemblage and South African Birth Narratives." *Feminism and Psychology* 27 (4): 489–509.

Clarke, Jennifer G., and Rachel E. Simon. 2013. "Shackling and Separation: Motherhood in Prison." *AMA Journal of Ethics* 15 (9): 779–785.

Connor, Jay. 2019. "Kamala Harris Reintroduces Bill Addressing the Black Maternal Healthcare Crisis." Root, May 22, 2019.

Davis, Dána-Ain. 2018. "Obstetric Racism: The Racial Politics of Pregnancy, Labor, and Birthing." *Medical Anthropology* 38 (7): 560–573.

D'Gregorio, Rogelio Pérez. 2010. "Obstetric Violence: A New Legal Term Introduced in Venezuela." *International Journal of Gynecology and Obstetrics* 111:201–202.

Diaz-Tello, Farah. 2016. "Invisible Wounds: Obstetric Violence in the United States." *Reproductive Health Matters* 24 (47): 56–64.

Donovan, B. M., C. N. Spracklen, M. L. Schweizer, K. K. Ryckman, and A. F. Saftlas. 2016. "Intimate Partner Violence during Pregnancy and the Risk for Adverse Infant Outcomes: A Systematic Review and Meta-analysis." *BJOG: An International Journal of Obstetrics and Gynaecology* 123 (8): 1289–1299.

El Kotni, Mounia. 2018. "Between Cut and Consent: Indigenous Women's Experiences of Obstetric Violence in Mexico." *American Indian Culture and Research Journal* 42 (4): 21–41.

Hern, Warren M. 2019. "Pregnancy Kills. Abortion Saves Lives." *New York Times*, May 21, 2019.

Hill, Nicole. 2019. "Understanding Obstetric Violence as Violence against Mothers through the Lens of Matricentric Feminism." *Journal of the Motherhood Initiative for Research and Community Involvement* 10 (1–2): 233–243.

Howard, Jacqueline. 2018. "C-Section Deliveries Nearly Doubled Worldwide since 2000, Study Finds." CNN, October 11, 2018.

Khozimannil, Katy Backes, Elaine Hernandez, Dara D. Mendez, and Theresa Chapple-McGruder. 2019. "Beyond the Preventing Maternal Deaths Act: Implementation and Further Policy Change." *Health Affairs*, February 4, 2019.

Kuhlik, Lauren. 2018. "Congress Just Took a Big Step toward Ending the Shackling of Pregnant Prisoners." ACLU, December 20, 2018.

Kukura, Elizabeth. 2018. "Obstetric Violence." *Georgetown Law Journal* 106 (April 23, 2018). https://papers.ssrn.com/sol3/papers.cfm?abstract_id=3167375.

MadameNoire. 2018. "Listen to Black Women: How Can We Combat Obstetric Violence and Infant Mortality in Our Community?" MadameNoire, September 21, 2018.

Mays, Kimberly. 2014. "Shackled during Labor: My Experience." *Women's Health Activist Newsletter*, May/June 2014.

Miller, Suellen, and Andrew Lalonde. 2015. "The Global Epidemic of Abuse and Disrespect during Childbirth: History, Evidence, Interventions, and FIGO's Mother-Baby Friendly Birthing Facilities Initiative." *International Journal of Gynecology and Obstetrics* 131 (S1): S49–S52.

Miltner, Olivia. 2019. "'It Felt like I Had Been Violated': How Obstetric Violence Can Traumatize Patients." Rewire News Group, January 23, 2019.

Morris, Theresa, and Joan H. Robinson. 2017. "Forced and Coerced Cesarean Sections in the United States." *Contexts*, June 16, 2017.

Phillips, Ruth. 2019. "Obstetric Violence: The Threat Facing Women in the Delivery Room." BodyandSoul, April 19, 2019.

Raymond, Elizabeth G., and David A. Grimes. 2012. "The Comparative Safety of Legal Induced Abortion and Childbirth in the United States." *Obstetrics and Gynecology* 119 (2, pt. 1): 215–219.

Rich, Adrienne. 1976. *Of Woman Born: Motherhood as Experience and Institution*. New York: W. W. Norton.

Sacks, Emma. 2017. "Defining Disrespect and Abuse of Newborns: A Review of the Evidence and an Expanded Typology of Respectful Maternity Care." *Reproductive Health* 14:66.

Sadler, Michelle, Mário J. D. S. Santos, Dolores Ruiz-Berdún, Gonzalo Leiva Rojas, Elena Skoko, Patricia Gillen, and Jette A. Clausen. 2016. "Moving beyond Disrespect and Abuse: Addressing the Structural Dimensions of Obstetric Violence." *Reproductive Health Matters* 24:47–55.

Savage, Virginia, and Arachu Castro. 2017. "Measuring Mistreatment of Women during Childbirth: A Review of Terminology and Methodological Approaches." *Reproductive Health* 14:138.

Shabot, Sarah Cohen. 2015. "Making Loud Bodies 'Feminine': A Feminist-Phenomenological Analysis of Obstetric Violence." *Human Studies* 39:231–247.

Vedantam, Shankar, Maggie Penman, Jennifer Schmidt, Tara Boyle, Rhaina Cohen, and Chloe Connelly. 2017. "Remembering Anarcha, Lucy, and Betsey: The Mothers of Modern Gynecology." NPR, *Hidden Brain*, podcast, MP3 audio, 27:38, February 7, 2017.

Warren, Elizabeth. 2019. "Senator Elizabeth Warren on Black Women Maternal Mortality: 'Hold Health Systems Accountable for Protecting Black Moms.'" *Essence*, April 30, 2019.

Wells Oseguera, Talita. 2019. "Black Women's Experiences of Stereotype-Related Gendered Racism in Health Care Delivery during Pregnancy, Birth and Postpartum." PhD diss., U.C. San Francisco. ProQuest (WellsOseguera_UCSF_0034M_11895).

Wetsman, Nicole. 2019. "Here's Exactly How Restricting Abortion Harms Public Health." Popular Science, May 16, 2019.

Wolf, Jacqueline H. 2018. *Cesarean Section: An American History of Risk, Technology, and Consequence*. Baltimore, Md.: Johns Hopkins University Press.

World Health Organization, Department of Reproductive Health and Research. 2011. "Intimate Partner Violence during Pregnancy." Information sheet, WHO/RHR/11.35.

———. 2015. "The Prevention and Elimination of Disrespect and Abuse During Facility-Based Childbirth." WHO statement, WHO/RHR/14.23.

OHIO

Behringer, Bruce, and Gilbert H. Friedell. 2006. "Appalachia: Where Place Matters in Health." *Preventing Chronic Disease* 3 (4): A113.

Bushak, Lecia. 2018. "CDC: Ohio's Infant Mortality Rate Remains One of the Highest in US." Ideastream, January 5, 2018.

Candisky, Catherine. 2018. "Ohio Infant Deaths Fall Overall, but Rate for Black Babies Increases." *Columbus Dispatch*, December 6, 2018.

Catte, Elizabeth. 2018. "Passive, Poor and White? What People Keep Getting Wrong about Appalachia." *Guardian*, February 6, 2018.

Centers for Disease Control and Prevention. 2020. "Infant Mortality Rates by State." National Center for Health Statistics, April 24, 2020.

DiPietro Mager, Natalie A. 2017. "Labor of Love: Initiatives to Reduce Ohio's Infant Mortality Rate." Ada Chats, March 14, 2017. Video, 19:47. https://digitalcommons.onu.edu/ada_chats/20/.

First Year Cleveland. n.d. Last accessed September 27, 2021. https://www.firstyearcleveland.org/.

Halverson, Joel A. 2004. "An Analysis of Disparities in Health Status and Access to Health Care in the Appalachian Region." Appalachian Regional Commission, November 1, 2004. https://www.arc.gov/report/an-analysis-of-disparities-in-health-status-and-access-to-health-care-in-the-appalachian-region/.

Harlan, Becky. 2015. "A Fresh Look at Appalachia—50 Years after the War on Poverty." *National Geographic*, February 6, 2015.

Healthy Lucas County. n.d. "Combating Infant Mortality." Last accessed September 27, 2021. https://www.healthylucascounty.org/combating-infant-mortality/.

———. n.d. "Helping Moms & Babies Be Healthy." Last accessed September 27, 2021. http://www.healthylucascounty.org/initiatives/healthy-babies/.

Heaney, Katie. 2019. "New Law Would Force Abortion Doctors to Do the Impossible—or Face Charges." Cut, December 5, 2019.

Hurlock, Jaenique. 2020. "Black Mothers Grieve the Babies They Lost—and Help More Survive Their First Year." *National Geographic*, November 24, 2020.

Lovett, Laura. 2019. "Looking to Curb Infant Mortality Rates, Columbus, Ohio, Pilots On-Demand Ride App, Program." MobiHealthNews, January 2, 2019.

Marshall, Julie L., Logan Thomas, et al. 2017. "Health Disparities in Appalachia." Appalachian Regional Commission, August 23, 2017. https://www.arc.gov/report/health-disparities-in-appalachia/.

Ohio Department of Health. 2018. "2017 Ohio Infant Mortality Report." Office of Communications, December 6, 2018.

Percy Skuy Collection and Gallery. n.d. "Contraception Collection." Dittrick Medical History Center, College of Arts and Sciences, Case Western Reserve University. Last accessed September 27, 2021. https://artsci.case.edu/dittrick/collections/aritfacts/contraception -collection/.

Rizzo, Salvador. 2019. "The Surprisingly True Comparison between Infant Mortality in Ohio and Iran." *Washington Post*, June 4, 2019.

Rosenberg, Gabe. 2019. "A Bill Banning Most Abortions Becomes Law in Ohio." NPR, April 11, 2019.

Saker, Anne. 2019. "Baby Deaths Are Down in Cincinnati. Here's How That Happened, and What More Needs to Be Done." *Cincinnati Enquirer*, April 25, 2019.

Sega, Lauren. 2019. "Report: Infant Mortality Rate Drops Overall, Racial Disparity Persists." Columbus Underground, March 11, 2019.

Singh, Gopal K., Michael D. Kogan, and Rebecca T. Slifkin. 2017. "Widening Disparities in Infant Mortality and Life Expectancy between Appalachia and the Rest of the United States, 1990–2013." *Health Affairs* 36 (8): 1423–1432.

Toledo-Lucas County Health Department. 2017. "2016 Infant Mortality Data for Lucas County." October 12, 2017. https://lucascountyhealth.com/2016-infant-mortality-data-lucas-county/.

Viviano, JoAnne. 2018. "Franklin County Infant-Mortality Rate Drops, but Black Babies Nearly 3 Times More Likely to Die." *Columbus Dispatch*, September 21, 2018.

Weingartner, Tana. 2019. "As Infant Mortality Rate Decreases, Cradle Cincinnati Is Shifting Focus." Cincinnati Public Radio, April 25, 2019.

Wells, Karlynn. 2021. "Greater Cleveland RTA Program Aims to Fight Infant Mortality." Spectrum News 1, January 25, 2021.

Yao, Nengliang, Stephen A. Matthews, and Marianne M. Hillemeier. 2012. "White Infant Mortality in Appalachian States, 1976–1980 and 1996–2000: Changing Patterns and Persistent Disparities." *Journal of Rural Health* 28 (2): 174–182.

Zeltner, Brie. 2018. "Rate of Black Infant Deaths 6 Times That of White Deaths in Cuyahoga County in 2017: Saving the Smallest." Cleveland.com, March 14, 2018; updated January 30, 2019.

PLACENTA

Ahmed, Salah Roshdy, Abdusaeed Aitallah, Hazem M. Abdelghafar, and Mohamed Alkhatim Alsammani. 2015. "Major Placenta Previa: Rate, Maternal and Neonatal Outcomes Experience at a Tertiary Maternity Hospital, Sohag, Egypt: A Prospective Study." *Journal of Clinical Diagnosis and Research* 9 (11): QC17–QC19.

American Council of Obstetricians and Gynecologists. 2018. "Placenta Accreta Spectrum." Obstetric Care Consensus no. 7. (replaces committee opinion no. 529, July 2012).

American Pregnancy Association. n.d. "Placenta Accreta." Last accessed September 27, 2021. https://americanpregnancy.org/healthy-pregnancy/pregnancy-complications/placenta -accreta-921/.

———. n.d. "Placenta Previa." Last accessed September 27, 2021. https://americanpregnancy .org/healthy-pregnancy/pregnancy-complications/placenta-previa-923/.

Ananth, Cande V., Gertrud S. Berkowitz, David A. Savitz, and Robert H. Lapinski. 1999. "Placental Abruption and Adverse Perinatal Outcomes." *JAMA* 282 (17): 1646–1651.

Ananth, Cande V., and Allan J. Wilcox. 2001. "Placental Abruption and Perinatal Mortality in the United States." *American Journal of Epidemiology* 153 (4): 332–337.

Belluz, Julia. 2017. "California Decided It Was Tired of Women Bleeding to Death in Childbirth." Vox, December 4, 2017.

Blumenfeld, Deena H. 2013. "Placentophagy: A Pop-Culture Phenomenon or an Evidence Based Practice?" Lamaze International, June 20, 2013. https://www.lamaze.org/Connecting -the-Dots/placentophagy-a-pop-culture-phenomenon-or-an-evidence-based-practice.

Breathett, Khadijah, David Muhlestein, Randi Foraker, and Martha Gulati. 2014. "Differences in Preeclampsia Rates between African American and Caucasian Women: Trends from the National Hospital Discharge Survey." *Journal of Women's Health* 23 (11): 886–893.

Bryant, Allison S., Ayaba Worjoloh, Aaron B. Caughey, and A. Eugene Washington. 2010. "Racial/Ethnic Disparities in Obstetrical Outcomes and Care: Prevalence and Determinants." *American Journal of Obstetrics and Gynecology* 202 (4): 335–343.

Buser, Genevieve L., Sayonara Mató, Alexia Y. Zhang, Ben J. Metcalf, Bernard Beall, and Ann R. Thomas. 2017. "*Notes from the Field*: Late-Onset Infant Group B Streptococcus Infection Associated with Maternal Consumption of Capsules Containing Dehydrated Placenta—Oregon, 2016." *Morbidity and Mortality Weekly Report* 66 (25): 677–678.

Coyle, Cynthia W., Kathryn E. Hulse, Katherine L. Wisner, Kara E. Driscoll, and Crystal T. Clark. 2015. "Placentophagy: Therapeutic Miracle or Myth?" *Archives of Women's Mental Health* 18 (5): 673–680.

Erez, Offer, Lena Novack, Vered Klaitman, Idit Erez-Weiss, Ruthy Beer-Weisel, Doron Dukler, and Moshe Mazor. 2012. "Early Preterm Delivery Due to Placenta Previa Is an Independent Risk Factor for a Subsequent Spontaneous Preterm Birth." *BMC Pregnancy and Childbirth* 12:82.

Farr, Alex, Frank A. Chervenak, Laurence B. McCullough, Rebecca N. Baergen, and Amos Grünebaum. 2018. "Human Placentophagy: A Review." *American Journal of Obstetrics and Gynecology* 218 (4): 401e1–401e11. https://www.ajog.org/article/S0002-9378(17)30963-8/fulltext.

Ghulmiyyah, Labib, and Baha Sibai. 2012. "Maternal Mortality from Preeclampsia/Eclampsia." *Seminars in Perinatology* 36 (1): 56–59.

Johnson, Sophia K., Jana Pastuschek, Jürgen Rödel, and Tanja Groten. 2018. "Placenta—Worth Trying? Human Maternal Placentophagy: Possible Benefits and Potential Risks." *Geburtshilfe und Frauenheilkunde* 78 (9): 846–852.

Kaiser, Jocelyn. 2015. "NIH Sets Aside More Than $40 Million for Study of Human Placenta." *Science*, February 27, 2015.

Kristal, Mark B. 1980. "Placentophagia: A Biobehavioral Enigma (or, De gustibus non disputandum est)." *Neuroscience and Biobehavioral Reviews* 4 (2): 141–150.

Maccani, Matthew A., and Carmen J. Marsit. 2009. "Epigenetics in the Placenta." *American Journal of Reproductive Immunology* 62 (2): 78.

March of Dimes. 2013. "Placental Abruption." https://www.marchofdimes.org/complications/ placental-abruption.aspx.

———. 2013. "Placenta Previa." https://www.marchofdimes.org/complications/placenta -previa.aspx.

———. 2020. "Preeclampsia." https://www.marchofdimes.org/complications/preeclampsia .aspx.

Marcoux, Heather. 2018. "New Study Challenges the CDC's Stance on Consuming Your Placenta." *Motherly*, May 7, 2018.

Martin, Nina, and Renee Montagne. 2017. "The Last Person You'd Expect to Die in Childbirth." ProPublica and NPR, May 12, 2017. https://www.propublica.org/article/die-in -childbirth-maternal-death-rate-health-care-system.

Mayo Clinic. n.d. "Placenta Accreta." Last accessed September 27, 2021. https://www .mayoclinic.org/diseases-conditions/placenta-accreta/symptoms-causes/syc-20376431.

———. n.d. "Placental Abruption." Last accessed September 27, 2021. https://www.mayoclinic .org/diseases-conditions/placental-abruption/symptoms-causes/syc-20376458.

McNeill, Bryony. 2017. "No, You Shouldn't Eat Your Placenta, Here's Why." Conversation, November 14, 2017.

National Accreta Foundation. n.d. Last accessed September 27, 2021. https://www.prevent accreta.org/.

Office of Communications. 2021. "Human Placenta Project." NIH. Last updated May 17, 2021. https://www.nichd.nih.gov/research/supported/HPP/default.

Preeclampsia Foundation. n.d. "What Is Preeclampsia?" https://www.preeclampsia.org/what -is-preeclampsia.

Purtill, Corinne. 2017. "No Mothers in Human History Ate Their Own Placentas before the 1970s." Quartz, July 7, 2017.

Queen Mary University of London. 2018. "First Evidence That Soot from Polluted Air May Be Reaching Placenta." September 16, 2018. https://www.qmul.ac.uk/media/news/2018/smd/ first-evidence-that-soot-from-polluted-air-may-be-reaching-placenta.html.

Quill, Elizabeth. 2018. "Though Often Forgotten, the Placenta Has a Huge Role in Baby's Health." *Science News*, April 24, 2018.

Roberts, James M., and C. Escudero. 2012. "The Placenta in Preeclampsia." *Pregnancy Hypertension* 2 (2): 72–83.

Rosenberg, J. 2002. "Neonatal Death Risk: Effect of Prenatal Care Is Most Evident after Term Birth." *Perspectives on Sexual and Reproductive Health* 34 (5): 270.

Salihu, Hamisu M., Qing Li, Dwight J. Rouse, and Greg R. Alexander. 2003. "Placenta Previa: Neonatal Death after Live Births in the United States." *American Journal of Obstetrics and Gynecology* 188 (5): 1305–1309.

Sample, Ian. 2018. "Lab-Grown Placentas 'Will Transform Pregnancy Research.'" *Guardian*, November 28, 2018.

Shahul, Sajid, Avery Tung, Mohammed Minhaj, Junaid Nizamuddin, Julia Wenger, Eitezaz Mahmood, Ariel Mueller, Shahzad Shaefi, Barbara Scavone, Robb D. Kociol, Daniel Talmor, and Sarosh Rana. 2015. "Racial Disparities in Comorbidities, Complications, and Maternal and Fetal Outcomes in Women with Preeclampsia/Eclampsia." *Hypertension in Pregnancy* 34 (4): 506–515.

Shen, Tammy T., Emily A. DeFranco, David M. Stamilio, Jen Jen Chang, and Louis J. Muglia. 2008. "A Population-Based Study of Race-Specific Risk for Placental Abruption." *BMC Pregnancy and Childbirth* 8:43.

Stambough, Kathryn, Angela Hernandez, Sheila Gunn, and Oluyemisi Adeyemi-Fowode. 2019. "Maternal Placentophagy as a Possible Cause of Breast Budding and Vaginal Bleeding in a Breast-Fed 3-Month-Old Infant." *Journal of Pediatric and Adolescent Gynecology* 32 (1): P78–P79.

Teigen, Chrissy. 2020. "Hi." Medium. October 27, 2020. https://chrissyteigen.medium.com/ hi-2e45e6faf764.

Tucker, Myra J., Cynthia J. Berg, William M. Callaghan, and Jason Hsia. 2007. "The Black-White Disparity in Pregnancy-Related Mortality from 5 Conditions: Differences in Prevalence and Case-Fatality Rates." *American Journal of Public Health* 97 (2): 247–251.

Turco, Margherita, Lucy Gardner, Richard G. Kay, et al. 2018. "Trophoblast Organoids as a Model for Maternal-Fetal Interactions during Human Placentation." *Nature* 564:263–267.

Wootson, Cleve R., Jr. 2017. "Don't Eat Your Placenta, Researchers Warn." *Washington Post*, October 18, 2017.

Yehuda, Rachel, and Amy Lehrner. 2018. "Intergenerational Transmission of Trauma Effects: Putative Role of Epigenetic Mechanisms." *World Psychiatry* 17 (3): 243–257.

PREMATURITY

Alang, Sirry, Donna McAlpine, Ellen McCreedy, and Rachel Hardeman. 2017. "Police Brutality and Black Health: Setting the Agenda for Public Health Scholars." *American Journal of Public Health* 107 (5): 662–665.

Butler, Judith. 2004. *Precarious Life: The Powers of Mourning and Violence.* London: Verso.

———. 2009. *Frames of War: When Is Life Grievable?* London: Verso.

Centers for Disease Control and Prevention. 2020. "Premature Birth." Last updated October 30, 2020. https://www.cdc.gov/reproductivehealth/features/premature-birth/index.html.

Cunningham, Timothy J., Janet B. Croft, Yong Liu, Hua Lu, Paul I. Eke, and Wayne H. Giles. 2017. "Vital Signs: Racial Disparities in Age-Specific Mortality among Blacks or African Americans—United States, 1999–2015." *Morbidity and Mortality Weekly Report* 66 (17): 444–456.

Davis, Dána-Ain. 2019. *Reproductive Injustice: Racism, Pregnancy, and Premature Birth*, ix. New York: New York University Press.

DiGregorio, Sarah. 2020. *Early: An Intimate History of Premature Birth and What It Teaches Us about Being Human.* New York: Harper.

Edwards, Frank, Hedwig Lee, and Michael Esposito. 2019. "Risk of Being Killed by Police Use of Force in the United States by Age, Race-Ethnicity, and Sex." *Proceedings of the National Academy of Sciences* 116 (34): 16793–16798.

Glynn, Peter, Donald M. Lloyd-Jones, Matthew J. Feinstein, Mercedes Carnethon, and Sadiya S. Khan. 2019. "Disparities in Cardiovascular Mortality Related to Heart Failure in the United States." *Journal of the American College of Cardiology* 73 (18): 2354.

Krieger, Nancy, Jarvis T. Chen, Brent A. Coull, Jason Beckfield, Matthew V. Kiang, and Pamela D. Waterman. 2014. "Jim Crow and Premature Mortality among US Black and White Population, 1960–2009: An Age-Period-Cohort Analysis." *Epidemiology* 25 (4): 494–504.

Reedy, Elizabeth A. 2003. "From Weakling to Fighter: Changing the Image of Premature Infants." *Nursing History Review* 11:109–127.

———. 2011. "Care of Premature Infants." *Nursing, History, and Health Care*, Barbara Bates Center for the Study of the History of Nursing, University of Pennsylvania.

Sewell, Alyasah Ali, Justin M. Feldman, Rashawn Ray, Keon L. Gilbert, Kevin A. Jefferson, and Hedwig Lee. 2020. "Illness Spillovers of Lethal Police Violence: The Significance of Gendered Marginalization." *Ethnic and Racial Studies* 44 (7): 1089–1114. https://doi.org/10.1080/01419870.2020.1781913.

World Health Organization. 2018. "Preterm Birth." February 19, 2018. https://www.who.int/news-room/fact-sheets/detail/preterm-birth.

PRENATAL CARE

Al-Gailani, Salim, and Angela Davis. 2014. "Introduction to 'Transforming Pregnancy since 1900.'" *Studies of History and Philosophy of Biological and Biomedical Sciences* 47 (pt. B): 229–232.

Altman, Molly R., Talita Oseguera, Monica R. McLemore, Ira Kantrowitz-Gordon, Linda S. Franck, and Audrey Lyndon. 2019. "Information and Power: Women of Color's Experiences Interacting with Health Care Providers in Pregnancy and Birth." *Social Science and Medicine* 238 (October): 112491. https://www.sciencedirect.com/science/article/abs/pii/S0277953619304848?via%3Dihub.

Casper, Monica J. 1998. *The Making of the Unborn Patient: A Social Anatomy of Fetal Surgery.* New Brunswick, N.J.: Rutgers University Press.

Casper, Monica J., and Lisa Jean Moore. 2009. *Missing Bodies: The Politics of Visibility*. New York: New York University Press.

Centers for Disease Control and Prevention. 1999. "Achievements in Public Health, 1900–1999: Healthier Mothers and Babies." *MMWR Weekly* 48 (38): 849–858.

———. 2020. "Planning for Pregnancy." Last updated April 16, 2020. https://www.cdc.gov/preconception/planning.html.

Dahlem, Chin Hwa Y., Antonia M. Villarruel, and David L. Ronis. 2015. "African American Women and Prenatal Care." *Western Journal of Nursing Research* 37 (2): 217–235.

Madgett, Katherine. 2017. "Prenatal Care (1913), by Mary Mills West." *Embryo Project Encyclopedia*, Arizona State University. May 18, 2017; updated July 4, 2018.

Maloni, Judith A., Ching-Yu Chang, Cary P. Liebl, and Sharp Maier Jeanmarie. 1996. "Transforming Prenatal Care: Reflections on the Past and Present with Implications for the Future." *Journal of Obstetric, Gynecologic and Neonatal Nursing* 25 (1): P17–P23.

Murkoff, Heidi, and Sharon Mazel. 2008. *What to Expect When You're Expecting: Completely New and Revised*. 4th ed. New York: Workman.

Osterman, Michelle J. K., and Joyce A. Martin. 2018. "Timing and Adequacy of Prenatal Care in the United States, 2016." *National Vital Statistics Reports* 67 (3): 1–14. https://pubmed.ncbi.nlm.nih.gov/29874159/.

Schlesinger, Mark, and Karl Kronebusch. 1990. "The Failure of Prenatal Care Policy for the Poor." *Health Affairs* 9 (4): 91–111.

Scott, Karen A., Laura Britton, and Monica R. McLemore. 2019. "The Ethnics of Perinatal Care for Black Women: Dismantling the Structural Racism in 'Mother Blame' Narratives." *Journal of Perinatal and Neonatal Nursing* 33 (2): 108–115.

Waggoner, Miranda. 2017. *The Zero Trimester: Pre-pregnancy Care and the Politics of Reproductive Risk*. Berkeley: University of California Press.

Weese, Karen. 2018. "Almost Half of US Pregnancies Are Unplanned. There's a Surprisingly Easy Way to Change That." *Washington Post*, May 1, 2018.

QUIET

Casper, Monica J. 2013. "Biopolitics of Infant Mortality." Anthropologies, March 15, 2013.

Chloe. 2019. "To Family and Friends Choosing to Ignore My Child's Existence on Social Media." *Still Standing Magazine*, March 27, 2019.

Layne, Linda. 2003. *Motherhood Lost: A Feminist Account of Pregnancy Loss in America*, 68–69. New York: Routledge.

Michaud, Marisa. 2019. "Never Shying Away: How to Share Them." *Still Standing Magazine*, May 3, 2019.

Scheper-Hughes, Nancy. 1993. *Death without Weeping: The Violence of Everyday Life in Brazil*, 505, 508. Berkeley: University of California Press.

RACISM

American Public Health Association. n.d. "Racism and Health." Last accessed September 28, 2021. https://www.apha.org/topics-and-issues/health-equity/racism-and-health.

Artiga, Samantha, Olivia Pham, Kendal Orgera, and Usha Ranji. 2020. "Racial Disparities in Maternal and Infant Health." Kaiser Family Foundation, November 10, 2020. https://www.kff.org/report-section/racial-disparities-in-maternal-and-infant-health-an-overview-issue-brief/.

Bell, Derrick A. 1995. "Who's Afraid of Critical Race Theory?" *University of Illinois Law Review* 4:893–910.

Birth Justice Now and Every Mother Counts. n.d. "How Many Black, Brown, and Indigenous People Have to Die Giving Birth?" Paid advertisement. Last accessed September 27, 2021. https://everymothercounts.org/wp-content/uploads/2020/07/everymother-print-2.pdf.

Boyd, Rhea W., Edwin G. Lindo, Lachelle D. Weeks, and Monica R. McLemore. 2020. "On Racism: A New Standard for Publishing on Racial Health Inequities." *Health Affairs* (blog), July 2, 2020. https://www.healthaffairs.org/do/10.1377/hblog20200630.939347/full/.

Bridges, Khiara M. 2013. "The Dangerous Law of Biological Race." *Fordham Law Review* 82 (1): 21–80.

———. 2020. "Race, Pregnancy, and the Opioid Epidemic: White Privilege and the Criminalization of Opioid Use during Pregnancy." *Harvard Law Review* 133 (3): 770.

Centers for Disease Control and Prevention. 2019. "Racial and Ethnic Disparities Continue in Pregnancy-Related Deaths." Press release, September 5, 2019. https://www.cdc.gov/media/releases/2019/p0905-racial-ethnic-disparities-pregnancy-deaths.html.

Chatterjee, Rhitu, and Rebecca Davis. 2017. "How Racism May Cause Black Mothers to Suffer the Death of Their Infants." NPR, *Morning Edition*, podcast, MP3 audio, 7:01, December 20, 2017. https://www.npr.org/sections/health-shots/2017/12/20/570777510/how-racism-may-cause-black-mothers-to-suffer-the-death-of-their-infants.

Coates, Ta-Nehisi. 2013. "What We Mean When We Say 'Race Is a Social Construct.'" *Atlantic*, May 15, 2013. https://www.theatlantic.com/national/archive/2013/05/what-we-mean-when-we-say-race-is-a-social-construct/275872/.

Cooper, Lisa A., Mary Catherine Beach, and David R. Williams. 2019. "Confronting Bias and Discrimination in Health Care—When Silence Is Not Golden." *JAMA Internal Medicine* 179 (12): 1686–1687.

Crenshaw, Kimberle. 1991. "Mapping the Margins: Intersectionality, Identity Politics, and Violence against Women of Color." *Stanford Law Review* 43 (6): 1241–1299.

Dickson, E. J. 2020. "Death of Sha-Asia Washington, Pregnant 26-Year Old Black Woman, Highlights Devastating Trend." *Rolling Stone*, July 9, 2020. https://www.rollingstone.com/culture/culture-features/shaasia-washington-death-woodhull-hospital-black-maternal-mortality-rate-1026069/.

Du Bois, W. E. B. 1903. *The Souls of Black Folk: Essays and Sketches.* Chicago: A. C. McLurg.

Gill, Paramjit, and Virinder Kalra. 2020. "Racism and Health." *British Journal of General Practice* 70 (697): 381. https://bjgp.org/content/70/697/381.

Kendi, Ibram X. 2016. *Stamped from the Beginning: The Definitive History of Racist Ideas in America.* New York: Nation.

Khazanchi, Rohan, Charlesnika T. Evans, and Jasmine R. Marcelin. 2020. "Racism, Not Race, Drives Inequity across the Covid-19 Continuum." *JAMA Network Open* 3 (9): e2019933. https://jamanetwork.com/journals/jamanetworkopen/fullarticle/2770954.

Knight, Hannah E., Sarah R. Deeny, Kathryn Dreyer, Jordan Engmann, Maxine Mackintosh, Sobia Raza, Mai Stafford, Rachel Tesfaye, and Adam Steventon. 2021. "Challenging Racism in the Use of Health Data." *Lancet* 3 (3): E144-E146.

Kozhimannil, Katy B. 2020. "Indigenous Maternal Health—a Crisis Demanding Attention." *JAMA Health Forum* 1 (5): e200517. https://jamanetwork.com/journals/jama-health-forum/fullarticle/2766339.

Krieger, Nancy, Rhea W. Boyd, Fernando De Maio, and Aletha Maybank. 2021. "Medicine's Privileged Gatekeepers: Producing Harmful Ignorance about Racism and Health." *Health Affairs* (blog), April 20, 2021. https://www.healthaffairs.org/do/10.1377/hblog20210415.305480/full/.

Mazzia, Claire, and Kelsey McLaughlin. n.d. "Black, Indigenous and People of Colour and Pregnancy." Conscious Pregnancy. Last accessed September 27, 2021. https://www .consciouspregnancy.ca/bipoc.

McFarling, Usha Lee. 2021. "'Health Equity Tourists': How White Scholars Are Colonizing Research on Health Disparities." STAT, September 23, 2021. https://www.statnews .com/2021/09/23/health-equity-tourists-white-scholars-colonizing-health-disparities -research/.

Milano, Brett. 2021. "With COVID Spread, Racism—Not Race—Is the Risk Factor." *Harvard Gazette*, April 22, 2021. https://news.harvard.edu/gazette/story/2021/04/with-covid-spread -racism-not-race-is-the-risk-factor/.

Oluo, Ijeoma. 2019. *So You Want to Talk about Race*. New York: Seal.

Omi, Michael, and Howard Winant. 2014. *Racial Formation in the United States*. 3rd ed. New York: Routledge.

Rawls, Anne Warfield, and Waverly Duck. 2020. *Tacit Racism*. Chicago: University of Chicago Press.

Robert Wood Johnson Foundation. n.d. "Racism and Health." Last accessed September 28, 2021. https://www.rwjf.org/en/library/collections/racism-and-health.html.

Tabobondung, Rebeka. n.d. "A Story of Indigenous Birth Justice." *MICE [Moving Image Culture Etc.] Magazine*. Last accessed September 27, 2021. https://micemagazine.ca/issue-two/ story-indigenous-birth-justice.

Thulin, Lila. 2020. "What 'Racism Is a Public Health Issue' Means." *Smithsonian Magazine*, July 20, 2020. https://www.smithsonianmag.com/science-nature/what-racism-public -health-issue-means-180975326/.

Timothy, Roberta K. 2019. "9 Ways Racism Impacts Maternal Health." Conversation, May 8, 2019. https://theconversation.com/9-ways-racism-impacts-maternal-health-111319.

Williams, David R. 1994. "The Concept of Race in Health Services Research, 1966–1990." *Health Services Research* 29 (3): 261–274.

———. 1996. "Racism and Health: A Research Agenda." *Ethnicity and Disease* 6 (1, 2): 1–6.

———. 1997. "Race and Health: Basic Questions, Emerging Directions." *Annals of Epidemiology* 7 (5): 322–333.

———. 2002. "Racial/Ethnic Variations in Women's Health: The Social Embeddedness of Health." *American Journal of Public Health* 92 (4): 588–597.

Williams, David R., and Chiquita Collins. 1995. "US Socioeconomic and Racial Differences in Health: Patterns and Explanations." *Annual Review of Sociology* 21:349–386.

Williams, David R., and Selina A. Mohammed. 2013. "Racism and Health I: Pathways and Scientific Evidence." *American Behavioral Scientist* 57 (8): 1152–1173.

———. 2013. "Racism and Health II: A Needed Research Agenda for Effective Interventions." *American Behavioral Scientist* 57 (8): 1200–1226.

Williams, David R., and Michelle Sternthal. 2010. "Understanding Racial/Ethnic Disparities in Health: Sociological Contributions." *Journal of Health and Social Behavior* 51 (S1): S15–S27.

Williams, Patricia J. 1991. *The Alchemy of Race and Rights: Diary of a Law Professor*. Cambridge, Mass.: Harvard University Press.

RAINBOW BABY

Ashe, Catherine. 2018. "Pregnancy after Loss: It Isn't All Rainbows." *Still Standing Magazine*, July 23, 2018.

Benson, Ren. 2017. "Why My Child Isn't a Rainbow Baby." Mother Load, October 29, 2017.

Bologna, Caroline. 2018. "What Is a 'Sunshine Baby'?" *HuffPost*, January 17, 2018.

Denney, Victoria. 2018. "3 Lessons on Loss from My Rainbow." *Still Standing Magazine*, May 6, 2018.

Grorud, Emily. 2018. "My Rainbow Baby Pulled Me from the Land of the Dead." *Still Standing Magazine*, August 18, 2018.

Henke, Lindsey. 2017. "14 Truths of Bringing Home a Rainbow Baby." Scary Mommy, March 31, 2017; updated May 27, 2020.

Howland, Genevieve. 2020. "What Is a Rainbow Baby? (Pregnancy after Loss)." Mama Natural, March 5, 2020.

Kittel, Kelly. 2014. *Breathe: A Memoir of Motherhood, Grief, and Family Conflict*, 140. Berkeley, Calif.: She Writes Press.

Reed, Katie. 2016. "I Was a Rainbow Baby." It's a Mother Thing, January 9, 2016; updated January 24, 2021.

Tabo, Cherlaine. 2019. "What Is a Rainbow Baby?" Bump, January 2019.

Theoi Project. n.d. "Iris." Last accessed September 27, 2021. https://www.theoi.com/Pontios/Iris.html.

Willets, Melissa. 2018. "What It Means to Be a Rainbow Baby and Why Rainbow Babies Are Beautiful." *Parents*, March 19, 2018.

REPRODUCTIVE JUSTICE

Asian Communities for Reproductive Justice. 2005. "A New Vision for Advancing Our Movement for Reproductive Health, Reproductive Rights, and Reproductive Justice." https://forwardtogether.org/wp-content/uploads/2017/12/ACRJ-A-New-Vision.pdf.

Luna, Zakiya. 2020. *Reproductive Rights as Human Rights: Women of Color and the Fight for Reproductive Justice*. New York: New York University Press.

Roberts, Dorothy. 1997. *Killing the Black Body: Race, Reproduction, and the Meaning of Liberty*, 48. New York: Pantheon.

———. 2015. "Reproductive Justice, Not Just Rights." *Dissent*, Fall 2015.

Ross, Loretta J., Lynn Roberts, Erika Derkas, Whitney Peoples, and Pamela Bridgewater Toure. 2017. *Radical Reproductive Justice: Foundations, Theory, Practice, Critique*. New York: Feminist Press.

Ross, Loretta, and Rickie Solinger. 2017. *Reproductive Justice: An Introduction*, 9. Berkeley: University of California Press.

Silliman, Jael, Marlene Gerber Fried, Loretta Ross, and Elena R. Gutiérrez. 2004. *Undivided Rights: Women of Color Organize for Reproductive Justice*. Boston: South End.

SisterSong. n.d. "Reproductive Justice." Last accessed September 27, 2020. https://www.sistersong.net/reproductive-justice.

STILLBIRTH

Bell, Bethan. 2016. "Taken from Life: The Unsettling Art of Death Photography." BBC News, June 4, 2016.

Biggs, Lucy. 2019. "'Please Find Some Words for Me': The Conversations That Helped after Our Son's Stillbirth." *Guardian*, August 17, 2019.

Cacciatore, Joanne. 2010. "The Traumatic Contradiction: When Birth and Death Collide." In *They Were Still Born: Personal Stories about Childbirth*, edited by Janet C. Atlas, 19–28. Lanham, Md.: Rowman and Littlefield.

Centers for Disease Control and Prevention. 2020. "What Is Stillbirth?" Last modified November 16, 2020. https://www.cdc.gov/ncbddd/stillbirth/facts.html.

————. n.d. "Family Stories." Last accessed September 20, 2021. https://www.cdc.gov/ncbddd/stillbirth/family-stories/index.html.

————. n.d. "How Does CDC Identify Severe Maternal Morbidity?" Last modified December 26, 2019. https://www.cdc.gov/reproductivehealth/maternalinfanthealth/smm/severe-morbidity-ICD.htm.

Count the Kicks. n.d. Last modified September 27, 2021. https://www.countthekicks.org/.

Daley, Elizabeth. 2016. "My Baby Was Stillborn. but I Refuse to Hide Him from the World." Narratively, September 22, 2016.

de Bernis, Luc, Mary V. Kinney, William Stones, et al. 2016. "Stillbirths: Ending Preventable Deaths by 2030." Lancet 387 (10019): 703–716.

Editorial Board. 2018. "How My Stillbirth Became a Crime." New York Times, December 28, 2018.

Edwards, Ashley Alese. 2019. "A Migrant Woman Had a Stillbirth in ICE Custody. Officials Won't Call It a Death." Refinery29, February 26, 2019.

Fleck, Alissa. 2013. "Capturing the Briefest of Lives." Narratively, September 27, 2013.

Fretts, Ruth. 2010. "What We Know about Stillbirth." In They Were Still Born: Personal Stories about Childbirth, edited by Janet C. Atlas, 185–197. Lanham, Md.: Rowman and Littlefield.

Frøen, J. Frederik, Sanne J. Gordijn, Hany Abdel-Aleem, et al. 2009. "Making Stillbirths Count, Making Numbers Talk—Issues in Data Collection for Stillbirths." BMC Pregnancy and Childbirth 9 (58). https://bmcpregnancychildbirth.biomedcentral.com/articles/10.1186/1471-2393-9-58.

George, Phillip. 2015. "Momento Mori—Remember That You Have to Die." Conversation, June 21, 2015.

Godel, Margaret. 2008. "Images of Stillbirth: Memory, Mourning, and Memorial." Visual Studies 22 (3): 253–269.

Green, Hannah Harris. 2019. "We Had No Idea How Much Physical Danger Stillbirth Can Cause." Rewire News Group, August 14, 2019.

Healy, Andrew J., Fergal D. Malone, Lisa M. Sullivan, et al. 2006. "Early Access to Prenatal Care: Implications for Racial Disparity in Perinatal Mortality." Obstetrics and Gynecology 107 (3): 625–631.

Hochberg, Todd. n.d. "About." Touching Souls. Last accessed September 27, 2021. http://www.toddhochberg.com/about.html.

Horton, Richard, and Udani Samarasekera. 2016. "Stillbirths: Ending an Epidemic of Grief." Lancet 387 (10018): 515–516.

Jepsen, Kristine. 2018. "This Is What No One Tells You about Having a Stillborn Child." HuffPost, October 4, 2018; updated January 13, 2021.

Komaromy, Carol, Sarah Earle, and Linda Layne. 2013. Understanding Reproductive Loss: Perspectives on Life, Death and Fertility. Surrey, U.K.: Ashgate.

Lancet. 2016. "Ending Preventable Stillbirths: An Executive Summary for The Lancet's Series." January 2016.

Lens, Jill Wieber. 2018. "I Gave Birth to a Stillborn Baby. Here Is My Heartbreaking Story." HuffPost, May 12, 2018.

Lewin, Tamar. 2007. "A Move for Birth Certificates for Stillborn Babies." New York Times, May 22, 2007.

London School of Hygiene and Tropical Medicine. 2016. "Slow Progress on Stillbirth Prevention: Parents of 2.6 Million Babies Suffer in Silence Each Year." EurekAlert!, January 18, 2016.

March of Dimes. 2020. "Stillbirth." https://www.marchofdimes.org/complications/stillbirth.aspx.

Martin, Nina. 2014. "A Stillborn Child, A Charge of Murder and the Disputed Case Law on 'Fetal Harm.'" ProPublica, March 18, 2014.

Matthews-King, Alex. 2019. "Black Women Almost Twice as Likely to Suffer Stillbirths, Study Shows." *Independent*, July 29, 2019.

MISS Foundation. n.d. "Home." Last accessed September 27, 2021. http://www.missing angelsbill.org/.

Muglu, Javaid, Henna Rather, David Arroyo-Manzano, et al. 2019. "Risks of Stillbirth and Neonatal Death with Advancing Gestation at Term: A Systematic Review and Meta-analysis of Cohort Studies of 15 Million Pregnancies." *PLoS Medicine* 16 (7): e1002838.

Muthler, Sarah. 2016. "Stillbirth Is More Common Than You Think—and We're Doing Little about It." *Washington Post*, May 16, 2016.

New York Times. 2015. "Stillbirth: Your Stories." June 26, 2015.

Now I Lay Me Down to Sleep. n.d. "History." Last accessed September 27, 2021. https://www .nowilaymedowntosleep.org/about-us/our-mission-vision-reach/history/.

Osman, Nikki. 2020. "Stillbirth: 3 Women Share Their Journeys through an Unspeakable Loss." *Women's Health*, December 10, 2020.

Paltrow, Lynn M. 2015. "When Pregnancy Leads to a Prison Term." Open Society Foundations, June 24.

Paltrow, Lynn M., and Jeanne Flavin. 2013. "Arrests of and Forced Interventions on Pregnant Women in the United States, 1973–2005: Implications for Women's Legal Status and Public Health." *Journal of Health Politics, Policy and Law* 38 (2): 299–343.

Pieklo, Jessica Mason. 2014. "Murder Charges Dismissed in Mississippi Stillbirth Case." Rewire News Group, April 4, 2014.

Qureshi, Zeshan U., Joseph Millum, Hannan Blencowe, et al. 2015. "Stillbirth Should Be Given Greater Priority on the Global Health Agenda." *BMJ* 351:h4620.

Ro, Christine. 2019. "Parents Mourning Stillbirth Follow Familiar Patterns on YouTube." *New York Times*, April 16, 2019.

Saint Louis, Catherine. 2015. "Stillbirths Now Outnumber Deaths among Infants, Study Finds." *New York Times*, July 24, 2015.

Sani, Livia, Anne-Charlotte Laurenti Dimanche, and Marie-Frédérique Bacqué. 2019. "Angels in the Clouds: Stillbirth and Virtual Cemeteries on 50 YouTube Videos." *OMEGA—Journal of Death and Dying* 82 (4): 587–608.

Stevens, Allison. 2007. "The Politics of Stillbirth." *American Prospect*, July 14, 2007.

Thebault, Reis. 2019. "A 24-Year-Old Honduran Woman's Pregnancy Ended in a Stillbirth at an ICE Detention Center." *Washington Post*, February 25, 2019.

U.S. Immigration and Customs Enforcement. 2019. "Joint Statement from ICE and CBP on Stillbirth in Custody." February 25, 2019; updated October 8, 2020. https://www.ice.gov/ news/releases/joint-statement-ice-and-cbp-stillbirth-custody.

Wall-Wieler, Elizabeth, Suzan L. Carmichael, Ronald S. Gibbs, et al. 2019. "Severe Maternal Morbidity among Stillbirth and Live Birth Deliveries in California." *Obstetrics and Gynecology* 134 (2): 310–317.

Walshe, Sadhbh. 2014. "If Stillbirth Is Murder, Does Miscarriage Make Pregnant Women into Criminals?" *Guardian*, March 26, 2014.

Willinger, Marian, Chia-Wen Ko, and Uma M. Reddy. 2009. "Racial Disparities in Stillbirth Risk across Gestation in the United States." *American Journal of Obstetrics and Gynecology* 201 (5): 469.e1–469.e8.

World Health Organization. n.d. "Every Newborn Action Plan." Last accessed September 27, 2021. https://www.who.int/initiatives/every-newborn-action-plan.

SURVIVAL

Crockford, Susannah. 2021. "Survivalists and Preppers." In *Critical Dictionary of Apocalyptic and Millenarian Movements*, edited by James Crossley and Alastair Lockhart. https://www.cdamm.org/articles/survivalists-and-preppers.

Darwin, Charles. 1859. *On the Origin of Species by Means of Natural Selection, or the Preservation of Favoured Races in the Struggle for Life*. London: John Murray.

Gender and Disaster Network. n.d. "Gender Equality and Disaster Risk Reduction." https://www.gdnonline.org/sourcebook/chapt/ind.php?id=1.

Kelly, Casey Ryan. 2015. "The Man-Pocalypse: *Doomsday Preppers* and the Rituals of Apocalyptic Manhood." *Text and Performance Quarterly* 36 (2–3): 95–114.

Kurbegovic, Erna. 2014. "Social Darwinism." Eugenics Archive, April 29, 2014. http://eugenics archive.ca/discover/tree/535eee377095aa0000000259.

Marche, Stephen. 2017. "America's Midlife Crisis: Lessons from a Survivalist Summit." *Guardian*, August 2, 2017.

Ordover, Nancy. 2003. *American Eugenics: Race, Queer Anatomy, and the Science of Nationalism*. Minneapolis: University of Minnesota Press.

Osnos, Evan. 2017. "Doomsday Prep for the Super-Rich." *New Yorker*, January 23, 2017.

Spencer, Herbert. 1910. *The Principles of Biology*. New York: D. Appleton.

Stern, Alexandra Minna. 2016. *Eugenic Nation: Faults and Frontiers of Better Breeding in Modern America*. 2nd ed. Berkeley: University of California Press.

Wilson, Robert A. 2018. "Eugenics Today." Aeon, May 21, 2018.

TAHLEQUAH

Center for Whale Research. 2020. "A Brand New Calf in J Pod!" Press release, September 6, 2020. https://www.whaleresearch.com/.

Chiu, Allyson. 2018. "'What Extinction Looks Like': A Young Orca's Presumed Death Cuts Endangered Whale Population to 74." *Washington Post*, September 14, 2018.

Cuthbert, Lori, and Douglas Main. 2018. "Orca Mother Drops Calf, after Unprecedented 17 Days of Mourning." *National Geographic*, August 13, 2018.

Dwyer, Colin. 2018. "After Calf's Death, Orca Mother Carries It for Days in 'Tragic Tour of Grief.'" NPR, July 31, 2018.

Gaydos, Joe. 2018. "Is Southern Resident Killer Whale J35 Really Mourning?" SeaDoc Society, August 2, 2018. https://www.seadocsociety.org/blog/is-southern-resident-killer-whale-j35 -really-mourning.

Holohan, Meghan. 2018. "Why So Many People Are Connecting with the Orca Mom Mourning Her Calf." *Today*, August 8, 2018.

Pulkkinen, Levi. 2019. "A Pod of Orcas Is Starving to Death. A Tribe Has a Radical Plan to Feed Them." *Guardian*, April 25, 2019.

Quinton, Sean. 2018. "'I Have Not Slept in Days': Readers React to Tahlequah, the Mother Orca Clinging to Her Dead Calf." *Seattle Times*, August 5, 2018; updated May 13, 2019.

Selk, Avi. 2018. "Update: Orca Abandons Body of Her Dead Calf after a Heartbreaking, Weeks-Long Journey." *Washington Post*, August 12, 2018.

Wallington, Natalie. 2020. "Tahlequah the Orca—Famous for Carrying Her Dead Calf for 17 Days—Gives Birth Again." *Guardian*, September 6, 2020.

Yong, Ed. 2018. "The Lingering Curse That's Killing Killer Whales." *Atlantic*, September 27, 2018.

TRAUMA

Blossom, Priscilla. 2016. "My Nightmare Didn't End after I Lost My Child 8 Hours after Birth. The PTSD Carried over to a New Pregnancy." *Washington Post*, January 6, 2016.

Carlson, Arica. 2017. "Living in a Swamp: PTSD after Baby Loss." *Still Standing Magazine*, August 15, 2017.

Casper, Monica J., and Eric Wertheimer, eds. 2016. *Critical Trauma Studies: Understanding Violence, Conflict, and Memory in Everyday Life*. New York: New York University Press.

Centers for Disease Control and Prevention. n.d. "Preventing Abusive Head Trauma." Last accessed September 27, 2021. https://www.cdc.gov/violenceprevention/childabuse andneglect/Abusive-Head-Trauma.html.

Deutsch, Stephanie A. 2021. "Abusive Head Trauma (Shaken Baby Syndrome)." KidsHealth. Last modified March 2021. https://kidshealth.org/en/parents/shaken.html.

Limone, Noa. 2017. "The Silenced Trauma of Late-Term Pregnancy Loss." *Haaretz*, April 15, 2017.

Solnit, Rebecca. 2010. *A Paradise Built in Hell: The Extraordinary Communities That Arise in Disaster*. New York: Penguin.

Still Standing Magazine. 2018. "Facing Trauma While Grieving." January 29, 2018.

World Health Organization. n.d. "Why We Need to Talk about Losing a Baby." Last accessed September 27, 2021. https://www.who.int/news-room/spotlight/why-we-need-to-talk-about -losing-a-baby.

URGENCY

Bellingham, Bruce, and Mary Pugh Mathis. 1991. "Race, Citizenship, and the Bio-Politics of the Maternalist Welfare State: 'Traditional' Midwifery in the American South under the Sheppard-Towner Act, 1921–29." *Social Politics: International Studies in Gender, State and Society* 1 (2): 157–189.

Centers for Disease Control and Prevention. 1999. "Achievements in Public Health, 1900–1999: Healthier Mothers and Babies." *MMWR Weekly* 48 (38): 849–858.

Cohn, Meredith. 2018. "Baltimore Just Saw the Worst Spike of Sleep-Related Infant Deaths since 2009—Sparking Review of Program." *Baltimore Sun*, March 19, 2018.

Gardner, Lloyd C. 2004. *The Case That Never Dies: The Lindbergh Kidnapping*. New Brunswick, N.J.: Rutgers University Press.

Helm, Angela. 2019. "In Baltimore, 6 Babies Died in Their Sleep in 6 Weeks. Most of Them Were Black." Root, March 21, 2019.

Ladd-Taylor, Molly. 1988. "'Grannies' and 'Spinsters': Midwife Education under the Sheppard-Towner Act." *Journal of Social History* 22 (2): 255–275.

Meckel, Richard A. (1990) 2015. *Save the Babies: American Public Health Reform and the Prevention of Infant Mortality, 1850–1929*. Illustrated ed. Rochester, N.Y.: University of Rochester Press.

Milwaukee Community Journal. 2019. "Milwaukee Receives $5 Million Grant to Focus on Maternal-Infant Health." April 12, 2019.

Moehling, Carolyn M., and Melissa A. Thomasson. 2012. "Saving Babies: The Contribution of Sheppard-Towner to the Decline in Infant Mortality in the 1920s." NBER Working Papers Series 17996, National Bureau of Economic Research, Cambridge, Mass., April 2012.

Owens, Deirdre Cooper, and Sharla M. Fett. 2019. "Black Maternal and Infant Health: Historical Legacies of Slavery." *American Journal of Public Health* 109 (10): 1342–1355.

Phelps, Edward Bunnell. 1910. "A Statistical Survey of Infant Mortality's Urgent Call for Action." *Publications of the American Statistical Association* 12 (92): 341–359.

Schwabe, Amy. 2019. "Milwaukee Doulas Ask for the Community's Help to Lower Black Maternal and Infant Mortality." *Milwaukee Journal Sentinel*, March 18, 2019.

UNICEF. 2018. "Every Child Alive: The Urgent Need to End Newborn Deaths." UNICEF Data, February 2018. https://data.unicef.org/resources/every-child-alive-urgent-need-end -newborn-deaths/.

Wilson, Jan Doolittle. 2007. *The Women's Joint Congressional Committee and the Politics of Maternalism, 1920–30.* Urbana: University of Illinois Press.

VULNERABILITY

Abramowitz, Sharon A. 2005. "The Poor Have Become Rich, and the Rich Have Become Poor: Collective Trauma in the Guinean Languette." *Social Science and Medicine* 61:2106–2118.

Angier, Natalie. 2006. "The Cute Factor." *New York Times*, January 3, 2006.

Bourgois, Philippe, Seth M. Holmes, Kim Sue, and James Quesada. 2017. "Structural Vulnerability: Operationalizing the Concept to Address Health Disparities in Clinical Care." *Academic Medicine* 92 (3): 299–307.

Centers for Disease Control and Prevention. 2020. "CDC Social Vulnerability Index (SVI)." Last modified February 13, 2020. https://data.cdc.gov/Health-Statistics/CDC-Social -Vulnerability-Index-SVI-/u6k2-rtt3/data.

Cutter, Susan L., Bryan J. Boruff, and W. Lynn Shirley. 2003. "Social Vulnerability to Environmental Hazards." *Social Science Quarterly* 84 (2): 242–261.

Dunsworth, Holly. 2016. "Labor Pains and Helpless Infants: Eve or Evolution? (Part I)." Sapiens, May 10, 2016.

Dunsworth, Holly M., Anna G. Warrener, Terrence Deacon, Peter T. Ellison, and Herman Pontzer. 2012. "Metabolic Hypothesis for Human Altriciality." *Proceedings of the National Academy of Sciences* 109 (38): 15212–15216.

Ehrlich, Paul R., David S. Dobkin, and Darryl Wheye. 1988. "Precocial and Altricial Young." Stanford Birds, Stanford University. https://web.stanford.edu/group/stanfordbirds/text/ essays/Precocial_and_Altricial.html.

Farmer, Paul. 2006. *AIDS and Accusation: Haiti and the Geography of Blame.* Berkeley: University of California Press.

Faust, Katerina M., Samantha Carouso-Peck, Mary R. Elson, and Michael H. Goldstein. 2020. "The Origins of Social Knowledge in Altricial Species." *Annual Review of Developmental Psychology* 2:225–246.

Gould, Stephen Jay. 2008. "A Biological Homage to Mickey Mouse." *Ecotone* 4 (1 & 2): 333–340.

Langley, Liz. 2017. "Go Baby! These Animals Grow Up without Any Help from Parents." *National Geographic*, September 9, 2017.

Scheiber, Isabella B. R., Brigitte M. Weiß, Sjouke A. Kingma, and Jan Komdeur. 2017. "The Importance of the Altricial-Precocial Spectrum for Social Complexity in Mammals and Birds—a Review." *Frontiers in Zoology* 14 (3). https://frontiersinzoology.biomedcentral .com/articles/10.1186/s12983-016-0185-6.

Taylor, Jamila, Cristina Novoa, Katie Hamm, and Shilpa Phadke. 2019. "Eliminating Racial Disparities in Maternal and Infant Mortality: A Comprehensive Policy Blueprint." Center for American Progress, May 2, 2019.

Wong, Kate. 2012. "Why Humans Give Birth to Helpless Babies." *Scientific American*, August 28, 2012.

WASHINGTON, D.C.

Boone, Margaret. 1989. *Capital Crime: Black Infant Mortality in America*. Thousand Oaks, Calif.: SAGE.

Franke-Ruta, Garance. 2013. "When America Was Female." *Atlantic*, March 5, 2013.

Giaratelli, Anna. 2016. "DC Council Approves Name Change If City Becomes State." *Washington Examiner*, October 18, 2016.

Gonzales, John. 2018. "Latest Data Reveal Appalling Gaps between Black and White Infant Mortality Rates." Center for Health Journalism, USC Annenberg, March 5, 2018.

Greeley, Horace. 1864. *The American Conflict: A History of the Great Rebellion in the United States of America, 1860-'64*. Hartford, Conn.: O.D. Case.

Hauslohner, Abigail. 2015. "Poor D.C. Babies Are More Than 10 Times as Likely to Die as Rich Ones." *Washington Post*, May 4, 2015.

Hawkins, Summer Sherburne. 2010. "Maternal Mortality Is Worse in Washington, D.C. Than Syria. Abortion Access Is One Reason Why." Think, NBC News, February 18, 2020.

Humphrey, Robert L., and Mary Elizabeth Chambers. 1977. *Ancient Washington: American Indian Cultures of the Potomac Valley*. Washington, D.C.: George Washington University.

Jacob, Angela. 2018. "DC Has Highest Maternal Mortality Rate in US; Council Wants to Learn Why." NBC4, February 8, 2018.

Jones-Taylor, Myra. 2019. "Let's Make Our Babies a National Priority." *Hill*, March 12, 2019.

Kellogg, Alex. 2011. "D.C., Long 'Chocolate City,' Becoming More Vanilla." NPR, *Morning Edition*, podcast, MP3 audio, 7:49, February 15, 2011.

Lazere, Ed. 2018. "DC's Growing Prosperity Is Not Reaching Black Residents, Census Data Show." DC Fiscal Policy Institute, September 26, 2018.

Lefrak, Mikaela. 2021. "51st: With Democrats in Charge, Is DC Destined for Statehood?" WAMU, January 7, 2021.

McQuirter, Marya Annette. 2003. "A Brief History of African Americans in Washington, D.C." Cultural Tourism DC, https://www.culturaltourismdc.org/portal/a-brief-history-of-african-americans-in-washington-dc.

Miller, Michael E. 2020. "In D.C., Black Families Reel from the Pain of Hundreds Lost to COVID-19 and Killings." *Washington Post*, December 30, 2020.

NCC Staff. 2020. "How Philly Lost the Nation's Capital to Washington." *Constitution Daily* (blog), National Constitution Center, May 14, 2020.

U.S. House of Representatives. 2017. *Washington, D.C. Admission Act*. H.R. 1291, 115th Cong., 2017–2018. Introduced March 1, 2017.

Vargas, Theresa. 2018. "Why Washington Is One of the Worst Places to Be Black and Pregnant." *Washington Post*, June 16, 2018.

Vinik, Danny. 2015. "Washington, D.C. Has the Highest Infant Mortality Rate of 25 Rich World Capitals." *New Republic*, May 5, 2015.

Washington.org. n.d. "History of Washington, D.C." Last accessed September 27, 2021. https://washington.org/dc-information/washington-dc-history.

———. n.d. "Home." Last accessed September 27, 2021. https://washington.org/.

Wiener, Aaron. 2015. "D.C.'s Infant Mortality Rate: An 'International Embarrassment'?" *Washington City Paper*, May 5, 2015.

WEATHERING

Cargle, Rachel. 2017. "Erica Garner: More Than the Battle against Police Injustice; Maternal Mortality in the U.S." Medium, December 30, 2017.

Demby, Gene. 2018. "Making the Case That Discrimination Is Bad for Your Health." NPR, *Code Switch Podcast*, January 14, 2018. https://www.npr.org/sections/codeswitch/2018/01/14/577664626/making-the-case-that-discrimination-is-bad-for-your-health.

Dennis, Jeff. A. 2019. "Birth Weight and Maternal Age among American Indian/Alaska Native Mothers: A Test of the Weathering Hypothesis." *SSM—Population Health* 7:100304.

Geronimus, Arline T. 1992. "The Weathering Hypothesis and the Health of African-American Women and Infants: Evidence and Speculation." *Ethnicity and Disease* 2 (3): 207–221.

———. 2003. "Commentary: Weathering Chicago." *International Journal of Epidemiology* 32 (1): 90–91.

———. 2013. "Deep Integration: Letting the Epigenome Out of the Bottle without Losing Sight of the Structural Origins of Population Health." *American Journal of Public Health* 103 (S1): S56–S63.

Jones, Rachel. 2019. "Why Giving Birth in the U.S. Is Surprisingly Deadly." *National Geographic*, January 2019.

Roeder, Amy. 2019. "American Is Failing Its Black Mothers." *Harvard Public Health*, Winter 2019.

Semprini, Jason. 2018. "Black Births Matter: Institutional Racism and Infant Mortality Rates in the United States." *Chicago Policy Review*, March 2, 2018.

Wang, Vivian. 2017. "Erica Garner, Activist and Daughter of Eric Garner, Dies at 27." *New York Times*, December 30, 2017.

WOMEN'S HEALTH

Acevedo, Nicole. 2019. "Nearly 900 Women's Health Clinics Have Lost Federal Funding over Gag Rule." NBC News, October 22, 2019.

Bailey, Moya, and Whitney Peoples. 2017. "Articulating Black Feminist Health Science Studies." *Catalyst: Feminism, Theory, Technoscience* 3 (2): 1–27.

Block, Jennifer. 2008. *Pushed: The Painful Truth about Childbirth and Modern Maternity Care*. Cambridge, Mass.: Da Capo.

———. 2019. *Everything below the Waist: Why Health Care Needs a Feminist Revolution*. New York: St. Martin's.

Clarke, Adele E., and Virginia L. Olesen, eds. 1999. *Revisioning Women, Healing, and Healing: Feminist, Cultural, and Technoscience Perspectives*. New York: Routledge.

Dusenbery, Maya. 2019. *Doing Harm: The Truth about How Bad Medicine and Lazy Science Leave Women Dismissed, Misdiagnosed, and Sick*. New York: HarperOne.

Green, Monica H. 2008. "Gendering the History of Women's Healthcare." *Gender and History* 20 (3): 487–518.

Morgen, Sandra. 2002. *Into Our Own Hands: The Women's Health Movement in the United States, 1969–1990*. New Brunswick, N.J.: Rutgers University Press.

Murphy, Michelle. 2012. *Seizing the Means of Reproduction: Entanglements of Feminism, Health, and Technoscience*. Durham, N.C.: Duke University Press.

Nichols, Francine H. 2000. "History of the Women's Health Movement in the 20th Century." *JOGNN* 29 (1): 56–64.

Norsigian, Judy. 2019. "Our Bodies Ourselves and the Women's Health Movement in the United States." *American Journal of Public Health* 109 (6): 844–846.

Price, Kimala. 2011. "It's Not Just about Abortion: Incorporating Intersectionality in Research about Women of Color and Reproduction." *Women's Health Issues* 21 (S3): S55–S57.

Reverby, Susan M. 2002. "Feminism and Health." *Health and History* 4 (1): 5–19.

Ruzek, Sheryl Burt, Virginia L. Olesen, and Adele E. Clarke, eds. 1997. *Women's Health: Complexities and Differences*. Columbus: Ohio State University Press.

XENOPHOBIA

Abraido-Lanza, Ana F., Sandra E. Echeverria, and Karen R. Flórez. 2017. "Latino Immigrants, Acculturation, and Health: Promising New Directions in Research." *Annual Review of Public Health* 37:219–236.

ACLU. n.d. "Timeline of the Muslim Ban." Last accessed September 27, 2021. https://www .aclu-wa.org/pages/timeline-muslim-ban.

Bacon, Perry, Jr. 2018. "Trump Had Made U.S. Policy Much More Resistant to Immigration— without the Wall." FiveThirtyEight, December 6, 2018.

Bhopal, Raj S. 2017. "Intertwining Migration, Ethnicity, Racism, and Health." *Lancet* 390 (10098): 932.

Briggs, Laura. 2018. *How All Politics Became Reproductive Politics: From Welfare Reform to Foreclosure to Trump*. Berkeley: University of California Press.

Chavez, Leo R. 2017. *Anchor Babies and the Challenge of Birthright Citizenship*. Palo Alto, Calif.: Stanford University Press.

Clarke, Adele E. 1944. "Subtle Forms of Sterilization Abuse: A Reproductive Rights Perspective." In *Test Tube Women: What Future for Motherhood?*, edited by Rita Arditti, Renate D. Klein, and Shelly Minden, 188–212. Boston: Pandora.

Collinson, Stephen. 2019. "Cornered: Trump Escalates Shutdown Crisis." CNN Politics, January 7, 2019.

Dominguez, Kenneth, Ana Penman-Aguilar, Man-Huei Chang, et al. 2015. "Vital Signs: Leading Causes of Death, Prevalence of Diseases and Risk Factors, and Use of Health Services among Hispanics in the United States—2009–2013." *MMWR* 64 (17): 469–478l.

Enarson, Elaine, and P. G. Dhar Chakrabarti, eds. 2009. *Women, Gender, and Disaster: Global Issues and Initiatives*. New Delhi, India: SAGE.

Escobar-Valdez, Miguel. 2014. "Reflections on Immigration, Binational Policies, and Human Rights Tragedies." In *Binational Human Rights: The U.S.-Mexico Experience*, edited by William Paul Simmons and Carol Mueller, 27–43. Philadelphia: University of Pennsylvania Press.

Foster, Carly Hayden. 2017. "*Anchor Babies* and *Welfare Queens*: An Essay on Political Rhetoric, Gendered Racism, and Marginalization." *Women, Gender, and Families of Color* 5 (1): 50–72.

Galvez, Alyshia. 2011. *Patient Citizens, Immigrant Mothers: Mexican Women, Public Prenatal Care, and the Birth Weight Paradox*. New Brunswick, N.J.: Rutgers University Press.

Giuntella, Osea. 2016. "The Hispanic Health Paradox: New Evidence from Longitudinal Data on Second and Third-Generation Birth Outcomes." *SSM—Population Health* 2:84–89.

Hoggatt, Katherine J., Maria Flores, Rosa Solorio, Michelle Wilhelm, and Beate Ritz. 2012. "The 'Latina Epidemiologic Paradox' Revisited: The Role of Birthplace and Acculturation in Predicting Infant Low Birth Weight for Latinas in Los Angeles, CA." *Journal of Immigrant and Minority Health* 14 (5): 875–884.

Holpuch, Amanda, and Sabrina Siddiqui. 2019. "Trump to Make Border Wall Speech on Primetime TV." *Guardian*, January 7, 2019.

Human Rights Watch. n.d. "United States: Events of 2017." Last accessed September 27, 2021. https://www.hrw.org/world-report/2018/country-chapters/united-states#.

Hummer, Robert A., Daniel A. Powers, Starling G. Pullum, Ginger L. Gossman, and W. Parker Frisbie. 2007. "Paradox Found (Again): Infant Mortality among the Mexican-American Population in the United States." *Demography* 44 (3): 441–457.

Jawetz, Tom. 2019. "Immigration Priorities in the 116th Congress." Center for American Progress, January 8, 2019.

Krogstad, Jens Manuel, and Ana Gonzalez-Barrera. 2019. "Key Facts about U.S. Immigration Policies and Proposed Changes." FactTank, Pew Research Center, May 17, 2019.

Lichtenberger, Anna Laura. 2018. "Undocumented Citizens of the United States: The Repercussions of Denying Birth Certificates." *St. Mary's Law Journal* 49:435.

Lugo-Lugo, Carmen R., and Mary K. Bloodsworth-Lugo. 2017. *Feminism after 9/11: Women's Bodies as Cultural and Political Threat.* New York: Palgrave Macmillan.

Martínez, Airín D. 2012. "Reconsidering Acculturation in Dietary Change Research among Latino Immigrants: Challenging the Preconditions of US Migration." *Ethnicity and Health* 18 (2): 115–135.

McCormick, Ty. 2021. "The 'Muslim Ban' Is Over. The Harm Lives On." *New York Times,* January 23, 2021.

McGlade, Michael S., Somnath Saha, and Marie E. Dahlstrom. 2004. "The Latina Paradox: An Opportunity for Restructuring Prenatal Care Delivery." *American Journal of Public Health* 94 (12): 2062–2065.

Metzl, Jonathan M., and Dorothy E. Roberts. 2014. "Structural Competency Meets Structural Racism: Race, Politics, and the Structure of Medical Knowledge." *AMA Journal of Ethics* 16 (9): 674–690.

Neumayer, Eric, and Thomas Plumper. 2008. "The Gendered Nature of Natural Disasters: The Impact of Catastrophic Events on the Gender Gap in Life Expectancy, 1981–2002." *Annals of the Association of American Geographers* 97 (3): 551–566.

O'Leary, Anna Ochoa, and William Paul Simmons. 2017. "Reproductive Justice and Resistance at the U.S.-Mexico Borderlands." In *Radical Reproductive Justice: Foundations, Theory, Practice, Critique,* edited by Loretta Ross, Lynn Roberts, Erika Derkas, Whitney Peoples, and Pamela Bridgewater, 306–325. New York: Feminist Press.

Olivares, José, and John Washington. 2020. "'A Silent Pandemic': Nurse at ICE Facility Blows the Whistle on Coronavirus Dangers." Intercept, September 14, 2020.

Project South. 2020. "Lack of Medical Care, Unsafe Work Practices, and Absence of Adequate Protection against COVID-19 for Detained Immigrants and Employees Alike at the Irwin County Detention Center." Institute for the Elimination of Poverty and Genocide, September 14, 2020. https://projectsouth.org/wp-content/uploads/2020/09/OIG-ICDC-Complaint-1.pdf.

Sammen, Joe. 2018. "The Racism of US Immigration Policy." Center for Health Progress, August 1, 2018.

Schmidt, Susan. 2018. "Endangered Mothers or 'Anchor Babies'? Migration Motivators for Pregnant Unaccompanied Central American Teens." *Vulnerable Children and Youth Studies* 13 (4): 374–384.

U.S. Immigration and Customs Enforcement. 2020. "Joint Statement from ICE and CBP on Stillbirth in Custody." Press release, February 25, 2019; updated October 8, 2020. https://www.ice.gov/news/releases/joint-statement-ice-and-cbp-stillbirth-custody.

Vidili, Monica. 2018. "Why We Must Engage Women and Children in Disaster Risk Management." *Sustainable Cities* (blog), World Bank, March 7, 2018.

Williams, David R., and Michael Sternthal. 2010. "Understanding Racial-Ethnic Disparities in Health: Sociological Contributions." *Journal of Health and Social Behavior* 51 (S): S15–S27.

YEARNING

Beau's Beginning: Life after Infant Loss. n.d. "Home." Facebook. Last accessed September 27, 2021. https://www.facebook.com/pg/beausbeginning/posts/.

Goldstein, Richard D., Ruth I. Lederman, Wendy G. Lichtenthal, et al. 2018. "The Grief of Mothers after the Sudden Unexpected Death of Their Infants." *Pediatrics* 141 (5): e20173651.

HealGrief.org. n.d. "Grieving the Death of a Child." Last accessed September 27, 2021. https://healgrief.org/grieving-the-death-of-a-child/.

hooks, bell. 1999. *Yearning: Race, Gender, and Cultural Politics.* Boston: South End.

Kersting, Anette, and Birgit Wagner. 2012. "Complicated Grief after Perinatal Loss." *Dialogues in Clinical Neuroscience* 14 (2): 187–194.

ZIP CODE

Bhatt, Jay. 2018. "Your Zip Code, Your Health." American Hospital Association, May 16, 2018.

Clark, Anna. 2013. "The Tyranny of the ZIP Code." *New Republic*, March 7, 2013.

Connolly, N. D. B., LaDale Winling, Robert K. Nelson, and Richard Marciano. 2018. "Mapping Inequality: 'Big Data' Meets Social History in the Story of Redlining." In *The Routledge Companion to Spatial History*, edited by Ian Gregory, Donald DeBats, and Don Lafreniere. London: Routledge.

Katcher, Margaret. 2018. "A Mother's Zip Code Could Signal Whether Her Baby Will Be Born Too Early." *Atlantic*, August 23, 2018.

Nierenberg, Andrew A. 2018. "Zip Codes Are More Predictive Than Diagnosis Codes." *Psychiatric Annals* 48 (3): 130.

Parks, Troy. 2016. "Death by ZIP Code: Investigating the Root Causes of Health Inequity." American Medical Association, August 25, 2016.

Roeder, Amy. 2014. "Zip Code Better Predictor of Health Than Genetic Code." News, Harvard T. H. Chan School of Public Health, August 4, 2014.

Rutledge, Mike. 2018. "6 Local ZIP Codes Targeted in Infant Mortality Fight." *Journal-News*, September 3, 2018.

Semuels, Alana. 2017. "The Barriers Stopping Poor People from Moving to Better Jobs." *Atlantic*, October 12, 2017.

U.S. Postal Service. n.d. "About the United States Postal Service." Last accessed September 27, 2021. https://about.usps.com/who/profile/.

U.S. Postal Service Office of Inspector General. 2013. "The Untold Story of the ZIP Code." Report no. RARC-WP-13–006, April 1, 2013.

Wong, Qing Wai. 2018. "Zip Codes Matter for Infant Mortality." *Public Health Post*, March 23, 2018.

Zeltner, Brie. 2018. "A Promising Win against Infant Mortality: 'One Community' Celebrates Zero Deaths." Cleveland.com, September 30, 2018; updated September 19, 2019.

INDEX

ABOUT THE AUTHOR

MONICA J. CASPER is a professor of sociology and the dean of the College of Arts and Letters at San Diego State University. She is the author of the award-winning book *The Making of the Unborn Patient: A Social Anatomy of Fetal Surgery* and many other works on women's health, bodies, and inequality.